# A CHART OF

# CAPTAIN TRUX~~~~~~LD

### Showing the Cours~~~~

AN~~

*Various Tracks ~~~~*
*East Indies, China, Europe, &c.*

D0856725

*~tain spent*
*~ his life*

Calcutta

Canton.

Macao.

Bombay

Madras

SOUTH
CHINA
SEA

30° E

60° E

90° E

120° E

SUMATRA

1790

Str. of Sunda

Batavia

JAVA

Johanna

1794

I. de France

NEW
HOLLA~

Homeward Bound
1787  1789  1791

1788

1786

~ape Town

St. Paul I.
Amsterdam I.

# TRUXTUN OF THE CONSTELLATION

# TRUXTUN

## OF THE

# *Constellation*

*NAVAL INSTITUTE PRESS Annapolis, Maryland*

THE LIFE OF
COMMODORE
Thomas Truxtun, U.S. Navy

1755-1822

*by* EUGENE S. FERGUSON

Library of Congress Cataloging in Publication Data
Ferguson, Eugene S.
    Truxtun of the Constellation.
    Reprint. Originally published: Baltimore :
Johns Hopkins Press, 1956.
    Bibliography: p.
    Includes index.
    1. Truxtun, Thomas, 1755–1822.    2. Constellation
(Frigate)    3. Seamen—United States—Biography.
4. United States.    Navy—Biography.    I. Title.
E182.T7F43    1983        973.4'5'0924 [B]        81–18734
ISBN 0–87021–712–7                                AACR2

Printed in the United States of America

# CONTENTS

# FOREWORD

ONE OF THE BEST WAYS in which to appreciate the history of one's country is to make actual contact with the things and events that shaped a nation. Museums exist for that purpose, but other experiences are invaluable, too. In Baltimore's inner harbor, at a place of honor, floats an admirable opportunity. It is the frigate Constellation, one of the great ships in our naval history, and a visit to it will inflame imaginations.

At a time when opportunities for vicarious visits to early America are becoming increasingly difficult to find, this famous old ship preserves a fascinating story. And in an age when history books must eliminate much old material to provide space for new, I find that certain choice episodes of our past are apt to be overlooked.

One period that has suffered is the formative era between the Revolutionary War and the War of 1812. This was a turbulent time for fledgling America, both politically and economically, for although our Constitution was in the process of being written, adopted, and launched, its greatness was not yet accepted, and foreign powers felt free to test it.

It was during these years that citizens of the new country awakened to the fact that their prosperity would be tied to foreign trade, and this required that American ships and crews must be ensured safe passage anywhere on the oceans. But the young country was not yet strong enough to enforce this rule of free passage; the British and French plundered our ships and arrested our crews, pressing them into service in their own fleets.

Without a strong and daring navy to protect its commerce, the beginning nation would have been powerless.

*Truxtun of the Constellation* details the political maneuvering that occurred between President George Washington and the Congress before the United States Navy could be launched. The building and manning of a group of adventurous frigates is an exciting part of our early national life.

The *Constellation* was the first of these frigates authorized and built. She was also the first to be victorious in battle. Her first captain, Thomas Truxtun, is considered one of our truly great naval officers.

In this book Eugene S. Ferguson has researched and written about a significant era in the development of America's character, and has given us as well a portrait of the noble old ship and its crew.

*James A. Michener*

Admiral of the Chesapeake Bay
September, 1980

# PREFACE

FLANKING the stage of the magnificent white marble amphitheater in Arlington National Cemetery are two impressively brief rosters of eminent Army and Navy officers. On the left, as one faces the stage, are the well-known names of the generals—George Washington, Anthony Wayne, and a dozen more. On the right are the names of captains and admirals. First is John Paul Jones; next is Thomas Truxtun; he is followed by Edward Preble, Isaac Hull, Stephen Decatur, and nine others of a later day.

This book is about Thomas Truxtun, an outstanding captain in the annals of the United States Navy. He was an able commander of men. He exerted a lasting influence upon his juniors in the service and, through them, upon succeeding generations of naval officers.

Thomas Truxtun was first and last a ship commander. In his early twenties, during the American Revolution, he commanded privateer ships. He was thirty years old when he brought Benjamin Franklin home from his long wartime service in France. For the next eight years he was a China hand, pioneering in the newly established trade to that distant corner of the world. In his forties he was the popular hero of the little-known and quickly forgotten war of 1798–1800 between the United States and France. In the *Constellation,* the frigate whose building he superintended and which he coolly commanded through two savage contests with French frigates in the West Indies, he earned renown as a brave and gallant man of action. He was among the first—only John Paul Jones was earlier—who won the sea battles that made the United States Navy respected and feared upon the ocean. He has often been called the Father of the Navy, because of the heritage he bestowed upon it. Some of the officers who were prominent in the Barbary Wars and the War of 1812 were tutored by him; many others were not. It is a fact, however, that the influential Board of Navy Commissioners, created in 1815 to advise and assist the Secretary of the Navy, was dominated for more than twenty years by officers who had been lieutenants or midshipmen in Captain Truxtun's ships.

His most important and permanent legacy to the United States Navy is the quiet and untheatrical tradition of command that he established. He drew upon precedents in the British Royal Navy, whose regulations he studied and whose system he often observed at first hand. He, more than any other individual, was responsible for transmitting to the new United States Navy, in effective form, the Royal Navy's way of doing things.

His doctrine was based upon the "honor and sacred trust" reposed in those who mount the quarter-deck of a man-of-war. He preached and practiced firm and fair government of his ship. At the same time he recognized, as few men did in his time, the truly autocratic nature of naval command, the necessity for a captain's absolute and unquestioned control of his ship. Captain David Porter, who began his naval career as a midshipman under Captain Truxtun, must surely have had his old commander in his mind's eye when he wrote, "A man of war is a petty kingdom, and is governed by a petty despot."

The captain of a ship of war has—and in this respect conditions have changed almost none at all in two hundred years—a continuously sustained, minute-by-minute responsibility that can be understood only imperfectly by a landsman. From the moment the anchor is apeak, when his ship is preparing to get under way, until the voyage is completed and his ship is safely moored again, the captain must be unremitting in his attentions to the safety of his command. Furthermore, he must always be ready to take his ship into action on a moment's notice. He must be able to use his ship as a single weapon in the way a swordsman uses his sword. To be effective the ship, like the sword, must be completely under the control of its wielder. It must respond instantly to his slightest muscle-twitch. In order to be ready for action—the sole purpose for which the ship exists—the captain has the never-ending task of training and exercising his crew and of keeping his ship and its armament in a state of perfect repair.

If a naval captain uses the personal pronoun when he describes an action or evolution of his ship, if he begins his statements with "I fought" or "I sailed," it is not because his ego has carried him away. There simply is no other way to say accurately what the captain is trying to express. A ship commander, after all, must always be a supreme egoist when he mounts his quarter-deck, when he "struts his few fathoms of scoured plank." He is indeed a petty despot. He is, as Captain Porter wrote, "a solitary being in the midst of the ocean." Such a man was Thomas Truxtun.

No deep-water ships were driven by steam while he commanded ships. Only the power of wind, the set of tides, and the brawn of seamen were available to him to move his ships and to hoist his anchors and set his sails. He regularly demanded of his men and of himself labor on an heroic scale, labor that would distress the hardiest of men today. He faced problems completely unknown to the modern mariner. He took full responsibility for vessels that were by their very nature sensitive to every change in the weather, at the mercy of every passing squall. Yet he had at hand none of the modern aids to navigation—no weather forecasts; no daily or hourly reports of weather conditions that might later affect him; no clear understanding, even, of the general course and nature of storms in many parts of the world. Ceaseless vigilance in watching and interpreting the face of the sea and sky provided his only means for safeguarding his ships.

I have been confronted by two difficulties in writing his life. First, it would be easy to conclude that he was out of date, a quaint individual who was something of a fool to know so little about things that we take for granted today. Second, I have often been tempted to paint him bigger than life as his struggles against the sea have come alive again from the thousands of documents I have studied. I think I have entirely avoided the first difficulty, and in my attempt to guard against the second, I have been supplied many times by my subject with an appropriate phrase to restore him to proper proportions.

This portrayal of the character of an important officer who should be better known by Americans both in and out of the Navy is, within the compass of my ability, an honest one; it is an accounting of facts as I have been able to see and understand them.

It is impossible to spend years in the virtual company of a man (unless he is a thoroughly evil man), searching out the intimate details of his life and trying to divine the workings of his mind, without developing a certain affection for him. Thus it becomes impossible to avoid a subjective appraisal of his actions, particularly his mistakes. This is as it should be, however. Even the cat, when he looks on the king, must have a point of view.

I have found a man whose first forty-five years were studded with periods of intense activity. The times in between were crammed nearly to the last hour with the study of such subjects as navigation, the masting of ships, signals, naval tactics, and naval organization. Most of his contemporaries in the sea service either took no notice of these subjects or had an active aversion to their study. Until he was eased out of the Navy in 1802, he had little time to engage in idle gossip or invective against those with whom he disagreed. He was too busy becoming a peerless ship commander. But after his ejection from the Navy—an event that could have been avoided by a more diplomatic and less hostile Secretary of the Navy—he became increasingly resentful of his treatment at the hands of an unfriendly government. At length he grew noisy and finally tiresome. I have not glossed over the unfortunate years he was forced to live out after he came ashore for the last time, but I have tried to put this anticlimactic period in proper perspective.

One may wonder why, if Commodore Truxtun is an important officer, this is the first biographical notice of him that exceeds a dozen pages in length. The answer lies partly in the widely scattered material and the endless searching required to locate it. If I had understood the magnitude of this task when I started, it is probable that the biography would still be unwritten. In spite of broad efforts, however, I still know little about his forebears. Unless important new material is turned up in England or on the island of Jamaica, he will remain the founder of a family, the progenitor of a proud line of numerous descendants.

Biographers have neglected him also because he wrote nothing expressly for their benefit. He was surprisingly unconcerned about what posterity's appraisal of him would be. While other men, such as John Paul Jones, always fancied the eyes of history peering over their shoulder whenever they took up their quills, Commodore Truxtun wrote as though he cared only about what his contemporaries thought of him.

This, then, is the story of an eminent naval officer, popular alike with the public and the men in his ships. In twenty-seven years of command of merchant ships and ships of war, he was never spoken to disrespectfully by a seaman under his orders, nor did he find it necessary—as many captains did—to maintain discipline by flogging. He was a navigator in a day when navigators were rare. He was a brave and skillful fighter and tactician. Unfortunately, he never voiced during the heat of battle a succinct and quotable slogan. Nevertheless, the United States Navy is a better service because he gave to it the seven most vigorous years of his life.

AMES, IOWA                                      *Eugene S. Ferguson*
*August, 1956*


## ACKNOWLEDGMENTS

MY PRINCIPAL DEBT is to Jo, my wife, whose constant encouragement, constructive criticism, patience, and understanding have made this work possible.

I owe a handsome acknowledgment to the following individuals who, by their interest, advice, suggestions, encouragement, and often plain hard work, have given me assistance without which this biography in its present form could not exist. They are responsible for none of its shortcomings, however; those are chargeable solely to me.

Dr. John H. Powell, by the exercise of his unique talent for transmitting to others his enthusiasm for history as a living and vital thing, started me on this work nearly ten years ago. Through the many vicissitudes that inevitably beset an author, he has supplied valuable advice and help at opportune moments.

The late T. Truxtun Hare, Esquire placed at my disposal his important and extensive collection of Truxtun papers, graciously opened his home to me, and read the manuscript. His advice and encouragement were of inestimable value.

Lieutenant Commander M. V. Brewington, USNR (ret.) suggested numerous sources that otherwise I should not have found; he answered dozens of questions, and read much of the manuscript. Dr. Robert G. Albion's painstaking criticism has enabled me to correct many errors of fact and interpretation. Mr. William Bell Clark generously gave me copies of manuscripts and eighteenth-century newspaper items that he had laboriously searched for and collected over a period of more than twenty years. Dr. Earle D. Ross read the manuscript and offered many valuable suggestions.

Mrs. Edward Truxtun Beale, who gave her collection of Truxtun manuscripts to the Office of Naval Records and Library; Mr. Clinton V. Black, Archivist in Jamaica, B.W.I., and Mrs. Hazel E. Hall, who sought material for me in the Islands; Mr. Truxtun Brodhead, who gave me a copy of genealogical data recorded by the subject of this work in the Truxtun family Bible, without which we should have almost no trustworthy information about the Commodore's family; Mr. Barney Chesnick, whose cheerful assistance and advice I enjoyed during many, many visits to the Ridgway Library; Mr. Robert W. Hill, who set me on the trail of the Constable-Pierrepont Papers in the collections of the New York Public Library, which gave another dimension to the China voyages; Mr. Edward B. Morrison, who helped me in numberless ways during the time I was able to spend in the New York Public Library's Manuscript Division, and who has been tireless in his search—on my behalf—for obscure Truxtuniana; Mr. Lewis M. Johnson, who furnished information concerning the Commodore's Perth Amboy home; Mrs. Alma R. Lawrence, who made my visits to the Office of Naval Records and Library particularly fruitful; Mr. Jesse Merritt, whose knowledge of Nassau County history provided useful leads; The Honorable Samuel Seabury, who supplied information concerning Thomas Truxtun's attendance at the Reverend Mr. Samuel Seabury's school; Mrs. John Hall Wheelock, who directed me to David Porter's vivid description of "the little tyrant"—all of these and many other people have helped me with no thought of personal return or recognition.

A special mention is due Commander Robert W. Copeland, USNR. I met him in the first days of 1945, a few weeks after he had lost his ship to a formidable Japanese fleet in the hopeless action off Samar. He is responsible for the awakening of my interest in naval history.

I have made much in this book of Captain Truxtun's bravery and calm demeanor, his talent for command, and of the traditions he established for the Navy to cherish and maintain. While I studied about his cruises and sea fights, I thought often of Bob Copeland. Bob, commanding the *Samuel B. Roberts,* a destroyer escort that mounted two five-inch guns and three torpedo tubes, acting as part of the screen for a half-dozen escort carriers in the Philippine Sea, one morning found himself faced by a Japanese force of battleships, cruisers, and destroyers. Characteristically, Bob attacked. He closed to within 4,000 yards of a cruiser before launching his torpedoes; a short time later, after retiring unscathed from this attack, the *Roberts* was mortally hit by a succession of salvos from the battleships and cruisers. Literally, the *Roberts* went down with her guns firing.

As long as men like Bob Copeland command ships of the Navy, I shall know that the traditions of bravery, audacity, and steadfast devotion to the honor and glory of the national flag are in strong hands.

When I was spending my days in libraries and ferreting out the materials of which this work is composed, I often made a mental note, when a member of a library staff was particularly sympathetic and helpful in guiding my research, that I would adequately acknowledge my debt to him or her when the writing of my book was complete. But now that I sit down to offer my thanks, I find that many of my mental notes have been obliterated by time and that my written notes of favors received are in no wise complete. Librarians being what they are, it is perhaps only necessary for me to point out to the reader that my hundreds of demands have always been met with patience and courtesy.

I have been helped by the following institutions, all but the last six of which I have visited in the course of this work:

Iowa State College Library, Ames; State University of Iowa Library and State Historical Society of Iowa, Iowa City; Chicago Historical Society and John Crerar Library, Chicago; Tippecanoe County Historical Association Museum, Lafayette, Indiana; Tracy W. McGregor Library, University of Virginia, Charlottesville; Office of Naval Records and Library, Library of Congress, and National Archives, Washington; Maryland Historical Society, Enoch Pratt Free Library, and Peabody Institute Library, Baltimore; United States Naval Academy Museum, Annapolis; Pennsylvania State Library, Harrisburg; Historical Society of Pennsylvania, Ridgway Branch of the Library Company, Free Library of Philadelphia, American Philosophical Society Library, University of Pennsylvania Library, Franklin Institute Library, Commercial Museum, and the indispensable Union Library Catalog, Philadelphia;

New Jersey State Library, Trenton; Perth Amboy Public Library; New York Public Library and New York Historical Society, New York; Public Library, Jamaica, N.Y.; New York State Library, Albany; Boston Public Library, The Boston Athenaeum, Archives of the Commonwealth of Massachusetts, Boston; Peabody Museum and Essex Institute, Salem; Massachusetts Historical Society, Boston; William L. Clements Library, Ann Arbor; Henry E. Huntington Library, San Marino; Mariner's Museum, Newport News, Virginia; Virginia State Library, Richmond; The Island Record Office, Spanish Town, Jamaica, B.W.I.

*TRUXTUN OF THE CONSTELLATION*

PART ONE

# Apprentice to the Sea

---

## CHAPTER I

## LONG ISLAND BOYHOOD

  ✌  ·  ·  ✌  ·  ·  ✌  ·  ·  ✌  ·  ·

LONG ISLAND in 1755 was a desolate and partly barren finger of land lying between the Sound and the Ocean and pointing eastward toward the open sea. It was here, within sight and smell of salt water, that Thomas Truxtun was born on February 17, 1755. His birthplace was on the north side of the great Hempstead plain, a fertile band that slashed across the island some twenty miles east of the seaport town of New York. It was a lonely place; neighbors were often separated by miles of roads that were deep-frozen ruts in winter and axle-deep mud in spring. Only a few farms were fenced off from the plain. Mostly the great reaches of meadow were used for pasturage of the "general flock" of sheep owned and earmarked by residents of the town of Hempstead. The sheep were put out to graze in spring and were then rounded up and claimed by their owners late in the fall of each year.[1]

He lived his earliest years on "a very pleasant and compleat Farm," owned by his father and situated near one of the bays that indent the shore of the Sound. The focal point of the two hundred acres of salt meadow, orchards, and wood lots was a "handsome and commodious Dwelling House, four Rooms on a floor, and Fire Places in them all." There were a big barn, a coach house, a store house, and other outbuildings; horses for riding, for driving, and for working the farm; cows for milk; sheep for meat and wool.[2]

Long Island was part of New York, which in 1755 was a British colony—one of the thirteen that skirted the Atlantic seaboard. The colonies were involved in a war when Thomas was born, although the King of England had not yet officially declared it. The French and Indians were harassing British settlers on the western and northern frontiers of Pennsylvania and New York. Fighting at the outposts was sometimes only 150 miles away, but the effects of the war were never acutely felt out on the Hempstead plain. Some of the Truxtuns' neighbors rode off to fight alongside the King's regulars while others took the fight to the enemy by sea, embarking in privateers that were owned by New Yorkers and fitted out nearby. Thomas, as he grew to understand such things, listened to stories about the war from those who had fought in it, but as a youngster he heard none of the noise of war. His were the later wars; first the Revolution, and then the naval war with France, in which he firmly established his fame.

The towns on this part of Long Island—Hempstead, Jamaica, Oyster Bay, New Town, to name a few—were small and widely separated. They were managed by local men, selected each year at public town meetings. Nearly a day's journey from New York, at that time a metropolis of perhaps 18,000 inhabitants,[3] they were not bound closely by the customs and usages of the city, but they were inevitably influenced by them.

At least two popular race tracks, one on the Hempstead plain and one near Jamaica, the town next west of Hempstead, attracted huge crowds, sometimes numbered in the thousands. Many spectators came from as far away as New York. Crossing on the Brooklyn ferry the evening before the races, hundreds of people journeyed out to the race track in chairs and chaises—two- and four-wheeled horse-drawn vehicles—and on horseback.[4] To these gala performances the Truxtuns and their neighbors were no doubt attracted as much by the crowds as by the races. The dress and equipage of the fashionable gentlemen and their ladies who had ridden out from the city were of high interest.

Thomas was born to that class of society whose men were called "gentlemen." He came of a family that remained obscure until he wrote his name boldly across the pages of history. His father, Thomas Truxtun, was an English barrister, a vocation which placed him high on the social scale. When the elder Truxtun came to Long Island from the island of Jamaica in the West Indies, he was probably close to fifty, for he left behind him a wife from whom he had been separated for many years and at least two grown daughters by a former marriage.[5]

The mother of the infant Thomas was Sarah Axtell Truxtun; she appears to have been the third wife of the barrister. She may have been a native of Long Island, but it seems more likely that she was a member of the prominent Axtell family in the West Indies. In keeping with generally accepted custom, the elder Thomas and Sarah were bound by common-law marriage when their son was born. It was only after they had received news of the death of Mary, his legal wife, that they were married in proper form by the Church of England. This was about a year after the arrival of the baby.[6]

The Truxtuns were a genteel family. Since they had a station in life to maintain, they looked for guidance in social vogues to the polite people of New York who, from the Royal Governor down, reflected as faithfully as they could the latest in manners, styles, and amusements of old London.

The elegant gentleman of 1755 wore a powdered wig under a cocked beaver hat, black velvet or scarlet breeches that met white silk stockings just above the knees, a tailored coat over a waistcoat trimmed with lace and adorned by buttons and flaps, and a shirt of fine linen complete with ruffles of lace at the throat and at the wrists. Shoes were decorated with shiny buckles and often with spurs.[7]

The gentleman's lady was even more elegant. She wore her hair in elaborate puffs, curls, and towers. Her hands, wrists, and neck were bedecked with jewelry. She was not properly attired unless she wore a hoop skirt. Splendid dresses were fashioned from silks and damasks, satins and mohairs, muslins and dimities, materials brought into New York from all over the world. The dresses were lavishly ornamented with spangled gold and silver lace or with exquisite embroidery. High heels on embroidered silk shoes, peeking out from beneath a spacious hoop skirt, were high style in 1755.[8]

The gentlemen and their ladies had little time or inclination for the day's work, occupied as they were in maintaining their elegance. There were, of course, black slaves to do most of the menial tasks. Between the top and bottom of the social scale were white yeoman farmers and freeholders, who worked and owned small farms; tradesmen, who tended their own shops; and craftsmen and mechanics—leather-aprons—who made and mended the tools of living. These were the men, these middle classes, who largely peopled the towns where Thomas first saw a street, a shop, a tavern, and a church.

There was really one more class in the society of 1755. The minister of the gospel was a person somewhat apart, definitely not a gentleman and usually less encumbered by worldly goods than many of the tradesmen and mechanics in his flock. At an early age Thomas came under the influence of one of these good men, the Reverend Mr. Samuel Seabury.

Samuel Seabury was parish priest of the Church of England in a parish that covered twenty square miles of territory east of Jamaica township. His home church was St. George's, in Hempstead, where Thomas's parents were married. He preached regularly in Oyster Bay, ten miles away, and occasionally he journeyed down to the mission at Rockaway.[9] The preacher was an intelligent and kindly man, yet his face bore signs of decision and unyielding firmness. He wore plain clothes, a three-cornered hat above and riding boots below. Day after day he traveled over his parish on horseback. Thomas could see him occasionally, a man of medium height, solidly built, seated on a strong sorrel horse, with his saddle bags strapped to the saddle. He rode well and he rode much.[10]

This preacher had a family to provide for, so he found time to practice medicine as well as preach the gospel. For bleeding, tooth drawing, giving an emetic or cathartic, or for a blister plaster he charged a shilling. A visit was usually two shillings except when he also wrote a patient's will, for which he charged an extra shilling.[11] He also found time to run a boarding school.

Thomas Truxtun spent a year, or at the most two years, in the Reverend Mr. Seabury's school. This may have been the only formal education he ever had. Certainly he had little enough time for any schooling before he went off to sea at the age of twelve, and from that time on he embarked upon one voyage after another. Yet he appears later as a literate man, better skilled in rhetoric and better acquainted with the literature of his day than many men whose schooling was much more extensive. If he did not have time to learn many facts from Samuel Seabury, he learned at least how to go about learning; and the preacher must have accomplished that which few teachers are able to do: he gave his pupil the desire to learn things for himself.

Thomas was six, going on seven, when he was sent to Mr. Seabury's boarding school. The boy's mother was dead. His father was preparing to marry again and to leave the country when, late in the summer of 1761, the schoolmaster-preacher wrote in his account book, "Thomas Truxtun came to me to board and school at 28 £ p annum." [12]

The school was a classical one "for the instruction of youth in Latin, Greek, and the mathematics," or if so desired, "in reading, writing, and arithmetic." The schoolhouse was separate from the parsonage, but the pupils boarded in the home of the preacher and his faithful wife. The £28 per year included not only schooling and meals and a place to sleep, but also washing and a supply of wood for the schoolhouse. Mrs. Seabury must have been busy indeed looking after the needs of her husband's pupils—entertaining them, as he had advertised, "in a genteel manner." [13]

A few months after Thomas had been placed in school, his father drew up his will. According to its provisions, almost all of his property was to go to his son; his daughters in the West Indies were to receive only a small bequest, since they were already married. He named his good friend John Troup, gentleman, of the town of Jamaica, as executor of his estate and as "Guardian o'er the Body of my said Son Thomas."

After writing his will, the elder Truxtun sold his farm, was married to his new bride, and then disappeared from the records. He probably returned to Jamaica, because in his will he mentioned "being bound out on a Voyage to parts remote beyond the Seas." He died four years later, when Thomas was ten years old. [14]

For a time John Troup looked after the well-being of his friend's son. Being a wealthy merchant with shipping interests in New York,

[5]

he knew about ships and the men who sailed them to "parts remote beyond the seas," to England, the West Indies, the African coast, and beyond. He was part owner of the *Sturdy Beggar,* a New York privateer ship that mounted twenty guns.[15] He could have entertained young Thomas by the hour telling him about the exploits and adventures of his friends and relatives who sailed in her during the late war.

Surrounded as the youngster was by salt water, nurtured on a potion of adventure and mystery of far places, it is natural to find him developing a longing and a love for the sea and for the spreading white sails that could carry him over the horizon to the exotic lands that lay beyond. No doubt it was John Troup who arranged to have Thomas, an orphan boy with a genteel background, apprenticed to the sea when he was twelve years old. He was placed in the ship *Pitt,* Captain Joseph Holmes, bound out for Bristol in old England.[16]

CHAPTER 2

APPRENTICE SAILOR

℘ • • ℘ • • ℘ • • ℘ • •

WHEN Thomas Truxtun turned twelve years old, all that he knew about the big world that lay beyond his immediate horizons he had learned from books or by listening to the tales of people who had been there; but a day in 1767 changed all that. He found himself suddenly at grips with the reality of learning through hard personal experience.

He journeyed from the quiet remoteness of Long Island into the bustling city of New York. While he was crossing on the Brooklyn ferry he could see the extensive group of buildings that made up the metropolis, huddled together at the lower end of Manhattan Island. The monotony of low roofs was punctuated by spires and steeples and interrupted by streets cutting across the island. The city wore an air of smug complacence, built as it was of brick and stone, its houses lined up in orderly rows. On this day, when Tom approached it, the city was merely the backdrop for a scene that must surely have com-

[6]

manded his unwavering attention. On the river front were piers and docks, and in the foreground was a forest of masts, spars, and ropes standing on hulls that lay moored well out in the stream. Some of these were vessels that had just come in from beyond remote horizons; others were waiting for a tide and a wind to carry them out to distant ports of call.

Somewhere in that shoal of sailing vessels ahead was the ship named *Pitt*. Could he pick her out? Three towering masts, crossed by a dozen wooden yards and held in place by hempen shrouds and stays. Bluff bows and a square stern. Less than one hundred feet in length and a third as broad. This was the ship that would carry him across a thousand leagues of open sea and bring him back after many long weeks to the same berth in the East River.[1]

Once in the city, Tom had to get himself and his belongings to his ship. His ship! What a thought! Soon he would be a sailor, a member of the ship's company of a "regular trader," which took American products to England and brought back the goods of polite living—clothing, cosmetics, books, window glass, teas, wines, and spices —that were produced in England or transferred from the great ships of the East India Company.

The "regular traders" to England, unlike the "transients," whose itineraries were dictated by the destinations of their cargoes, usually carried on a trade between two ports only; but here the regularity ended. They depended upon freight for their chief revenue, and if a cargo did not materialize when the advertised sailing date arrived, a "regular trader" would wait for days, and often for weeks, until her hold was filled.[2]

Thus Tom, the young sailor, could expect to spend six weeks at sea on the outward passage, another six or eight weeks at sea on the return passage, and an indefinite number of weeks in Bristol, whence the *Pitt* was bound. It was unlikely that he would hear any word from home during all this time, because news generally traveled no faster than the ship he was in.

A waterman for a few pennies would pull a sailor and his dunnage across to a vessel anchored out in the stream. It was probably thus that Tom completed the last leg of the journey to his new home.

It was a complex and bewildering place, this sailing ship. The captain and his mates constituted the afterguard, which arrogated to itself the cabin space back aft. This they shared with genteel passengers who had money enough to pay the cabin price. Other passengers, not so well off, were forced to take shelter in the steerage, a bare and dimly-lit compartment below the cabin. The sailors, similarly less fortunate in their station in life, all swung their hammocks in a single cramped compartment just before the foremast. Because the boy Thomas was neither a foremast hand nor yet a member of the afterguard, he probably slept wherever he would be most handy to the captain's summons.

His duties as cabin boy, for which, since he was an apprentice, he was paid nothing, were subject to the captain's slightest whim. Cabin boys usually carried food from the caboose, where the cook held forth, down to the captain's table. They might be assigned the duties of chambermaid to the cabin passengers as well as sweeper of the captain's cabin, and to insure their proper introduction to the sea service they would be responsible for emptying the cabin chamber pots. If the cook should take a fancy to the boy he could expect the best of the ship's food, and if he found favor with the passengers he might occasionally be invited to enjoy a share of the private stocks of delicacies that experienced sea travelers always carried with them. The life of a cabin boy might be extremely pleasant. On the other hand, a crotchety captain and a malicious mate could make his existence unbearable. Probably Tom's experience during his first voyage lay somewhere between the two extremes.

When at last the moment of sailing approached, when the hatch covers had been battened down, when the mail bags had been stowed in the cabin, and when the crew and passengers and finally the captain had come on board, Tom could begin to observe what this sea life consisted of.[3]

He added his inconsiderable weight to the all-hands evolution at the capstan and helped to inch the bars around as the anchor was weighed and catted. He watched the rest of the activity that accompanied the maneuver of getting under way. He might see the mate sending the hands aloft to unfurl the sails, urging them with a rope-end to step lively; and he might marvel as the experienced hands, making sense of the babel of shouted commands, trotted about the deck heaving on a line here, making one fast there, and again slacking off on another.

No doubt he had an opportunity to watch the city recede astern as the *Pitt* worked her way down the Bay toward the open sea. The

Battery of Fort George, with its cannon in a hundred-odd embrasures, kept watch over the seaward approach to the city. On the skyline were the church steeples, Trinity's towering above them all. Over on the larboard quarter of the ship as it sailed down the Bay were the wooded bluffs of Brooklyn. Somewhere not far beyond those peaceful green hills, Tom was leaving his childhood forever behind.[4]

After the *Pitt* crossed the bar and sailed out into the wide and rough Atlantic, Tom probably found that his stomach would no longer behave. He, like many men who follow the sea, was never entirely free of the threat of turning quite green when he went to sea after spending too long a time on shore. After his viscera settled down, he was able to take notice of his new surroundings and to begin to store up the bits and pieces of sea-knowledge that all together made him a distinguished mariner when he reached the zenith of his career.

Often a ship's boy might be popular with some of the foremast hands, if not with the captain or mate. Since nearly all men enjoy displaying their knowledge to an appreciative audience, what more satisfactory way was there to spend the long hours of watches below than to introduce a bright lad to the intricacies of a vessel under sail and to the endless mysteries of the sea? During this voyage and the voyages that followed, Tom learned the names of the masts of a ship: fore, main, and mizzen; the difference between a sloop, with one mast, and a brig or snow, with two. He learned the names of the sails belonging to each mast: courses, topsails, topgallant sails, and royals; he learned to recognize and tie knots and hitches and bends; he learned the names of ropes, stays, and shrouds. He soon knew which lines were sheets and which were braces, which were clewlines and which bow-lines and bridles; he boxed the compass; after a while he found courage to scramble aloft and lie out on a swaying, plunging yard; and in good time he came to understand the multiplicity of details that had to be mastered before a man was capable of standing a watch at sea.

Tom survived his first voyage to Bristol and return. What he saw he liked well enough to make him stay with his new-found way of life. When he embraced the sea he accepted, whether he realized it or not, the prospect of sailing with an autocratic captain, a bullying mate, and a recalcitrant crew; of pitching through the wild North Atlantic with wind and wave providing the only motive power; and of living on pickled meat—often spoiled—and ship's bread from which the weevil worms had to be driven before it was fit to be eaten. For seven years, however, until he was over nineteen years old, he stayed with British merchant ships. After one or two voyages in the *Pitt,* he shifted—at his own request, according to his first biographer—to another "regular trader." Most of the seven years he probably spent in the ship *London,* Captain James Chambers commanding.[5]

Only one incident, which nearly changed the course of his whole career, broke the pattern of his life in the merchant service. Early in 1771, when Tom was just sixteen, he found himself suddenly and unceremoniously impressed on board His Majesty's ship *Prudent,* a 64-gun ship of the Royal Navy.

CHAPTER 3

HIS MAJESTY'S SERVICE

   ᘒ  .  .  ᘒ  .  .  ᘒ  .  .  ᘒ  .  .

DEPARTING from New York in December, 1770, on board the *London,* it appeared that Tom would celebrate his sixteenth birthday in London and then return to New York ahead of the warm weather; but in planning to spend Maytime ashore in Long Island, he did not reckon with the press gangs of the Royal Navy.

In September, a warship of the Royal Navy had sailed up the English Channel, crowding on all the sail she could carry, hurrying to get into her home port to deliver momentous news. She had been insulted—insulted and humiliated by a few arrogant Spaniards in the far distant Falkland Islands, down off Cape Horn. Spain and Great Britain both claimed the islands for their own. An argument had arisen, and a small Spanish force had overcome an even smaller British force, which consisted merely of a single ship of war. It was agreed by the Spaniards that the British might return to England, but not until after the Spanish governor had arrived to take account of the situation. In order to make sure that the British, living in their ship, complied with the agreement and did not slip away ahead of time under cover of fog or darkness, the Spaniards took ashore some of the ship's sails, and—indignity of indignities—unhung her rudder, took it ashore, and placed it under guard. This was the comic-opera news that reached England late in 1770.[1]

Nations as well as individuals go to great lengths to save face. The reaction in England to this insult in the remote Falklands was immediate and violent. How dare those Dons? Call out the Navy. Where is the Navy? Sixteen sail of the line, peacefully rotting away in ordinary, were put back in commission immediately. Appropriations for the Navy were more than doubled.[2] But the suddenly expanded Navy needed many thousands of additional seamen, and these were not so easily obtained as the money and ships.

His Majesty offered a bounty of thirty shillings to every able seaman who would enter the naval service, and the cities of London, Bristol, and several others offered additional bounties to induce seamen to sign up.[3] These inducements unfortunately were overbalanced by the nature of the royal sea service. Crowded quarters, rotten food, months and sometimes years on board a ship with no liberty to go ashore lest a man desert: all of this was common knowledge. Still, men were needed; so the Navy met the need in traditional fashion. Press gangs were called out. They would find the men.

Impressment of any able-bodied British subject, no matter what his occupation or family obligations might be, was legal when men were needed for the Navy. Only those who had influence in official circles could buy their way out of the service if the press became hot. A hapless man, beset by a press gang, might be torn from his family for years, or forever, without warning and without recompense.

The press gangs usually consisted of fifteen to thirty men, armed always with cutlasses and sometimes with pistols besides. A lieutenant commanded the gang, which included two or three midshipmen, several ratings, and seamen big enough and strong enough to do the job effectively and expeditiously. They were put ashore from warships, generally in and around the cities and larger towns. Occasionally they would range through the countryside, traveling on foot and in coaches from one place to another.[4]

This was the sort of gang that Tom Truxtun encountered as his ship came into London early in 1771. The seamen on board merchant ships, as long as they even looked like British subjects, were fair game for the press gangs. Working afloat, the gangs would surround an incoming ship and prevent the escape of any of her crew. So hot did the press become in London that the Lord Mayor had to ask the Admiralty office for "protections" for enough merchant seamen to bring vessels loaded with food up to the city.[5] But this happened after Tom already had been taken by a press gang and sent on board a British man-of-war.

Tom was in the Royal Navy only for a few months, serving all of his time in the 64-gun ship *Prudent*. He was alert and eager; the captain found him to be an uncommonly good boy. Before long the captain showed his confidence in him by sending him ashore as a member of a press gang.[6] He talked to Tom about the naval service, painting a pleasant picture of the life it afforded. The captain, according to Tom Truxtun's first biographer, "endeavoured to prevail on him to remain in the service, and assured him that all his interest should be used for his promotion."[7] Tom took naturally to the routine and discipline of the service, and indeed was greatly and lastingly influenced by the laws, customs, and traditions of the Royal Navy. Twenty-five years later, when he was wrestling with the organization of his own ship of war, he leaned heavily on what throughout the years he had learned of the ways of the British sea service. However, in 1771, after the British had within a few months' time settled their little altercation with Spain and press gangs were no longer being sent ashore, Tom decided he would prefer the peacetime merchant service to the peacetime Navy. He may have read in a London newspaper what he might expect of the Navy after the peace: "After the navy has been reviewed by his Majesty, and paraded round Spithead, with Music playing, Guns firing, Flags flying &c. all the Ships are to be distributed among the several Sea Ports of this Kingdom—to rot, until the next Spanish Encroachments rouse them from their Lethargy."[8] Perhaps Tom wondered what officers did while their ships were rotting. In any case, as soon as he was released from the Navy he returned to his old ship *London*.

On board the *London* for another three years, Tom completed his training in merchant ships, still under the tutelage of Captain Chambers, who it has been said was "a celebrated commander in the London trade."[9] He was probably a good commander, because Tom learned his sea trade well; but when Captain Chambers is remembered it is not for his seamanship: it is for the infamous part he played in the New York tea party, a most uncelebrated event.

CHAPTER 4

## THE NEW YORK TEA PARTY

℮    .    .    ℮    .    .    ℮    .    .    ℮    .    .

THE arrival of the ship *London* in New York usually caused only a ripple of excitement. She was announced in the Exchange, where maritime traders gathered to transact their business, and in the newspapers. Ordinarily, the townspeople were interested in her arrival only if she brought them mail or freight from England.

When she arrived in the early spring of 1774, however, the *London* received more attention than her commander had bargained for. A special committee was waiting for the ship when she arrived at the entrance to the Bay. A mob greeted her when she tied up at her wharf in the city. Her captain, James Chambers, had the warmest homecoming of his career; he was fortunate to get through the day unharmed. And all of this because somebody had reported that there was a small amount of tea on board his ship.

This trouble over tea was the result of the latest in a series of ill-considered moves made by the British Ministry to maintain its right to tax the commerce of the colonies. It was attempting, said one New Yorker, "to enslave this country." Some inhabitants of Boston had agreed with this sentiment when, in December of the preceding year, a band of "Mohawks"—citizens faintly disguised as Indians—had thrown 352 chests of tea into Boston harbor. In New York, just before Captain Chambers had set out on his latest voyage, he had received public thanks from "most of the merchants and many other inhabitants" because he had ostentatiously refused henceforward to carry any British tea in his ship. When he returned from England, merchants and many other inhabitants greeted him, but there were no thanks to be heard anywhere.

The third week in April, 1774, passed as follows. On Tuesday, the

*Nancy,* Captain Lockyer commanding, arrived off Sandy Hook at the entrance to the Bay with a full cargo of tea on board. A Committee of Observation, appointed by the Sons of Liberty (another committee), was waiting in boats to greet the ship when she arrived. Captain Lockyer was told flatly that the people of New York would not permit his tea to be landed; and furthermore, that if he was interested in the safety of his ship and his skin, he would turn the *Nancy* right around and sail her back to England. When the captain pointed out to the committee that he could not return until he had taken on more provisions and made some repairs to his ship, he alone was permitted to go up to the city. The committee remained where it was and watched the *Nancy* around the clock, in order to make sure that no attempt was made to run the tea ashore.

From London, by way of Philadelphia, had come word that the *London,* Captain Chambers, would be arriving any day in New York. This was a routine bit of news; but the rest of the message astonished and angered the Sons of Liberty. According to a Philadelphia shipmaster, who by chance had seen her cargo lists in London, she was carrying in addition to her regular cargo eighteen boxes of fine tea! Here, it appeared, was Captain Chambers, who had so recently refused to carry tea in his ship, coming home with some tea on board. The matter must be carefully looked into. The Sons of Liberty immediately alerted the Committee of Observation.

On Friday, about noon, the *London* arrived off Sandy Hook. She was boarded by the Committee of Observation, who demanded to see her cargo lists. Captain Chambers immediately produced them, and since no evidence of tea could be found on the lists, the committee gave the ship leave to sail on up to her berth in the city. This may have been the first inkling that Tom Truxtun, by this time a veteran member of the *London*'s crew, had that this might be his last voyage with Captain Chambers. He knew about the "Liberty Boys": he had been hearing of them off and on ever since the Stamp Act troubles of nearly a decade before. He knew that the committee that called itself "Sons of Liberty" was composed of men of the trader and working classes, and that Isaac Sears, a merchant and sometime privateer captain, was the principal leader. "Sons of Licentiousness," some called them; "Sons of Violence," led by "King Sears." They were radicals, and they were extremely vocal. They had managed in the past to influence and coerce more conservative citizens. They had made themselves heard, and they had sometimes gained their ends by violent means. They were not to be taken lightly.

By late Friday afternoon, the *London* was tied up to her wharf. Four more committees had been detailed by the Sons of Liberty to watch the ship, night and day, until her cargo was all discharged. Tom found himself in the midst of a nasty situation when some men came on board and demanded to know whether the ship carried any tea. Perhaps this was Tom's first opportunity to see Isaac Sears in action. When Sears' band threatened to break out every piece of cargo until they should find the tea, Captain Chambers finally confessed that he had the eighteen boxes on board and that they belonged to him. Thus ended abruptly his little adventure in tea.

Following Boston's lead, New York had made preparations for "Mohawks" to dump the tea into the harbor at an appointed hour; but the mob that gathered at the wharf became impatient. By eight o'clock in the evening, the mob had found the tea, broken open the boxes, and had dumped the "detested herb" overboard. No other damage was done to the ship or to the cargo, and by ten o'clock the mob had dispersed and the city was quiet.

Early Saturday morning the quiet was broken by the clangorous pealing of bells. The Sons of Liberty had organized the epilogue of the New York tea party. Bells all over the city were ringing. Crowds were converging on the Coffee House; a large flag had been hoisted to the top of the Liberty Pole; a band of musicians was ready to animate the proceedings. A handbill, issued two days before, explained what it was all about. When Captain Lockyer, of the *Nancy,* was ready to leave the city to return to his ship, said the handbill, "it is the desire of a number of the citizens . . . that he should see, with his own eyes, their detestation of the measures pursued by the Ministry and the India Company, to enslave this country." It was to be a celebration of detestation.

Captain Lockyer was escorted by the mob from the Coffee House to Murray's Wharf at the end of Wall Street. The band struck up "God Save the King," not because it was particularly appropriate but probably because it was the tune they played best. Lockyer was put off in a boat to go down to his ship off Sandy Hook, whence he would sail her back home with her cargo still intact. The mob called for Captain Chambers. "Where is he? Where is he? Captain *Lockyer* must not go till we find Captain *Chambers,* to send him with the tea ship." But Chambers was prudently nowhere to be found. Several days later the newspaper announced that he had boarded the *Nancy* before she departed, and that he too was on his way to safety in England. Thus ended the week of the New York tea party.

This incident, placed against Tom's Long Island background, gave him much to consider, and in time he was faced with some difficult decisions. After the action of committees—committees of correspondence, committees of observation, the Committee of Fifty-One, committees to detect conspiracies, and as one result of all these committees, the Continental Congress—began to point toward serious trouble with the royal government, many people in Long Island and elsewhere began actively to oppose government by committee and to call themselves Loyalists. John Troup, Tom's legal guardian, was at the forefront of this movement. He would never submit to these upstart committees, in his opinion composed of the rabble and dedicated to lawlessness.

Finally the issues all simmered down to a single question: would Tom continue to be a loyal British subject, believing in the wisdom of the King and his ministers, or would he cast his lot with the people who called themselves Patriots and who seemed to be gaining the upper hand in the contest for control of government of the colonies? Would he go back with the people among whom he had grown up in Long Island, or would he become one of King Sears' subjects? At length Tom decided to follow Sears; he might still be a British subject, but he concluded that he was first of all an American.[1]

# PART TWO

# Young Mariner

## CHAPTER 5

## *CHARMING POLLY*

ꝫ . . ꝫ . . ꝫ . . ꝫ . .

ON THE twenty-seventh of February, 1775, just ten days after his twentieth birthday, Tom was married. His bride was Mary Vandrau, fifteen years of age.[1] Probably they were married in Perth Amboy, New Jersey, near the entrance to New York harbor. One searches in vain for the story of this romance. When and where Tom met Mary, and under what circumstances, it is not likely that one will ever know. Nothing beyond the simple fact of their marriage appears to have been recorded.

Perhaps there is reason enough for this void in the story of Tom Truxtun's life. In the American colonies it was normal for a man to marry early and a woman even earlier. Once married, the woman could expect to devote much of her remaining life to the rearing of children. Large families were the rule, and to this the Truxtuns conformed. Over the next thirty years, Tom's wife bore him twelve children in all, ten of whom survived childhood. While the children were growing up he was a devoted family man. He provided a comfortable home and, unlike many of his contemporaries, he was faithful to his marriage vows as long as he lived. In spite of all this, one can only conclude from a study of his life that his first love was, after all, the sea. It was the sea, stretching to the outermost ends of the earth, that set his imagination afire and enticed him on long and hazardous voyages. The sea had first call on his time and his exertions. In later life it was only the sea that figured in his recollections.

Tom and Mary's first year as man and wife set the pattern for many more to follow. Tom was home for scarcely three months out of the twelve. Six weeks after they were married, he was ready to embark on the first of three voyages to "parts remote beyond the seas," sailing this time as master of his own vessel.

Captain Truxtun! A handsome title for a young man of twenty. His first command was the *Charming Polly*, named quite naturally for his young bride (Polly was a common diminutive of Mary). Tom went to the King's customhouse in New York early in April, 1775, to have his vessel cleared for departure to the island of Jamaica in the West Indies.[2] The *Charming Polly* was a small vessel—merely a sloop, carrying a few rags of sail on a single mast.[3] Three or four hands only, besides the captain, would be needed to sail her. Nevertheless, Tom was her master. He was responsible for the safety of his vessel and the welfare of his crew. It was up to him to steer his way across trackless seas and to find a safe harbor at the end of a several-weeks' voyage. Out in the open sea his word was law, but he had to be ready to enforce his law as well; as long as he maintained the respect or fear of his men, he was ruler supreme of a tiny kingdom, a kingdom apart and remote from all the rest of the world.

Tom owned half of the vessel and her cargo, and it may have been Isaac Sears who owned the other half.[4] Usually, a cargo to the West Indies consisted of the products of farm and of forest—Indian corn, flour, salt beef, and salt pork, shingles, staves, and common lumber.[5] From Jamaica, a vessel in normal times would return with sugar, rum, molasses, and with dye woods and mahogany.[6] But these were anything but normal times: sugar, rum, and molasses could no longer be brought home in American vessels, because the nonimportation agreements, designed to keep all English goods from entering the colonies, were already in effect. The nonexportation agreements, which would cut off the export trade to the West Indies as well as to England, were to go into effect in November. But it was not yet November; in spite of some changes in the cargoes carried, trade to the islands was exceptionally brisk.

The *Charming Polly* departed from New York for Jamaica just a few days before the nineteenth of April, 1775. When Tom returned home in July, he found the whole situation changed. The shots at Concord Bridge were still echoing down the land. The armed rebellion had begun. The Continental Congress, which many people had hoped would smooth over the differences between the colonies and the royal government, was now in the business of raising and supplying an army. General Washington was at Boston, sorely perplexed by a lack of supplies, particularly gunpowder. "Our want of powder," he said, "is inconceivable. . . . A daily waste, and no supply, presents a gloomy prospect." [7] General Schuyler, at Fort Ticonderoga, was more specific. "I am extremely apprehensive," he wrote, "that a want of powder will be fatal to our operations." [8] Since almost no powder was being made in the colonies, it was at once clear that the war could not go on unless a supply was found immediately. Some powder might be captured from the British, perhaps; but most of it would have to be brought in ships from other shores. It was to this trade, patriotic as well as profitable, that the merchants turned at once.

Tom's second voyage was to Hispaniola in the West Indies. He returned with a cargo of powder and was soon ready to depart in search of another. On the thirteenth of November, 1775, one might read in a New York newspaper the first paid notice of a Truxtun voyage: "For Antigua, St. Christophers, and St. Eustatia; the Sloop *Charming-Polly,* Thomas Truxtun, Master: Has good Accomodations for Passengers, and will sail by the fifteenth of November: for Passage only, apply to the Master on board said Vessel, now lying at Hallet's Wharf." [9] For passage only. The nonexportation agreements were in effect; the war was already a reality.

This voyage, Tom's third in the *Charming Polly,* ended in virtual disaster when he was caught under the guns of a British warship. The encounter changed his role in the impending Revolution from one of passively supplying the Army with powder and supplies to one of actively seeking revenge for the loss and humiliation he suffered during this voyage.

## ROUND THE STATE HOUSE YARD

  *&*    .   .   *&*    .   .   *&*    .   .   *&*    .   .

THE islands of St. Christopher, commonly called St. Kitts, and St. Eustatius lie side by side in the chain of Leeward Islands; Antigua lies nearby. Since the Dutch were neutral in the argument between England and her colonies, St. Eustatius had become one of the busiest spots in the West Indies. The Dutch proprietors reaped a handsome profit while trade that could no longer be carried on directly between the mainland and the British islands was shunted through their warehouses. It was primarily to St. Eustatius that Tom was bound, searching for a cargo of arms and powder, the shortage of which was the most serious and immediate threat to the success of American campaigns.

When she was approaching St. Eustatius, the *Charming Polly* was brought to by a British sloop-of-war, the *Argo* of 28 guns. A 28-gun ship—twelve guns on a side and at bow and stern a pair of chasing guns—was a small one in a Navy that boasted hundred-gun line-of-battle ships; but to Tom, who may have had not even so much as a pistol in his own vessel, the *Argo* was a formidable antagonist. When he carried his papers on board the warship, he no doubt vociferated his protest at being molested, but the British commander would hear none of it. Since the colonies were in a state of rebellion, all rebel vessels were being seized. The fact that there was no law permitting the Royal Navy to take private property from a British subject—this was still 1775—did not disturb the *Argo*'s captain. His admiral was confident that there soon would be such a law. All of Tom's arguments fell on deaf ears. The Royal Navy was willing to let him wait awhile until the proper law had been enacted, and then the question could be settled in a British Court of Vice-Admiralty. Tom had no choice but to sail his vessel down to St. Kitts. There he lost her.

For more than two months he languished in the Islands waiting for the Court to release his property. He was not alone in his misery, however; twenty or thirty other American vessels had been captured. Back home, it was reported that some of the Americans were shackled and thrown into dungeons "for only expressing their sentiments." This report no doubt was greatly exaggerated; but the loss of a score of vessels was no exaggeration. In mid-March, the *Charming Polly* was condemned as a prize of war. It was only then that he learned that word had just arrived from England authorizing the capture of American merchantmen. The British admiral had anticipated the action of his government by almost three months; his clairvoyance had cost Tom dearly. His vessel and cargo were gone, irretrievably lost.[1]

A commander with nothing to command, Tom's next move was clear enough. Going to neutral St. Eustatius, he took passage in the first vessel he could find that was bound for an American port. Early in the spring of 1776, Tom arrived in Philadelphia, where the Second Continental Congress was in session.[2]

The grass and trees in the State House yard were beginning to take on the green of another season. Inside the State House the representatives from the colonies, in congress assembled, were debating issues that would be remembered for an age. Outside, a fiery pamphlet that argued openly for independence of the colonies was selling by the thousands. Advertised in newspapers and ale houses, Tom Paine's "*Common Sense* for eighteen pence" was helping to push the Congress toward the brink of independence.[3] The colonies actually had been at war with England since that memorable nineteenth of April of the year before; but many people thought that there was still hope for reconciliation. Word had just been received from London that a shipload of Peace Commissioners was supposed to be on the way to bring the colonies back into the fold without any further bloodshed. But the Congress already knew—and this was no news to Tom Truxtun—that the King had suspended all trade with America and had made American vessels fair game for British guns upon the high seas.[4]

The merchants of Philadelphia decided that they too could play that game. They asked the Congress to let them send out privateers with authority to capture any British vessels they might find. After much discussion and some delay, the permission was granted.[5] Letters of marque and reprisal, which made legal the capture of enemy vessels by privately-owned American vessels, were prepared by the Continental Congress, and during the course of the Revolution many hundreds were issued.

Tom, still smarting from the loss of his sloop in St. Kitts, was ready for immediate action. When he heard that two privateers were to sail from Philadelphia, he went at once to the owners. The captains had already been chosen, but there was a place for a prize lieutenant in one of the vessels. Tom would have to sail as a subordinate officer. No matter: the sooner he got to sea the better.

The *Congress* and *Chance* were the first two privateers to be given letters of marque by the Continental Congress.[6] Tom was to sail in the *Congress,* under Captain McAroy. Both vessels were small; both were sloops. The *Congress* mounted six guns and the *Chance* but four. Each vessel carried a crew of forty-five, a multitude by peacetime standards. But these were vessels of war: the guns needed crews to serve them; and prize crews, to manage the vessels they might capture, had to be taken along.

It was an arduous task to fit out a war vessel in Philadelphia in 1776. The privateers had to share men and materials with the Army. There was no gunpowder to be bought at any price. The Continental Congress was figuratively sitting on all the powder in the city; a secret committee was responsible for its distribution.[7] In truth, the quantity at the disposal of the Congress was pitifully small. The few vessels that could elude the British blockade off the Delaware capes brought in only a dribble of powder. The Continental Navy, which had sailed from Philadelphia in February, took with it its share of powder and ship's stores. The Pennsylvania fleet, to be used for river defense, was calling for materials and powder.

In spite of all these difficulties, the *Congress* and *Chance* were fitted out by the middle of April.[8] They had four hundred pounds of gunpowder and three hundred pounds of assorted shot between them.[9] Not a plentiful supply, but enough to cow a totally unarmed merchantman or two.

There remained one more obstacle in their way. A few miles down the river, the Committee of Safety had built a maze of *cheveux-de-frise* to discourage any British vessels that might attempt to sail into the port of Philadelphia. The *cheveux-de-frise* consisted of heavy timber caissons, anchored in position and topped by huge iron spikes, "the bigness of a Man's thigh."[10] Only the river pilots knew all the details of the works, and they could only guide the way of vessels approved by the Committee of Safety. This approval was forthcoming for the two privateers, however.[11] At last they were ready to sail.

On the very next tide the *Congress* and *Chance* dropped down the river together. They ran safely through the *cheveux-de-frise;* they continued down the widening river, taking advantage of every slant of wind to speed them on their way. Keeping a sharp lookout for the blockading frigate, they discharged their pilot near Cape May and continued unmolested out into the open sea.[12]

Tom looked over the side at the clean white water, curling back from the bow-wave, as the *Congress* heeled to a stiff western breeze. He took a deep breath of the fresh sea air. His gaze drifted aloft as he noted the set of the sails. Once again he was going out to sail beyond the horizon, to learn a little more of the ways of the ever changing sea. His mind took him back ashore for a moment, to Mary. A new bride but a year before, Mary had spent most of the time since then waiting for her sailor husband to come home from the sea. Perhaps this time he could please her by bringing home a rich prize. At any rate, a prize would please him; it would help compensate for the loss of his first command.

CHAPTER 7

## *CONGRESS* AND *CHANCE*

℘ . . ℘ . . ℘ . . ℘ . .

HEADING south from Delaware Bay, holding a fair wind day after day, the *Congress* and the *Chance* saw nothing to interest a prize master until after they reached their chosen cruising grounds. Coming onto the coast of Cuba, the two privateers, still sailing in company, were ready to patrol the tract of sea between Florida and Cuba called the Gulf of Florida. It would be hard to find a better place to cruise at this particular time of year. The Jamaica fleet, homeward bound for England, heavily laden with tropical plantation products, sailed unescorted up through these waters. If there were slave ships bound for home after selling their human cargo in the Islands, they would be carrying hard money—gold doubloons and Spanish milled dollars—in addition to exotic produce. Best of all, they would be entirely unaware that American privateers might be cruising here. The news that the colonies had decided to venture out with privateers was brought by the *Congress* and the *Chance* themselves.[1]

The first prize to be taken was not a Jamaicaman, however. The *Thistle,* a small schooner from Mobile bound for the Leeward Islands, was brought to by the *Congress,* which pretended to be a tender for a British frigate. The master of the *Thistle* was ordered to come on board. When he clambered over the rail onto the deck of the little privateer, he was prepared to display his papers and receive clearance to sail on with no further ado. When he found that this was not a British tender and that he was about to lose his own vessel, he turned livid, screaming execrations at his captors. "Pirates," he called them; "worse than Pirates and Highway Robbers." He was no enemy, he argued. He was merely taking a cargo of flour and lumber to be traded off in St. Kitts for a cargo of sugar and rum. Mobile was a British city, to be sure, and not in the thirteen united colonies; but the owners of his vessel, said the master of the *Thistle,* were merely peaceful merchants who were not in the least angry at the colonies. Furthermore, he was not carrying supplies to the British Army. If his flour should eventually find its way to the Army, that was entirely beyond his control. Captain McAroy of the *Congress* listened to this tale but decided to send the *Thistle* into an American port. The Court of Admiralty in Philadelphia could decide whether she was an enemy vessel.

Just after this prize schooner, sailed by a prize crew, had been dispatched to a friendly port, two more strange sails appeared on the horizon; the *Congress* filled away in pursuit, carrying with her the master of the *Thistle,* his clothes, his papers, his money, his quadrant, his negro man named Lewis, and his negro man named Jack.[2]

The two strange sails vanished, and another week or ten days of empty cruising brought the *Congress* and the *Chance* up to the ninth of May, 1776, with no further captures. On that day, however, three ships of the Jamaica fleet hove in sight. Each of them was larger than the privateers, but two of them were completely unarmed and the other was not much better off. Without a struggle, the *Congress* took the *Reynolds,* largest of the three, while the *Chance* took the *Lady Juliana.* The third ship, the *Juno,* was armed with "two Great Guns and six Swivel Guns"; but the two privateers together, mounting a total of ten guns, had little trouble persuading the master of the *Juno* that a fight would be futile. He promptly struck his colors and surrendered his ship.[3]

There was no question about the status of these ships. Coming from Jamaica as they had and being bound for their home ports in England, they carried contraband cargoes toward enemy ports. This first privateering cruise, less than a month old, would turn out to be a fabulous success if only these prizes could be gotten safely into friendly American ports. Three more prize crews would be needed; one had already been sent off in the *Thistle;* and some men would have to remain in the privateers to sail them home. Here was reason enough for the magnitude of the privateers' original crews.

The prisoners from the three ships just captured were disposed of at once. The master of the *Juno,* the mate of the *Reynolds,* and twenty sailors were put off in a large boat. They had no trouble pulling into the harbor of Matanzas, nearby.[4] Ten hands, shifting their allegiance as readily as they shifted their clothes, entered immediately into the privateers' service.[5] The masters of the other two ships, the rest of their crews, and their passengers were placed in a passing "Spanish vessel that was leaky," which put them ashore in one of the Bahama Islands where they could arrange for passage home to England.[6] The master of the *Lady Juliana,* who was returning home with his new Jamaican bride, was permitted to take her with him, but her dowry, a considerable fortune in cash and silver plate, was taken from him by the privateers.[7] The ships were then dispatched under prize crews for American ports.

Tom was told off as prize master of the *Reynolds,* largest of the ships. Going on board with his prize crew, Tom surveyed the ship with a critical eye; he checked to make sure that he had ample stores and water on board. No doubt he was pleased with what he found. The ship was larger than any he had sailed in, save only the British man-of-war. The living quarters were the best he had ever had in any vessel; and the stores, intended to be sufficient for the British officers and passengers for two months or more, would keep him and his small crew well fed for as long as his voyage might conceivably last. When he was satisfied that he had ship enough and crew enough to make a safe voyage reasonably certain, he laid down his course and got his ship under way. With a wave of his hand he dismissed the tiny fleet that had brought him here to find his latest command.

In order to avoid the risk of running the blockade off the Delaware capes, he chose to take his ship to a New England port. After nearly three weeks of uneventful sailing, steering toward the Massachusetts coast, he made a landfall on the island of Martha's Vineyard. He anchored there for a few days, until he could make sure that there were no British ships lurking between the island and the mainland; then he sailed into the closest mainland harbor, which was Bedford in Dartmouth—now New Bedford.[8]

The other two prize ships also arrived safely in American ports. The *Lady Juliana* went to Boston. She was accosted off Boston by a "Scotch vessel of force" carrying soldiers and supplies to the British Army in America. The prize master of the *Lady Juliana* told the Scottish captain that he was bound from Jamaica for London, but because he thought his cargo of sugar and rum might bring a better price in Boston, he was going to call there first. The Scotsman, thinking that the British still held Boston, asked the prize master to lead him in to Boston, since he was not acquainted with these waters. The result of this encounter was that the *Lady Juliana* arrived safely in port and the Scottish vessel fell prey to two vessels of the Continental Navy that were cruising nearby.[9] The *Juno*, last of the prize ships to be accounted for, eluded the blockading frigates and made her way into Philadelphia.

Eventually Tom would get a share of the prize money realized from the sale of all the ships and cargoes. The owners of the *Congress* and *Chance* claimed half of all prize moneys; the other half was to be divided among the officers and crews. The total prize was rich indeed. Over $22,000 in cash and 180 pounds of silver plate were taken from the *Lady Juliana*.[10] The cargo of Tom's ship, typical of the others, consisted of "302 Hogsheads of choice Sugars, 74 Puncheons of Rum; 52 Pipes, 10 half Pipes, 10 Butts and 4 Hogsheads of Wine; 42 Bags of Pimiento, 40 Planks and 11 Logs of Mahogany, 16 Tons of Lignum Vitae, and 7 Tons of Fustick."[11]

Before there was any money to be divided, the prize ships and their cargoes had to be libeled by the captors, regularly condemned by a Court of Admiralty, and then sold at public auction. Long before the *Reynolds* was condemned and sold, Tom had turned over to somebody else the paper work, the waiting upon judges, and the attendance at auction sales that had to be done by a member of the captor's crew. He was in a hurry to get back to New York; he had not seen Mary for at least three months and possibly not since the previous fall; and if the *Congress* and *Chance* were going out for another cruise he would want to be ready to go with them. But while he was in New York he talked to Isaac Sears. He decided then and there that the *Congress* and *Chance* could sail without him, because he had more important business to attend to. Sears, in company with two other merchants in New York and one in New Haven, was nearly ready to send out the first vessel of what eventually became an extensive privateer fleet. Would Tom like to command this privateer? Yes! How soon could she be made ready for him?

CHAPTER 8

## *INDEPENDENCE* TO *MARS*

℘   •   •   ℘   •   •   ℘   •   •   ℘   •   •

TOM knew, when he sailed in his new privateer, that he might not be able to return to New York when his cruise was over. This was the summer of 1776. General Howe, with his army in transports, had arrived off Sandy Hook at the end of June. After being driven from Boston by General Washington's troops, Howe had repaired to Halifax. Now he was back; on the eighth of July he landed his men on Staten Island, athwart the entrance to New York Bay.[1] General Washington already had his army in the city, at the upper end of the Bay.

On the eighth of July, in Philadelphia, the Declaration of Independence was, according to one eye witness, "published and proclaimed from that awful stage in the State House yard."[2] On the ninth, General Washington had it read to his troops in New York.[3]

It was about this time that Tom received a letter of marque for his privateer. It arrived when he was almost ready to sail. His vessel, a seventy-ton sloop called—as one might expect—the *Independence,* was complete with arms and provisions. For a crew of sixty men, he had on board thirty barrels of salt beef and fifteen of salt pork; for the ten carriage guns, he carried five hundred pounds of powder and a quantity of four-pound shot—about three inches in diameter; if a fight at close quarters developed the crew could make good use of the thirty muskets and twenty pistols in the arms chest.[4]

Since the British controlled the entrance to the Bay, it would be foolish to try to run through their blockade as long as there was another way out. Rather than risk being captured before his voyage was fairly under way, Tom sailed the *Independence* up the East River, through the narrow and treacherous strait called the Hell Gate, and out into the Sound safely beyond the reach of British guns.[5]

Crossing and recrossing the tract of sea where the Gulf Stream veers eastward from the American coast, Tom captured a brig that had strayed from a homeward bound convoy of British merchantmen from the West Indies. On board this vessel he had the good fortune to find a copy of the signals being used in the convoy, a fleet of nearly eighty sail. Nonchalantly he sailed the *Independence* into the convoy and took up a station at its center. Knowing what the signals were, he had no fear of being challenged. All day he sailed along peacefully in this fleet, arousing no suspicion, answering every signal that was addressed to him. As evening approached, he began to drop back toward the rear, keeping a sharp eye peeled for a ship that would make a likely prize. When it was quite dark, he worked his way over toward a ship that appeared to be both valuable and vulnerable. Coming close alongside, he menaced her with his guns and ordered her to surrender. Without alarming the rest of the convoy, he managed to cut this ship out from its rear. Before morning he had a prize crew in the ship, the ship's company was imprisoned aboard the *Independence,* and the convoy, after plodding on throughout the night, was nowhere to be seen.[6]

Tom cruised in the *Independence* for about two months. He captured two brigs and two ships, all of them British merchantmen homeward bound from the West Indies.[7] One of the ships was recaptured by a British man-of-war before her prize crew could bring her into an American port;[8] and one of the brigs Tom returned to her crew after taking out a few bags of cocoa, a bale of cotton, some quarter-casks of wine, and after he had relieved himself of his prisoners.[9] Probably this brig was the last of the four captures. If so, he had already dispatched three prize crews and had taken as prisoners, on board the *Independence,* the officers and crews from the three prize vessels. Short of men for prize crews and long on prisoners, he again chose a prudent course of action. He took out of the brig only such cargo as he could conveniently carry, then gave the vessel over to the prisoners and headed for home.

This cruise, like the first cruise of the *Congress* and *Chance,* was successful and immensely profitable. In addition to the cocoa, cotton, and wine that he took from the brig, Tom sent into New England a cargo of whale oil in the other brig, and a cargo of sugar, rum, and cotton in the ship. The vessels themselves undoubtedly brought a good price because they could be refitted as privateers and, in their turn, they could bring in more prizes and more prize cargoes.

Putting into Boston at the end of his cruise in the *Independence,* Tom was greeted by Isaac Sears, who had recently fled from New York when the British took the city in September, 1776. The two of them, jubilant at their success in privateering, were full of schemes for bigger and richer enterprises in the future. The *Independence* had grown too small for Tom. The number of men and guns she could carry were limited; and as for prizes out in the sea, waiting to be taken, there seemed to be no end to them. Besides, if British sail were plentiful in American waters, how much more plentiful they must be in British waters. Tom proposed to take the war to the British, but he decided he would need a bigger ship to do it. Very well; let someone else take the *Independence* out next time; meanwhile, find a ship to suit the appetite and talents of this able commander.

Sears and company were not the only people who talked, ate, and slept privateering. It had spread like a rash over the whole eastern seaboard. The fabulous profits that the privateers were making distressed the leaders who were trying to organize the war against the British Army and Navy. The American Commissary-General found it virtually impossible to buy supplies because he could not outbid the privateers.[10] One American general said, "Nothing impedes the recruiting of the Army so much as the present rage for privateering." [11] Another said, "The success of privateering has set all the troops distracted." It was said that many of the men "pant for the expiration of their inlistments," in order that they might go out in privateers.[12] A man could not be expected to enter or stay in the Army while he was reasonably sure of earning a handsome share of prize money in a privateer. No money could be borrowed by the government at a moderate rate of interest because the merchants seemed to be concerned only with "privateering, buying up prize cargoes, and monopolizing them at any price." [13] On the other hand, some of the leaders of the Revolution, like John Adams, felt that the privateers would shorten the war. "It is by cutting off supplies," he said, "not by attacks, sieges, or assaults, that I expect deliverance from enemies." [14]

Tom, in his early twenties, had in the privateer service a better opportunity to further the cause of the thirteen United States than in any other place he might have served. In either the Army or Navy he could have been only a very junior officer. His talent for command would have been largely wasted. But in privateers he was in a position where his audacity and ability to lead men could pay dividends to his country in destruction of the enemy's commercial fleet. His job also paid Tom good dividends; but that is not to his discredit. It is not always necessary to starve in order to be useful.

In the months following his arrival at Boston, he must surely have gone home to see Mary, but not for long. After the prize business of the *Independence* was completed in December, the fitting out of his next ship demanded all of his time in order to have her ready for departure early the following spring.[15]

In May, 1777, Tom was about to depart for a six months' cruise in European waters. His ship was ready for sea. The *Mars,* a ship of 280-tons burden, was probably somewhat larger than the British traders in which he had served as an apprentice. She had a battery of 22 carriage guns and 12 smaller swivel guns, enough to subdue almost any merchantman afloat. Somewhere he had located more than a ton of gunpowder. His ship, staunch and roomy, was well found with provisions enough to last his crew of 150 men for the full six months.[16]

Captain Tom Truxtun, aboard his ship *Mars* in Boston harbor, comes into sharp focus for the first time as he strides his quarter-deck, giving orders to cast off all lines and to spread sail enough to get his ship under way. He is only twenty-two years old, yet already he is accustomed to command. His two lieutenants and 150 men look to him as the ultimate authority in his ship. His position is secure; it is based on respect for the reasonableness of his orders and his discipline. He derives none of his power from the fear of the cat. Flogging, a common punishment for seamen, is practically unknown in his ship. Not that he is afraid to rule by force should it ever become necessary. If his authority were challenged directly, he would not hesitate to break a man's jaw or his head. Something about his demeanor tells a man that this is so: his orders are never challenged. He does not understand fear in a personal sense. Cowardice is a trait that he cannot comprehend.

He is a man of medium height, about five feet seven inches tall, well built, with brown hair, a fresh complexion, tanned by the sun and bleached by the constant sea wind, and blue eyes that are never at rest.[17] Telling him, as they must, many things about his men and his ship and the sea, his eyes shift constantly, from a hand at the pin-rail to a loose rope-end he had not noticed before; from a hand on the ratlines to the water beyond the ship, where he continually studies and tries to interpret the face of the sea. His gaze is forever drifting aloft, noting the set of his sails and the condition of his rigging.

His appearance arrests the attention because he is mounted on his own quarter-deck. He carries easily his responsibility; he is accustomed to endless days and nights of constant vigilance. He is the master of the fate of his men and his ship.

He will grow as he goes from command to command, each a little more important than the last. He will show his mettle when the full shattering force of a hurricane finds him undismayed. Finally, he will attain his full stature when the noise of war engulfs all those around him and leaves him cool, calm, and in full command.

The cruise of the *Mars,* which occupied the latter half of 1777, was Tom's last and most successful adventure in privateering. He cruised for several weeks at the western end of the English Channel, where most of England's trade routes converged. The *Mars* was but one of many American privateers in these waters, and several vessels of the Continental Navy were here also, preying upon British commerce; but Tom managed to capture five vessels—two sloops, two brigs, and a ship—all of which his prize crews took safely into the nearby friendly ports of France.[18]

It was convenient to send captured vessels into Nantes and other

French ports, where they could be disposed of and turned into cash and supplies without having to risk the rigors of the long passage across the Atlantic or the danger of recapture by British men-of-war. The British Ambassador to France, Lord Stormont, complained bitterly about this use of French ports by the Americans. It was contrary to treaties, he reminded the French Minister; furthermore, it did not comport with "the General Interest of all civilized Nations." [19] This traffic was responsible in part for the open French alliance with the United States and her declaration of war against Great Britain during the following year.

Tom was in Nantes in September to replenish his supplies and to look after the business of disposing of his prizes.[20] One prize at least, the sloop *Jenny*, he sent back to America, perhaps because his own ship could not carry all the prize freight that he wanted to send home.[21] In January, 1778, he returned to Boston in the *Mars*. The ship was repaired and refitted and in a few months went out to cruise again, but Tom did not go along. He decided, for reasons unknown, to quit the privateering trade, to leave the expanding fleet of Isaac Sears, and to depart from the city of Boston.[22]

At this point, he took time out from the war to attend to some personal business. When the British Army had departed from Philadelphia in the spring of 1778, after holding the city captive throughout the winter—this was the winter that General Washington and his ragged army had spent at Valley Forge—Tom took Mary and their belongings and moved to Philadelphia. Here, in the largest city in America, they soon had for the first time—after more than three years of married life—a home. That fall, when the first frosts were painting the Pennsylvania countryside with streaks of crimson and patches of brown and when the days were warm and the nights crisp and clear, the Truxtuns were happily together, awaiting the arrival of their first-born. On the twenty-fourth of October, 1778, the baby arrived. They named her Sarah, after Tom's mother. She was baptized by the Reverend Mr. William White, rector of Christ Church in Philadelphia.[23]

Now that Tom was a family man as well as a successful shipmaster, he probably considered his duty to his family when he chose his next job. From the many opportunities he had for employment, he decided on a connection in Philadelphia with the Caldwell brothers, whose merchant ships were bringing in war supplies. He abandoned privateering and returned to a merchant captain's berth, but this had no noticeable effect upon his opportunities for adventures at sea nor upon his capacity for being at the scene of action when action was imminent.

## CHAPTER 9

## ANDREW CALDWELL

                    

AS THE War of Revolution dragged on into its fifth year in the spring of 1779, Tom sailed a new ship over the familiar route to the West Indies. The *Andrew Caldwell,* armed with ten guns to protect her from British privateers and the "refugee galleys" that infested the lower reaches of the Delaware River, carried a crew of only thirty or forty men, not enough to be engaged in a privateering voyage; but she carried a letter of marque in order to legalize any prizes she might happen to take in the course of her normal business.[1]

Tom, seeking a cargo of rum and salt, was bound for the Dutch island of St. Eustatius. The island was in sight, barely an hour's sail away, when he repeated his experience of three and a half years before. While he was yet trying to reach the haven of the neutral roadstead, he found himself under the guns of another warship of the Royal Navy. To give battle with his few small guns would be but a futile gesture; bowing to the inevitable, he surrendered his ship. Once again he sailed under guard down to St. Kitts, where the *Andrew Caldwell* was taken over by a British crew.

Tom was detained in St. Kitts for a short time only.[2] When he was released he hurried back to St. Eustatius in order to find passage to Philadelphia, or at least to North America. St. Eustatius, seven miles northwest of St. Kitts, was a rocky, barren island ending abruptly at a bold coast line, a rough stone in a jewel-like setting. All the nearby islands were lush and green, capped with verdant mountain peaks that pierced low-hanging clouds. On the lower slopes were plantations, neatly kept and prosperous in appearance. But not

St. Eustatius. One traveler who visited the island about this time described it as "a place of vast traffick from every quarter of the globe. The ships of various nations which rode before it were very fine, but the Island itself the only ugly one I have seen. . . . It is however an instance of Dutch industry little inferior to their dykes; as the one half of the town is gained off the Sea, which is fenced out by Barracadoes, and the other dug out of an immense mountain of sand and rock; which rises to a great height behind the houses, and will one day bury them under it."[3]

There was only one street in the town. Lined with the stalls of shopkeepers from many lands, the narrow street was a cosmopolitan bazaar. "Here hang rich embroideries," the traveler observed, "painted silks, flowered Muslins, with all the Manufactures of the Indies. Just by hang Sailor's Jackets, trousers, shoes, hats, etc. Next stall contains most exquisite silver plate, the most beautiful indeed I ever saw, and close by these iron-pots, kettles and shovels. Perhaps the next presents you with French and English Millinary-wares. But it were endless to enumerate the variety of merchandize in such a place, for in every store you find every thing, be their qualities ever so opposite."[4]

Contemplating his next move, Tom no doubt wandered past the colorful shops; his way led him at length to the trading firm of Aull and Morson. After explaining his predicament to the merchants, he received from them a bold offer which he promptly accepted. Aull and Morson advanced him money to buy another vessel to replace the *Andrew Caldwell* and to buy a cargo to take back to Philadelphia. It was only a matter of days, after that, until he bought the *Lydia*.[5] She may have already carried the name—many other vessels did—but it is perhaps significant that Andrew Caldwell's wife was named Lydia. At any rate, he loaded her with salt, rum, and some loose freight, including "A Package containing a Bible in Twelve Volumes" for a Jewish merchant in Philadelphia, and in September, 1779, he was homeward bound, carrying to the Caldwells the news that they had just bought another ship.[6]

The voyage was a hard one. The *Lydia* met with foul winds; she was becalmed; several times she was chased out of her way by British men-of-war; and finally, off Cape Hatteras in the middle of September, the hurricane month, she found herself in a roaring gale.

Tom took in sail as the wind increased. When the first full fury of the storm hit his ship, he brought her head up into the wind's teeth to avoid being swamped. The gale mounted to hurricane force and for more than two days and two nights the *Lydia* lay to, drifting steadily to leeward, not daring to show a rag of canvas. The hurricane pounded the little ship unmercifully; the wind thrummed a terrifying tune in the rigging. Stays, stretched taut as wires, strained against the wind's force until they reached their limit and parted with reports like cannon shots; then masts and spars, lacking any support, gave way with a series of splintering shocks. There was nothing Tom could do to save his upper works from destruction; his ship lost all her masts—fore, main, and mizzen—and her bowsprit as well.

On the third day, when the hurricane blew itself out, the hulk of the *Lydia* lay helpless somewhere at sea. Surveying the wreckage and deciding what next to do, Tom placed no blame on his ship. "If she had not been the best sea boat in the world," he recounted later, "we never could have survived the tempest." Fortunately, he had had enough sea room to avoid being driven ashore on Diamond Shoals off the pitch of Cape Hatteras.

Within a short time he had lashed together the few small spars that remained on board and had fished those to the splintered stump of a mast. On this jury-mast he was able to hoist a small spread of sail. Thus he continued on his way, slowly and laboriously working the *Lydia* up the coast toward Norfolk, a hundred miles distant. He sailed under the jury-rig day after day while the wind came out of the north, making headway almost impossible; it was almost two weeks before he finally reached the sheltered waters of Chesapeake Bay. During this time he was carefully inspected, at a safe distance, by two privateers. One of them, a brig of twelve guns, hovered about all one night, then at daylight came up fast as though she were going to attack. She held the weather gauge; that is, she had the advantage of being able to close the action or avoid it as she chose. Tom, slogging along with barely enough sail to steer by, could not maneuver his ship; but he was not content merely to wait for the attack. He bore away to leeward, losing precious headway, and at the same time hoisted his colors and "gave her a shot." The brig made no reply, but hauled her wind and went off. She chose not to come to action with a captain who, in spite of the shattered condition of his ship, had the audacity to invite an attack. For fifteen days Tom slept only when exhaustion forced him to it; even then he turned in all standing, completely dressed—coat, shoes, and all—and ready to tumble out on deck at an instant's notice.[7]

When at last the *Lydia* arrived in the bay, Tom took her up to Portsmouth, opposite Norfolk, where he could obtain the materials he would need to refit her. With furious energy, hardly taking time even to eat, he supervised every detail of the repairs and refitting. He disposed of the cargo, storing some, sending some up to Baltimore. He expected at first to offer the rum and salt to the government for army supplies, but upon learning that prices had risen because of "some speculators from the Noreward" he decided it would be to his owners' advantage to send it up the James and Rappahanock rivers to be traded for tobacco, which he could sell for a substantial profit on his next voyage to the West Indies.

As soon as he felt he could be spared at Portsmouth, he took the rest of his cargo up to Baltimore. It would then take him but two or three more days to make the journey to Philadelphia to see his wife and year-old baby. If he was home at all, it was only for a few days, because he was soon back in his ship, sailing again to the West Indies to recoup some of the losses he had suffered in his scrapes with the Royal Navy and the angry sea. One thing more he did before he departed from Portsmouth. To change his luck, he changed the name of his ship. Looking back upon his privateering days, he borrowed the name of a happier vessel. The *Lydia* became, for better or worse, the *Independence*.[8]

It seemed, for a time, that it was definitely for worse. Returning to Philadelphia from his second voyage to St. Eustatius early in February, 1780, the perils of the sea once again threatened to put an end to his ship. This time it was ice that plagued him.

All the way up through the wintry seas north of the latitude of the Bahamas, the *Independence* had been battling one continuous gale of wind. Fifty miles offshore from the Delaware capes, Tom saw a sight that strikes terror in the very soul of a deep-water sailor. White water—breakers—appeared on the horizon. Knowing that there were no charted shoals in these waters, he ventured closer and found the sea breaking over great islands of ice. The Delaware Bay was a field of broken ice; when Mike Dawson, the pilot who conned Tom's ship up the bay, came aboard from the pilot boat, he told Tom that he had never seen anything like it. At Philadelphia, the river had been frozen over since before Christmas.[9]

Creeping slowly along through the drifting ice in the bay, the *Independence* rammed into one huge cake that refused to give way. As the ship came to a shuddering halt, the ice tore a gaping hole through her planking below the water line. Water immediately began to pour into the hold; almost as quickly Tom sprang to action. Upon his order a loose sail—any sail that happened to be handy—was lowered down around the bows of the ship; it was then made fast by lines leading aft to the deck. In casting about for something else to help check the rush of water into the ship, Tom thought of his mattress. In an instant it was snatched from the Captain's bunk and was lowered over the side to stanch the flow; but in spite of all his exertions the ship continued to fill. Within fifteen minutes there was five feet of water in the hold. There was only one thing left to do. With his ship settling rapidly, Tom with great difficulty ran her aground before she foundered.

At low water he was able to patch the leak and pump out the hold. As soon as she was refloated, he sailed up the river to a wharf in New Castle. Later, when he sat down in his cabin to write a report of the accident to his owners, he explained all the circumstances and described his actions. "I must add," he added, "that I believe few ships in a similar situation was ever saved." [10]

Tom made a third voyage to St. Eustatius that spring with happier results. All the way down to the Islands he chased and brought to every vessel he saw except one, and that one, a British frigate, chased him for half a day but failed to overtake him. He had decided before he left home that he needed a prize to ease the pinch of "the variety of vicissitudes I went through with that ship." [11] He carried a letter of marque, which permitted him to take prizes, if any should offer, in the course of his regular trading voyage. But all the vessels he saw were friendly except the frigate. On the return passage, however, while she was sailing in company with two brigs, the *Independence* took a prize.[12] The prize was a brig named *Clyde,* and she put up no resistance. Nevertheless, Tom watched her closely all the way up to Philadelphia. The proportion of the prize that each of the captors was entitled to was decided by the Court of Admiralty, but in view of his "extraordinary Care, and attention" to bringing the prize in safely, the others who were present when the capture was made decided that Tom should have a larger share than the Court had awarded him.[13]

The cargo of the prize brig, consisting entirely of rum, was sold for a fantastic price. It was valued at more than £300,000, almost a million dollars.[14] Nearly eighty dollars a gallon for rum sounds impossible; but this was June, 1780.

Prices had been rising ever since the Continental Congress started to print paper money almost five years before. Price fixing had been tried, but merchants with few goods and customers with many wants had soon wrecked that system. The individual states had followed the lead of the Congress, and printing presses in every state were spewing out money by the bushel. Now the spiral of inflation whirled through every town in the land, accelerating with each new day. In March, 1780, when the Congress created a new Continental dollar, it publicly admitted that its money was backed by nothing but lame faith. This new dollar was to be worth, by law, forty of the continentals then in circulation. Already, the old continentals were "not worth a continental." They found their way to the trash barrel when the rate finally fell to a thousand to one.[15]

This explosive inflation was but one indication of the low ebb to which the American cause had fallen after more than five years of war. The patriotic spirit of '76 had, according to one observer, "given place to avarice and every rascally practice. . . . Its depreciation," he said, "is equal to that of the currency—*forty for one*." [16]

Tom Truxtun did not seem to be much concerned about his country's fortunes at this time. His next voyage, in the course of which he deliberately got himself into a scrape with John Paul Jones, added no luster to his career; but eventually he was a better man for having exchanged words with that ardent patriot.

## CHAPTER 10

# INDEPENDENCE II AND JOHN PAUL JONES

ℰ . . ℰ . . ℰ . . ℰ . .

THE *Independence* crossed the North Atlantic in the late summer of 1780. The passage took six or seven weeks—disagreeable weeks for the crew and trying weeks for the Captain. His crew had complained about rotten meat that was being served to them even before the ship left the Delaware; and with good reason. Tom admitted that the provisions were the worst he had ever gone to sea with. "We have not a barrel of beef or pork but what smells," he had told his owners, "which I am verry sorry is the case." But there was nothing better to be had.[1]

There had been a shortage of meat all spring and summer. Prices were unconscionably high and quality had dropped to a new low. While Tom had been able to keep peace in his ship by promising his crew that they should have, as soon as they reached France, the very best provisions that money could buy, General Washington's armies were virtually without meat, and their faith in promises had long since vanished. When the government could find a few cattle to be killed, salt for preserving the meat was lacking because, as the President of Pennsylvania complained, "we cannot get a Bushel [of salt] as we have neither Specie nor Continental Money & our Merchants will not touch State Money."[2]

Near the end of September, the *Independence* arrived in L'Orient, a seaport on the Brittany coast of France. This port was built to serve the French East India Company and was named for the source of its wealth; its principal trade was in the treasure of the Indies. Great vaulted stone warehouses lined attractive streets and quays. Sailors from the far corners of the earth congregated here, swapping money and exotic goods for the pleasures of the beach.[3]

In the roadstead, under the Ile de Groix, ships from many oceans lay at anchor, waiting to discharge their cargoes or to take others on board. When Tom's ship came into these roads he saw Captain John Paul Jones's *Ariel*, a ship of the Continental Navy, lying at anchor. Tom was flying at the main truck of the *Independence* a long pennant, the signal of command. When he passed close under the stern of the *Ariel*, he showed no mark of respect for this Navy ship nor for her captain. In the face of a resolution of the Continental Congress that no American privateer or merchant vessel be permitted to wear pennants when in company with vessels of the Continental Navy, Tom continued to fly his command pennant. He sailed on, according to Captain Jones, "with a long Pendant Flying and without lowering any Sail or Colour or even shewing any mark of Politeness." [4] Reflecting widespread opinion of the moment, Tom had little but contempt for the Continental Navy. It was an exalted service only in its own eyes. Tom no doubt agreed with others that the privateers had done a better job of commerce raiding than had the Navy; and the Navy had done little else.

Captain Jones was not the sort of officer to command the respect of a merchant captain who was developing some awareness of his own importance. Jones was lionized by the natives on this Brittany shore; many people called him "king of Brittany" because of his great influence with the officialdom of L'Orient; the King of France had sent him an elegant sword; all of this tickled his vanity.[5] He was forever jealous of his good name and fame. One of his officers said, "Jones has a wonderful notion of his name being handed down to posterity." [6] But his inordinate vanity was tightly bound up with a consuming patriotic zeal; he was as jealous of the good name and fame of the Continental Navy as of his own. He countenanced no action that might be construed as an insult to its dignity.

While Tom was arranging for a cargo for his ship, the *Ariel* departed, bound out for America. The master of the *Independence* affected nonchalance and unconcern when, five days later, the *Ariel*, dismasted and wrecked, crept back into a berth near his ship.[7]

Captain Jones had sailed out into a gale that threatened to drive his ship onto an angry lee shore. The men in the *Ariel* spent a terrible night, expecting each moment to hear the grinding of hull on rocks, expecting each hour to be their last. In the middle of this blackest of nights, with his ship standing almost on her beam ends, Captain Jones called his officers together on the quarter-deck to consult about whether to cut away the foremast and to let go the sheet anchor. This was agreed to; before the night was over the main and mizzenmasts had followed the foremast over the side.[8]

Tom could sympathize with Jones; he had lived through a storm in which his ship had been dismasted; but apparently he paid scant notice to the arrival of the *Ariel*. From the masthead of the *Independence* flew a broad pennant now, flaunting Tom's disdain for the Continental Navy as here represented by John Paul Jones. It is small wonder that Tom's insolence rankled in Jones's mind. His patience reached its limit when the *Independence,* still wearing the broad pennant, weighed anchor and dropped down the river, again steering close to the *Ariel*. Jones sent a boat with an officer to remind Tom of the resolution of Congress. This mission was rebuffed; the mate on deck told Jones's officer that he had orders to "treat with contempt and disobey any order" Jones might send regarding the pennant. In addition, the hands in the boat were menaced by Tom's men.

Jones then sent his first lieutenant, Richard Dale, at twenty-four a "clever, good natured sea officer," with two boat loads of armed men to remove the offending pennant.[9] As the boats approached the *Independence* the pennant was hauled down, and the Continental Navy once more reigned supreme in the harbor of L'Orient; but the issue was not quite put down.[10] During the next two days, the broad pennant flew again aboard Tom's ship.[11] No doubt he was enjoying the intense rage that was revealed in the letters he received from Jones.

Captain Jones finally had the last word when the *Independence* was preparing to sail for home. He wrote to the Board of Admiralty in Philadelphia and reviewed Tom's conduct. "Is not this," he asked, "bidding defiance to Congress and the Continental Flag? Congress will Judge what punishment is equal to such a Crime when committed in Sight of the Flag and Forts of our Illustrious Ally." [12] Then he sent his letter off to Philadelphia in Tom's care.[13] The Board of Admiralty treated this letter from Jones as it treated many of his letters. No record survives to show that the Board did any more than politely ignore it. Tom was headstrong and his judgment had not matured, but the cause would not be furthered by depriving him of his command. He was still an able shipmaster.

The incident of the pennant was closed; but it had its effect on Tom Truxtun, even though it was many years before the effect became evident. Perhaps, in the long monotony of night watches on deck, he turned Captain Jones's carefully chosen words over and over in his mind. At length he came to the realization that a cause or a nation needs passionate men like Jones to set the standards and to guard their inviolability. Some of Jones's ideas he put away in a corner of his mind. Many years later, when he commanded an American ship of war, he echoed the words that the ardent patriot had written to him: "It is not me you have offended. You have offended the United States of America." [14]

He arrived home in December, 1780, after an expeditious passage of less than five weeks from France. Mary was expecting her second baby; but Tom was off to the West Indies before the baby arrived. The sea came first.

When the *Independence* dropped down the Delaware with the tide, the old year of 1780 was ebbing fast. On the last day of the year, his new daughter was born in Philadelphia, even as he sailed between the Delaware capes and once more stood out to sea.[15]

This was to be his last voyage as master of the *Independence*. The Caldwell brothers were having built a new and larger ship for Tom to command. He hoped to be able to take her out for France in the spring.

"Hurry," he wrote to the Caldwells before he dismissed his pilot, "with the ship." [16]

CHAPTER II

## ST. JAMES

℘  .  .  ℘  .  .  ℘  .  .  ℘  .  .

IT WAS a fine October day in 1781—clear, warm, with a pleasant breeze blowing from the Delaware shore—when Tom sailed his brand new ship, the *St. James,* out to sea, carrying with him as passenger Thomas Barclay, the new consul-general to France. The ship had just come from her builders, and her crew had been aboard for only a few days. Her guns had already been fired in anger, however, while she lay at anchor in a fog off Reedy Island. Just as the fog was lifting, Tom noticed that he was virtually surrounded by "refugee galleys"—hostile, shallow draft gunboats manned by fugitive Americans who espoused the enemy cause. He scattered the galleys with a few shots because he was prepared for such an attack.[1] However, it would take yet a few days at sea to shake down the ship and crew, and a few more to learn the many idiosyncrasies that, taken all together, made up the individual character of the ship itself.

The *St. James* was running before the wind, steering an easterly course. The great brick lighthouse on the dunes of Cape Henlopen was dropping rapidly astern. A lookout at the fore topmast head scanned the monotonous sea rim, from northeast to south, where it merged into the sky. As sailormen have done from earliest times, he was looking for a sail, for a cloud, for anything that time and the sea and the sky might choose to disclose.

The *St. James* was only three hours outside the capes when a scrap of sail appeared on the southern horizon. Keeping a close and anxious watch, Tom saw the sail grow larger. It appeared to belong to a ship at least as large as his. She might be friendly, but Tom decided it would be foolish to wait for her to come up to find out. Reaching up the coast as she was, apparently headed for a northern port, it was more likely that she was a British ship, either a man-of-war or a New York privateer, with neither of which Tom wished to speak. Considering his new ship, his green crew, and his important passenger, he did not care to risk an action if he could honorably avoid it. Tom steered his ship away two points to northward, letting his sails take full advantage of every ounce of wind. He crowded on all the sail he could set—jibs, staysails, courses, topsails, topgallants, spanker, and ringtail.[2]

Throughout the afternoon and evening, the stranger slowly closed the distance between the two ships. At midnight, gazing astern, Tom imagined that his ship was outsailing the other by a slim margin. On through the small hours of the midwatch the chase continued. As the watch ended, at four in the morning, the breeze died down completely. When a new spurt of wind came up from the southwest, it caught the chasing stranger first, reducing the lead that Tom had been trying so hard to hold.

Now came the time for desperate measures. Knowing that his ship was slightly down by the head and hoping that by shifting his trim he might improve her sailing, Tom ordered the anchors cut from the bows; next he ordered every man on board, crew and passengers alike, to sit down on the quarter-deck. Very quickly and effectively, Tom shifted some ten tons of weight to where it might do the most good. In spite of everything he could do, the stranger still gained, so at last Tom ordered all hands to quarters and "got every thing in as good order as was possible for a new Ship only out a few hours."

When the late dawn at last arrived, the stranger was scarcely a mile away. The breeze was becoming fluky; a dead calm threatened. Since it appeared that an action could no longer be avoided, Tom hauled up his courses, hauled down jibs and staysails, hove to, and waited for the ship to come up alongside. He could see by this time that she was a copper-bottomed ship mounting twenty-four or twenty-six guns—the *St. James* had but twenty—and that she was British; there was no mistaking the uniforms of the officers and marines on her quarter-deck.

She came up abreast of him, and as soon as he saw the British ensign being hoisted at the mizzen peak, Tom ordered his whole broadside fired into her. His laconic report of the action said simply, "She immediately returned it. This brought on a severe action for three glasses," an hour and a half. Early in the action a shot carried away the enemy's tiller ropes; after that she was unable to steer except with her sails. Tom took advantage of his antagonist's misfortune by maneuvering his ship into a raking position, athwart her hawse. He raked her thrice, pouring his whole broadside down her length while she was unable to bring any of her guns to bear to return his fire. He brought down her foreyard, he shattered her mainmast with three hits, and he cut her rigging to bits.[3]

The *St. James* fared not much better. Balls from the enemy's cannon were coming on board all too often. One man was killed instantly; four others were badly hurt. But the captain and his crew did not give up the fight. One tale, probably apocryphal, tells of a foremast hand who, in the thick of the action, found a spent ball lying against the mainmast. He took the ball, carried it to the gunner, and said, "Here, gunner, take this shot, write post paid upon it, and send it back to the rascals." [4]

The action ended with both ships badly shattered. The enemy drifted into a raking position only twenty yards ahead of the *St. James,* and Tom was unable for the moment to move his ship because of her crippled condition. But the enemy did not rake. She had no fight left.

Tom stood off a little way to refit in case the action should be resumed. His ship was a desolate sight. Her sails and rigging were cut to tatters; great Irish pennants were hanging everywhere. One man was dead and others were dying. In spite of all this, when the Britisher seemed to be making sail once more, Tom's crew gave her three cheers, "which she did not return."

This sea fight was one of those that established Tom's "character . . . as a brave and skillful commander." Almost thirty years later, one of his officers recalled this scene. "The impression of that character was indelibly stamped upon my youthful mind," he said, "in a contest [both] unequal and meritorious." [5]

The British ship, which turned out to be the *Goodrich,* a New York privateer, had three men killed and four wounded. According to a Loyalist who was in British-held New York when she arrived home from this action, she "was glad to get off." [6]

The *St. James* was less than a day's run from the Delaware capes, but instead of limping back into port to refit, Tom chose to continue his voyage as soon as he could make repairs at sea. After nearly three days of hard work—made more difficult by a worthless first mate—he was ready to sail on. As an anticlimax, the *St. James* had to battle contrary winds almost all the way to France. By the time she arrived in L'Orient, three of the injured men had died and another was not expected to survive. The final count was four or five killed and four injured. One of the passengers, Joseph Erwin, who was badly injured by a musket ball that came to rest in his shoulder, finally recovered after losing his right arm. When he offered Tom his passage money, Tom not only refused to accept it but also offered Erwin the privilege of shipping home a hundred guineas' worth of merchandise, freight free.[7] Thomas Barclay, the consul-general, was unhurt but thoroughly shaken. He rested for several days in L'Orient before he set out for Paris.[8]

While Tom was in L'Orient, he took advantage of the generous offer made to him by the "Commandant of the Mareen" to break off from the French seventy-four, then under construction, enough caulkers and carpenters to sheathe the bottom of the *St. James* with copper. Tom was following the latest European practice of coppering the bottom of a ship to prevent its fouling.[9] He was glad to spend the money on the *St. James* because, according to him, "Their is no better ship than the *St. James*. She has every good Quality, sails verry fast and when Coppered may justly be called a Non-such." [10]

Tom returned home just as winter was ending. By leaving his ship in New Castle and hurrying overland to Philadelphia, he was able to be present at a dinner given for General Washington on March 17, 1782, five months after Cornwallis' surrender at Yorktown. Many years later, Tom wrote about this meeting with the great General. "Washington . . . knew," he recalled, "the early and seasonal supplies I brought into the United States at different times, of powder, arms, cloathing, &c, &c, from the dawn, quite to the close of the revolution— [He] spoke of my conduct in the most honorary manner, and told me at a public dinner . . . that I had been as a regiment to the United States." [11]

It is evident that Tom carried many valuable cargoes. This latest one in the *St. James* was, according to him, the most valuable single cargo brought into the United States during the Revolution. No doubt it was, since cargoes are valued in terms of the money they will bring in the market place. But when this cargo is considered in terms of its usefulness to the Army, the ratio of "forty for one" comes immediately to mind.

No complete list of this cargo survives, but it was probably much like the cargo that he had brought from L'Orient a year or so before. That one consisted of "102 bales, 14 boxes, 45 chests, 2 hogsheads, 3 trunks and 5 packages European merchandize, 20 pipes brandy, 10 chests tea, 9 bales linen, 9 bales sail cloth, 9 casks allum, 5 casks copperas, 16 baskets oil, 1 box olives, 39 boxes window glass, 8 bags shot, 3 kegs musket balls, 2 kegs and 24 sheets lead, 20 barrels gunpowder, 10 cases claret, 1 case spices, 2 trunks thread, 476 bags salt." [12] The "European merchandize" included Britannia linens, Flanders sheeting, white swanskins, elegant embroidered waistcoats, Paris ruffles, white silk hose, elegant artificial flowers, and gold and silver laces.[13]

Lest General Washington's praise sound too extravagant, it must be remembered that service in the Revolution was a relative thing. One can accept his estimate with confidence, even though it must be admitted that he was forever the perfect diplomat. However, one wonders, if Tom had been more patriot and less merchant, whether he might not have been as a division rather than a regiment.

Tom Truxtun, in 1782, appears neither worse nor better than other prosperous men whose profits were not in proportion to their patriotism. Captain Truxtun the patriot did not appear until later; but on these voyages Captain Truxtun the commander appeared in unmistakable terms. In his report of his action with the *Goodrich,* he used the personal pronoun throughout. He shared with no one the responsibility for heaving overboard two large anchors. Never while he commanded a ship did he mention what was in his lifetime customary—the conference of officers to decide on a course of action when an emergency arose or disaster impended. Even the redoubtable John Paul Jones was quick to call a conference of his officers, and then he was careful to gather evidence in writing to show that his officers felt that his decisions were beyond reproach.[14] Tom experienced many disappointments as a result of mistaken judgment or failure of his plans. As long as he held the deck as captain, however, he blamed no man but himself for his failures.

If he had not survived the Revolution, he would have left a few years' record of good seamanship, of fearlessness and enterprise. He assumed command wherever he went not because of his family or his connections—he had none of the former and he had not yet developed the latter—but because of his talent for command. All of that, however, is not enough to give a man a place in history. It took a long period of maturing judgment; it took endless nights of crowding thoughts on a lonely plunging deck in the seas beneath the Southern Cross; finally it took another war to bring out in him the fervent patriot spirit that shines through the record that his deeds—not he, for he was not concerned about posterity's judgment—wrote for the future.

CHAPTER 12

## *COMMERCE* AND DRY GOODS

   ❧  •  •  ❧  •  •  ❧  •  •  ❧  •  •

A SHIPMASTER, if he has been able to put aside a fair amount of money from his earnings and his share of prize monies, may at some time begin to consider critically the lot of his employer. He sees the owner of his ship as a merchant who is always at home, who visits the quarter-deck of his ships only when the weather is fair and a voyage has been safely completed. He is able to sleep clear through a night, undisturbed by shifting winds or changes in the weather. The merchant is accustomed to profits of ten to a hundred per cent and more for doing nothing but issue orders to buy things and to sell things. His profits from a single cargo may be as much as a shipmaster's earnings for half a lifetime. He proves that money is the seed from which money grows. He is a respected, if not particularly esteemed, member of the community. When all of the advantages are added together, the lot of the merchant seems to approach, at the very least, a sinecure. When this line of thinking engages the mind of a prosperous shipmaster, he is well on his way to becoming a merchant.

While he was sailing for the Caldwell brothers, Tom bought shares in vessels and cargoes whenever he had the money and the opportunity.[1] After his last voyage in the *St. James,* he put all the money he could spare in the business house of Randall and Company. During a hot Philadelphia summer he attended closely to the task of fitting and sending out a small schooner, the *Harlequin,* owned by Randall and Truxtun,[2] and he looked after the owners' interest in a new ship being built for the two of them in Joshua Humphreys' shipyard.

In September, 1782, the schooner *Harlequin* was captured in Delaware Bay by refugee galleys.[3] That venture was, therefore, a dead loss. When the new ship was ready for sea, there would be perhaps enough business to keep Randall occupied in Philadelphia, but Tom could be spared nicely. He could assume one more command.

The *Commerce,* a square-sterned ship of one hundred and fifty tons burden, made one voyage to the West Indies under the auspices of the house of Randall and Company. That was voyage enough, however, to get Tom involved in another sea fight.

While sailing near the Virgin Islands in company with two smaller vessels from Philadelphia, he was attacked by two enemy privateers, a brig and a copper-bottomed schooner, each mounting fourteen guns. The action was close—at some thirty yards, severe—and lasted for about twenty minutes. Tom broke off the engagement when two more enemy vessels came up to join battle. By that time the two American vessels accompanying him had had time to run for safety into a nearby port. The enemy's vessels were badly shattered; their losses of men totaled fifteen killed and twenty-four wounded. Tom had one man killed and two wounded.[4]

For this action Tom and his crew were publicly applauded by the masters of the other American vessels. They, with their owners, sent Tom a "tribute of our thanks . . . for your gallant and disinterested conduct in engaging two privateers off Tortola, on the 14th of November, of superior force, in order to preserve these vessels from capture."

"Gentlemen," Tom replied, "nothing gives me more sincere satisfaction than to have it in my power to render any service to my fellow-citizens, more especially when I can at the same time check the common enemy."[5] There is a hint of pompousness here; but pompous or not, Tom Truxtun never hesitated to fight when to fight seemed the right thing to do.

He returned to his fireside in time for the Christmas, 1782, holiday season. A few days before his coming, Mary was delivered of a fine set of twins, a boy and a girl. There were now four children: Sarah, four; Mary, two; and the new twins, Thomas and Elizabeth.[6]

The Truxtuns probably were happier at this time than they would ever be again. The years of the Revolution were about at an end. Peace and Britain's recognition of the United States were being discussed, and word of a treaty was expected soon. If Tom should go to sea again, Mary would no longer have sea fights to worry about; she would have only her usual anxieties about the perils of the sea. And whatever happened, she would have a comfortable home.

They had moved from the lower part of Dock Ward uptown to a house in the vicinity of Christ Church.[7] Mary had Hannah, a young negro woman whom Tom had bought for £160 hard money, to help with the house and the children.[8] Their home was well furnished, and as their fortunes were enlarged it was increasingly adorned by expensive pieces of silverware. They owned a phaeton and two horses. Only such prominent men as Dr. Benjamin Rush with his chariot rode in more elaborate conveyances; most families owned simply a two-wheeled "chair."[9] The Revolution had been kind to Tom Truxtun. He had come a long way in the few years since he had been prize master of one of the ships captured by the *Congress* and *Chance*. He was well known in Philadelphia, and his reputation as a brave and skillful ship commander was spreading.

The talk of this Christmas season was full of his next adventure.

What seemed to be an opportunity to multiply his fortune manyfold had just presented itself. James Collins, who was reported to be "a genteel man, of a good family, and . . . strongly recommended," had come to town.[10] He proposed a partnership of Truxtun, Collins, and Charles Biddle, the latter a shipmaster whose judgment of people was sharper than Tom's would ever be, and of whom much more will be heard. Captain Biddle declined to enter the partnership, later making the observation that "Without you can place the utmost confidence in the honor, integrity, and prudence of your partner, your mind must be always uneasy, for it is in the power of a partner to ruin you."[11] If only he had made this observation to Tom now, before the house of Collins and Truxtun was formed.

Collins and Truxtun opened a large dry goods store in Water Street, down near the wharves.[12] Since the war was so near to an end they, like most other merchants in the United States, were busy with schemes to import British goods that had been scarce during the war and for which the markets were now starved. This new firm bought out Thomas Randall's interest in the *Commerce*, and presently it was decided that Tom would take the ship to London at once to buy a fresh stock of goods for the new store. He sailed in June, 1783, three months before the definitive treaty of peace ending the Revolution was signed, and brought back "A Great variety of Dry Goods Suitable for the ensuing season." [13] He turned his ship around within a month and was off again for London to take full advantage of this trade before the American market became saturated with British wares.

During the year and a half following his first departure from Philadelphia, in 1783, Tom was home from the sea for only a few weeks. For all the rest of the time, Collins handled the business alone. Tom made three voyages to London, remaining in Philadelphia only long enough to unload his cargoes of dry goods, to have voyage repairs made by Joshua Humphreys' ship carpenters, and to load for London his burden of tobacco, rice, tar, flax, and pig iron.[14]

The house of Collins and Truxtun moved from Water Street to another store in Front Street, five doors above the Market. Even a partial listing of their stock of dry goods required more than forty lines in the newspapers. They had an endless variety of piece goods: flannels, corduroys, swanskins, serges, velveteens, dorseteens, calimancoes, and many more. And handkerchiefs, gloves, shoes, hats, buckles and buttons, pins, needles, and combs; chinaware, writing paper, locks and hinges, window glass and nails, sailcloth and gunpowder, bellows and sconces, "With a variety of other hardware, ironmongery, &c, &c." [15]

The possibilities of trade after the end of the war seemed unlimited. The manufactured goods of the British Isles rolled across the sea in an ever increasing flood. Within one six weeks' period more than two hundred vessels brought foreign goods to the port of Philadelphia alone.[16] But the American people could not be forever buying and never selling. Markets at length were glutted; and when buying stopped, merchants frequently had to sell their stocks at a loss to pay their creditors. When the bubble of speculation burst, late in 1784, the house of Collins and Truxtun tottered and threatened to collapse.

Tom and his partner were forced to sell the *Commerce* to pay their creditors; but even that did not help much, since they were able to salvage only a quarter of their original investment in her.[17] Their situation was serious. Not only did they stand to lose their business; but their friends, who had endorsed notes for them at various times, would become liable for the full amount of the notes if the business failed. The partners could resort to the legal procedure of bankruptcy, and for them the slate would be wiped clean. Their friends would be losers, but Collins and Truxtun could start over again with no outstanding debts.

Charles Biddle, who had endorsed some of their notes, had this to say about the eventual end of the partnership: "Collins not having the means of doing anything for his creditors, took the benefit of the Bankrupt Law; but Truxtun would not do this. . . . declaring that not one of the endorsers should be a loser by him, and he was as good as his word, paying the endorsers every farthing due from the house." But not until after many years and many voyages.

"Such conduct," Biddle concluded, "will always make a man esteemed and respected, and every one will endeavor to push him forward in the world." [18]

The month of January, 1785, when Collins and Truxtun dissolved their partnership, became more bleak than ever when the Truxtuns' fifth child, a girl, died before she was three weeks old.[19]

The pain of this disastrous winter was softened a bit when spring came once more to Philadelphia. Tom had failed as a merchant, at least in his choice of a partner, but he had lost none of his stature as a mariner. The shipbuilder, Joshua Humphreys, had just completed another new ship, this one for the house of Donnaldson and Coxe.[20] The command of the ship, the *London Packet,* was offered to Tom and he accepted it at once.

In the newspaper of February 18, 1785, the thirty-year-old shipmaster could read an advertisement that announced the sailing and proclaimed the virtues of his next command. "This ship," said the notice, "is built in the strongest and best manner, is well found, has very elegant and convenient accomodations for passengers, and is intended for a regular London trader." [21]

Those elegant accommodations were ready at precisely the right moment. Before the summer was over they would house a most distinguished passenger. Venerable old Benjamin Franklin, Minister Plenipotentiary to France, was nearly ready to come home.

CHAPTER 13

DOCTOR FRANKLIN COMES HOME

ℰ  .  .  ℰ  .  .  ℰ  .  .  ℰ  .  .

CAPTAIN Tom Truxtun was in London, probably at the Pennsylvania Coffee House in Birchin Lane, when he learned that the great Doctor Franklin wanted to engage a ship to carry him home.

Benjamin Franklin had attended the Court of Versailles for more than eight years, during almost the whole of the Revolutionary War, obtaining for the United States incalculably important aid from the French government. A man who enjoyed the company of learned men and charming women, he was about to leave a circle of friends and acquaintances who admired and loved him. "I have continu'd to work till late in the Day," he said; "tis time I should go home, and go to Bed." [1] He was an old, old man, already in his eightieth year. He was afflicted with the stone and with the gout. As he put it, "I feel the infirmities of Age come on so fast, and the Building to need so many Repairs, that in a little time the Owner will find it cheaper to pull it down and build a new one."[2] The stone bothered him greatly. The motion of a carriage caused him unbearable pain. He was not at all sure that he could survive the journey to the coast; and even if he got that far, he still might not be able to bear the motion of a ship.[3] But he wanted to go home to be with his daughter and his grandchildren. He was determined at least to attempt the long journey; if he could not withstand it, there would be time enough then to think of returning again to his friends in Paris.

As soon as he learned that his term as Minister was completed and that he was at last free to go home, Franklin had looked about for a comfortable ship. In Amsterdam and Dublin, in London and Paris, his friends tried to locate accommodations that would be fine enough for one so old and so greatly esteemed.[4]

On the fourth of July, 1785—it was now nine years since Franklin had helped frame the Declaration of Independence—he decided on the ship that would take him back to his beloved Philadelphia. Through a merchant doing business at the Pennsylvania Coffee House, he engaged the *London Packet,* which was to meet him in Havre if possible, or if not, then at Cowes on the English side of the Channel.[5] He reserved the whole cabin for himself and his party in order that he "might not be intruded on by any accidental disagreable Company."[6]

Captain Truxtun was happy to accommodate the great man in any way he could, but to call at Havre would greatly increase his insurance costs; charging the increase to Franklin would almost double the amount he would have to pay for his passage.[7] Therefore it was agreed that the *London Packet* would meet Franklin's party at Cowes; a French paquet boat would bring the party from Havre to meet the ship.

In London, Captain Truxtun hurried the loading of his cargo of "Shone's best porter in casks," chinaware, ship anchors of all sizes, and an assortment of pigments for inks and paints.[8] He took on board thirteen German redemptioners, who were berthed in the steerage and who would pay for their passage by selling themselves into bondage for a stated number of years upon their arrival in America.[9] When he was on the point of departure, he took in fresh provisions for his cabin passengers, consisting of a dozen pigs and sheep, several hundred chickens, ducks, turkeys, and geese,[10] and a goat to furnish fresh milk.[11]

In Paris, Franklin and his two grandsons, William Temple Franklin and Benjamin Franklin Bache, were hard at work on the final preparations for their departure. Most of their belongings already had been sent on a barge down the river Seine with the expectation that it would be waiting for them when they arrived at Havre; but they had yet to pack the things they were going to carry with them. They managed finally to squeeze them all into twelve trunks, twelve boxes, three baskets, and a bale.[12]

M. de Castries, French Minister of Marine, learned of Franklin's intended departure only at the last minute. Had he heard of it sooner, he wrote to the American, he would have suggested that the King order a French frigate to take him home "in a manner suitable to the known importance of the services you have been engaged in, to the esteem you have acquired in France, and the particular esteem which his Majesty entertains for you." [13] But it was too late to alter the plans already laid. Franklin was to be carried in a royal litter to Havre, where he would take passage in the paquet boat for Cowes.

On the twelfth of July, 1785, a heroic recessional began amidst a great crowd that had gathered to bid him farewell. There was a mournful silence, interrupted only by a few sobs, as the great man was helped into his stately conveyance. He rode in the litter—a sort of sedan chair, covered and curtained and supported by poles running fore and aft. It was slung between two very large Spanish mules, and a proud muleteer rode alongside the leading mule. Franklin was followed by his two grandsons and M. Le Veillard in a carriage; the baggage was consigned to a wagon that followed them.[14]

Within a week the little party was in Havre, where it was joined by Antoine Houdon, one of Europe's foremost sculptors, and his three assistants. He was on his way to Mount Vernon; he had been engaged by Franklin on behalf of the State of Virginia to execute a statue of General Washington.[15] Houdon's baggage and his clay and tools also had been sent down the river Seine; but when the paquet boat was ready to depart with the company for Cowes, neither his baggage nor Franklin's had yet come down the river. The inconvenience to Franklin was slight, because he had brought a wagon load of luggage with him; but a "subscription of shirts and stockings" was taken up during the voyage to America in order to keep Houdon and his helpers properly clothed, and the sculptor had to buy new tools and materials when finally he arrived in America.[16]

The venerable Franklin had survived his journey in the royal lit-ter; and when he reached the English shore of the Channel after two days and two nights of being buffeted about by choppy seas he was able to say, "I was not in the least incommoded by the voyage"; [17] while his grandson Ben added, a little ruefully, "All the passengers had been sick except my grandfather." [18] It was apparent that Frank-lin would have no trouble with the motion of a ship.

While Franklin's friends and admirers flocked to see him at the Star Inn, in Southampton, he followed the progress of the *London Packet* with keen interest. "Our Ship was at Gravesend the 22d," he wrote, and was expected in the Downs on the 24th.[19] And finally, on the 26th, Jonathan Williams told him, "Capt. Truxtun is arrived at the Mother Bank," off Cowes. "Don't let Ben forget to bring all the mattrasses." [20] Jonathan Williams, Franklin's grandnephew, who had arrived from Dublin to join the party, took care of the transfer of baggage from the paquet boat to the ship while Captain Truxtun went up to the Star Inn to meet his famous passenger.[21]

Finally, on the twenty-seventh, Captain Truxtun, accompanied by Franklin, his grandsons, Houdon and his assistants, and a host of visitors, returned to his ship. He entertained them all at dinner on board his ship, after which the entire company decided to stay on board overnight and to depart early in the morning. When Franklin next awoke, however, the ship was under way. The visitors had been put ashore at four and the Captain had weighed anchor at five o'clock in the morning.[22] Franklin's old friend David Hartley, hur-rying down from London, was yet a mile from Cowes when he met one of the guests returning from the ship.[23] So little late, and yet he would see the great man no more. Benjamin Franklin had quitted the shores of Europe for the last time. His day's work done, he was going home.

Franklin was in better health and spirits than he had been for some time. He was well situated in a stout ship whose commodious quarters were entirely at his disposal, and he was sailing with an amiable and capable captain. It is easy to picture a very old man, his life's mission completed, seated in a comfortable chair on the sunny leeward side of the deck, bundled in blankets to keep out the chill of the North Atlantic air, dozing fitfully as he watched the heaving horizon and listened to the gentle chuckling of the seas as they spent themselves under the bows of the ship.

But the old philosopher fits no such picture. The *London Packet,* throughout this voyage, was a hive of activity, most of it a result of Franklin's insatiable curiosity about all manner of things. At his behest, Jonathan Williams started a special log even before they cleared the English Channel. Morning, noon, and evening, Williams lowered a thermometer into the water and recorded its temperature. He recorded also the usual information about wind direction, courses steered, and distance run.[24] Franklin wanted the log in order to learn more about the relation between geographical position and water temperature. He thought that the thermometer could become an important aid to navigation, particularly to ships sailing in or near the Gulf Stream. He convinced Captain Truxtun that this novel idea was a good one, and for many years the Captain went about plunging thermometers into most of the seas of the world.

Young Ben Bache, a lad of sixteen, kept a journal of the voyage and the other grandson, Temple, also kept one, though his was very brief.[25] Franklin made only sporadic entries in his own journal, but his literary output exceeded that of all the others on board. Intending originally to bring his autobiography up to date during this voyage,[26] he launched forth instead on some "Maritime Observations" that had been shifting about in his mind for some time.[27] He discussed some of his ideas with Captain Truxtun, and the Captain's future was the richer for it. Franklin pointed out that sailors could sometimes profit from the advice of landsmen since it was certain that the first vessel ever built was the invention of a landsman. The echo of his words rang down through the years. "It was a Landsman who first invented a Ship," wrote Captain Truxtun twenty years later.[28] Franklin talked over an idea he had for a collapsible sea anchor, to keep a vessel's head up into the wind when lying to; and when the Captain arrived in Philadelphia, he had one built for his ship.[29]

Franklin went on to list in some detail the things that a passenger about to embark on a long voyage should consider. The choice of captains was important, he said, "as you must for so long a time be confined to his company, and under his direction." A sociable, good-natured captain would make for a happy voyage but if he were only "skilful, careful, watchful, and active in the conduct of his ship," then excuse the rest, for these were the essentials.[30] Temple's judgment of the Captain of the *London Packet* seemed to fit the requirements laid down by his grandfather. "It would be impossible for anyone," he said, "to be more careful or forehanded." [31]

Whatever image one may have of a frugal, sparing Poor Richard, it will be quickly destroyed by the instructions he wrote regarding personal stores, to be carried in addition to those provided in the ship. "It is good," he said, "to have some particular things in your own possession, so as to be always at your own command. 1. Good water, that of the ship being often bad. . . . 2. Good tea. 3. Coffee ground. 4. Chocolate. 5. Wine of the sort you particularly like, and cider. . . ." and so on, through "11. Jamaica spirits. 12. Eggs, greas'd. 13. Diet bread. 14. Portable soup. 15. Rusks." Even if the ship's provisions were good enough to make some of these unnecessary, Franklin pointed out that "there are frequently in the ship poorer passengers, who are taken at a lower price, lodge in the steerage, and have no claim to any of the cabin provisions, or to any but those kinds that are allowed the sailors." He continued, "These people are sometimes dejected, sometimes sick; there may be women and children among them. In a situation where there is no going to market to purchase such necessaries, a few of your superfluities, distributed occasionally, may be of great service, restore health, save life, make the miserable happy, and thereby afford you infinite pleasure." [32] The steerage passengers in the *London Packet* were fortunate to have the good Doctor Franklin aboard.

When Franklin's nautical budget was exhausted in an essay of some ten thousand words, he launched into another ten thousand words on the cause and cure of smoky chimneys; and the world was the loser because he never quite got around to his autobiography. Meanwhile, his shipmates continued to plunge thermometers into the sea and into bottles and kegs of water brought up from the bottom, in order to learn more about the waters, tides, and currents. [33]

Half way across the Atlantic, the *London Packet* sailed into a furious squall. Captain Truxtun furled his sails as the wind increased until at last he was scudding under a single rag of canvas. When the squall was at its height this last sail carried away with a terrible crash, so loud that young Ben Bache thought surely the ship must have lost a mast. The ship rolled and pitched, dipping her main yard, normally fifty feet aloft, into the mountainous seas. Sculptor Houdon and young Ben stayed out on deck all through the storm "enjoying the beauty of this scene." The seas boiled into the staterooms, and the passengers spent the next day repairing and drying their damaged effects. When the squall had passed, Captain Truxtun told his passengers what every merchant master says, what even Charon must tell the dead souls as he ferries them across the Styx, that he "had never seen anything equal to it." [34]

After six and a half weeks at sea, the *London Packet* made her landfall some distance south of the Delaware capes, and on the evening of September 11, 1785, a pilot clambered aboard. Early on the morning of the 13th, the ship entered the bay, and by sunset of the same day she was abreast of New Castle; the pilot pressed on up the river by moonlight as long as the tide and the wind held out and then came to anchor. [35]

"With the flood in the morning," Franklin wrote in his journal, "came a light breeze, which brought us above Gloucester Point, in full view of dear Philadelphia!" The little city, basking in the sunshine of this warm September morning, was busily preparing a welcome for its most illustrious citizen. The old man could see row on row of three-story red brick houses, rising beside the river and marching inland for half a dozen blocks. If he looked sharp, he could just see the tiny spire on top of the State House, where he had labored so long and so well. He could pick out his church, the old Christ Church, whose steeple towered high above the whole city. In a little while his long journey would be at an end. At long last he was home.

All the vessels in the river were decked out with flags and pennants, and houses in the city were decorated with the flags of all nations. Cannon were discharged and bells everywhere rang out a joyous peal of welcome. [36] A great concourse of people had gathered to welcome him as he was rowed ashore at the Market Street wharf. Grandson Temple, swept along in the press of the crowd, told a friend, "I cried for joy all through the streets and my tears were doubled when I saw I was not the only one thus moved." [37]

In his unassuming way, Franklin described his welcome. "We were received by a crowd of people," he wrote, "with huzzas, and accompanied with acclamations quite to my door. Found my family well."

"God be praised and thanked for all his mercies." [38]

This voyage was more than merely another event in the life of the young shipmaster. His whole future was affected in some degree by this encounter with the world-renowned statesman and philosopher.

He added to his mental storehouse many facts and ideas during the six weeks at sea. More importantly, however, his intellectual curiosity was whetted by his observation of the many and varied activities of Doctor Franklin. Henceforth, the Captain seldom failed to study any work he could lay his hands upon that would increase his knowledge and understanding of the ways of the sea and of vessels that swam on its surface.

# PART THREE

# China Hand

## CHAPTER 14

## THE NEW CHINA TRADE

IN John Dunlap's printing office on Market Street, the type dropped into the stick with a monotonous click, click, click as the compositor set up another advertisement for Friday's newspaper. It was a routine notice announcing the proposed sailing of another ship. The ship was the *London Packet* and the destination was again London; "will positively sail on the 8th day of October next." [1]

October 8, 1785, positively! Captain Truxtun was preparing to sail for London again. With reasonable luck, this voyage would pay him more than enough to meet the current expenses of his growing family; perhaps he could even pay off some of the debts that he had assumed voluntarily when he quit his partnership with Collins. But how many years of sailing to London it would take to discharge these responsibilities was an unanswerable question. A little item in the newspaper that carried his advertisement caught his attention. "The *United States,* Indiaman, captain Bell, is arrived at Reedy Island."

The *United States!* He had passed her in the river a year and a half before, when she was outward bound for the Far East and he was returning home from London.[2] He had been to London three times since then. A year and a half was a long time for a single voyage, but if one voyage to the East Indies could pay him more than three or four to London then he could not afford to ignore the possibilities of the trade.

As long as the thirteen American colonies were a part of the British Empire, their vessels were free to trade with the mother country and with the islands of the West Indies; but India and China were closed to them because of the British East India Company's monopoly in the Far East. Privately-owned ships of the British Empire were not permitted to share in that lucrative trade.

However, when the colonies became the United States of America, the situation was reversed. British ports in the West Indies were closed to them, but they were free to trade, if they could, with the distant countries of India and China.

The *Empress of China* was the first American ship to embark on the sea route to the Far East. She sailed from New York on February 22, 1784—General Washington's fifty-second birthday.[3] She displayed the American flag in the Chinese port of Canton, and in May of the following year returned to New York with a cargo of teas, silks, and chinaware. The *Empress* had opened new vistas to American traders. It was reliably reported that her voyage had earned a clear profit of twenty-five per cent on the investment, which included the cost of the ship; and the profit might have been greater if the agent for the owners had not stolen over two thousand dollars in cash, which should have been used to purchase China goods.[4]

The *United States,* of Philadelphia, followed soon after, departing from the Delaware capes in March, 1784. Plagued by scurvy and a drunken chief mate, she changed her destination from China to Coromandel, the eastern coast of the Indian peninsula. This voyage, which ended in Philadelphia in September, 1785, was not particularly profitable, but it helped to demonstrate that the Eastern seas were not beyond the reach of American mariners.[5]

When the eighth of October came, Captain Truxtun did not sail for London. Nor did the *London Packet,* under that name, ever leave the port of Philadelphia.

The Captain succumbed to the lure of the distant Indies. Perhaps he could, in a voyage or two, pay off his debts and repair his personal fortune. If that were so, then the long absence from home and his family would be amply compensated. Regardless of the fortune involved, the distant seas held a powerful attraction for an adventurous spirit. He would see for himself what lay beyond the far horizons; he would command an expedition that would take him to the outer ends of the earth. The preparations that had to be made before he could sail involved numberless details, but if he hurried he might be able to get his ship out in time to reach the China seas in proper season, before the arrival of the unfavorable monsoon. At any rate, he would try.

As a result, his ship became one of the very earliest China traders to sail from America. There were only four other American vessels preparing to go out to China this season, and one of these was the *Empress of China,* undertaking her second voyage.

Donnaldson and Coxe, who had had the *London Packet* built the year before, were unwilling or unable to underwrite the whole adventure; so they shared the risk with the Captain, who scraped together a little more money on credit, and with two other business houses. Thus the general arrangements for financing the voyage were settled; many of the details could be attended to by John Frazier, who was appointed supercargo.[6] As supercargo he would act throughout the voyage as the owners' business agent. On a voyage as long as this, the supercargo was necessary in order to relieve the Captain of the manifold duties of buying, trading, and selling cargoes and to give him freedom to attend to the management of his ship.

Captain Truxtun took his ship, still called the *London Packet,* to Joshua Humphreys' shipyard, where she was to be prepared for the long voyage. At Humphreys' wharf, long tackles were fastened to the ship's masts and anchored firmly ashore, and the ship was hove down to expose first one half of her bottom and then the other. Her seams were caulked and paid with tar and her bottom was sheathed over, probably as a result of Franklin's suggestion that double sheathing a ship's bottom would make her tighter and stronger. Finally, her quickwork was caulked in order to keep her dry throughout the long stormy months that lay ahead.[7]

After her overhaul in the shipyard, the question of a name arose. *London Packet* was hardly a proper name for a China trader. Perhaps the inscrutable Orientals, to whose shores she was sailing, would be impressed by a more appropriate one. Accordingly, and without any great display of imagination, she was renamed the *Canton*.[8]

In sailing out to the Eastern seas, his ship might be attacked by pirates or by the warships of hostile powers, so Captain Truxtun decided that she would need some armament. The Algerines, of the Barbary coast, already had sent their raiders beyond the Pillars of Hercules and had captured two American vessels in the Atlantic.[9] While he was yet bringing Franklin home, during the last voyage, it was rumored in London that Captain Truxtun's ship had been captured by the Barbary corsairs and that all aboard, including the great Franklin, were consigned to slavery in Algiers.[10] Even if the danger of attack in the Atlantic were ignored, the passage through the China seas would be made under the constant threat of an encounter with proas and junks of roving pirate bands.

The Captain looked about for cannon and ammunition, but there were none to be bought. In less than three years, the sinews of war had shriveled up. He asked the State of Pennsylvania to lend him "Four brass nine Pound Cannon one hundred round nine Pound Shot and Fifty double head Nine Pound Shot"; but the state had no nine-pounders; he had to be content with sixes instead.[11]

As additional protection, to be used in case he was accosted by a vessel he could not subdue with his four small cannon, he applied for a "sea-letter," a sort of official passport. The Confederation Congress still governed the United States in form, but it was by this time merely a frayed remnant of the wartime Congress. It granted him a sea-letter with the seal of the United States affixed, but a document from such a debilitated body could insure little protection. It could only pray that the Captain be received with kindness and treated in a becoming manner. The United States had no Navy to stand back of any claim it might make to equal rights with other nations on the waters of the deep or in the ports of the world. A generation later, when the Navy was firmly established, a passport could say peremptorily, "Suffer [this vessel] to pass." But in these feeble years after the Revolution, while the Confederation fell quietly asunder and before the Constitution had yet been fashioned, the Congress spoke more softly. Its aim was to offend no one, but the result was not likely to enhance the reputation of the new nation.

In part, the sea-letter read: "Most serene, serene, most puissant, puissant, high, illustrious, noble, honourable, venerable, wise and prudent emperors, kings, republicks, princes, dukes, earls, barons, lords, burgomasters, counsellors, as also judges, officers, justiciaries, and regents, of all the good cities and places, whether ecclesiastical or secular, who shall see these presents, or hear them read. . . . our prayer is to all . . . where the said Thomas Truxtun shall arrive with his vessel and cargo, that they may please to receive him with goodness, and treat him in a becoming manner, . . . whereof we shall be willingly indebted." [12] This was meager protection against arrogant despots whom he might find in the far lands.

With the *Canton* overhauled and insured by guns and paper against unknown hazards, the question of cargo was next to be considered. The usual goods of American commerce—tobacco and timber, liquor, candles, corn, and chairs—found no market in China. It was about this time that the Chinese told a foreign ambassador: "The Celestial Empire possesses all things in prolific abundance and lacks no product within its borders. There is therefore no need to import the manufactures of outside barbarians in exchange for our own products." [13] On this note of contempt was all foreign trade carried on by the Chinese. There was only one port—Canton—open to foreigners, and all trade was carefully supervised by the Celestial Government. What, then, could Captain Truxtun take that might titillate the tastes of these celestial people?

There was only one American product that the Chinese wanted, and that was ginseng. Sometimes it sold for its weight in gold. Ginseng was grown in the northern part of China, where its harvesting was carefully regulated in order to prevent its extinction. It grew wild in America, and for many years it had been harvested and sent to England, there to be transferred to the ships of the East India Company and carried out to the market in Canton. The root was used to make a syrupy bitter-sweet tea, a stimulant of a kind, "chiefly used by weakened men and youths." It was an aromatic root that grew in the shape of a man; therefore it was supposed to increase or restore sexual vigor. The appearance of the ginseng was very important to the Chinese. It must be gathered during the month of September, at a time when the juice of the plant was all in the root;

otherwise the skin of the root might wrinkle. It must be garbled, or picked over, to remove the stringy root ends. Next, it must be "well rounced in Hair Bags—it gives a fine face to the parcel." In a hair bag some two feet wide and six feet long, with a black man holding onto each end, the ginseng was rounced—thrown and jostled—back and forth for several minutes to impart a good polish to its surface. Finally, it had to be packed in perfectly dry barrels to keep it firm and healthy looking.[14]

On board the *Canton* were loaded 41 hogsheads and 226 barrels of ginseng.[15] The only other items of cargo were a few rolls of lead, which sometimes brought a good price in Canton, and a few chests of silver dollars, the only money acceptable to the Chinese.

The return cargo was specified by those who provided the money for its purchase. Benjamin Fuller, an elderly dry goods merchant, gave Captain Truxtun and his supercargo fifteen hundred Spanish milled dollars. He wanted half of them spent for chinaware, a third for tea, and the balance for silks and nankeens. The owners of the ship were entitled to twenty per cent of the Chinese goods to pay for the freight of the rest; the Captain and supercargo were to have two per cent in addition to the twenty for their trouble in purchasing the goods.

Mrs. Fuller gave the Captain eighty Spanish milled dollars on her own account; she wanted "two pieces of Black Sattin of the first Quality, Two Fanns & Two Green Silk Umbrellas, & two genteel Rich China Punch Bowls." If there should be any money left over, he might buy her anything "suitable for the use of a Lady, upwards of Sixty." The freight for this consignment was paid in best wishes for a "happy and prosperous Voyage, and a safe return to the Embraces of his Good Family & Friends." [16]

As though the fitting out, loading, and provisioning of his ship and the recruiting of a crew were not trouble enough for Captain Truxtun, he was beset by another Oriental worry in the person of Sick Keesar.

Sick Keesar, leading a band of thirty lascars, natives of Bengal and China, descended on him when Keesar learned that the *Canton* was bound for the Orient. Would he please take them home? They would gladly work for their passage and would expect no wages. They were so persistent that they soon became a nuisance.

Captain Truxtun learned that they had come from Canton by way of Batavia in a ship just lately arrived in Baltimore. They had expected to sail only as far as Batavia, but they had been forced at gun point to stay on board their ship when she sailed for America. When they heard that the *Canton* was about to sail for China, they trooped from Baltimore up to Philadelphia. They were destitute. Only because of the charity of Levi Hollingsworth, a local merchant, did they have a roof over their heads and food to eat.

Captain Truxtun wanted no part of the lascars as crew members. They might be fair enough sailors and he might have no trouble with his crew on the outward voyage, but he knew that there were no American or European sailors to be recruited in China and that his ship would be quite useless in China without a crew. He told Sick that he would take them only if he had an order from the Supreme Executive Council, governing body of Pennsylvania, and that for the passage he would have to charge forty guineas per man. Sick Keesar and company promptly flung themselves upon the mercy and charity of the Council.

Hollingsworth, who had opened one of his vacant houses for the lascars, talked to Captain Truxtun to see whether he might not reduce the fare below the forty guineas he had fixed; but the Captain had received twelve guineas for a steerage passenger crossing the Atlantic, and it was four or five times as far to China.[17] Apparently he could not see his way clear to reduce his price. The only thing left for Levi Hollingsworth to do was to add his voice to those imploring help from the Council.

Benjamin Franklin, who was by this time President of the Supreme Executive Council, thought it a matter of national concern. Neither he, nor many of his fellow citizens, had yet developed fully the conviction of natural American superiority, so he was anxious lest these people carry home with them "any well-founded prejudice" against the United States. But the Council did not care to pay for their passage home. When Captain Truxtun departed from Philadelphia, the lascars were still an unsolved problem; and so they remained for the better part of a year, until the shipmaster who brought them to America in the first place finally took them home on his next outward passage.[18]

The year 1785 was ebbing fast; it was December and time to be gone if the favorable monsoon was to be met. This parting from home, family, and friends for at least a year and a half was—according to a letter Captain Truxtun wrote a few days later—the most difficult part of the whole business; but at length he tore himself away from Mary and the four children, leaving them at home in Third Street, just north of Market. As he rode overland to join his ship at New Castle his thoughts were of the five "sympathetick objects of affection, constantly before me, to rouse the tender sensations of the heart; and employ the mind with pain and Constant distress, for at least two days before I left sweet Philadelphia." [19]

As the year ended, the *Canton,* with some thirty men on board, dropped down the river from New Castle, past the wharves off Reedy Island, through the widening bay and out to sea. As the new year dawned, the Captain turned his eyes to the sunrise; and beyond, to the golden shores of ageless Cathay.

CHAPTER 15

IN *CANTON* TO CANTON

℘ . . ℘ . . ℘ . . ℘ . .

WHEN Captain Truxtun laid down his course for Cape Town, his first port of call, seven thousand miles of open sea lay before him. He steered east-southeast from the Delaware capes, sailing clear across the Atlantic to the Cape Verde Islands, just off the western bulge of Africa, where he expected to find the northeast trades that would carry him down into the Ethiopic—South Atlantic—Sea.

Just north of the Equator, the *Canton* ran into calms, squalls, and baffling winds. For days on end the ship moved so slowly that she could scarcely be steered; then suddenly there would come "deluges of rain, and the most tremendous thunder and lightning known in any part of the globe; strong currents, and often violent tornadoes, in which a ship cannot show a rag of canvas for an hour or two; after which it falls of a sudden calm." The currents in these waters, the Captain thought, were strong and variable; sometimes they set to the west, sometimes to the east, "and frequently in all other directions." Here, said he, "I experienced the most disagreeable fortnight of my life."[1]

The calms gave the crew an opportunity to catch fresh food, since their ship was surrounded by an abundance of albacore, dolphins, skipjacks, and kingfish; and the heavy rains were not all wasted. Fresh water was caught in pieces of canvas that were rigged to lead it into water-casks; thus the ship's water supply was replenished while she was yet at sea.

Here, in the tropics, the Captain carefully avoided exposing his men to the hot sun that rode high overhead, because he believed that "by proper precautions in this tract of sea, the scurvy may be avoided perhaps during the whole voyage, as it is here frequently that the seeds of it are generated." He paid particular attention to his crew's food, and he tried to keep their quarters dry, clean, and free from mildew by "frequently washing with hot vinegar, burning powder and fumigating below," and by building fires to dry out the living spaces.[2]

While the *Canton* rolled slowly southward through the doldrums, Captain Truxtun entered for the first time into Neptune's kingdom. The boisterous ritual of plunging the uninitiated "over head and ears in a tub of water" as they crossed the line was a long established custom. In some vessels, the ceremony was observed at the Tropic of Cancer; the Old Man of the Tropic came aboard with his face blacked and painted and crowned by a swab whose long coarse strands hung down about his shoulders. The neophytes were daubed with tar and grease and then shaved with a notched wooden razor. A boat, filled with water, was used for the inevitable ducking. Whether the ritual took place at the Tropic or at the Equator, all of the gentlemen on board could buy their way, dry and unmolested, into the kingdom by furnishing a round of grog for the sailors.[3]

After leaving the doldrums, the *Canton* sailed southward through the Ethiopic Sea with gentle swells and pleasant breezes, to the Tropic of Capricorn and beyond. Continuing south to the latitude of the Cape of Good Hope, the ship met the southern trades and then headed east toward Cape Town. On the fifth of April, 1786, after three months at sea, the Captain sighted a strange sail on the horizon. He steered for the stranger and in a short while spoke her, finding her to be the *Empress of China,* just two months out of New York and bound also for Canton.[4] The *Empress* was inherently a faster sailer than the *Canton,* and in addition she had by luck avoided that dreadful tract of sea where the latter ship had spent two miserable weeks.[5]

Finally, after three more weeks of sailing eastward, Captain Truxtun brought his ship to anchor in Table Bay, just off the Dutch settlement of Cape Town, which was nestled at the foot of mesa-like Table Mountain.[6] Established by the Dutch East India Company more than a century before, this outpost provided a welcome break in the long voyage from America to China. Here was an opportunity to refit, to fill up water-casks, and to obtain fresh provisions. In addition, as the Captain learned when he went ashore, the Dutch would buy miscellaneous merchandise such as Philadelphia Windsor chairs; pine lumber, any wood being very scarce in Cape Town; and such wines and liquors as caught their fancy.[7] He made a mental note to bring along, on his next voyage, a suitable cargo for Cape Town, since his ship now was largely in ballast while she carried only ginseng and lead for the Chinese market.

Looking about the town, he found evidence of the heavy hand of Dutch authority on all sides. The British, whose East India Company ships called at St. Helena for refreshment, looked on Cape Town with a covetous eye because of its superior location. The Dutch settlement was well fortified, and a large body of troops was stationed there. Lookouts were maintained high on the towering mountains—Sugar Loaf and the Lion's Rump—and on Robben Island at the entrance to the harbor. Every approaching vessel was carefully scrutinized long before she dropped her anchor before the fort. On Robben Island, also, were "three gibbets for the sailors, one for the Soldiers & one for the Slaves" in sight of vessels sailing into and out of the harbor.[8] From these gallows, the bodies of luckless transgressors against the Dutch East India Company were left swinging in the breeze as a warning to all who might pass that way.

The town itself was a pleasant place, built of brick and stone, neat and clean as the cities of Holland. Surrounding the governor's palace was a beautifully kept garden, laid out in large squares with walks in between. Some day, these walks would be shaded by the young oak trees planted around each square. Now, however, the garden served a more utilitarian purpose, vegetables for the troops being grown there. Adjoining the garden there was a zoo, where the visitor might see ostriches, baboons, zebras, tigers, buffaloes, hart springbucks, and many kinds of birds.[9]

The Company provided a convenient watering place, water being piped to the end of a long pier, where ships' boats could fill their casks without having to take them ashore.[10] When Captain Truxtun had filled up every tier of water-casks and had his ship once more ready for sea, he weighed anchor, sheeted home the jibs and topsails, and with a favoring breeze stood out to sea. Skirting the high booming surf that exploded on a rocky ledge a few miles south of the pitch of the cape,[11] the *Canton* filled away to eastward, sailing into seas that were navigated by dhows, proas, and junks and, in the opinion of many sailors, still peopled by mermaids and sea monsters.

He steered his ship due east for several weeks. In that long lonesome waste of sea eastward from Africa, stretching all the way to the shores of New Holland (Australia), only two tiny islands break the monotony of the ceaseless curving horizons. After nearly three thousand miles of the heave and run of long hurrying swells, after wearisome weeks of running his easting down, Captain Truxtun raised a desolate bit of barren land, volcanic Amsterdam Island. He had no intention of pausing there nor at St. Paul Island nearby. These islands did, however, provide him with a check on his navigation thus far. He sailed on, making another few days of easting; then he steered away to northward, toward the Strait of Sunda, gateway to the China seas.

His next landfall was on the southern coast of Java, a hundred miles east of the Strait.[12] Having come more than two thousand miles since his last sight of land, it would not be surprising to find that his reckoning was in error by a hundred miles. On closer investigation, one finds that the British Tables Requisite, which he used, fixed the position of Java Head a hundred miles east of its true position at the entrance to the Strait of Sunda.[13] Had the Strait been where the Tables Requisite said it was, he would have made almost a perfect landfall. Next voyage, when he knew the true position of the Strait, he had no difficulty steering directly to its entrance. He demonstrated great skill as a navigator at a time when few mariners understood the intricacies of celestial navigation and when the methods in use were both cumbersome and inherently inaccurate.

Having made this landfall on the southern coast of Java, he followed the coast, trending to the northwest until he rounded Java Head. After passing through the Strait of Sunda, he threaded his way cautiously past countless islands in waters that teemed with reefs and banks and shoals. Through the China Sea to his destination, to Canton in China, he took his ship.

Sailing past the Ladrones, which lie across the mouth of the Canton River, he entered into a strange river in a strange land. Here was an ancient people, disdainful of the barbarians who inhabited the rest of the world. With great condescension they had opened to foreign vessels this one port in all the Empire; here they had developed an elaborate mummery to which all foreign traders were forced to submit. When he dropped his anchor in the mud of the Canton River off Macao, Captain Truxtun was already within the celestial precincts. For the next six months he could neither buy nor sell, come nor go without the permission of some representative of the Celestial Emperor.

CHAPTER 16

TRADER AT CANTON

❧ . . ❧ . . ❧ . . ❧ . .

LIKE nearly all the rest of China, the old walled city of Canton, lying eighty miles up the Canton River from Macao, was forbidden territory so far as westerners were concerned. Foreign devils were forced to deal with Chinese merchants outside the city gates, and even to get that far required a tedious ritual. It was a carefully circumscribed performance that tested the patience and pocketbooks of all who came to trade.

The first act was at Macao. This town, unique in the Empire, was a Portuguese colony and had been for two hundred years. Here, some four thousand Portuguese and seven thousand Chinese lived in an uneasy state of truce.[1] Leaving his ship anchored in Macao Roads, Captain Truxtun went ashore to get the first chop—permission to proceed with his ship up river to the anchorage at Whampoa. Usually it was a day or two before the chop was issued. The Chinese explained the delay by saying that it was necessary to get permission from Canton to issue the chop, but since the round trip of 160 miles was a great deal more than a day's journey, the delay can probably be better explained by an Englishman who, after waiting two days for his chop, understated the case by observing that "The Chinese are not very expeditious in transacting their business"; and, he added, "there is no remedy for these delays but patience." [2]

With his patience a bit frayed but with chop in hand, Captain Truxtun returned to his ship, took a Chinese pilot on board, and after a careful look about him, weighed anchor and sailed up the river. The prospect here in the muddy estuary was anything but pleasing. The bold, rocky hills of Macao were capped by a decrepit old fort; the off-lying islands were barren, dreary little hummocks. There was as yet no hint of the fabulous golden shores of old Cathay.[3]

Working his way slowly up the river, using sampans hired by the pilot to act as buoys on the various banks and shoals, tacking and reaching while the wind served, anchoring when both wind and tide were contrary, and embracing the set of the tide between ebb and flood, he came at length to Boca Tigris, "the Bogue," a narrow passage defended by a paltry fort on each bank of the river. Here he came to anchor again. The pilot from Macao was discharged, and another was engaged to take him the rest of the way to the final anchorage. He was boarded by a mandarin boat, a sort of sampan, armed with carriage guns and fitted to comport with the exalted station of the customs officials who rode in it. After they had inspected his chop and had given him permission to continue on his way, one or two of the government men remained on board. They went with him to the anchorage at Whampoa in order to make sure that he carried on no illicit trade on the way.

The countryside brightened as the *Canton* worked her way upstream beyond the Bogue. The river wound through gentle sloping hills and swampy fields of cane and rice, with every bend affording a new and pleasing vista. The rising ground was adorned with trees, and the hills were crowned by lofty and ancient pagodas. There were many villages and towns, bright spots on a distant landscape; but they lost much of their appeal when approached more closely. They were dirty and crowded; oppression and poverty and want were apparent on every hand.[4]

The impoverished state of the populace was even more evident on the river. The *Canton* was forced to pick her way among the shoals of river craft that clogged the stream. There were thousands upon thousands of sampans, each one occupied by a whole family, living their whole lives on the river, eking out a miserable existence by fishing and by some trivial employments they occasionally found for their boats or themselves. On the river, too, were the tall, ungainly junks, with great eyes painted on their bows to spy out evil spirits; mandarin boats, with red sashes decorating the muzzles of their cannon; flower boats, gaily decorated houses of pleasure; and passage boats, some fitted with sumptuous cabins that contained a table and eight or ten chairs for passengers, enclosed by lattices decorated with mother-of-pearl, and covered by neat arched roofs of bamboo. All the boats on the river had a place at the stern for a lavishly ornamented joss-house; there sat the idol that the people worshiped. At night the river was eerily lighted by thousands of tiny fires, each one keeping watch over its joss and protecting him from the terrors of darkness.[5]

At last, after toiling northward through a string of low, flat islands that lay athwart the channel, the *Canton* sailed into that reach of the river known as Whampoa Anchorage. Here was an imposing array of ships of many nations. Bluff-bowed British East Indiamen, comprising well over half of those present, lay in a line with ships from Holland, Denmark, Sweden, France, Spain, and America.[6] After warping his way clear through the fleet, Captain Truxtun brought his ship to anchor near the Americans, at the very head of the line. About the first of September, 1786, the long outward passage from Philadelphia was finally at an end.

Three American ships had arrived this season ahead of the *Canton*. The eighty-ton sloop *Experiment* was first, then the *Empress of China*, and finally the *Hope*.[7] All had sailed from New York. The Salem ship *Grand Turk*, arriving soon after the *Canton*, completed the American fleet for this trading season.[8]

Captain Truxtun learned that the master of the *Hope* was James Magee, who, nearly ten years before, had succeeded him in command of the first vessel of Isaac Sears' privateer fleet, the sloop *Independence*. In the *Hope* had come Isaac Sears himself, trying to regain in the China trade the fortune he had lost at the end of the Revolution. This early Son of Liberty, now fifty-six years old, had completed his last voyage. He was ill of a fever when he arrived; he grew steadily worse, and here, aboard the *Hope,* he died. His body was taken ashore and buried on nearby French Island, some fourteen thousand miles from home.[9]

After long months at sea, living on salt meat, dried peas and beans, and ship's bread that was baked before the voyage began, Captain Truxtun's first duty was to arrange for a steady supply of fresh provisions during his stay in China. He had no choice but to buy all of them from a comprador, who was licensed by the government to carry on the trade. Mandarin boats, with customs officers living aboard, hovered about his ship to prevent his buying any foodstuffs from anyone else. Not satisfied with the profits from this exclusive trade, the comprador always demanded an additional cumshaw, or gratuity, of two or three hundred dollars.[10]

The next step of the intricate routine of trading was to engage a linguist, or interpreter, in order to be able to carry on the rest of the business. To the linguist went another cumshaw.[11]

The selling and buying of cargoes all had to be done in the factories outside Canton, a dozen miles up river from the anchorage. Leaving his ship in charge of the first mate, with instructions for overhauling the running and standing rigging, mending the sails, caulking, painting, and making other routine repairs, he engaged a passage boat which, for a dollar or two, took him and his supercargo up to the factories at Canton.[12] Although he lived in a factory during his stay in China, Captain Truxtun had to return frequently to his ship in order to attend to the visits of customs officers and to oversee the repairs and the stowage of cargo.

All of the factories, so named because factors, or business agents, lived in them, were located on the river bank outside the walls of old Canton. They formed "a tolerably handsome range of buildings," about a quarter of a mile in length, being disposed in several rows parallel to the river. Between the factories and the city's walls lay the "suburbs" of Canton, where foreigners could observe from the factory compound, but could not enter, the "exceedingly narrow and inconvenient, but . . . tolerably clean" streets, lined on both sides by ramshackle rows of shops and warehouses.[13] The factories were two-story buildings, the first floor being used as a godown, or warehouse, for the teas and silks and porcelain that made up return cargoes, and the second floor for living quarters. Foreigners rented the buildings from Chinese merchants. After a lease had been signed, a factory comprador would, within a few hours' time, furnish the living quarters completely with beds, tables, chairs, and dishes, and in addition would provide a cook and two or three servants.[14]

Foreign trade at Canton all passed through the hands of a powerful association of ten or a dozen Chinese merchants comprising the "Co-hong," whose monopoly on foreign trade was absolute by virtue of a decree of the Celestial Emperor.[15] In return for their monopoly, the hong merchants, as they were called, were responsible to the government for the payment of all customs duties and port charges, and for the proper conduct of all transactions. The foreign trader had no choice but to do business with the Co-hong; he did have his choice of hong merchants, however. He might select Shy Kinqua or Chouqua or Pinqua or one of the others to handle his business, to purchase his ginseng and lead and to arrange for the procurement and delivery of his return cargo.[16]

Before anything could be unloaded or any new cargo could be taken on board, a ship had to be inspected and measured for tonnage, from which the port charges might be computed. Of the total cost of doing business in Canton, the port charges amounted to an important part, so it was only fitting that an important personage be present while the charges were determined. Therefore, it was usual for the Grand Hoppo, Superintendent of the South Sea Customs, personally to visit the foreign ships as they arrived.[17] And so it was that Captain Truxtun, after hurrying back from the factories to his ship one day in order to prepare for the grand visit, was boarded by the Grand Hoppo and his large retinue.

Wearing the rich embroidered robes of a mandarin, his hair close cropped except on top of his head, whence grew his long braided queue, the Hoppo came alongside the *Canton* in a fine barge, regally furnished, decorated with many flags and pennants, and propelled by ten oars.[18] With the Hoppo was the hong merchant whom Captain Truxtun had selected and a company of soldiers and musicians. As the Hoppo came on deck, his own people saluted him on bended knee, and his band of musicians, comprising two small drums and three or four pipes, provided, according to one British observer, "a harmony resembling a sow-gelder's horn and the cackling of geese." [19] His attendants measured the ship for tonnage, taking only two dimensions, the length and the breadth. The length was established as the distance from foremast to mizzenmast, or sometimes from foremast to taffrail; the breadth was measured near the gangway.[20]

Considering the caprice with which a vessel's dimensions were determined, the port charges could have been as easily levied in the Hoppo's private chambers, since the total charge for every vessel was very nearly a constant sum. To the government went a few hundred dollars, but the Hoppo invariably demanded a cumshaw of about three thousand dollars, regardless of the size of the vessel.[21] The total cost to each vessel was, therefore, practically independent of tonnage. In return for this exorbitant cumshaw, the Hoppo sent on board a standard gift, variously described by those who received it. It consisted, according to one, of "two Bulls a sack of dirty Sugar and a fiew Bottles of Samshaw"; [22] and to another, "two poor buffaloes, eight jars of samshu, (a spirit so bad that we threw it overboard) and eight bags of ground rice, about forty pounds each." [23]

After being visited by the Hoppo, Captain Truxtun was officially admitted to do business with the Empire. He could now unload his cargo and get on with the business that he had come so far to transact. His linguist, who was also a government man, arranged for "chop boats" to carry his cargo to Canton, and kept a tally of the ginseng and lead as they were discharged, in order to insure the payment of all import duties.[24]

While the return cargo was being assembled by the hong merchant, Captain Truxtun had ample opportunity to make necessary repairs to his ship. In order to overhaul and restow his supplies, it was convenient to take some of them ashore. Accordingly, for about two hundred dollars, the enterprising Chinese built a banksall on a nearby island for his exclusive use. The banksall was a sizable building, framed with bamboo and covered with a roof of grass mats and straw; as soon as the owner was finished with it, the Chinese tore it down in order that they might rebuild it later for another owner for another two hundred dollars.[25]

All of these impositions on foreign traders, sanctioned and encouraged by government officials great and small, resulted in lower profits for those who had risked their money in the trade, but few if any adventurers were discouraged by them. Port charges, chop fees, cumshaws, and other extraordinary expenses amounted to a few thousand dollars for each ship, while the investment represented by each ship was generally upwards of a hundred thousand dollars; and fifty per cent profits were not uncommon.

Early in December, the return cargo began to arrive in Canton; [26] but it was after Christmas when Captain Truxtun finally got all of his cargo on board and his ship ready for sea. Then there was but one more act to be performed in the elaborate ritual. The last chop —the Grand Chop—was procured from the Grand Hoppo. An imposing document, neatly inscribed in Chinese characters and decorated with fanciful birds and dragons, the Grand Chop served as clearance from the port of Canton, indicating that all duties and charges had been paid; it served also as a passport through the China seas, charging all Chinese officials to "let the said vessel pass without interruption," and incidentally without carrying on any illicit trade with the vessel.[27] Captain Truxtun, making application through his linguist to the Hoppo for his Grand Chop, waited only for it and a fair wind to begin the long homeward passage. On the third of January, 1787, the *Canton* weighed anchor and departed for Philadelphia.

CHAPTER 17

## SUMMER AT HOME

෴ . . ෴ . . ෴ . . ෴ . .

AFTER a homeward bound voyage of a hundred and thirty-six days, Captain Truxtun brought his ship up the Delaware River on a Sunday afternoon in May, 1787.[1] An experienced China hand now, the first from Philadelphia, he was back home after an absence of more than sixteen months.

The *Canton* was moored to her wharf and the unloading began. The tea chests and bales of nankeens and boxes of chinaware were swayed up out of the hold, loaded into wagons, and conveyed to the stores of the ship's owners and to stores and warehouses of those who, like Benjamin Fuller, had ordered goods on their accounts. As the wagons rumbled and careened through the uneven cobblestone streets, passersby paid them scant notice.[2] It was no novelty in Philadelphia to see the wagon loads of chests and bales with the Chinese markings; the only novelty was in the fact that they had come directly from China; it was no longer necessary for China goods to come to America by way of Europe.

Sixteen months was a long time to be away from home; and this had been in China, according to the American consul there, "the worst year for trade ever known before or expected again";[3] but when the returns from this voyage were totted up, there was no question about where Captain Truxtun's next voyage would take him. He would go to China again. First, however, he would have several months at home, his departure being regulated by the season of the southwest monsoon in the China seas. But he would not be idle; it was not his nature to be idle.

When he was not completely occupied by the business of his ship, he was apt to become involved in affairs that he would do better to avoid. For example, his sense of honor had been affronted by John Green, captain of the *Empress of China,* while they were both in Canton. The nature of the controversy cannot be divined from surviving documents, but a letter written by a Philadelphia newspaper editor gives an idea of the reaction that could be expected from Captain Truxtun when he imagined that his good name was in jeopardy. "You have doubtless heard," the editor wrote to a friend in New York, "that Capt. Truxtun did not escape the general and particular insinuations which, it is alledged, Capt. Green threw out, on various Occasions, to the Disadvantage of almost all the other American adventurers to that distant Country."

"Capt. Truxtun," he continued, "since his arrival here, has behaved with becoming Spirit, and commenced the avenger of his own Injuries. He possesses such Materials as would, if published to the World, render Capt. Green quite odious and contemptible—but his Employers have prevailed on him to suppress them, at least for the present."[4]

The American consul in China characterized Green as "a diabolical scoundrel";[5] and Captain Truxtun certainly was not the aggressor in the Canton affair; but when he was attacked, or when he fancied that his name might be besmirched, it was all his friends and well-wishers could do to keep him from publishing "to the World" his side of any controversy. It was probably just as well that this altercation never reached the public prints. His energies could be better spent on plans for his second China voyage.

The ownership of the *Canton* was expanded to include seven new shareholders, and all of those who invested money in the first voyage held onto their shares; so a total of thirteen persons were now interested in the ship.[6] Two new supercargoes, identified only as Wilcox and McCall, were appointed to replace John Frazier, who had made the first voyage.[7] Frazier wanted to go out to China again, but this time he contracted to go with Captain Truxtun's friend John Barry, who was also preparing to leave in time for the next trading season. Barry, a former captain in the Continental Navy and now in his early forties (Captain Truxtun was thirty-two), was commander of the *Asia,* a new ship slightly larger than the *Canton* and owned by no less than seventeen shareholders.[8] Another ship, the *Alliance,* an aged vessel that had served during the war as a frigate in the Continental Navy, had already sailed for China, attempting by its early departure to gain a trading season.[9]

Captain Truxtun may have found time to call on his friend and neighbor, Benjamin Franklin, who was spending his free time in the pleasant little garden at the rear of his home just off Market Street, near Third. The old man, now eighty-one, would want to know how the sea anchor had worked out; he would be interested in the results of Captain Truxtun's taking the temperature of the Eastern oceans; and he would surely have many questions to ask about people and customs in Canton; all of this in order to increase his already tremendous fund of information about a wide variety of subjects.

During the summer, Captain Truxtun could see the old philosopher in his sedan chair, carried on the shoulders of trusty convicts, going to and from the State House, where the Constitutional Convention was attempting to fashion an instrument that would help make the United States—united by the exigencies of war—into a permanent republic.[10] There were other great men of the age on the streets of Philadelphia that summer. General Washington, Alexander Hamilton, James Madison, and many others were attending the convention. While Captain Truxtun, like everyone in Philadelphia except the members of the convention, heard little of its secret proceedings, he was still present in September when the Constitution was finally published and the great public controversy arose over whether it should be ratified by the several states. Many thousands of words by the Federalists, in favor of the Constitution, and the Antifederalists appeared in newspapers and pamphlets; public meetings were held; occasional clashes between factions were marked by physical violence and the flinging of rocks.[11] It was not until after he had been out to China again that he could learn that the Constitution was ratified, and that the issue had finally been settled in favor of "a more perfect Union."

It was during this summer of 1787, also, that John Fitch demonstrated, in the presence of many members of the Constitutional Convention, that his steamboat would go through the water under its own power.[12] Captain Truxtun must surely have seen the contraption that Fitch had put together, but he no doubt dismissed the scheme of the inventor as a chimerical one. Indeed, it was not until twenty years later, when Fulton's boat was running on the Hudson, that it began to be generally realized that the steamboat might become anything more than an ingenious toy.

As the chill days of autumn marched by and the lamplighter went his rounds earlier and earlier in the short afternoons, Captain Truxtun was completing preparations for his second voyage. Old Benjamin Fuller gave him seven hundred Spanish milled dollars to be spent for tea, nankeens, chinaware, and nutmegs. "The China that I rec'd last voyage," he told Captain Truxtun, "was packed very badly, and I lost a considerable part in Breakage; therefore have to request your care in haveing this (now order'd) pack'd in the most Carefull Manner." Mrs. Fuller wanted some chinaware, too: a 160-piece set of the most fashionable kind of blue and white porcelain, with the Fuller coat of arms to be skillfully reproduced in full color on every piece. His commission, about twenty dollars, paid him small return for the time and trouble he had to expend in fulfilling the tedious instructions of the aging merchant and his wife.[13] Fuller insured his little adventure through a London broker. When he arranged for coverage, he told the broker that Captain Truxtun was "a Gentleman well known at Lloyds." [14] He referred, of course, to the group of maritime underwriters, formerly customers of Lloyd's Coffee House in London, who now had rooms in the Royal Exchange.

Charles Biddle, sometime sea captain, who had just completed a term as Vice-President of the Supreme Executive Council of Pennsylvania, was a friend and admirer of the young mariner. When Captain Truxtun was away from home, he depended on Biddle to attend to his personal affairs. On the first of December, he left with Biddle a list of bills to be collected when they came due and a number of other accounts, still remaining from his partnership with Collins, to be settled. "What Mrs. Truxtun wants for Family Use," he said, "I will thank you to supply." [15]

On the eighth of December, 1787, the *Canton* dropped down the river to New Castle, where the livestock was put on board; and on the thirteenth, holding a fair wind, Captain Truxtun discharged his pilot at the Delaware capes and took his departure from the light on Cape Henlopen, laying down his course once more for the far lands.[16]

CHAPTER 18

SECOND VOYAGE TO CANTON

۶۹   .   .   ۶۹   .   .   ۶۹   .   .   ۶۹   .   .

VEERING southward before he reached the Cape Verde Islands, Captain Truxtun carefully avoided the tract of sea near the Equator where, last voyage, he had lived through a fortnight of thoroughly wretched weather.

Entirely unknown to him until years later, another ship, about the same size as his, crossed his wake not far from the Equator, sailing just a few days astern of the *Canton*. His Majesty's ship *Bounty,* Captain William Bligh, was outward bound for the South Seas. The mutiny on the *Bounty,* that well-known epic of the sea, occurred before Captain Truxtun had returned home from this voyage.

After calling again at Cape Town for refreshment, Captain Truxtun sailed toward the Sunda Strait. Being certain of its position this time, he made a perfect landfall. Two months after leaving Cape Town, the *Canton* was working her way up through the Strait; past bold Java Head; between the mainland of Java and the lofty cone of volcanic Krakatau Island, whose rumblings occasionally shook the waters in the Strait; [1] past Fourth Point, where lay the town of

Anjer; and at last into the Java Sea. On the eleventh of June, 1788, Captain Truxtun spoke the *Asia,* which had departed from Philadelphia a week, and from Cape Town two days, after the *Canton.*[2] The *Asia* continued northward toward Canton, but Captain Truxtun bore away eastward for Batavia, on the north coast of Java.

On this second voyage he was making use of information about indirect trade with China that he had obtained in Cape Town and Canton. By trading at intermediate ports of call, he hoped to enter the Canton market with more trade goods and fewer hard dollars. Tin, pepper, shark's fins, edible bird's nests, and sandalwood were in demand at Canton; he was calling at Batavia to trade his cargo of tar, iron, and spirits for the tin, pepper, and other items that would yield a handsome profit at Canton.[3]

Batavia, a Dutch stronghold in the bitter early struggle for monopoly in the Spice Islands, was the principal outpost of the Dutch East India Company. It was well fortified, but its location, on the swampy shore of a bay, was abominable. Captain Truxtun heard that the unhealthful location had "cost the lives of at least a million of the innocent natives."[4] Nevertheless, the houses were built of brick, the streets were straight and wide, and beyond the city were the elegant country seats of government and Company officials. Balls and concerts were held often and were attended by the Europeans and their ladies. Some of the ladies had succumbed to the native habit of chewing the betel nut, and a lady when chewing was accompanied by a little female slave who carried a gilt or silver jar into which the lady might spit when necessary.[5]

While visiting one day at the home of an old and respected Dutch resident in Batavia, Captain Truxtun saw a funeral procession passing by. He observed to his host that this city seemed to be the most sickly place he had ever seen.

"Yes, it is," the old gentleman agreed, "a sickly place indeed; but, I have had my seasoning, and now I do not mind it."

Pressing him for ways to avoid the fever, Captain Truxtun learned a little more of the white man's ways in the East. His host told him that during the sickly season he ate "soups, an abundance of vegetables, and but little flesh, . . . drank moderately of weak Holland gin and water, of porter, and other things well diluted, and seldom exceeded two or three glasses of wine after dinner." He made it "a rule always to let in his appartments the pure fresh air of the day, and never expose himself improperly to the effects of sun or moon, dews or night vapours." [6] Like much of the incidental information he chanced upon, he filed the old man's wisdom in his mind for future reference.

When, a few weeks later, he brought the *Canton* into Whampoa Anchorage, he found there only one other American ship, the *Asia.* The *Alliance* had already departed for home. She had, in spite of a six months' voyage during which nearly half of her crew was disabled by scurvy, indeed stolen a season.[7] Two more American ships were expected. When one of them, the *Jenny,* arrived, she bore a letter for Captain Truxtun.

Benjamin Fuller had written to him. He had changed his mind. Would Captain Truxtun please buy none of the blue and white porcelain he had ordered, but buy the same pieces in enameled ware instead? He had decided that a year hence the enameled ware would suit the market better than the other variety. Considerately, he had added, "Your Family and all your Friends within my Knowledge are well—Mrs. Fuller Desires to be remember'd to you." [8]

Captain Truxtun and his supercargoes moved into a factory at Canton, where they arranged to do their trading with Equa, one of the hong merchants. A contract was prepared in English, written "in a full hand on a Large Sheet of paper," to impress the Chinese, and was, following the usual tea-drinking ceremony, witnessed, signed, and sealed. "When you have the name of a China man to his agreement," one trader wrote, "he is much more observant of it." [9] Besides Equa, they had some business with Lysingsang, better known as the Black Doctor. He was not a hong merchant, but he operated under Equa's chop; that is, he had Equa's permission to deal with the barbarians.

After arrangements for the return cargo had been completed, the inevitable wait of several months began. The American captains and supercargoes and the American consul, Samuel Shaw (serving "without being entitled to receive any salary, fees, or emoluments whatsoever"), went occasionally to French Island for refreshment and recreation, the island being in "a delightful situation, and the resort of the gentlemen generally, of all nations." The crew of the *Canton* also could go ashore on French Island, a privilege accorded to the "common sailors" of only American and French vessels.[10]

While ships were overhauled and gentlemen drank and talked the evenings away, return cargoes for their vessels were collected in the back country, from whence they eventually began to trickle into the factory godowns outside Canton, preparatory to being taken in chop boats down to Whampoa Anchorage.

All of the various grades of tea, packed in chests, half chests, and quarter chests, were brought to the godowns. The quality ranged from cheap Bohea black, grown in the mountains of Wu Yi, to the very best Hyson skin. Besides the naturally grown tea, the Chinese "made a vast deal of counterfeit tea" of such things as the leaves of the sweet potato, sometimes mixing it with genuine tea and sometimes simply preparing it with "such colour and taste as they judged proper." [11]

Much of the chinaware was made by farmers during their spare time, each farmer making only a single article such as cups or saucers or bowls. Merchants then went about the countryside, collecting the individual lots and sending them on to Canton, where they were combined to form complete sets.[12]

Some of the goods were carried into Canton on the backs of coolies, some came in boats down canals that slashed across hundreds of miles of open plains, and some were brought in wheelbarrows aided by the wind. The wheelbarrow porters, spreading a light sail on a bamboo mast, sailed across the open country at a pattering clip. Sometimes they traveled in fleets; it was said that one might see as many as three hundred sail of wheelbarrows a hundred miles from the nearest water.[13]

When he was almost at the point of sailing from Canton, early in January, 1789, Captain Truxtun did what was common in his day, when a mariner was ever conscious of the uncertainty of a sea voyage: he wrote a long letter to his wife. No doubt he delivered it into the care of his friend Captain Barry, who also was ready to sail. If the *Canton* should not survive the long passage home, he wanted Mary to have this last remembrance, something to help fill the emptiness that follows the disappearance of a ship at sea. In addition, he wrote for the first time to one of his children.

Addressing this letter to Sarah, now ten years old, he told her that he was writing to her first only because she was the eldest, "for I love you all and all alike." He advised and counseled her on matters that must have been strange and incomprehensible to her; but then he was consciously writing what might well be his last letter to his children as well as his first.

"As mental and personal accomplishments depend in a great measure on example," he wrote, "you must carefully observe all the dictates of your good Mama, impress on your mind all her minute actions, take notice of every step as she walks and let her will (in all cases) be your criterion, for it is impossible for you to have a better pattern." A year's absence will color in any mind the picture of domestic felicity; but he voiced the same sentiments in Philadelphia as in Canton.

He charged Sarah with the "duty incumbent on the elder branch of a family, to interest themselves in the instruction of the younger." Referring to Sarah's brother and two sisters—he had not yet heard of Evelina, born four months after his departure from home—he continued, "You should instruct them all you can and inspire them with a proper sense of the excellence of a superior education, the duty they owe their affectionate Mama, for her care in nursing and bringing them up and of the many anxious moments she has had for your and their happiness."

Knowing that she was attending Schoolmaster Andrew Brown's academy a block or two from home, he admonished her to "take especial care and not lose a single moment, in improving yourself in every useful branch of female education and knowledge . . . you are now arrived at a period which will not admit of idleness and inattention to books, for by and by it will be too late to regain what you may now let slip." On the sort of books to be read, he said, "the Spectator I have, and will give you out of my collection, when I come home."

"In your general deportment," he wrote, "you should be easy and affable but not over volatile. . . . let me always see and hear, that you are, in the *eyes of everybody truly amiable*." All of this, he assured her, was "the advice, and early desire, of an affectionate father who from unforeseen and unexpected misfortune, is obliged, to his heart felt pain, to be so great a proportion of his time absent from you and your dear Mama, your brother and sisters as he is."

"Kiss your Mama heartily for me and your brother and sisters." [14]

Within a day or two after writing this letter, Captain Truxtun had his cargo completed and his ship ready for sea. Since Captain

Barry's *Asia* was also ready to depart, the two captains decided to sail in company through the China seas, as far as the Strait of Sunda, for mutual protection from the pirates that ranged the China coast.

The two ships watered at an island in the Sunda Strait, and then, because each found it easy to regulate her sailing to the other, they kept company as far as Cape Town, where they watered again and stood out on the last leg of the long voyage home. From Cape Town to the Delaware capes, the *Canton* steered a direct course, sailing steadily northwestward for ten weeks. The ships parted company in a storm soon after leaving Cape Town, but they arrived in Philadelphia only a day apart, in June, 1789.[15]

This was the second and, as it turned out, the last of Captain Truxtun's voyages to Canton. The trade in tea and silk was becoming less and less attractive as the limited American market became satiated. He believed that the really lucrative trade was between the coasts of India and China, with calls at intermediate islands. He decided at length that his next voyage would take him to new lands.

He was still working for the creditors of the house of Collins and Truxtun when he went about the business of getting the *Canton* out for her third Eastern voyage. Slowly he was whittling down the debts he had assumed, but at the same time he was putting into his next adventure every dollar he could command. This time he intended to take out two ships instead of one.

CHAPTER 19

## AND A VOYAGE TO INDIA

ᘒ　·　·　ᘒ　·　·　ᘒ　·　·　ᘒ　·　·

ONE day in June, 1789, Captain Truxtun walked into Mr. Morris's countinghouse to talk over plans for his next voyage.[1] Robert Morris, statesman, banker, and probably the wealthiest merchant in Philadelphia, had been one of the first businessmen to enter the China trade. Now he was proposing a new scheme. He and some business associates would help Captain Truxtun buy out the shareholders in the *Canton;* then they would prepare her for a voyage to China by way of India. Furthermore, they would send out another ship with a cargo for India. In India, they would sell the extra ship, and the *Canton* would bring back the proceeds of the sale. Thus it was that the *Canton* became the property of William Constable, Isaac Hazelhurst and Company (Robert Morris was the company), and Captain Truxtun.[2]

Constable, a New York merchant, had for many years been dreaming of the profits he might make in the China trade.[3] He was confident that this plan, if it was carried out by the right person, could hardly lose. Judging by his reputation, Captain Truxtun was the right person. Before long, Constable ran across a bargain ship, the *New York,* which he promptly bought for this venture.

The command of the *New York* went to Robert Mercer, who had been first mate in the *Canton.*[4] His pay, £8 per month, and his privilege of carrying home three tons of freight, were the same as though he had continued as first mate, but his duties and responsibilities were greatly increased;[5] and his ship was not one to delight the heart of a seaman.

Captain Truxtun had hoped that the *New York* would sail as far as India with only minor repairs, but his hopes were dashed when he journeyed to New York to look at her. She needed two new topmasts, a new suit of sails, a new anchor and cable, and some internal repairs; and he decided it would be necessary to heave her down to repair her bottom.[6] She appeared to him to be a dull sailer, slow to answer her helm, a dangerous ship on a lee shore. Still, he hoped that she might sell for twenty thousand dollars in Johanna or Bombay. Accordingly, he reminded Mercer, "you know the necessity of letting all the good Qualities of the Ship be known, whenever you have an Opportunity."[7]

Hazelhurst arranged for the cargoes: bar iron, tar, pine lumber, porter, shrub, and Windsor chairs in the *Canton,* and a cargo of masts and spars in the *New York.*[8] The *Canton* would call at Cape Town, but the *New York* would go directly to Johanna, off the east coast of Africa. There she would wait twenty days for the *Canton* and then proceed to Bombay. If, after waiting fifteen days longer in Bombay, the *Canton* had not yet arrived, Mercer was instructed to sell his ship and cargo. It was clearly understood that whenever Captain Truxtun was present, at sea or on shore, his commands would take precedence over any written instructions that Mercer might have.[9]

Even before the ships sailed, there was talk of another, newer ship to replace the *Canton* next voyage. Messrs. Morris and Constable had one in mind, now absent on an India voyage, that they might buy; or they might build a new one. Whichever they did, Captain Truxtun wanted his next to be a copper-bottomed ship. He knew how foul a bottom could become in warm seas where, on long voyages, grass was known to grow to a length of two feet or more.[10] But coppering was outside the ken of American shipyards, so the new ship would have to be sent to England to have the job done.

On the eve of his departure from Philadelphia, Captain Truxtun walked out Market Street to call on Robert Morris at his mansion, the finest in the city.[11] He told Morris that he expected to make a most successful cruise, even though he was leaving later than he would have liked. He also mentioned Hazelhurst's handling of the details, which he thought had been done quite satisfactorily. He stayed but a few minutes and then walked down to spend another few minutes with Hazelhurst, to settle the accounts. But the accounts were not ready for him, so he took off his coat and sat down to help get them straightened out. The hours passed; it was almost midnight when he suddenly remembered that he had told his friend Charles Biddle that he would be home by eight o'clock.

Next morning, still mortified by his lapse of memory, he scrawled a note to Biddle; "I ask you ten thousand pardons," he wrote, "for not meeting you according to my appointment . . . I thought nothing could have prevented me, but. . . ." [12]

Nor did he see Charles Biddle before he left Philadelphia. He took long leave of his family, left a little money with Mary to answer her immediate needs ("for which I am to bring back the amount for the lender in India Goods, this is paying a heavy Interest but what can I do?"), and boarded the stage for New Castle, where his ship lay waiting for him.[13]

While he waited for a wind to take him out to sea, he wrote a letter to Biddle, asking him to attend to some business that was still pending. He accepted Biddle's offer to keep Mary supplied with money during his absence and reminded him "that I have made no other arrangements for this purpose, relying intirely on your kind offer and promise."

He wanted Biddle to push the suit he had brought against Tench Coxe, who is remembered as a political economist and an early advocate of American manufactures. Coxe had been a shareholder in the previous voyage. Upon his recommendation, Captain Truxtun had lent £1,000 to Joseph Harrison, but soon afterwards he had heard on every hand that Harrison was not to be trusted for a shilling. Coxe had not endorsed the note, but he had visited Captain Truxtun on board his ship one day and told him he had gotten security from Harrison; however, he had never delivered it up, and no move had been made to repay the £1,000. Captain Truxtun felt that Coxe had made him look foolish, and he was determined to try to make him pay, even though he had small chance of success. "You well know," he told Biddle, "that Coxe is a very Cunning, artfull, and deceitfull general, though dam him, I do not believe him to be a brave one, but as he is a great proficient in Manuvering, he . . . without fighting, may defeat my whole army of lawyers." [14] No record has been found of this war, if indeed it ever materialized. It is likely that Charles Biddle discussed the situation with Tench Coxe, and then quietly let the issue die.

Sailing from a Philadelphia winter into a South African summer, Captain Truxtun called again at Cape Town. While talking to an old acquaintance in the India trade, he outlined his plan to carry on an indirect trade with China by way of India, Batavia, and intermediate points. He received such encouragement that he wrote to Isaac Hazelhurst at once, telling him that if he and Morris and Constable were going to build a new ship, they should make it half again as large as they had originally planned. [15]

He continued on to Bombay, the British East India Company's stronghold on the west coast of India. No record of the disposition of the *New York* has been found, but it is likely that he found her waiting for him in Bombay and that he sold her there.

Ten months out of Philadelphia, he had sailed as far as Calcutta, where the British were at war with one of the numerous native princes. However, the Governor General, Lord Cornwallis, whose defeat at Yorktown had marked the virtual end of the Revolutionary War, took time to be a cordial host. An amiable man, "universally esteemed," he won Captain Truxtun's instant admiration. [16] The Governor General welcomed him to Calcutta. He assured him that, in spite of the Company's rule against it, he was always glad to see an American ship arrive. He said that he wished a hundred sail a year might come out from America. The Americans had a salutary effect on British captains who, as long as they had a monopoly, charged "three to six" prices for the goods they brought from England.[17]

Captain Truxtun was enthusiastic about the India trade. He formulated ambitious plans for keeping one ship constantly plying between India and China with another occasionally to take the earnings back to America. This year, however, it was too late to continue on to China, so he took in a cargo of piece goods and spices and set sail for Philadelphia. He was anxious to get the *Canton* home; he was beginning to lose confidence in his ship "owing to her stearing so very ill that she is scarcely governable with a press of Sail when before the Wind, or going large."[18] Although he complained about many things, Captain Truxtun almost never complained about his ships; but the *Canton,* now six years old, had carried him more than seventy thousand miles, and her age was beginning to tell.

The passage from India was the worst he had ever had. In his haste to get home, he may have omitted his usual call for refreshment at Cape Town. Whatever the reason, he was in serious trouble before he reached the northern tropic; his crew was so badly stricken by scurvy that he was scarcely able to sail his ship into a port in the West Indies, being forced to take some hands on board to help him anchor and to pull a boat ashore with the sick. He resumed the homeward passage as soon as his crew was partly recovered, but he was forced to leave five seamen in the hospital in Martinique.[19]

Scurvy was still likely to appear during a long voyage. The disease had yet to claim many more thousands of victims before the absence of fresh vegetables from the diet was recognized as its true cause. A specific preventive was not yet generally agreed upon. Lime juice, regular use of which was prescribed for all Royal Navy vessels a few years later, was now merely one of many antiscorbutics. Captain Truxtun was not alone in his belief that scurvy might be prevented by taking particular care to keep his crew away from the direct rays of the tropical sun, and to keep their living spaces and clothes dry, sweet, and well aired. Such things as tea and sugar, Peruvian bark, and fresh meats were thought by some to be "excellent antiscorbutics." By drawing an erroneous conclusion from the observation that a few days ashore would often revive a victim of the disease, "land air," as opposed to sea air, was considered a tonic for seamen engaged in long voyages.[20]

It was nearly the end of April, 1791, more than six months after the *Canton* departed from India, when old Benjamin Fuller wrote, "I received an account that the Ship *Canton* Thomas Truxtun Esqr Commander was in the River and would be up in a few Tydes— The Letters by her are in Town and I hope to see the Captain in a few hours." [21]

## CHAPTER 20

## OWNER OF THE GOOD SHIP *DELAWARE*

℘ · · ℘ · · ℘ · · ℘ · ·

IT ALWAYS took a few days to bring Captain Truxtun up to date on the Philadelphia story when he returned home from his China and India voyages. This time there seemed to be so much news; so many things had happened while he was gone. He could agree completely with the man who had recently written, "We live in a day, when one year of life is worth many in dull common times." [1]

To be sure, the most important event was the arrival in May, 1790, of his second son, named William, who was now almost a year old. His wife and other children—Sarah, Mary, Thomas, Elizabeth, and Evelina—were all well. He had to renew his acquaintance with Evelina, now three; he had been home only for seven months of her lifetime thus far; and unless his present plans were changed, he would be home for just another seven months before time to leave again. Sarah, twelve, was becoming quite worldly with all her learning at Mr. Brown's academy. Thomas, eight, was old enough now to be an attentive audience when his father told him about Tipoo Sahib, who was fighting against Captain Truxtun's friend Lord Cornwallis way off there in India, about all the strange animals in the zoo at Cape Town, and about the thousands of little boys in China who were born and reared in sampans on the Canton River.

He learned that his friend Benjamin Franklin had died at the age of eighty-four. It was already more than a year since his body had been laid to rest in the Christ Church burying ground. Although the population of Philadelphia was less than 30,000, some twenty thousand people had watched the ceremony or followed the funeral procession.

The government of the new republic had moved from New York to Philadelphia during the winter just past. George Washington was again in the city, this time as President of the United States, living in the Morris mansion on Market Street, going about the city in his elegant cream-colored carriage, drawn by two—and sometimes four—handsome Virginia bays, driven by a proud German coachman.[2]

The State House again was at the center of the national stage, having been given over to Congress and the Supreme Court. Across the street, on the north side of Chestnut, was the War Office, presided over by General Henry Knox, an enormous paunchy gentleman who carried a gold-headed cane, flourishing it as he talked to add emphasis to words that rolled out in a voice "deep as a thunder-growl."[3] He was charged with management of the land and naval forces of the United States. His Army was small, his Navy non-existent.

There had been talk of a naval force to be used against the Barbary pirates, in order to reduce the price of ransom for a number of American seamen who were being held in slavery at Algiers. They had already been there six years, ever since their vessels were captured by the Algerines in 1785. This Navy talk had raised a storm of opposition. One congressman wrote in his diary, "Eleven unfortunate men, now in slavery in Algiers, is the pretext for fitting out a fleet to go to war with them. . . . it is urged we should expend half a million dollars rather than redeem [ransom] these unhappy men."[4] Secretary Knox had inquired into the cost of building a fleet, and even those who favored a Navy agreed with him that the government could not yet afford one.[5] Eleven Americans remained in slavery while plans for the Navy were quietly laid aside.

Throughout the summer months, Captain Truxtun followed the

progress of his new ship, being built in Joshua Humphreys' ship-yard. Named the *Delaware,* she measured nearly 400 tons, was 105 feet long on deck with a beam of 29 feet, larger than the *Canton* by 150 tons.[6] The new ship incorporated a basic improvement in steering; instead of ropes, usually used to transmit motion from wheel to rudder, she was fitted with cast iron gears. Positive action was assured; there were no ropes to fail at a crucial moment when the safety of the ship depended upon the rudder's instant response to the helmsman's will.[7]

In December, as usual, Captain Truxtun stood out to sea, this time bound for England, where he was to have his new ship coppered. While there, he loaded a cargo of attractive luxury goods for British gentlemen and their ladies in India; then he departed on his fourth Eastern voyage. In distant Madras, on the coast of Coromandel, he traded this cargo for one of pepper, sugar, and rich India piece goods.[8] Finding that he had more than the *Delaware* would carry, he dispatched over a hundred tons of pepper and piece goods in a French ship, the *St. Jean de Lone,* sending his purser along to insure their safe arrival in Europe. He sailed his own ship to Hamburg, Germany, where he disposed of most of his cargo, and then he returned with his ship to London.[9]

He left the *Delaware* in London under the care of his associate, William Constable, who had just come from New York; and then, in the unfamiliar role of passenger, he took passage for America in another man's vessel.[10] While he was yet upon the ocean, his family was saddened by the death of the second eldest girl, Mary, age twelve. Before he arrived home, she had been buried in St. Peter's churchyard.

Coming back to Philadelphia in the spring of 1793, Captain Truxtun was too late to see the French aeronaut Blanchard astound the inhabitants by making several ascensions in his hot air balloon, but there was excitement aplenty in the city when he did arrive. The French craze had captured the popular imagination. Within the memory of all but the very young, the Army and Navy of France —and timely supplies from her shores—had made possible the successful outcome of the American Revolution. Now the French Revolution was in full flood. The king had been put to death; gory tales of the Reign of Terror were just beginning to be heard when the new French envoy, Citizen Genêt, arrived in Philadelphia. Even if the United States could offer no material assistance, its citizens thought they should lend moral support to the citizens of their "sister Republic." Citizen Genêt was warmly received; his entry into the city was a triumphal procession.

Enthusiasm for everything French was displayed by old and young alike. A liberty pole, reminiscent of those put up by the Sons of Liberty, was erected, and the *"bonnet rouge,"* red cap of liberty, was placed atop it. Gangs of boys wearing French cockades, shouting *"Vive la République"* and singing popular French airs, marched through the streets at all hours of the day and night. The populace was excited to a frenzy when the crew of a French frigate, then lying in the river, manned the yards and gave a stirring rendition of the *"Marseillaise."*

Citizen Genêt was royally entertained on the first of June, 1793, at Oeller's Hotel; presiding at the banquet was none other than Captain Truxtun's friend Charles Biddle. Many bizarre toasts were proposed and drunk; each toast was answered by the roar of a park of artillery drawn up in the street outside. As the climax of the occasion, the *"bonnet rouge"* was solemnly placed on Genêt's head and as solemnly passed from head to head, all around the table.[11]

But France was at war with Great Britain. For Americans to continue in this vein would sooner or later invite war with the British. Three hundred merchants and traders, protesting this fad of republicanism, celebrated the birthday of King George III, on the fourth of June, with a dinner at Richardet's tavern.[12] Unshaken by popular clamor, President Washington steadied the ship of state by issuing a proclamation of neutrality.

Captain Truxtun, who did not share the passion for *liberté* and *egalité,* welcomed the President's proclamation, because his ship was lying in a London dock. When a letter from William Constable reached him in July, he was doubly certain that war with Great Britain would be a calamitous blow to his fortunes. The *St. Jean de Lone,* still carrying his pepper and piece goods, had been captured by a British privateer![13]

To confound the situation still further, Philadelphia was visited late in the summer with a disastrous epidemic of yellow fever. Perhaps, as one witness believed, the plague was a sign of divine disapproval of the "unhallowed orgies" celebrating "the dismal butcheries in France." [14] It might well have been so: men could agree neither upon its cause nor its cure. Some reasoned that the fever was caused by "the torrid sun acting upon a moist soil, or upon impure and stagnant water." Others thought it might follow the breathing of the foul exhalations of one already infected. [15]

The deaths each day were counted in scores; the carters made their rounds by night, furtively hauling the dead to their graves. Bonfires were built, bells were rung, and guns were discharged from morning until night to clear the air. A small cannon was hauled through the streets, the men with it loading and firing, loading and firing. Indoors, householders burned gunpowder and sprinkled vinegar on their furniture and themselves. [16]

For a patient who had suffered an attack of the fever, the treatment was often as violent as the disease. The most moderate believed in "bleeding, keeping the body open, and the patient cool and clean." [17] Others, equally sincere, thought calomel, "a greater poison than the fever," would drive out the disease, since "it is difficult for any two poisons to exist in the human frame at the same time." [18] There were as many modes of cure as there were doctors —even more. One need not be a physician to invent a cure for a disease whose cause seemed impossible to discover. One traveler noted that "mosquitoes torment the whole city of Philadelphia," but that was merely an observation that neither he nor anyone else related to the fever. [19]

"It is not easy to describe," Charles Biddle wrote, "the consternation of the inhabitants at this time; the streets were almost deserted." [20] The federal government was in the van of the exodus. President Washington retired to Mount Vernon; others flew in all directions. By the first of September, possibly half of the residents had gone from the city. Terrified of the fever, Captain Barry, living several miles out in the country, barred his door to anyone who had been near the city. [21]

Captain Truxtun had seen the fever at work in the Indies. He thought he had learned how to avoid its evil effects; but his flight with his family was headlong nevertheless. [22] He took Mary and the children to Perth Amboy, his wife's girlhood home. When they had reached safety, he wrote to his friend Biddle, "the Malady, with which our city is visited, has obliged me to leave it, with my affairs much deranged, but I am always, I am afraid, to be unfortunate in

America, *for I never come into it, without, meeting with some disagreeable rub or other—which is not the case elsewhere.*"²³

In October, 1793, he took passage from New York to London, expecting to join his ship and take her out to India again; but after he had talked to William Constable he began to reconsider his plans.²⁴ Constable painted for him a dark picture and predicted that it would grow darker. The possibility of war between Great Britain and America seemed much more serious in London than it had in Philadelphia. He advised Captain Truxtun against embarking on a voyage lasting a year and a half; the war might start long before his ship was safely home again. Besides, they were short of capital because of the loss of their cargo in the *St. Jean de Lone.* That ship had been condemned and her cargo sold at auction, the part belonging to them having brought nearly £25,000.²⁵ Constable had entered a claim for this amount immediately, but the claim had yet to go through the courts; indeed, he would be surprised if it were settled in less than a year.²⁶ The uncertainty of war or peace and the gnawing doubt as to the ultimate outcome of the *St. Jean* affair finally caused the harassed Constable to exclaim, "I hate ships & every thing belonging to them!" ²⁷

At length they decided to abandon their plans for the next voyage and, if possible, to rid themselves of the whole business and close their accounts. They would sell their one liquid asset, the *Delaware.* Accordingly, in an auction at Lloyd's, the ship was knocked down to the highest bidder for a little over £3,000; the highest bidder was Captain Truxtun.²⁸ The net result was that he had bought out the shares belonging to Constable, Morris, and Hazelhurst, the auction serving merely to place a fair value on the whole.

The end of 1793 found the Captain, now thirty-eight years old, in an enviable position. He was owner, as well as master, of a fine copper-bottomed ship. He was by this time out of debt to the creditors of the house of Collins and Truxtun, and he was beginning to build up an estate for the protection of his already large and still growing "young helpless family." ²⁹ He was well known in business houses in England, in America, and in the Orient. By his determination to stand responsible for his debts and by his exertions in going "over and over the Globe" to pay them off, he had established unlimited credit in many ports of the world.³⁰ His industry and integrity were recognized by merchants and traders everywhere; he was widely known as a skillful and prudent mariner.

President Washington, among many others, had occasion to mention his superior "character and talents." Alexander Spotswood, husband of the daughter of Washington's half-brother, was in the habit of asking favor upon outlandish favor of his illustrious relation.[31] One day he decided that his son John should go to sea. With the naïveté that sometimes comes of gentle birth, he sent off a letter to the President, requesting that he arrange for his son to sail with Captain Truxtun.

Patiently, President Washington explained to Spotswood that Captain Truxtun was away at present and was not expected to return for a year and a half; but he was sure that if his son John still wanted to go to sea when he did return, a berth could be arranged. "But," he added, "he must not expect the place of Chief mate in his first voyage to India; for great dependance [is] placed on the Chief mate of those Ships in respect to Seamanship and Experience." If he did not care to wait for Captain Truxtun's return, then the President felt sure that he might find a place in another ship, but he enjoined him to be sure that the captain was a capable seaman and a good commander.[32]

From surviving accounts of expenditures for the *Delaware* and from Captain Truxtun's personal account in London, one is able to follow the Captain as he went about the routine of preparing his ship for the voyage home to Philadelphia.[33]

From his lodgings near the Royal Exchange, he could easily make his daily rounds on foot. He would first visit Lloyd's and the New York Coffee House, where he usually found the captains and traders with whom he had business; [34] then he might go to the hairdresser's; or visit John Troughton's shop to have his sextant cleaned and adjusted; or buy navigation books, tables, and charts from Sewell the bookseller; or take three tickets for the Irish state lottery and one for the English state lottery; or make sundry purchases of clothing, including sixteen shirts complete with neck handkerchiefs, two hats, boots and shoes, stockings and socks, and razors, hair powder, and medical supplies.

Just before Christmas, 1793, he purchased the bulk of his cargo, which consisted of 100 hogsheads of Shone's best porter (to be ripe in April or May), 300 dozen of Shone's best bottled port, four trunks of hosiery, and 1,000 grindstones which ranged in size from one to seven feet in diameter. On the bill of lading he described these items as the "Captain's Private adventure." In addition, he arranged to carry a few odds and ends of freight for several Philadelphia merchants.

Repairs to his ship, lying in a dock at Limehouse, required the skills of ship carpenters, riggers, blacksmiths, ropemakers, sailmakers, blockmakers, painters, and plumbers; supplies were furnished by a ship chandler; and the water-casks were overhauled by a cooper. Throughout the time she was in the Thames above Gravesend, there was no evidence of a crew for the ship. She was attended by watermen, who moored and unmoored her and moved her from place to place. The watermen also carried workmen back and forth in their boats and brought supplies and provisions alongside.

Captain Truxtun ordered a dozen barrels of corned beef and pork for the crew and "1 Barrel nice corned Beef picked pieces for cabbin use" and "1 ditto corn'd pork Nice pieces with legs &c." He sent the old ship bread ashore to be repacked, bought several barrels of new ship bread and three hundredweight of cabin bread. His list of provisions for cabin use was a long one, including fifteen dozen bottles of sundry spirits, several hampers of fresh vegetables, a dozen varieties of condiments, tea, coffee, chocolate, butter, cheese, a hamper of red herring, and a keg of tripe.

He engaged first, second, and third mates and a purser. He arranged to carry, as passengers, Mr. and Mrs. Potter in the cabin and four nameless persons in the steerage—a man and wife and two other men. His crew, consisting of a carpenter, captain's steward, ship's steward, cook, ten seamen—six of whom were able to sign their names to the articles—and a boy, was being recruited with the indispensable help of crimps and boarding-house keepers. Because of the war between Great Britain and the French republic, press gangs were active up and down the river, and it was customary to hire crimps to procure men for the crew—no questions were asked about methods employed—and boarding-house keepers to conceal them ashore until almost time for the ship to sail.

When the *Delaware* was ready for sea, early in February, the first mate, assisted by watermen, took her down the river to Gravesend, where the livestock—sheep, pigs, chickens, and ducks—was loaded on board. Captain Truxtun then applied to the Lord Mayor of London for "protections," which would permit him to sail away with his men after the crimps had delivered them on board at Gravesend.[35] When Captain Truxtun had completed his business in London, he settled his board bill, paid his washerwoman, left gratuities for his cook and for servants at the coffee houses, and took a postchaise down to join his ship.

He had sailed as far as the Downs, at the eastern end of the English Channel, when contrary winds arrested any further progress for nearly a fortnight.[36] While he waited impatiently for a change of weather, he sent ashore several times for more rum and gin, more butter, eggs, and fresh provisions, in order to keep his inventory of sea stores intact. It was nearly the end of February, 1794, before he was able to sail through the Channel and into the Atlantic toward home.[37]

While he was yet in London, he had agreed with Thomas Mills, a merchant there, to make another voyage in the *Delaware* after this one was completed. Mills wanted a shipload of French brandy, but since Britain and France were at war, he could not have it carried in an English bottom. Therefore, Captain Truxtun was to sail from Philadelphia to France and take the brandy back to Philadelphia, where it could be reshipped to Mills.[38] Although this contract caused trouble later on, it was neither illegal nor unusual. Trading with the enemy was seldom frowned upon as long as the profits were commensurate with the risks involved.

When he sailed his ship up the river toward Philadelphia it was early spring. His mind no doubt buzzed with plans for a quick departure for France. It is quite unlikely that he had any suspicion that the present voyage was the last he would ever make as master of a merchant vessel.

PART FOUR

# Petty Despot

CHAPTER 21

## CAPTAIN, UNITED STATES NAVY

THE "eleven unfortunate men, now in slavery in Algiers" were still there in the spring of 1794, enduring their ninth year of imprisonment; and recently over a hundred more Americans had been added to this number. The Algerine corsairs were loose in the Atlantic, and within another year they were expected to be cruising on the American coast. Several attempts to ransom the captives and to make peace with Algiers had been made, but to no avail. The Barbary powers were forever at war with some country or other. Since he had just declared a truce with Portugal and Holland, the despotic Dey of Algiers was in no mood to treat with the Americans.[1]

"If I were to make peace with every body," he said, "what should I do with my corsairs? What should I do with my soldiers? They would take off my head, for want of other prizes."[2]

Soon after the first American vessels were captured, in 1785, Thomas Jefferson had advocated war as the only way to arrive at a lasting peace. "Honor favors it," he wrote, and "I think it least expensive." [3] The idea of a Navy to bring the arrogant Barbary rulers to terms had been gaining a few adherents through the years, but the opposition to any naval force was still strong. Because the European powers were reconciled to paying tribute to the Barbary states, it was argued that the United States, as an infant nation, would do better to follow the lead of the older and more experienced nations and not be quite so independent. Also, it was feared that a Navy formed to suppress the Barbarians would be but the opening wedge for a standing Navy, which, in the opinion of one congressman who spoke for many, "would hereafter involve this country in immense debts and maritime wars." [4]

After a long and bitter debate, the Congress finally, on March 27, 1794, agreed to the building of a small Navy; but in order to obtain support for its passage, the Navy bill contained an important proviso: if peace were established between the United States and Algiers, then the Navy would immediately be abandoned. Without this proviso, the bill would not have passed. [5]

By the time Captain Truxtun came home, in May, the broad outlines of the new naval force had been sketched in. Congress had authorized six ships—four of forty-four guns and two of thirty-six—to be built or purchased and fitted out; and President Washington, for reasons that will appear later, had decided to have the ships built.

When it came to finding qualified officers for the Navy, it was natural for the President to turn to survivors of the Continental Navy, men who had fought in the sea service during the Revolution; accordingly, a list of these officers was prepared for his information. [6]

As soon as it was first hinted that a naval force might be raised, a deluge of importunate applications began to descend on the Executive and his Secretary of War. [7] Many of the requests for commissions came from Continental officers, but there were dozens of others who would be happy to serve—for example, Alexander Spotswood's son John. Alexander naturally wrote directly to the President, from whom he got this slightly chilly reply: "It is impossible he can be contemplated by me as commander of one of the Frigates." John might qualify as second or third lieutenant, Washington added, but even that he would not promise.[8]

John Barry, one of the senior surviving officers of the Revolution, informed the President that he would be glad to take chief command of the proposed squadron. Sam Nicholson, of Boston, asked Barry to mention his name to those responsible for appointments "after establishing yourself in such command as may be pleasing to you."[9]

No record of Captain Truxtun's application, if indeed he wrote one, has been found. Being at the seat of government, he may have enlisted the aid of Robert Morris, whose influence upon the President was well known; he may have accosted Secretary Knox, marching up Chestnut Street, and he may have been told with a flourish of the gold-headed cane that his name would be considered. He must have known that he might be appointed to the Navy, because, near the end of May, he dispatched his ship, the *Delaware,* on the voyage to France under another master.[10]

Early in June, 1794, the appointments were announced. Captain Truxtun was duly notified that "The President of the United States, by and with the advice and consent of the Senate, has appointed you to be a Captain. . . . It is understood that the relative rank of the Captains are to be in the following order—

> "John Barry
> Samuel Nicholson
> Silas Talbot
> Joshua Barney
> Richard Dale
> Thomas Truxtun."[11]

The first five men on the list had all held Continental commissions during the Revolutionary War. Captain Truxtun, who during the Revolution had been commander of privateers and merchantmen only, was in a class with those whom John Paul Jones had called "those licensed robbers . . . actuated by no nobler principle than that of self-interest."[12] But Jones's opinion was not shared by all naval officers, since at least four of the five ranking captains had served in privateers at some time during the Revolution.

Nevertheless, Captain Truxtun's appointment was a reflection of his unimpeachable reputation as an able mariner and gallant ship commander. If any of his friends championed his cause when the selections were being made, it was because they were convinced that he would serve his country with distinction, not because they felt that his past services obliged the government to employ him. Nor was any accident of geographical location involved. The commissions were not distributed by states or sections of the country. Three of the captains were Philadelphians.

It is quite remarkable that he was invited to enter a service so conscious of rank and seniority. Had he not been appointed, the War Office would have suffered no embarrassment in explaining the omission. As it was, there were dozens of former Continental officers who would be wounded by the appearance of an outsider on the list. One can only conclude that his character and ability were highly regarded by the men who picked him.

It was nearly three weeks after his notification that he took the oath of office; but his decision to serve could not have required more than a few minutes.[13] Probably he was with his family in Perth Amboy when he heard of his new post.

The pay of a naval captain was no inducement. Seventy-five dollars a month and six rations a day—the rations brought his monthly pay to less than 120 dollars a month—would not maintain him and his family in their accustomed manner; but he was free of any considerable debts, and his ship and other trading interests would provide him with a comfortable income. In the best tradition of arms, therefore, he repeated the rhetorical question, "Does any man enter into that profession for the sake of subsistence? Are not glory and fame the grand incentives?" [14]

CHAPTER 22

## NAVIGATOR

ℰ  ·  ·  ℰ  ·  ·  ℰ  ·  ·  ℰ  ·  ·

ALTHOUGH the Navy had first call on his time, Captain Truxtun somehow managed to ready a manuscript for the printer during the summer of 1794. It was a book on navigation, designed to supply some of the deficiencies and omissions of standard works on the subject.[1] This was five years before publication of the first American edition of John Hamilton Moore's *New Practical Navigator,* with corrections and emendations by Nathaniel Bowditch; and eight years before Bowditch published his own *New American Practical Navigator.* Moore, a British author, was in 1794 the reigning authority in Britain and America.

Captain Truxtun submitted his work to the Reverend Doctor John Ewing, President and Professor of Natural Philosophy of the University of Pennsylvania, Fellow of the American Philosophical Society, and authority on astronomy, for his "candid opinion" of its worth. He was publishing it, he said, in order to be "useful to the public" and with the idea that nautical information should be "more generally diffused, and more clearly understood by the present rising generation of seamen."

Professor Ewing's response was somewhat less than candid, but it made pleasant reading. He had no suggestions for improvement; he simply hoped that the book would have a "desireable tendency to promote the useful and important art of navigation." Being a theorist, he said, he could hardly hope to add anything to a work by "a gentleman of experience, in every situation of seas, wind, and weather; and who has justly acquired the character of the first navigator that has ever sailed from the ports of the United States."

"I very well know," he added, "the indolence of masters of vessels, and their aversion to the trouble of calculation, when they apprehend themselves able, by the common mechanical mode of conducting a vessel, after many circuitous windings, to reach an intended port." [2]

When the master of a ship could take her out of an American port, sail half way around the world, and then confidently expect to return once more to the very port from which he sailed, he must know something about navigation, even though it might be only the "common mechanical mode of conducting a vessel." Almost all mariners at this time could find their latitude at sea by measuring the altitude, or angle above the horizon, of the noonday sun or of the pole star; but to fix one's position in longitude was to most of them one of the unsolved riddles, on a level with perpetual motion.

The usual approach to the problem of navigating a vessel over long distances at sea was by dead reckoning. In dead reckoning, the navigator kept an approximate record of time, course, and speed. Each day he laid down on his chart the courses and distances run, and from these he could deduce his position. This method had grave disadvantages, however, and steered many a stout vessel onto unexpected rocks and shoals. After a long voyage, the only safe way to approach a coast was to sail during daylight hours, keeping a sharp lookout ahead and a deep sea lead sounding for bottom, and then to cease all progress at nightfall, lie to, and wait for the sunrise once more.

Captain Truxtun, when he brought Benjamin Franklin home from France, navigated by dead reckoning. After he had been out of sight of land for more than a month, he overtook another vessel that had been at sea for about the same length of time. He asked her what longitude she made and then compared his own figures with hers. They disagreed by four degrees, nearly two hundred miles. Two days later, thinking that he was still over a day's run from the Delaware capes, he spoke two whalers from New York, who informed him that he was almost on soundings. When he took a pilot on board, he found that his actual position was more than two hundred miles farther west than he thought it was. On the other hand, the vessel he had overtaken had been nearly four hundred miles from her calculated position.[3]

Errors in dead reckoning were easily made and accumulated rapidly. For example, there was no simple way to correct for drift of a vessel due to ocean currents. The navigator could determine approximately how fast he was moving through the ocean, but he could not tell how fast the ocean was moving. Even without any drift, the gauging of speed was subject to gross errors. Speed was determined by a chip log. The chip, a triangular piece of wood weighted at one end, was fastened to the end of a reel of light log line, the line having knots tied in it at uniform intervals. A sand glass completed the necessary equipment. The log was heaved out astern, the log line was paid out freely, and the number of knots that came off the reel while the sand ran through the glass was counted. The sand glass was usually timed at twenty-eight seconds; the number of knots dragged out by the nearly stationary chip in twenty-eight seconds could then be converted to a rate of speed. But either the line or the glass might be in error. The *Empress of China* had once made land two days before she expected to, because a twenty-eight-second glass actually measured only twenty-five, an error of more than ten per cent.[4]

Captain Truxtun realized, when he entered the China trade, that he would be able to make quicker and safer passages if he knew something about celestial navigation. Accordingly, he purchased books and tables published by the British Commissioners of Longitude—"for no others are sufficiently exact," he wrote, "or printed with equal care"—procured a first-class sextant, and then assiduously applied himself to unraveling the mysteries of finding the longitude at sea.[5]

The now-famous John Harrison chronometer Number 4—this Englishman had spent most of his life building and perfecting his timekeepers—had been proven in 1762, during a 6,000 mile voyage, to be an accurate and dependable instrument. However, chronometers had not by 1794 been generally adopted for use at sea, and they would not be for another thirty or forty years.[6] Moore and Bowditch each devoted little more than a page to finding the longitude by chronometer. In both works, the recommended approach to the problem was to use "Lunar Observations." This method involved the measurement of angular distance between the sun and moon or between the moon and a fixed star. After measuring this angle and checking local time—the latter a relatively simple task—the navigator could, by using the British tables, work out his longitude. However, the observation of angles had to be made with "the greatest imaginable nicety," because an error of observation of one minute of arc could result in an error of position of almost thirty miles.[7] Also, the required calculations were formidable. When Captain Truxtun wrote his book, he was one of perhaps less than half a dozen Americans who could fix his longitude "within a very few miles, (often within five miles, and always within fifteen)." [8] It was more than a generation before the practice of celestial navigation became general in American ships.[9] An officer in the Navy during the early eighteen-hundreds recalled later that "Chronometers were unknown . . . sextants were very rare, and their use still more so. The navigators who could ascertain the longitude by lunar observations were few in number, and the process of calculations a mystery beyond ordinary attainments." [10]

There were no new theories or methods presented in Captain Truxtun's book; nor did he pretend that there were. He called the book simply "Remarks, Instructions, and Examples relating to the Latitude & Longitude"; feeling that it was necessary to provide numerous worked-out examples that the neophyte might use as a guide while he followed the standard instructions, and to caution him against some of the errors he might make when he used methods outlined in the British works. He included an essay on the use and care of instruments, one on the "Variable Winds, Trade Winds, Monsoons, Hurricanes, Tornadoes, Tuffoons [typhoons], Calms, Currents and Particular weather met with" on his Oriental voyages, and a chart of the world, which he "caused . . . to be engraved, at a great expence," and on which he laid down the course of the Gulf Stream and the routes he had followed to China and India.[11]

Bowditch, in his *New American Practical Navigator,* first published in 1802, wrote, "We are chiefly indebted to Doctor Franklin, Commodore Truxtun, and Jonathan Williams, for the knowledge we possess of the direction and velocity of this stream. . . . They all concur in recommending the use of the thermometer, as the best means for discovering when you are in or near the stream."[12]

An appendix to Captain Truxtun's book included a system of masting that he had worked out and an outline of the general duties of officers of ships of war, for the information of other officers in the Navy. In its final form, this compendium of naval lore was impressive. It filled a folio-size volume of about a hundred and twenty pages; it displayed an extensive understanding of marine arts and science; and it represented an immense amount of work.

Undoubtedly, he expected some recognition for this enterprise. When at length it was published, he sent copies of his book to men high in the national government—the Secretary of State, among others—and he probably directed a copy to the President's attention.[13] He gave the Secretary of War enough copies to distribute to each of the other naval captains.[14] But it would be ungenerous to say that his book was produced with the aim of impressing his seniors; he wanted as well to instruct and inform his juniors. Later on, many members of the rising generation of naval officers, at least on board Captain Truxtun's ships, spent untold hours struggling through examples that paraded parallax and refraction up one side of the page and six-place logarithms down the other. As for the system of masting and general duties of officers, he wanted the Navy to be a closely knit organization, whose aims and procedures were uniform and generally understood throughout the service. He did not expect his work to be definitive; he invited discussion and comments; but he recognized that talk of improvement was idle unless there was first something to improve.

## CHAPTER 23

## FRIGATES ARE PLANNED

ও    •    •    ও    •    •    ও    •    •    ও    •    •

AN EXTRAORDINARY lot of thought and work had already been expended on the naval force that, according to the Act of Congress, was merely to be used to make peace with Algiers. It was beginning to appear that this Act might indeed be the opening wedge for a standing Navy. And so it was.

President Washington, in deciding to build rather than buy the ships, was clearly flouting the wishes of the majority of Congress, which included those who had agreed to the Navy only on condition that it be used solely against Algiers, as well as those who were unalterably opposed to it under any circumstances. To build the ships would take longer, and the cost would be greater, than to buy them. But he was looking at a broader picture than was the Congress. He was considering not only depredations by Algerine corsairs; he was also concerned about British interference with American commerce as a result of her war with France. Britain denied the right of neutral vessels to enter her enemy's ports, and under this policy she had searched and seized many American ships suspected of carrying war supplies to France. Without a Navy, there was nothing that Americans could do except protest, and protestations were treated with contempt. Therefore, the President was eager to build a respectable naval force that would, if it became necessary, be useful against European as well as Barbary powers. He directed the building of such ships as would, in his view, best comport with the national dignity and honor.

Soon after the Naval Act was passed, Secretary Knox had invited several shipbuilders to help him lay plans for the six vessels that it called for. He asked John Hackett, who had built the Continental frigate *Alliance,* to come down from Newburyport in Massachusetts; he enlisted the aid of Joshua Humphreys, Philadelphia's leading builder; John Wharton, in whose yard Humphreys had gotten his start; and William Penrose, another Philadelphian.[1]

Humphreys, a good friend of Captain Truxtun and builder of three of his ships,[2] had been a master builder for nearly twenty years. He had never been to sea; he had never seen a ship of the line; but he had studied every work on naval architecture he could find; he had built and repaired hundreds of vessels; and he was always ready to talk about the building and working of ships.[3] He was prepared to lead the discussions in the War Office. He had been thinking for a long time about the problem of building a Navy, and he had worked out a bold but well-reasoned plan of action. In the first place, he wanted ships that would be a match for the individual ships of any navy: large, fast sailing frigates of well over a thousand tons, mounting about thirty heavy guns on a single gun deck and a few smaller ones on the quarter-deck. Such a vessel would be able to attack a double-deck ship of the line in blowing weather, when the double-decker could not open her lower gun ports; in light winds, the frigate could avoid an action by outsailing the heavier ship.[4]

He was opposed by Penrose, who thought the proposed frigates were too large and who pointed out that the British never built single-deckers so large. Humphreys said that the French had cut down some of their double-deckers, seventy-fours, to make heavy frigates whose dimensions were almost the same as those he was proposing. He said further that he thought that when it came to naval architecture the French were superior to the British. He concluded with the claim that "we have not followed the tracts of that nation, but in my opinion have gone before them, & let me say we cannot excell if we are to travel after them."[5]

Humphreys carried the day, and the Secretary of War asked him to prepare a model showing his version of the proposed frigates. When the model was delivered, Secretary Knox asked for further criticism and opinions "in order to make them the Most perfect ships." Finally, when Knox had gathered together many ideas and had adjudicated diverse opinions, he returned the model, with some slight alterations, to Humphreys and directed him to prepare the drafts, or plans, for the frigates.[6]

While Humphreys toiled over his drawing board, the Secretary went on to another problem. Having settled on the size and lines of the ships' hulls, he now wanted to establish spar dimensions. He asked Captain Truxtun's help on this job.[7]

Before he had even thought of the Navy, Captain Truxtun had spent many long watches beneath tropical skies thinking about and drawing sketches of the masts and yards that always towered above him. At length he had worked out a system that could be used in fitting out a new ship. "To find the length of the main-mast," he wrote, "I take twice the breadth of the beam, and one-sixth of the sum, and add them together; and to find the length of the main yard, I take twice the breadth of the beam. . . ." and so on, through the forest of spars, from jib boom to ensign staff and from lower masts to royal yards.

Applying his system of masting to the new frigates, he compiled a list of spar dimensions which he submitted to the War Office with the wish that "the most experienced sea-officers, of skill here, or other ingenious persons, who have been at sea," be consulted before his dimensions were considered final. "I mention sea officers," he continued, "because it is almost impossible that any other description of men, who have not had an opportunity of being often at sea, can form a proper judgment on this important subject." [8]

Builder Humphreys, disregarding his friend's deprecatory remark, found time to disagree in principle and detail with Captain Truxtun's system of masting. He had seen ships before and after masting, and he was acutely aware of the problems involved; moreover, he had over a period of years devised his own system.[9]

Captain Barry also submitted a list of spar dimensions; he agreed with neither of the other two.[10] Captain Truxtun's were on the conservative side; he believed that ships of war were generally oversparred. But any system of masting was but an empirical approach to the dimensions that would please a seaman's eye; "true principles" of masting were never found. Even Captain Truxtun admitted that if a ship spread her sails and worked satisfactorily "we ought never to forget to give *Mr. Chance* his proportion of Credit for it." [11] The Secretary of War neatly side-stepped the issue, when he found it unresolvable, by leaving the masting entirely to the discretion of the builder and captain of each individual ship.[12]

Captain Truxtun's views on the subject were contained in his book. To illustrate his system, he had asked Josiah Fox, a young marine architect who was helping Humphreys with his drafts, to draw for him a picture of one of the new frigates complete with spars and sails. "Be pleased to take pains with this draft," he said, and "let me have it, as soon as possible. . . . When you have done, I will make you a present, of a handsome piece of India cloth for your wife." [13]

Secretary Knox had agreed to have an engraving made of Fox's completed draft, "the same being wanted for the Public use." He then told Captain Truxtun he might borrow the plate to use in his book, "which if as complete as I augur from an estimate of your nautical talents," said Knox, "will be a valuable acquisition to the United States." [14]

Even while all of this was going on, Captain Truxtun was concerned with another aspect of the preparations for a Navy. He was to superintend the building of the ship he would one day command. It was soon determined that his ship was to be built in Baltimore.

CHAPTER 24

FRIGATES ARE BEGUN

ↄ    .    .    ↄ    .    .    ↄ    .    .    ↄ    .    .

PRESIDENT Washington decided that the six frigates should be built in six seaport towns, with due regard for the "wealth, and populousness" of the states in which they were located. Accordingly, the four 44-gun ships were assigned to Philadelphia, Boston, New York, and Norfolk; the two thirty-sixes to Baltimore and Portsmouth, New Hampshire. That "appeared to me," Captain Truxtun told Secretary Knox, "to be going great lengths for the gratification of a few individuals." [1] It would be expensive, requiring six separate establishments, six master builders, six sets of everything; and six times as many mistakes could be made. Just how expensive this arrangement would become, nobody—in 1794—could even guess.

Each naval captain was assigned to a building yard in order to superintend the construction of his ship. For each ship the government appointed a Navy Agent, to handle the money, a naval constructor, who was directly responsible for supervision of the workmen, and a clerk.

To the four senior captains went the four larger ships. Therefore, Captain Truxtun was assigned to a thirty-six. Captain Barry elected to superintend the ship nearest home, and presumably the one that needed the least watching since Joshua Humphreys was naval constructor. To Captain Nicholson went the Boston frigate; to Captain Talbot the one in New York. At this point, the question of rank was raised momentarily.

Joshua Barney refused to serve at all if he could not be senior to Captain Talbot. Thereupon, he promptly sailed off and joined the French Navy.[2] The fourth large ship, then, went to Captain Dale. Captain Truxtun had no pretensions to rank—not yet—but the abdication of Barney moved him up to number five on the list, so he was given the choice of the thirty-six at Portsmouth or the one at Baltimore. He chose the latter. To Portsmouth went the new sixth-ranking captain, James Sever, who had held a subaltern commission in the Continental Army.

All the arrangements for engaging agents, constructors, and clerks were carried on by correspondence with the War Office. Once the Navy Agent was selected, he could usually find suitable men for the other positions, but the difficulties of handling from a distance a business of such great magnitude were soon made manifest to Secretary Knox. For example, he wanted John Hackett, who had recently helped him with the planning of the ships, to be one of the naval constructors. Therefore, he directed the Navy Agent in Boston to employ him, but added the warning, "It is to be understood that there are three Hacketts, one of whom, named William I believe, and who is subject to temporary insanity—you will of course not engage."[3]

Before the summer of 1794 was far gone, the situation in Baltimore was as settled as repeated exchanges of letters could make it; but the Secretary decided that Captain Truxtun had better go down and talk to the people concerned, look over the ground, and do everything possible to get the building started "with all possible vigor."[4] Vigor was one thing that the Captain possessed in full measure. His judgment might some day be questioned, but his energy and activity never. He set off at once for Baltimore.

Another traveler going to Baltimore that same year described the route: "We next changed horses at Newark [Delaware], and completed our day's journey, soon after sunset, at Head of Elk, the name given to a few houses situated upon the Elk River, which we crossed in a boat, hauling upon a rope stretched across it." He resumed his journey next day before dawn, and "proceeded very slowly till break of day, and not very fast after, the road being exceedingly deep and rough." After at least two full days on the road to cover the ninety-odd miles from Philadelphia, the traveler rode into the courtyard of the "Indian Queen," a large Baltimore inn "of very respectable appearance."[5]

Captain Truxtun's principal task was to find a suitable building yard. The naval agency was in the hands of Samuel and Joseph Sterett, merchants, and the naval constructor was David Stodder, who for some years had been building vessels in his shipyard on Harris Creek. Most of the yards were located on Fell's Point, the commercial section of town; but when Captain Truxtun journeyed out to Stodder's yard, the better part of a mile beyond Fell's Point, he was convinced that this was the best that the city had to offer. By far the largest shipyard in the vicinity, it had plenty of room for the building ways and additional storage areas required for construction of a large ship. Moreover, it had along one side a natural basin, or wet dock, where ship timbers could be stored and preserved under water. It was at the point where Harris Creek flowed into the Patapsco, pleasantly situated, surrounded by fields and small woods; there was a rope walk just north of the yard; and directly across the river, on Whetstone Point, were the ruins of the fort built during the last war.[6]

Having settled upon Stodder's yard and having no further business in Baltimore for the time being, he returned to Philadelphia to report to the Secretary. "I stated to General Knox," he recalled, several years later, "that it was my Opinion, None of the ships . . . ought to be built to the southward of Philadelphia," because the facilities were inferior, there was "no choice of Artificers, Labourers scarce and indolent, every article higher in point of price than in the other parts of the United States N E of this." [7] Knox received his report politely, thanked him for his opinions, but told him that he did not care to upset the President's policy of spreading the benefits of the building program all up and down the land.

Progress in the building of the frigates was painfully slow. In its first sanguine report to the Congress at the end of 1794, the War Office reviewed the trials of that summer and fall, winding up with the statement that "Every thing, if not to be created, was to be modified. That the wood from which the frames were to be made was standing in the forests; the iron for the cannons lying in its natural bed; and the flax and hemp, perhaps, in the seed." The work was being vigorously pursued, added the report, and the ships might surely be launched during the ensuing twelvemonth.[8]

There was one obstacle that this report did not stress, but it was destined to plague the War Office and everyone concerned with the ships. It was needed to build the skeletons of the frigates. It was the cursed live oak.

CHAPTER 25

DELAYS AND LIVE OAK

☙    ·    ·    ☙    ·    ·    ☙    ·    ·    ☙    ·    ·

IF FURTHER evidence was needed to show that the Administration intended to have a standing Navy, one had only to look at the materials of which the ships were to be built. Live oak, whose life was estimated at five times that of the white oak that was used in Europe, was specified for the principal members of the frames; the best heart pitch pine was designated for deck beams and lower decks.[1] Not many American ships built during the eighteenth century survived for more than a few years' time. Cutting whatever timber was easiest to get out and using it before it was seasoned, the builders had little reason to wonder that their ships went to pieces in so short a time. But these new frigates were to be different. The builders were convinced "that their frames will be perfectly sound half a century hence, and it is very probable that they may continue so for a much longer period." [2]

Heavy, tough, dense, and extremely durable when properly seasoned, live oak was found in the low country and on numerous islands along the coast of South Carolina and Georgia. Secretary Knox heard that in 1776 the frames for two seventy-four gun ships of the line had been cut near the mouth of the Savannah River but had never been hauled away. If that timber could be found now, eighteen years later, he thought not unreasonably that "it would be excellent from its long seasoning." [3]

John Morgan, who expected to be naval constructor in Norfolk after the live oak was cut, was sent to Georgia to supervise that work. He was an able man, uncommonly tenacious; but weather, fever, fire, and the perils of the sea all conspired to make his task an impossible one. [4]

After a trying summer of preliminary arrangements, Morgan was joined in October, 1794, by sixty New England axemen, but the weather was so oppressive and the place so sickly that only three of them stayed. [5] He reported that the whole area was almost under water. "Never," he wrote, "was so much rain known in this Country." [6]

The oxen and heavy logging wheels to haul the timber out of the woods, and even grain and hay to feed the oxen, had to be sent in by sea. [7] The coastal islands, most of them uninhabited, afforded nothing but the live oak trees. Nevertheless, with the three remaining axemen and a few negroes he was able to hire, he was determined to get the live oak out. Late in October, after the molds, or patterns, for the timbers had finally arrived, John Morgan received a letter from Joshua Humphreys complaining about the lack of progress. Morgan was nearly at the breaking point when he replied, "These Moulds frighten me they are so long. . . . I cannot stand it, you say that if I was there I shou'd be mortified, if you was here you wou'd curse live Oak." [8]

Captain Barry was sent down to find out what caused the delays, but apparently he could not comprehend the nature of the problem; he returned shortly with the confident report that the work could be completed before spring. [9] Another inspector, who visited the scene when spring came, was of the opinion that the job would require at least another year. [10] Progress was hampered by fire, which destroyed some of the molds; at least one vessel carrying the hard won live oak was cast away on the treacherous shoals off Cape Hatteras.[11] Another, bound for Baltimore, after several attempts to enter Chesapeake Bay against contrary winds, finally found a safe harbor at Martha's Vineyard.[12] Some of the largest timbers proved defective after a great deal of work had been done on them.

Laboring under tremendous difficulties and with the situation well known in Philadelphia, Morgan still got little sympathy from Humphreys. "Your Letter & Box of Oranges came safe to Hand for which you will please to accept my thanks," Humphreys wrote just after Christmas, 1795, "but the oranges were so sowered by the most infamous Stern Piece that you sent that their Flavor is lost. I am sure you must never have seen it otherwise you would not have sent it, for the most ignorant negro [would know] it would not do." [13]

After many months of vain waiting, Captain Truxtun contrived with Humphreys to have another man sent to Georgia to insure that if any live oak were ready to be sent anywhere, it would be sent to Baltimore and to Philadelphia.[14]

Because of the unforeseen obstacles that blocked the delivery of suitable materials for ships so large, many compromises had to be made. Captain Truxtun eventually made excursions down Chesapeake Bay looking for white oak timbers, and Humphreys journeyed into the back country beyond the Catskills before he found trees large enough to meet his needs.[15] Nor was that the only impediment to progress. There were twice as many opinions about how the ships should be built as there were ships. Each naval constructor and each captain had his own ideas. This resulted in endless correspondence with the War Department, which was further complicated by changes of Secretaries. Timothy Pickering held the post for a few months following General Knox's resignation, and he was followed by James McHenry.

Joshua Humphreys spent much of his time in defense of his original plans. One of his most frequent antagonists was Captain Truxtun. Humphreys expected to use pitch pine deck beams in all the frigates, but "my friend Truxtun," he said, "frustrated that good plan & prevailed on the Secretary at War to substitute white Oak" for all the ships except the one at Philadelphia.[16]

When Humphreys added diagonal riders to the plans in order to stiffen the hull fore and aft and to keep it from hogging, or arching like a hog's back, Captain Truxtun was opposed to the idea. Again, he went directly to the Secretary of War. The British used no riders in their ships, he argued, and the riders would cut down on his storage space in the lower decks. Finally, he had his way. "At your instance and resting entirely on your experience," the Secretary wrote, "I consent that the Diagonal riders be omitted." [17]

While Captain Truxtun was relying on precedent in making positive statements about how a frigate should be built, Humphreys was trying to improve on the best designs already developed. His conclusions, based on reasoning and experience, were usually sound. When disputes arose, he was willing to accede to his "worthy Friends great experiance as a sea officer," but he thought that his friend might occasionally submit to his—Humphreys'—great experience in "building, repairing, strengthening Vessels many of which cases never came under his [Truxtun's] notice." [18] He was never as dogmatic as Captain Truxtun, and he demonstrated a much more secure grasp of mechanical principles. Humphreys, in his methodical way, was a creator and innovator. His friend, without peer as a ship commander, was always a little too willing to give advice and opinions on subjects that he had not mastered.

David Stodder, naval constructor of the Baltimore frigate, was as much vexed by delays and improvisations as anybody concerned in the business. Captain Truxtun had heard—at third hand—that Stodder was contemptuous of the whole proceedings, and that he thought he could do a much better job of drafting and molding a frigate than Joshua Humphreys had. Furthermore, he saw no need for a naval captain to superintend the building. He had declared—this was still at third hand—that he would follow neither draft nor molds nor any directions from the War Office, and that he would not take orders from any officer in his yard; in short, he would do just as he pleased.[19]

As it turned out, there was surprisingly little strife in the Baltimore yard, considering the tempers of the two men. Faced with a situation that could become quite impossible, Captain Truxtun was determined to make the most of it. Stodder, outnumbered by the aggressive Captain and an adamant Secretary of War, grumblingly consented to follow instructions.

The first task was to transform Stodder's yard into a Navy Yard.

Large and expensive building ways had to be erected; a great many piles had to be driven and a sizable quantity of fill was required. These ways might be used to launch a hundred ships later on, as Captain Truxtun pointed out, but they had to be built for the first one. Except for this project, however, there was little work needed to complete the transformation. The buildings seemed adequate—rigging loft, blacksmith shop, boatbuilder's shed, mast shed, and a few others—and the road connecting the yard with town, though rough, was passable.[20]

When the molds, or patterns by which to cut the timbers, arrived from Philadelphia that first autumn (1794), Captain Truxtun told David Stodder in "plain terms" that the frigate would be built according to the directions received from the War Office.[21] Stodder yielded, although he was impelled eventually to tell the Secretary of War that, had he been permitted to supply the materials, he could have furnished them "at least one hundred per cent cheaper"; and he could thus have saved a great deal on labor, too, being able to plan his work so the bulk of it could be done during "the long days," men working from sun to sun being paid by the day regardless of season.[22]

Stodder often had more or less serious trouble with his men, and Captain Truxtun, by way of keeping peace in the yard, interceded in some of the disputes. While his instructions charged him with responsibility for pushing the work with all possible vigor, he had no direct authority over Stodder or the workmen. Accustomed as he was to giving positive orders, he was often frustrated by being merely an adviser on labor problems. Therefore, he wrote to the Secretary of War requesting authority "to regulate disputes," which implied the power to hire and fire. He had to be satisfied with a negative answer, to which was added a mitigating compliment. "But by your prudence," the Secretary wrote, "you may reconcile disputants, & restore & preserve harmony in the yard."[23] Although he was never satisfied with his anomalous position, he continued, as he described it, "by a decided conduct, and independent spirit," to bend the efforts of all concerned toward the building of the best possible frigate in the shortest possible time.[24]

In spite of his exertions, the ship consisted of little more than a keel when the second annual report was made to Congress more than a year and a half after the start of the business. The live oak came slowly; mistakes were made by agents in ordering materials; [25] questions were answered only after protracted correspondence, and even then with little conviction because there were no precedents in American shipbuilding upon which to draw. When he surveyed the yard at the end of 1795, there was no towering ship to block his view of the surrounding wintry hills and brooding ramparts; and yet the Baltimore frigate was as far advanced as any of the others.[26]

Then came like a thunderclap the news that the Dey of Algiers had signed a treaty of peace with the United States. According to the Act of Congress, this was the end of the Navy.[27]

CHAPTER 26

CAPTAIN IN A QUANDARY

*ᐧ* . . *ᐧ* . . *ᐧ* . . *ᐧ* . .

PEACE with Algiers, the latest hindrance to the building of the United States Navy, left Captain Truxtun in a quandary. He had trimmed his personal affairs to the convenience of the service; and now, according to law, the service had expired.

During his first summer in the Navy, he was still deeply immersed in trade. He employed his own ship, the *Delaware,* and he was interested in at least two other vessels. He sent the *Delaware* to France for a cargo of brandy to comply with the agreement he had made with Thomas Mills in London.[1] This venture was complicated by Mills' attempt to break his contract, but eventually the cargo was procured, brought to Philadelphia, and reshipped in another vessel. To avoid payment of duties, the brandy was sent to Guernsey, one of the Channel Islands, whence it might be smuggled into England. Since there was some doubt whether the smugglers could safely handle it, the vessel carrying it was, by his order, "to call at Guernsey, as for water, and if she is suffered to land it is well. If not, she is to proceed to Hamburg." [2] Although there was no opprobrium attached to such dealings, the contract was one that a careful merchant would have shunned; it caused Captain Truxtun much trouble and anxiety; and to complete his distress, Mills turned out to be dishonest. He had already admitted to his friend Biddle that "I have too often misplaced my confidence." [3] It probably never occurred to him, but this was another way of saying that he was not a shrewd judge of men.

With the Steretts, Navy Agents in Baltimore, and William Patterson, another Baltimore merchant, he had invested money in the ship *Friends' Adventure* and the snow *John and Joseph*.[4] He made an agreement with the French envoy in Philadelphia to ship a cargo of sorely needed flour to France, but he relied heavily on the envoy's assurances that he would be paid in specie by the shaky French government, still in the throes of revolution.[5] Again, he found he had misplaced his trust, and he ended up with a bundle of assignats, nearly worthless paper money.

He had already recovered, through the High Court of Admiralty of England, at least a part of his money tied up in the cargo of the captured *St. Jean de Lone;* but he was again to have trouble with the British. The *John and Joseph* was detained by the British in Bermuda, and he spent many an anxious day before he managed, remote from the scene, to recover his vessel and cargo.[6]

As the building of the frigate had demanded more and more of his time, he had at length decided to withdraw himself from trade altogether and to invest his money in real property and securities, in order to give his full time and attention to the service.[7] Having done so, he now found to his dismay that there might be no service.

While he pondered the situation, he spent the Christmas holidays of 1795 with his family. They usually spent winter (the "dreary season") in Philadelphia, but by now they had, in addition to their home in town, a place in Cranbury, New Jersey, on the Brunswick Road fifteen miles beyond Trenton—Captain Truxtun sometimes styled it his "villa"—and a fine waterfront estate in Perth Amboy, where his wife and children stayed during the summer months.[8]

His family was growing up as well as still increasing in numbers. There were six girls, ranging from Mary, not yet two, to Sarah, just turned seventeen and soon to be married, and the two boys. Young Tom, thirteen years old, was the only child away from home. It was a foregone conclusion that he, being the first male child, should have the best possible education; to obtain it he was spending several years in England.[9]

Their Negro servant, Hannah, was still with the family; but Captain Truxtun, influenced by his late friend Franklin's stand on slavery, had set her free on condition that he should never be called upon to support her, should she leave his employ.[10] Apparently she had chosen to stay on.

Captain Truxtun, at forty, had reached another turning point in his career. Unquestionably, he could resume command of a merchant ship whenever he chose. On the other hand, the naval service, uncertain as it was, exerted a strong attraction. The conferences with the heads of state, the building and working of great ships, and perhaps the opportunity for fame and glory: all these were powerful incentives.

During the year and a half following the commencement of the Navy in March, 1794, the Administration had paid scant notice to raising a force designed exclusively to harass Barbary corsairs. All of the emphasis had been on size and durability of the ships. Drawing on his experience with the refugee galleys, Captain Truxtun had long ago suggested a naval force that could be raised quickly, at little cost, and one that was well calculated to hit the piratical enemies hard and often on their own shores. His idea was to build a squadron of small gunboats, whose frames could be carried to a friendly Mediterranean port for assembly. These boats, carrying the fight home to the enemy by negotiating the shoal and treacherous harbors, could attack the corsairs in waters that large ships could never enter. This was no visionary scheme. Gunboats eventually were used successfully on the Barbary coast, but when he first outlined his plan in a conference with President Washington and Secretary Knox, he enjoyed only their polite attention; nothing came of the scheme.[11] True, these heads of state were engaged at home by the western insurrection over whisky taxes; nevertheless, they found time to attend closely to the many details of building a durable Navy worthy of the "national character."

Now, at the beginning of 1796, there was talk of merely curtailing instead of abandoning the building program. In spite of the words in the original Act, which stipulated in case of peace with Algiers "that no farther proceeding be had under this act," it began to appear that the President might somehow find a way to keep opponents of the Navy from bringing to naught all the work expended on it. Perhaps a compromise, calling for completion of one of the forty-fours and one thirty-six, could be reached.[12] In any case, Captain Truxtun decided to see the thing through to its conclusion. He would stake his future on the Navy.

CHAPTER 27

## MARYLAND *CONSTELLATION*

ℭ . . ℭ . . ℭ . . ℭ . .

TEN years after the first American vessels were captured by the Algerine corsairs and after ten years of slavery for the surviving members of their crews, a treaty of peace was signed by the capricious and tempestuous Hassan Bashaw, Dey of Algiers.[1] The peace was concluded at the cost of nearly one million dollars.[2] When the first payment of tribute to the Dey was delayed because the American envoy could not immediately command so large a sum of money, the Dey threw one of "his usual Blustering Comvulsions of Passion" and threatened to abrogate the treaty.[3] Finally he was quieted by the promise of a present—a thirty-six gun warship—if he would wait three months longer for his money.

Those who knew the Dey predicted that peace could not last long. An American agent in Algiers said, "They are now going to War with Denmark, After that it is probable they will take Venice or Sweeden, or both, they will then try Holland again & perhaps Spain, and our turn will be the next."[4] Besides, all the Barbary pirates were not in Algiers. No treaties had yet been made with Tunis and Tripoli; and the treaty with Morocco, concluded some time before, could last only as long as the present emperor lived, since none of the Barbary rulers would recognize treaties made by their predecessors.

Taking careful note of this danger as well as the unsettled state of European politics, President Washington informed Congress that he had not yet halted construction of the Navy as he was required to do by law, because he feared that the sudden suspension of all activity would cause a considerable loss in money, materials, and men. He gave Congress another opportunity to change the law and to adopt the policy that he thought would "best comport with the public interest." Then he awaited further instructions.[5]

In the House of Representatives, the Navy fight broke out anew. All the old arguments for and against it were paraded again. The opposition contended that if the frigates were got to sea, they would surely find an enemy. This would be inviting disaster, because these few ships would give little protection against the great European powers. And the expense of completing the ships would be enormous. Those in favor of the Navy argued that these frigates could defeat a European antagonist piecemeal, taking on individual ships and small squadrons as they arrived in American waters. As for the expense, all of the money would be spent at home; the farmer, the merchant, the mechanic, all would be benefited; nobody would lose anything.[6]

At length the issue was settled and a new Navy bill was signed by the President on April 20, 1796. The Navy was saved. As a concession to those who wanted to scuttle the frigates before they were launched, the majority of Congress agreed to go ahead and finish only three of the ships, leaving it to the President's discretion whether the others should be completed or abandoned.

Long before this definite turn of events occurred, Captain Truxtun had made a frontal attack on the uncertainties that lay before him. Carefully setting down everything in favor of completing the Baltimore frigate, pointing out that the other thirty-six, in Portsmouth, was not nearly so far along, that Maryland white oak was superior to that of New Hampshire, and that more live oak was expected daily in Baltimore, he sent off his report to the War Office; but he was not content to rest his case there.[7] Upon hearing that General Anthony Wayne, just back from his brilliant successes in crushing the Indians on the Ohio frontier, might be appointed Secretary of War, he wrote to him and briefed him on the situation. Even if the President decided to continue with his ship, Captain Truxtun told the General, he had heard that Captains Nicholson and Talbot might try to use their influence "(or their friends for them)" to have him displaced by one of them, because they stood higher on the list of captains. That, he said, would be contrary to custom and usage in either the British or the French Navy, where a captain could expect to keep his own ship even when senior officers were in need of employment. "I have made great sacrifices, by My engaging in this business," he wrote; "I should be Mortified . . . if I am superceded." [8] He talked to Captain Barry, who assured him that he had nothing to worry about, but he placed little confidence in Barry's encouragement.

Leaving no bastion unbreached, he sat down one evening in Baltimore and wrote a letter to President Washington. He hoped the President could see his way clear to order his frigate to be continued. In which case, he wrote, "I shall take a particular pleasure, in exerting my utmost abilities, to have her speedily compleated, and in a way that will do honor to the United States." [9]

Shortly after the passage of the new Navy bill, in the spring of 1796, the pleasure of the President was made known. [10] Captains Nicholson, Barry, and Truxtun were permitted to continue with their ships in Boston, Philadelphia, and Baltimore. Captains Talbot and Sever were returned to private life; Captain Dale, away on a private voyage to China, was likewise put aside.

Except for occasional flying trips to expedite the business of the frigate, Captain Truxtun now spent nearly all of his time in Baltimore; he was determined that his ship should get to sea as soon as either of the others.

One day he journeyed up to Cecil Furnace, near Head of Elk, where he and Captain Barry were to inspect some cannon for their respective ships. They were told that thirty-five had already been proof-fired; but after making a visual inspection, they agreed to accept only twenty-nine of these. Furthermore, they doubted whether the guns had been adequately proven. They knew of too many cases where guns had burst in action with disastrous results. They thought the charge and wadding ought "at least to have been as much in proving as in time of Action." [11] Ironmaster Sam Hughes disagreed. His contract did not even require that the cannon be proved; he had done that solely from benevolence. He was merely to furnish so many guns at so much per ton. Captain Barry dryly commented to Captain Truxtun that the contract was the work of "your friend Tench Coxe." This altercation, which forced Captain Truxtun to make at least one extra trip to Philadelphia, had to be settled by the Secretary of War, who as a consequence took pains to spell out the requirements for proof-firing for all future contracts. [12]

The frigates had been named by President Washington more than a year before, but it was only after her "raising," early in 1796, that Captain Truxtun's ship began to be referred to by her proper name. When Joshua Humphreys first prepared the molds, he arbitrarily assigned a letter to each ship as a matter of convenience. The Baltimore frigate, according to her mold markings, was the "E." When names were being selected, Humphreys submitted to the War Office a list of some forty names ranging all the way from *Thunderer* and *Terrible* to *Virtuous* and *Modeste,* but none of his ideas was finally adopted. Timothy Pickering, who served during the first few months of 1795 as Secretary of War, made perhaps his sole contribution to the naval program when he prepared a much shorter list for the President. George Washington made the final selections by running his pencil across the page beneath the first five names suggested by Pickering.[13] The Boston frigate was named *Constitution;* Captain Barry's ship, in Philadelphia, the *United States;* and the Baltimore frigate became the *Constellation,* named for the American flag. It may have been Timothy Pickering who had remembered the resolution made by the Continental Congress twenty years before: "that the Flag of the United States be thirteen stripes alternate red and white; that the Union be thirteen stars white in a blue field, representing a new constellation." [14]

The names were chosen early in order to allow time enough to complete the figureheads and other carved work before launching. The *Constellation* and *United States* both were to be embellished by William Rush, a celebrated Philadelphia ship carver who, when he heard the names, hurriedly drew a few swatches from his grab bag of ideas and set down his "first thoughts" on how the work should appear.

"The *Constellation,*" he wrote, "should be represented by an elegant female figure, characteristick of indignant Nature, at the period of the American Revolution determined on forming a New Creation, from that Chaos of Ignorance, Vice and folly, which she had long been burthened with.—She should have a flaming torch in her right hand, setting fire to the bursting world under her feet, with the emblems of Tyranny Superstition Folly, &c issuing from it, and thrown into Confusion and fermentation, her left arm resting on the altar of Liberty. The American Eagle in the act of flight, a Sphere resting on his pinions with the Constellation inserted, soaring to heaven with one more great offering of Nature—or to adorn the new political fermament, with light and Glory, to Serve as a light to the Nations that have long Wandered in political Darkness; and to Strike with Wonder and Surprize the Wise Men of the East." [15]

In the same grandiloquent manner, the "raising" of the *Constellation* was noticed in one of the Baltimore newspapers.

There is a time in the building of a ship when the meaningless aggregation of timbers, properly scarfed and bolted together, suddenly assumes the definite shape and form of the finished work. This metamorphosis begins spectacularly when the stern frame is hoisted into place. Until that time, the building ways are encumbered only by the keel and some staging. Once the stern is raised, however, the structure takes on the appearance of a ship; its size and bulk stand out in sharp perspective.[16] It was after the raising, which occurred on February 5, 1796, that a writer for the *Maryland Journal* unleashed his pen and let it soar away on a flight of fancy.

This great ship, said the *Journal*, "reflects no small lustre on the state of Maryland, and particularly on those gentlemen concerned in this glorious undertaking. . . . Now may the servile instruments of a foreign despotism tremble; . . . For soon shall the genius of Columbia, adorning the prow of the *Maryland Constellation*, clear the seas of those marauding depredators, and extend our commerce in safety from pole to pole." [17]

When Captain Truxtun picked up the paper and read the item, he suspected that it might be "some of Stodders nonsense." He immediately asked the other publishers in town not to reprint it; then he went in search of Stodder. Upon being confronted with the piece, Stodder swore that he knew nothing about it until it was printed.

"I must confess," Captain Truxtun wrote to Josiah Fox, "I was very much ashamed, at seeing the piece, least some person might suppose, it was published by some one Concern'd in building the Frigate." [18]

Joshua Humphreys read the "Bombastical publication about your frigate" a few days later when it had been copied in a Philadelphia paper. He told Captain Truxtun that he thought it "was really laughable." [19]

In the evenings, when he could take time from writing letters, preparing his reports to the War Office, and checking over the endless lists of stores and materials, Captain Truxtun often dined and drank with the gentlemen of the city. It was a pleasant place, Baltimore, with clear wide streets, paved sidewalks, and wooden bridges over the rivulet called Jones Falls. Colonel Howard's beautiful park overlooked the city from a commanding hill north of the Court House. There were good eating and drinking places, a theatre in Holiday Street, and many gracious homes.[20] Captain Truxtun made numerous friends here, Doctor Rattoone and the merchant prince William Patterson among them. He made some enemies, too. It was here that he met the two Smiths, General Sam of the Maryland militia and his younger brother Robert, the latter of whom was destined eventually to frustrate his ultimate ambition for fame and glory. While Sam was always a friend to the Navy, he never forgave Captain Truxtun for some remarks that passed in Baltimore during a political argument. Robert, apparently snubbed by the Captain as being beneath his notice, lived to see the day when the situation was reversed.[21]

Captain Truxtun also found time to prepare another book for the printer. Realizing that unless some energetic measures were taken, the Navy, when finally it got to sea, would consist merely of a number of individual ships, each operating under the particular system devised by its captain, or under no system at all, he was anxious to bring the subject of organization and training to the attention of those who might be able to do something about it.

Already, in his first book—on navigation and assorted nautical lore—he had published a treatise on the general duties of officers "from an Admiral, Down to the most inferior officer." Wisely, he devoted the largest amount of space to the instruction of inexperienced midshipmen; but he did not pass over captains lightly. His belief was reinforced during the few following years that these were the officers who needed most to learn the details and philosophy of naval command.

In that treatise, which he compiled largely from the British naval regulations, he stressed the need for system in "our young navy." Since precedent was lacking in America, he recommended following, though not blindly, the customs and usage of an old and experienced sea power.[22] Basically, his pattern—the Royal Navy's way of doing things—was sound, and he was able by precept and example to pass on to his successors the best traditions of command at sea.

This second book, a quarto volume of forty pages, published in Baltimore in 1797, was entitled "Instructions, Signals, and Explanations, offered for the United States Fleet." Again drawing on the experience of the Royal Navy, he devised a system of signals to be used by a squadron or fleet of warships.[23] The day signals, designated by numbers, were to be displayed on a pennant hoist. Each number from zero to nine was represented by a particular pennant. Thus, with only three sets of pennants, a thousand different signals could easily be made. His list of signals contained something less than three hundred, among them the following: "21. Prepare for battle"; "224. Are your dead buried and the ship well washed?"; "187. A mutiny"; "188. Mutiny quelled and ringleaders secured"; "225. Prepare to hold a court martial as directed"; and "226. Execute the condemned criminal." He also prepared fog signals, which prescribed the firing of guns and muskets, the ringing of bells, and the beating of drums. His night signals required lights, flashes from the pans of muskets, and false fires.

His system of night and fog signals was in many ways cumbersome and impractical. The night signal of distress, for example, required a range of fifteen lights at one-fathom intervals on a halyard suspended from a yardarm. This string of lights would be not only enormously difficult to display but also was likely to be obscured by spars and sails. However, while his system was far from perfect, it was as good as most. It was common knowledge that the British signal book was so defective that each admiral commanding a squadron had to compose his own set of signals.[24] A simple and universal signal system was not devised until sixty years later.

Although Captain Truxtun was not an original thinker, he recognized and proclaimed the need for a system, however imperfect, for the government of the naval service. He characterized naval officers generally as "uninformed men, who mostly have an aversion to reading and studious application," and urged upon them the study of the literature of their profession. At the same time, he recognized the dearth of dependable marine works, owing mainly to the jealousy with which the principal maritime nations guarded the discoveries and advances that they had made in the naval arts. He advocated the founding of a national marine academy and a society for the study and improvement of naval architecture. If his present work "should be approved of," he declared that he was willing to spend his leisure hours in compiling a comprehensive treatise on naval tactics and evolutions, "but to do it completely and extensively," he wrote, "it will take some time." [25]

The larger work never materialized, and the only tangible approval of this book that he enjoyed was in having the War Department pay for its printing.[26] However, one is obliged to conclude that he was the only one of the first six Navy captains who was at all inclined to improve himself by "studious application" and to encourage his juniors to become proficient in anything more abstruse than the reefing, handing, and steering that were known to every common seaman.

In his own copy of his signal book, he wrote the only two surviving examples of any poetry he may have composed. The first is a five-line stanza of bad verse having to do with the protection of injured American commerce. The second is this:

> "The rights of America we'll maintain
> And then return to you, Sweet girl, again
>                     T. T." [27]

In the summer of 1797, three years after the Navy was first authorized, the Navy Yard in Baltimore resounded with the ring of the adze and the thud of the maul. The *Constellation* still rested in the stocks. The planking of her hull was complete and the bottom was being sheathed with copper sheets imported from England.[28] Some of the inside work was well under way and much of her top hamper was in the yard ready to go on board as soon as the ship was launched.[29]

The *United States,* in Philadelphia, had been launched in May, and it appeared that the *Constellation* might be ready before the end of the summer. The Philadelphia frigate had actually launched herself, having started to move before all the keel blocks had been knocked loose and before all the workmen were out from under the hull. In her precipitate haste to plunge into the river, she suffered some underwater damage that required heaving her down for repairs.[30] In order to avoid any similar troubles with the Baltimore launch, the Secretary of War asked—of all people—Joshua Humphreys, whose launch had gone awry, to go to Baltimore to "consult on the best Method to be pursued in Launching the Frigate *Constellation* into the Water (so as to float)." [31] One might idly wonder whether Humphreys was being sent to help out or to learn something.

He was received by David Stodder in a "very polite manner." The two constructors and Captain Truxtun discussed the prospects of a successful launch. Learning that the *United States,* when launched, drew nineteen feet of water, Stodder had soundings made off the end of his ways. Sixty feet out from shore, he found sixteen feet of water and eight feet of soft mud; three times as far out, a pole was pushed down over thirty feet without reaching solid ground. He observed that a high tide would add at least three feet to his figures. The three men carefully surveyed the situation of the ship; they checked the descent of the ways; and at length they agreed that there appeared to be nothing to prevent the ship from being launched in complete safety.[32]

As the month of August wilted away into September, the grand preparations were nearing an end. The Baltimore *Telegraphe* of August 29, 1797, announced the coming climax to three long years of delays, changes, mistakes, hard work, and worry. "Wind, weather and tide permitting, the United States Frigate CONSTELLATION, will be LAUNCHED on Thursday, the 7th of September." [33]

CHAPTER 28

## THE LAUNCH

*&* . . *&* . . *&* . . *&* . .

THE *Constellation,* poised in her stocks on the left bank of the Patapsco, was an imposing sight. As yet she was just a hull; none of the lofty masts was in place; but already she towered higher than a three-story house. She was 171 feet long on deck and 40 broad. Her great body, curving upward from the keel, bulged out like some vast puncheon, reached maximum width over ten feet below the deck, and then tumbled home, or curved inward again up to the railings. Her great weight was carried by keel blocks; she was steadied by multiple rows of heavy timber stanchions, planted firmly on the ground along each side of the hull. The copper sheets, which covered her entire bottom up to the water line, gleamed dully in the late afternoon sun.[1]

Everything here was on a heroic scale. The brow, or ramp, laid between the deck and the ground, was over one hundred feet long and broad enough to hold four workmen abreast.[2] The ship's boats, great guns mounted in their carriages, water-casks, blocks, deadeyes, and sundry other equipment lay about the yard.[3] A cargo of spars, cannon balls, and pig iron ballast had just arrived by a vessel from Philadelphia.[4] Shrouds and stays, comprising the bulk of the standing rigging, were ready to be set up when the masts were shipped after the hull was safe in the water.[5] All around the ways were scrap ends and chips of tough, odorous woods, trimmed and bored by adze and auger; here and there was a locust treenail, shivered by a maul as it was being driven home through the planking. The saw pits were banked with sawdust, by-product of countless gallons of sweat expended in shaping the massive timbers. A whipsaw flashed as it was drawn up through a log by the topman sawyer; a second later it was almost lost to sight as the pitman dragged it downward again.

The carved work was all in place, even to the cat faces that adorned the timbers called catheads, when readers of the *Federal Gazette,* attracted by a glowing description of the "super-excellent and masterly" work, began to arrive in the yard. Captain Truxtun, upon receiving an explanation of the allegorical meanings of the carvings from William Rush, who planned and executed the work, had forwarded it to the newspaper with a request that it be printed for the gratification of those who might wish to visit the ship.[6]

Nature, still an elegant female figure, was mounted high on the prow, just beneath the bowsprit; but she was no longer "indignant"; now that she had emerged from a block of wood she was represented "in pleasing extacy . . . she is crested with Fire, her waist is encircled with the Zone or signs of the zodiac, her hair and drapery loose and flowing, her right arm and hand elevated, her left arm lightly resting on a large sphere, on which the Constellation is rising, her feet on a rock." Flame ascended and water descended from the rock; it was flanked by a scale and mirror, emblematic of truth and justice, and a dove, symbolic of peace, resting in a liberty cap. The carvings extended back along the trailboards on each side of the bluff bows. The four seasons were represented there, "crowning the Muses," encouraging the "free and uninterrupted progress" of arts and sciences in the new world.

At the center of the stern was "a large sphere, with the Constellation inserted, resting on a massy pedestal." A panel sunk in the pedestal displayed the fasces, badge of Union. Three large volumes and a scroll, suggesting the three branches of government and the Constitution, were on one side of the pedestal, and the American eagle and shield were on the other. On the starboard side of the central figure, Fortitude was followed by the emblems of Order, Industry, and Agriculture, "supported by Ceres, the goddess of agriculture, in the starboard quarter-piece." To the larboard side, Justice stood next to the emblems of Science, Shipbuilding, and Navigation, "supported by Neptune, the god of the seas, in the larboard quarter-piece." [7]

The Navy Yard was, for a few weeks, the focal point of interest in Baltimore. Old William Faris, diarist, dentist, and silversmith of Annapolis, came up to the city one day; after completing his business he and a companion "went and took a View of the Frigat." [8] Captain Truxtun, approving highly of the appearance of the hull with its carved work and festooned galleries, was anxious to have the townspeople come to see his ship.[9] One visitor, however, disturbed the "pleasing extacy" of the scene. Styling himself "an admirer of *truth*, as well as beauty," he wrote a letter to the editor of the *Federal Gazette* after examining Rush's woodcarving.[10]

"Great was my disappointment," he complained, "on actual inspection, to find it infinitely beneath, and not at all corresponding with, Mr. R's description." Dipping his pen in vitriol, the anonymous critic launched into a lengthy diatribe, picking the work apart almost splinter by splinter. "How long, my *profound astronomer*," he carped, "has the goose or eagle, (for critics have not agreed which it is)," been one of the signs of the zodiac? He condemned the dove in the liberty cap "(or as some have facetiously called it, a duck in a bag)" because the dove seemed to be trampling the emblem of liberty. But his idea was no better: he thought the dove should be wearing the cap. Likewise, his judgment of Nature's figure was open to question.

"Nature is always represented," he wrote, "as having a row of breasts, wholly uncovered, to show her office of fostering all created beings: Mr. R's figure has but two." Furthermore, she should be as "naked as is consistent with modesty—on the contrary, this figure is cloathed to a preposterous degree of clumsiness." And so he continued, taking up each detail in turn, expressing his disgust with "such contemptible chopping," at the same time giving a much clearer picture of the whole work.

As the day for the launch approached, plans for the great event were perfected. Captain Staats Morris, who commanded the little Army garrison in the fort on Whetstone Point, had been extremely co-operative throughout the building period, even to the extent of giving up a dozen of his cannon to help arm the *Constellation*.[11] He had furnished guards for the Navy Yard and was willing to do so again for the launch, but the crowd promised to be more than his men could handle, so Captain Truxtun called for volunteers. These came forward in droves, most of them sporting uniforms of one kind or another.

Builder Stodder's preparations were carried out with admirable thoroughness. He bought a hundred and twenty dollars' worth of tallow and spread it on the launching ways, down which the ship would slide.[12] The bilge ways, which would carry the ship down the tallowed launching ways, were hauled up into place and made fast to the under side of the hull before the morning of the seventh. That would leave for Thursday morning only the wedging-up and the final launch.

After dawn on Thursday, David Stodder waited for the flood tide. The ship still rested on the keel blocks. The last operation was to raise the hull a few inches with wedges, in order to remove keel blocks and stanchions and to transfer the hull's weight to the bilge ways.

Even though the event was planned for an early hour, the surface of the Patapsco was covered with innumerable boats, and the low hills to the east, across Harris Creek, swarmed with spectators. Never before had such a concourse of people, of both sexes and all ages, been assembled in the city of Baltimore. One group of uniformed volunteers was stationed around the yard to prevent the entry of anyone but the workmen and invited guests. Another group of volunteers, carrying muskets, was admitted on board to make the thrilling descent with the ship. A park of artillery was planted on high ground within the yard.[13]

Captain Truxtun, who commanded on board, was resplendent in

his new uniform. He wore a full dress blue coat with long buff lapels, gold "anchor and eagle" buttons, and a standing collar; a cocked hat with cockade; and buff breeches. The golden epaulets on his shoulders sparkled as they caught the morning sunlight.[14]

The workmen—two hundred of them—were ranged up and down the ways beneath the hull in two rows. Armed with heavy mauls, they were ready for the wedging-up. David Stodder was in command of the actual operation of launching. Close by his side stood a drummer, who communicated his commands to the men. At a signal from Stodder there was a ruffle on the drum, and two hundred mauls rained down on the wedges. At another signal from Stodder the ruffle ended, the men stayed their blows, and a rally at the wedges was complete. This was performed, according to one observer, "with as much exactness and precision, as the manuel exercise by a regiment of veterans."

The rallies continued. As the hull was raised and the strain came off the stanchions, they were removed. When the keel cleared the blocks, they too were knocked aside. By nine o'clock the ship was ready to launch.

"And now," continued the observer, "description is beggared."

"Everything being in the most complete preparation, all the blocks taken away, every man from under the vessel, and the hull standing on almost nothing but the slippery tallow, orders were given for knocking away the last stanchion. This being done, she moved gracefully and majestically down her ways, amidst the silent amazement of thousands of spectators, to her destined element, into which she plunged with such ease and safety, as to make the hills resound with reiterated bursts of joyful acclamations." Another witness wrote, "Nothing could surpass the proud and stately movements of the ship—she seemed conscious of the occasion, and passed on to the embrace of her destined element, with an air of dignity and grandeur, inconceivable."

The volunteers on board fired a musket salute of sixteen rounds, one for each state in the Union, each star in the Constellation. This salute was answered by the park of artillery.

Her launch was perfect. She came to anchor within a hundred yards of shore. The opinions of the builder and captain repeated the superlatives that appeared in the newspapers.[15]

"I launched the United States frigate *Constellation*," Stodder proudly reported to the Secretary of War, "without the least appearance of the smallest accident happening." He praised his workmen for executing his orders "at the instant directed." [16]

Captain Truxtun was more eloquent. "The masterly manner in which the ways were laid by Mr. Stodder," he wrote, "and the other precautions he took to prevent the smallest accident, which had the desired effect, does him the highest honor as a master builder and professional man. In fact, Sir, I never witnessed in Europe, or any other country a performance of the kind better executed and more highly gratifying, and I am convinced a more sightly ship of the sort cannot be built." [17]

If he imagined for a moment that his troubles were over now that his ship was in the water, Captain Truxtun was sadly disillusioned as the fitting out period dragged on for many exasperating months. The first of a series of vexatious delays came within two days after the launching. Before the week was ended, Baltimore was struck down by the dreaded yellow fever.

CHAPTER 29

MORE DELAYS

    *℘*   ·   ·   *℘*   ·   ·   *℘*   ·   ·   *℘*   ·   ·

WORK on the *Constellation* was halted when the fever hit Baltimore. On the very weekend of the launch it was reported that the carters were hauling away a dozen bodies a night from Fell's Point.[1] As soon as he heard the alarm, Captain Truxtun sent out for a box of calomel pills, which he proceeded to take morning and night to keep his "bowels perfectly open." Harking back to his experience in Batavia, he watered his gin and porter and seldom exceeded two or three glasses of wine after dinner. In going to and from the yard, he gave a wide berth to every place where the fever had appeared. He carefully avoided breathing the noxious effluvia generated in the closed spaces of his ship because they were believed by many to cause deterioration of the human frame as well as rotting of ship timbers.[2]

When work was resumed more than a month later, news of another launch was arriving from Boston.[3] The *Constitution,* being built there, was ready for launching two weeks after the *Constellation.* John Adams, who was now President of the United States, was one of the huge crowd of spectators present in Boston when all the blocks and stanchions were removed and when—nothing happened.[4] Resting only on the tallow, the ship moved not an inch. Urged by "screws and other machinery," she grudgingly slid a few yards, but when the President went home that day, the ship was still resting on her ways in midpassage. Two days later, after another attempt to shove her into the water, she was thirty-one feet closer to it but still embarrassingly on dry ground. It took a third try, late in October, 1797, to get her safely afloat.[5] The *Constitution*'s launch was as deliberate as that of the *United States,* in Philadelphia, had been precipitate. Of the first three frigates, the one in Baltimore was the only one to be launched without incident.

Although Captain Truxtun's *Constellation* was off the ways, she was in no sense ready for sea. The masts, rigging, and guns all had to be put on board before the ship could leave her berth in the Patapsco; a very long list of supplies, stores, and provisions was required before she could go to sea. Throughout the fall and into the winter, her outfitting proceeded under Captain Truxtun's watchful eye. He attended her constantly, checking off hundreds of items of equipment and supplies as they were carried on board.[6] He had expected to take his ship down the bay early in December to the sheltered mouth of Patuxent River, halfway between Baltimore and Norfolk, where she would not be troubled by ice, but an early freeze thwarted his plans, and she remained in Baltimore all winter. Therefore, her captain went home to his family.[7]

In the diplomatic arena, the posture of foreign affairs was, as usual, tense. A treaty had been made with Great Britain, halting for a time her Navy's frequent insults to the unprotected American flag at sea. But the French government, construing the treaty as a threat to its security, had set out on a systematic program of retaliation. American vessels suffered unconscionable delays in French ports, and many were captured on the high seas by French naval vessels and privateers. In all, more than two hundred cases of French spoliations had been reported.[8]

Sympathy for the French revolutionists was subsiding in America. Charles Biddle, for example, had made the full swing away from the French mania, saying, "War [with France] in my Opinion would be infinitely better than remaining in the situation we are in at present";[9] but the steps being taken to protect foreign commerce from such depredations were halting and uncertain. The opponents of the Navy were still sniping at the Administration. In the opinion of one congressman, there was never "such a sink of expense as that of fleets." Another said he would rather see the ships burnt than completed and manned. A third claimed that it was well known that there had been "an extraordinary waste of public money on these frigates."[10]

Relations with the Dey of Algiers were still carried on in an atmosphere of meek submission. The *Crescent,* the frigate built to placate the Dey, already had sailed for the Mediterranean; there she was to be added to his piratical fleet. The Secretary of State was relieved to see her go, because he was anxious to comply with all the Dey's demands. "Nothing," he had said, "is to be done to hazard the good opinion of the Dey, or to excite the most distant idea of trespassing on his distinguished benevolence towards the United States."[11]

John Adams had been President for just a year when, in March, 1798, he heard ominous news from the peace commissioners he had sent to France. They had not been recognized officially by the French government as envoys of a free, independent, and powerful nation. They had been affronted and humiliated; they were forced to carry on their business with three nameless Frenchmen X, Y, and Z; finally they found that their negotiations were blocked until they would agree to the payment of bribes and gifts of money—"a great deal of money."[12] Within a few days, President Adams, the short, round man who looked like a drab little country squire, decided that the United States had tolerated French insults long enough. He would maintain American dignity, even though such a course might lead to war. Even before he consulted Congress, he made his policy known to his heads of department.[13]

Accordingly, by the middle of March, Captain Truxtun had his orders from the President, conveyed to him by Secretary of War McHenry. He was to return at once to Baltimore, to take his ship into deep water, fit her out, provision her, recruit a crew, and in every respect prepare her for sea.[14] This was the first link in a chain of events that, within a twelvemonth, was to find a formidable United States Navy at sea, with Captain Truxtun's fame shining above all, like the proud stars of the *Constellation*.

## CHAPTER 30

## FITTING OUT

𝒞ꞵ  .  .  𝒞ꞵ  .  .  𝒞ꞵ  .  .  𝒞ꞵ  .  .

EARLY in April, 1798, the *Constellation* got under way from her berth in Baltimore. Manned by a few temporary hands, she dropped down the Patapsco to the Chesapeake and, steering easily "like a boat" and outstripping every vessel with her, she sailed down the bay to the mouth of the Patuxent.[1] In this out-of-the-way anchorage, Captain Truxtun was faced by the months-long task of transforming his new ship, scarcely out of the builder's hands, into an invulnerable man-of-war.

One of his many responsibilities was to assemble a crew. Since the ease with which men could be persuaded to enlist in a ship depended upon the reputation of her captain, there was little doubt that he could command his share of available seamen in Baltimore, but the large number of men he needed—two hundred and twenty seamen and forty marines—was likely to exceed the supply. The manifest disadvantages of naval service—strict and often harsh discipline, overcrowding, enforced cleanliness in clothing and person—would lose him some men; the period of enlistment, one year "unless sooner discharged by order of the President," would alienate others, because a merchant voyage, the alternative open to most seamen, usually lasted only a few months.[2]

Some of his commissioned and warrant officers had already been appointed by the War Office. His first lieutenant and second in command was John Rodgers of Baltimore. Twenty-five years of age, Rodgers had for the past five years commanded Baltimore merchant ships, one of which he had lost to a French privateer.[3] He was taller than his captain, muscular, with seemingly boundless energy. His shock of coal-black hair, shaggy eyebrows, and dark eyes set in a handsome face, made a striking impression. His firmness and resolution demanded respect. He fitted perfectly into Captain Truxtun's scheme of organization and later adopted it for his own, after leaving the *Constellation*.[4] His devotion to his captain was unalloyed.[5]

Lieutenant Rodgers' first duty was to recruit as many men as he could find in Baltimore, where Captain Truxtun ordered him to open a rendezvous in Cloney's Tavern at Fell's Point. He could offer able seamen fifteen and ordinary seamen ten dollars a month, with an advance of two months' pay if a man could furnish "good and Sufficient Security" against running away before entering the ship. He was allowed one dollar for every man he engaged, to cover the expenses of the rendezvous, "fire, candle, Liquor, house rent, &c &c," in addition to a reasonable allowance for "music to indulge and humour the Johns in a farewell frolic." Whenever he enlisted ten men, he was to send them down to the ship in a pilot boat. He was strictly enjoined to "be at the rendezvous night and day, untill the object of your mission is completed." This he did for five weeks running, enlisting in all about a hundred men.[6]

When it became evident that Baltimore could not supply all the men needed, the second lieutenant, William Cowper, was sent to open a rendezvous in Norfolk. Lieutenant Cowper, brother of Captain Truxtun's good friend John, a Norfolk merchant, proved to be an imperious and hot-tempered officer, but he was able to convince another hundred men that they should cast their lot with the *Constellation*.[7]

After persuading an Army artillery officer, James Triplett, to act as lieutenant of marines (there was as yet no Marine Corps), and upon learning that some men who had just lost their ship to a French privateer were on their way to Alexandria, Virginia, Captain Truxtun sent him off to open a rendezvous there, thinking that the opportunity to go out in search of Frenchmen might be a strong incentive to enlistment.[8] He could offer marines only nine dollars a month for sergeants, eight for corporals, seven for drummers and fifers, and six for privates, with an advance of two dollars upon being sworn in. Nevertheless, Triplett managed to engage nearly forty marines and seventeen seamen besides.[9]

While stores and provisions for his ship demanded his frequent attention, Captain Truxtun's principal task was the organization and training of his crew, an undertaking that had already occupied his mind for many months.[10] He had previously prepared a quarter bill and a list of standing orders, both of which he now posted conspicuously alongside the Articles of War, where all might read and absorb the code by which the ship would be governed.

The quarter bill prescribed the station that each crew member was required to take when the drum beat to quarters and the ship was prepared for an engagement at sea. The standing orders, supplementing the rather unspecific Articles of War, explained in detail the routine to be followed both in port and at sea. Captain Truxtun had them printed, and distributed a copy to each of his officers, one of whom commented that it would take a sea lawyer to learn them all.[11]

To his first lieutenant he outlined his general policies. He looked for proper subordination from every officer and man aboard. "No Officer," he said, "must attempt to offer an opinion to me on the duty to be performed, without its being previously asked, but on the Contrary, Carry all orders into execution without hesitation or demur." He expected his officers to "be Civil and polite to every one . . . for Civility does not interfere with discipline." He warned against tyrannous practices, remarking that "too great a disposition to punish where we have power is not necessary either to facilitate business, or to keep alive good Subordination." On the other hand, he was convinced that nothing was quite so ruinous to authority and to respect due to officers as "improper familiarity with the petty Officers &c."

He outlined the etiquette to be observed when coming on board or leaving the ship, when addressing an officer, and when stepping onto the quarter-deck. In each case, officers "simply lift their hat." When delivering a message, petty officers, seamen, and marines "Speak holding their hats in hand."

Finally, he aired his views on "that detestable vice drunkenness," which he found too frequently among officers in the sea service. "I do not mean to insinuate," he said, "that a Convivial fellow is a drunkard, who may become Chearful in Company, the distinction is too great to make it necessary for me to draw any line on that subject." [12]

In order to make sure that every commissioned and warrant officer knew exactly what was required of him, he made it a practice to supply each one with a written statement of his duties and responsibilities. The lieutenants, the boatswain, the gunner, the carpenter, the armorer, and the master-at-arms received individual instructions to regulate their conduct.[13] All of his orders, to whomever addressed, kept one idea paramount: his ship and crew were to be organized "so that in a few minutes warning the ship may be ready at any time to go into an Engagement by night or day." Thus he demonstrated his understanding of the function of naval command. If all the rules and regulations were observed in spirit as well as letter, he was confident that he would have a "happy and well govern'd Ship."

"We have an Infant Navy to foster, and to organize," he said, "and it must be done." [14]

Little more than two months after dropping his anchor in the Patuxent, Captain Truxtun had developed what promised to be a spirited and efficient fighting organization. He had labored incessantly to get men and materials on board and to use both to the best advantage. Supplies arrived from time to time, and his head was filled with the details of equipage, from rammers and sponges and worms and ladles for the great guns down to bed pans and chamber pots for his sick bay.[15] He had some of the cannon powder made up into cartridges for scaling the guns; he had some fifteen thousand paper cartridges of musket and pistol powder filled and stowed away in padded barrels.[16] He was sorely vexed by the failure of the War Office to order the huge quantities of bread and cheese, rice, peas, potatoes, flour, and rum that his crew would consume. He was able to get them without protracted correspondence only because he knew William Pennock, the Navy Agent in Norfolk, who had sailed with him as his second lieutenant in the *Mars,* nearly twenty years before.[17]

When he moved his ship down to Hampton Roads, almost at the door to the ocean, his crew was complete except for a few men whom he was to receive from Norfolk. Finding more men there than he had hoped for, he was able to discharge "a Number of Rotten and inanimate Animals that found their Way into the Ship, by imposing on the recruiting Officers and Surgeon's Vigilance." [18]

He already had his orders for cruising. He waited only for the arrival of a dozen merchant vessels that he had agreed to convoy a few leagues beyond the capes, in order to protect them from the

French privateers he felt sure must be lurking nearby. He made good use of the delay, however. He fired the scaling charges in his guns, removing the rust that had accumulated inside them; the drum beat to quarters, the great guns were exercised, and the marines were drilled in the use of their muskets. He was determined to be prepared for a fight if one awaited him outside the Bay.[19]

In Philadelphia, meanwhile, the possibility of war with France was at last being discussed openly. The President called for a fleet of ships to cruise off the coast and for an Army to prevent invasion if it should be threatened.[20]

It had been recognized for a long time that James McHenry, Secretary of War, was not equal to his charge. He was, after all, a Hobson's choice. Three others had refused the appointment before it was finally offered to him.[21] He was completely "bewildered with Trifles," turning for help with Army affairs to Alexander Hamilton and gladly turning over to him the details of raising the Army.[22] But there was no one to take care of the Navy. In McHenry's hands it might remain but a paper fleet, while he busied himself with such projects as naming the new fort being built on Whetstone Point in Baltimore after himself.[23] The answer to this dilemma was not long in coming.

In a strong Federalist Congress, where mercantile interests were heavily represented, it was becoming easier to push through measures that led to a strong Navy. The opposition was noisy but it was not too numerous. McHenry's incompetence suggested the separation of naval affairs from the War Department and provided the excuse for the introduction of a bill calling for the formation of a Navy Department. In favor of the bill, it was argued that he was not conversant with naval business and because of the press of Army affairs the Navy was beginning to suffer. By spending a few hundred dollars to pay someone to direct the Navy, it was claimed, thousands could be saved. The other side of the debate was more lengthy. It was pointed out that there was no economy in creating a new department. The head of the Navy Department would try to make it as important as he could; soon the Army and Navy would be competing for men and materials. Perhaps the War Department might be enlarged; but if the claim that an executive must be conversant with all the details of his department was valid, then it would logically follow that the business of the War Office should be split up still further; it would soon be argued that it was necessary to have a Commissioner of Gun Barrels and a Commissioner of Ramrods.

The gentleman from North Carolina summed it up by saying that "the arguments in favor of the bill were derived from a want of knowledge of naval affairs in the War Department." In spite of the shaky ground on which the arguments rested, the Federalists managed, in April, 1798, to pass the bill and thus create an autonomous Navy Department.[24]

The newly chosen Secretary of the Navy was Benjamin Stoddert, at forty-seven a prosperous merchant from Georgetown, Maryland, near the site of the proposed capital city called Washington. He brought to the office boundless energy and a talent for organization. By the time Captain Truxtun was ready for sea, the plans for a greatly expanded naval force were framed, five ships had been purchased from private owners, others were being considered, and all were to be armed and sent out to cruise as soon as possible. Captain Richard Dale, who had just returned from India in the *Ganges,* had already armed his ship for war and was out looking for a French privateer reported off Sandy Hook, complaining that "Some *Dam rascal* has been giveing him information of my giting out." Captain Barry's *United States* was nearly ready to sail; in Boston the *Constitution* was yet a month from departure.[25]

On the point of sailing, Captain Truxtun sent off his letters to the War Office, because he did not yet know that the Navy Department existed. He wrote also to his friend Charles Biddle, telling him that if anything should happen to Mary, who was expecting another baby "(life is uncertain)," he would be greatly obliged to him for looking after the children until his return. Then his thoughts turned to his profession of arms.

"War is Certain," he wrote. "I am directed to send in all French Cruizers Only, but should I meet a fat Merchantman, or a Neutral Covering French property, it will seem hard to let such pass." [26] He was annoyed not so much by the possible loss of a valuable prize as by the reticence of Congress to admit that the proposed retaliations for French insults and plunder amounted to a full blown war. When he accepted his commission, he put aside for all time what he chose to call "the privateering Principle." [27] He had come up through the school of privateering, but he was soon to demonstrate by word and deed that his first concern was for the national honor. All of his actions were now attuned to "the Good of the Service." [28]

On the twenty-sixth of June, 1798, the *Constellation* was quite ready for sea. The water-casks were full; everything on board was stowed carefully and well; the guns were loaded, ready to be run out at a moment's notice and fired in anger if need be. At eleven o'clock, Captain Truxtun signaled the merchantmen to be convoyed that he was about to weigh anchor. By noon, his ship was under way. Rain squalls scudded before the wind across the open water. The high, square lighthouse on Cape Henry towered above the sandy beach and the low woods; its lime-whitened bricks stood out sharply against the dark rainy sky.[29]

At four o'clock in the afternoon, the pilot clambered down over the side into the pilot boat. Heading east, the *Constellation* stood out to sea.[30]

CHAPTER 31

SHAKEDOWN CRUISE

౭ళ   .   .   ౭ళ   .   .   ౭ళ   .   .   ౭ళ   .   .

CAPTAIN Truxtun was ordered to cruise from the capes of the Chesapeake to the southern limits of the United States. He had sailed but a few days down the coast when he began to sense that the crew's inevitable grumbling, which was to be expected wherever men were constrained by any sort of discipline, was taking on an unnatural and angry tone.

Setting out on a cruise with a large and untried crew—three hundred and thirteen men all told, including officers—and being anxious about the health of his ship, he had ordered a water ration of slightly more than two quarts per man per day, to be served out in four portions at specified hours. He believed that some men, like horses, would drink excessive quantities of water when hot and tired and that the practice would invite serious consequences, such as bloating and dysentery.[1] Apparently this measure, added to the generally strict and exacting discipline that he had enforced since the first men had arrived on board his ship, was more than some members of the crew thought they had bargained for. In little groups the men talked themselves into a state of agitation, and when the talk reached Captain Truxtun's ears, he thought he heard in it the prelude to mutiny.

Acting immediately and with resolution, he called all hands on deck. He had the Articles of War read first, and then a paper he had prepared, in which he took notice of "several mutinous Assemblies" that had occurred. He restated the Article providing that "Any Officer, Seaman, or Marine, who shall begin, excite, cause, or join in any Mutiny, or Sedition in the Ship to which he belongs, on any Pretence whatsoever, shall suffer Death, or such other Punishment, as a Court Martial shall direct." He cited the Article that gave him authority for the water ration, its size being fixed at two quarts per day for foreign voyages "and such further Quantity, as shall be thought necessary on the Home Station, but on particular Occasions the Captain may shorten this Allowance." He added that if he had erred in his discipline, it had been in "not observing that Rigor, which the infamous Conduct of some On board have deserved." He stated in peroration, "You have the Law before you, and, I repeat, you know the Consequence, if, in future, you transgress. I must and will do my duty." [2]

As a climax to the proceedings, he had a marine private seized up at the gangway and flogged "with one Dozen of Stripes on his bare Back, with a Cat of nine Tails, for Insolence to the Sergeant of Marines, and endeavouring to arest a Pistol out of his Hands." [3]

From this day forward, there was never any threat of mutiny in a ship commanded by Captain Truxtun. As this first cruise of the *Constellation* wore on, he increased the water ration, and finally he ordered the scuttle casks filled for all to use as they wished.[4]

On the very day that Captain Truxtun reasserted his authority, Secretary of the Navy Ben Stoddert in Philadelphia hurriedly dispatched an urgent message to him. The Speaker of the House had just given Stoddert an anonymous, bitter, complaining letter, evidently written by someone on board the *Constellation,* that indicated a "spirit of Mutiny" in some part of the crew. Anxious to warn the Captain at the earliest possible moment, he posted the letter to William Pennock, the Norfolk Navy Agent, with the request that he immediately send a pilot boat in search of the *Constellation.*[5]

The subject of mutiny was still fresh in the public mind because newspapers of the summer before had been full of the latest news of mutinies in the British fleet. Breaking out at Spithead, where ships could not be got to sea because their crews refused to carry out their regular duties, the idea of mutiny spread to the fleet in the Thames' mouth. The mutinies had started as peaceful protestations against intolerable conditions on board ships full of impressed men, but they became grim, cruel, bloody affairs when the King's justice was meted out by courts-martial. Thirty men were hanged; nine others were flogged, each receiving from forty to three hundred and eighty lashes.[6]

The mutiny that may have sparked the threatened uprising in the *Constellation* was one that occurred on the West India station. The British frigate *Hermione,* cruising in the Caribbean, was commanded by Captain Pigot, a young man who failed to understand the distinction between firm justice and brutality. Ordering some men down from aloft one day, he threatened to flog the last man down. In their haste to avoid punishment, two men lost their hold and plunged to the deck. Looking upon them with contempt, the captain ordered, "Throw the lubbers overboard." Justice of a sort was returned to him that same night, when his crew mutinied. He and most of his officers were murdered and heaved over the side, and the ship was voluntarily surrendered to the Spanish fleet, then at war with Great Britain. It was supposed at the time that some of the mutineers had made their way to America.[7]

When the pilot boat carrying Secretary Stoddert's dispatches found the *Constellation,* more than three weeks later, Captain Truxtun set about trying to find out who wrote the offending letter. One day he assembled his crew and read the names and descriptions of the men who were known to be in the *Hermione.* Shortly afterwards Hugh Williams, able seaman, was found "in a tremor" by one of the officers and was brought to the Captain's cabin, where he confessed that he had been one of the mutineers. Making his way to Norfolk after the mutiny, he had been in America only three days when he entered the *Constellation* under the false name he now bore.

Captain Truxtun was satisfied that he had gotten to the bottom of the affair. He clapped Williams in irons, and after he returned to

Norfolk he turned the prisoner over to the British consul. Even while he agreed that Captain Pigot was "not a disciplinarian but a brutal man," he could not overlook the fact of mutiny nor the treasonous surrender of the *Hermione* to the enemy.[8]

Captain Truxtun's rule of his ship was absolute but it never approached brutality. His senses revolted at having a man flogged. Throughout the rest of his naval career, he never found it necessary in his own ship to resort to the cat; and this included the period when Captain Nicholson, in the *Constitution*, was flogging as many as six men in a single day.[9] He preferred to stop a man's allowance of grog, which, at a quart a day, he thought was too great anyway.[10]

His officers gave him nearly as much trouble as the seamen and marines. It pained him to see the slovenly way Lieutenant Cowper stood his watch, with sails untrimmed, loose rope ends towing in the water, and petty officers scuffling on the quarter-deck while he talked and joked with the common seamen. He was wearied almost beyond endurance by Lieutenant Triplett's inattention to duty, his failure to appear on deck when speaking other vessels, and the altercations that continually occurred among the marines because of his neglect of the watch bill. A fist fight between two midshipmen on the quarter-deck, a midshipman asleep at his post, and a squabble among several petty officers—these were all situations that he had to deal with in one way or another. Usually he chose merely to reprimand the offenders, hoping to appeal to an officer's reason and self-respect, and recognizing that it was "much easier to make a deep Wound, than to heal a small one." [11]

David Porter, a lad of eighteen, was a midshipman in Captain Truxtun's ship for over a year. More than thirty years later, thinking back on his days in the *Constellation*, he painted a vivid picture of naval command, in the center of which stood his first captain.

"A man of war is a petty kingdom," he wrote, "and is governed by a petty despot. . . . The little tyrant, who struts his few fathoms of scoured plank, dare not unbend, lest he should lose that appearance of respect from his inferiors which their fears inspire. He has therefore, no society, no smiles, no courtesies for or from any one. Wrapped up in his notions of his own dignity, and the means of preserving it, he shuts himself up from all around him. He stands alone, without the friendship or sympathy of one on board; a solitary being in the midst of the ocean." [12]

The government of Captain Truxtun's ship struck different men in different ways. Lieutenant John Rodgers, for example, was entirely in accord with his Captain's system. So highly did he regard it, in fact, that he carried it with him to his next ship, where an observer noted that "The order on Board was *Great,* & *Probably* too much *all a mode L' Truxtun.*"[13]

Captain Truxtun was always aware that he was "Surrounded by a crew composed of so many Argus's," who watched his every move and expression;[14] but his actions were in the last analysis always guided by one overriding idea. The end of military discipline is the winning of battles. Everything else is subordinate to that end. Only when every man in a fighting unit obeys reflexively and without question or reservation, can its full force be wielded by its commander. To be effective in action, a ship must have an able captain, of course; but the ship in turn must become in his hands a single weapon, instantly answering to his will; it must be completely adaptable to the changing fortunes of battle. Captain Truxtun was one of very few men who understood this idea completely. His every effort was bent toward the moment when he would close with the enemy. Not knowing how soon that time would come, he was determined to be ready. He would have a happy ship if possible, but above everything else he would have an obedient ship.

After returning from this shakedown cruise, which lasted nearly two months, Captain Truxtun found orders awaiting him to take under his command the *Baltimore,* 20, Captain Isaac Phillips, to proceed with all possible speed to Havana, where it was reported that some sixty American vessels were assembled, waiting for a convoy, and to bring them home.[15] Twenty or thirty French privateers were thought to be lying in wait for this convoy in the Gulf of Florida; but in the course of the whole voyage Captain Truxtun saw only one French vessel, and that was a one-gun schooner, which he chased. While pursuing the schooner close in under the shore, the *Constellation* suddenly found herself becalmed. The French crew then had the satisfaction of watching the hoisting out of boats and the wearisome towing that it took to get their pursuer back into deep water.[16]

Otherwise uneventful, this convoy duty gave him an additional opportunity to exercise his ship and crew, and incidentally to purchase a barrel of oranges and a barrel of limes, which he forwarded along with two jars of sweetmeats to his family in Perth Amboy.[17]

Before the first cold weeks of autumn had arrested the yellow fever season of 1798 in Philadelphia, and before Secretary Stoddert had returned to the city from his temporary office in fever-free Trenton, Stoddert had decided how he would employ his growing naval force during the coming winter. Since the swarm of French privateers that was expected on the American coast had failed to materialize and since Congress had extended the limits of the retaliatory and as yet undeclared war, he hoped to be able to send a respectable fleet to the West Indies, where it would be easier to find and capture Frenchmen.[18]

Several new vessels were abuilding, authorized by an act of Congress that permitted the Navy to accept them from patriotic citizens—who were paid at the rate of six per cent for their patriotism—in return for government bonds. These vessels, added to those already purchased and built, brought the total number of vessels of all descriptions in the Navy to an encouraging twenty-one by the end of 1798.[19] Now the vessels were causing him little worry. It was the captains who kept him awake nights.

Captain Barry had gone with a small squadron to the West Indies, but he had already returned in precipitate haste, being afraid to stay on his station during the hurricane season. Unimpressed by his fears, Secretary Stoddert sent him out again. His performance this time was notable for his inactivity in seas that apparently swarmed with enemy privateers waiting to be caught.[20] Sam Nicholson, the second ranking captain, was described by the Boston Navy Agent as "a rough blustering Tar merely, he is a good Seaman probably . . . but he wants points much more important as a Commander in my view, prudence, judgement & reflection are no traits in his character, nor will he ever improve." He had already demonstrated his lack of prudence and judgment by capturing a British privateer, which act cost the government considerable embarrassment and ten thousand dollars for damages. Stoddert, who feared to trust him with a separate command, was forced to send him out in Captain Barry's squadron, because he was junior to no one else in the Navy.[21]

The captains who ranked after Barry and Nicholson were causing trouble of another kind. On George Washington's sixty-fifth birthday, in 1797, the year the first three frigates were launched, he had signed the commissions of the captains attending them. The commissions were numbered consecutively according to rank: Barry one, Nicholson two, and Truxtun three. That "No. 3" on Captain Truxtun's commission was to cause trouble for years to come. It will be remembered that Talbot and Dale, ranking third and fourth on the original list of captains, had been returned to private life when the building of their frigates was suspended. Now, when they were recalled to service, they found themselves junior to Captain Truxtun. Talbot would not serve unless his original rank was restored, and Dale, who had already been cruising in the *Ganges,* refused to continue until the issue was settled. Secretary Stoddert was anxious to pacify all parties, but he was afraid Truxtun would resign if he placed Talbot and Dale ahead of him; he wanted to avoid that if in any way possible. Therefore, he submitted the question to President Adams, who ignored it as long as he was able.[22]

When Captain Truxtun arrived in Philadelphia, near the end of November, 1798, the question of relative rank was still a long way from being decided. However, he had come not to contend for rank, but to plan a winter cruise.

After more than six months of almost incessant labor—he had been ashore only three days in all that time—he was satisfied that his ship and crew were equal to any service they might be called upon to perform.[23] Stoddert had given him the choice of leaving his ship at Norfolk or taking her round to New York, where he would be close to his family in Perth Amboy. Owing to the thinness of his sails and the possibility of meeting with wintry gales off the Jersey coast, he had decided it would be best to leave her where she lay. "I have not been able," he told the Secretary, "to get my own Consent, to run into a Northern Port at this Season." Instead of journeying on to Perth Amboy, he asked Mary to come down to Philadelphia to visit him, so he could return to his ship as soon as his business was concluded.[24]

While he was in the city, Secretary Stoddert asked him and Captains Barry, Dale, Decatur, and Tingey, to get together in order to revise the Articles of War for the government of the Navy, which had been in force since before the Declaration of Independence. These captains, meeting for a few days only in the Navy Office on Walnut Street, making use of the "room, pen Ink & paper" provided by Stoddert, added to but did not substantially change the original Articles. All subsequent Navy regulations have been based upon the rules that evolved from these sessions.[25]

In less than a month after he left her, Captain Truxtun was back on board his ship, ready to proceed to his assigned cruising grounds in the West Indies.[26]

While he was making final preparations for his departure, late in December, 1798, he took time out to eat Christmas dinner and spend "an agreeable Day" with the British admiral, George Vandeput, whose squadron was lying in Hampton Roads. He suggested to the admiral that they exchange salutes when the *Constellation* sailed. Admiral Vandeput, an old sea dog who had spent over forty years in the King's service, would be happy to oblige; following the custom of the British Navy, he would answer Captain Truxtun's salute with two guns fewer. Needless to relate, no salute was exchanged. The admiral outranked a captain in the Royal Navy, but in the United States Navy a captain was the highest ranking officer. "It is impossible for me to acquiesce," said Captain Truxtun, "without degrading the Flag of the United States." However, the old admiral was not offended; he simply could not understand how a mere captain could expect him to exchange a salute gun for gun.[27]

The United States brig *Richmond*, 16, Captain Samuel Barron, was ready to sail with the *Constellation,* as were four merchant vessels, bound for West Indian ports. In the *Thetis,* a small schooner from Alexandria, was a passenger whom Secretary Ben Stoddert had asked Captain Truxtun to pay particular attention to. A young French lady it was, bound for the island of Martinique; she was to have the best protection that the Navy could afford. She was probably of a royalist family that had fled to America after the French Revolution. For these reasons, and because he was a normally chivalrous man in uniform, Captain Truxtun was determined to see her safe to her destination. He had offered to take her aboard his ship, where she would be safe from capture by the "Pirates of her Nation," but he warned her it would be most uncomfortable. Therefore she chose to stay in the *Thetis.*[28]

As the new year, 1799, reached the Virginia coast, the *Constellation* was standing out to sea, bound out on a cruise that would bring glory to the infant Navy and fame to her gallant commander.

## CHAPTER 32

# PETTY KINGDOM

AFTER two weeks at sea, the *Constellation* was still shepherding the little schooner with the lady aboard toward her destination. Captain Truxtun had had "a vast Deal of trouble" with the master of the *Thetis,* whose vessel was a dull sailer and who, like most merchant masters under convoy, paid no attention to the signals or the sailing of his escorts. One of the other vessels had disappeared from the convoy the first night out, and the remaining two were being led to their intended port in the Virgin Islands by the *Richmond.*[1] The *Constellation* was almost half way down the chain of islands that rims the eastern end of the Caribbean Sea and separates it from the Atlantic Ocean when the steep rugged coast of Martinique hove into view on the larboard bow. The town of St. Pierre, menaced by the mile-high furrowed cone of Mount Pelee to the northeast and the abruptly rising Carbet Peaks to the southeast, was huddled on a shelf below the backbone ridge of mountains as though in imminent peril of being pushed into the sea. About four leagues offshore, Captain Truxtun peered through his long glass and inspected the bold coast on either hand of the town. Finding it perfectly clear of vessels of any description, he hailed the *Thetis.* Speaking through a trumpet, he told the master to make the best of his way up to the anchorage before the town; and then, unbending for a moment, he bade farewell to the young lady and wished her "a happy Sight of her Friends."[2] He recovered his dignity as he lowered the trumpet and gave orders to bring the ship about; within a few minutes he was standing northward by the wind toward Basseterre, St. Kitts, his port of rendezvous.

Next morning, still rolling northward with the wind coming in from her starboard side, the *Constellation* was almost abreast of the island of Guadeloupe, where French naval vessels and marauding privateers were based.[3] Since his cruising grounds were north of St. Kitts, Captain Truxtun chose to ignore the Frenchmen here until after he had looked over his own station. It was a fine morning, clear, with pleasant breezes.

While the "petty despot," arrogating to himself "his few fathoms of scoured plank" on the weather side of the quarter-deck (just abaft the poultry coops), struts up and down the line of twelve-pounders that were borrowed from the embrasures of Fort McHenry, one finds the opportunity to look about the ship and to investigate the nature of his "petty kingdom."

He commands a fast-sailing ship. He has hesitated to make any definite statement about her performance to the Secretary of the Navy because he has seen "so much in the public Prints of the Sailing of Barry's ship [*United States*], and so much more bombastical Nonsense of that at Boston [*Constitution*]." Should he meet those ships, however, he is confident that the *Constellation* will outsail them both.[4]

All the sails are spread to catch every ounce of the light winds. Under the bowsprit, the spritsail yard carries a square of canvas only a few feet from the water. Above is a cloud of canvas, with jibs, staysails, and spanker rigged fore and aft from the jib boom, between the masts, and from the spanker gaff and boom on the mizzenmast. The huge courses, lowest sails on the main and fore-masts, are suspended athwartship from the lower yards. The other square sails, duplicated on fore, main, and mizzenmasts, are top-sails, topgallants, and royals, towering skyward almost to the trucks. The main truck, highest point in the ship, is 150 feet above the deck.[5] Leading down from aloft is the maze of running rigging that is used to control the set of the sails. Hauling singly and in unison, the sailors can regulate the canvas from the deck. But when a sail is loosed or furled, men must go aloft. Up there, lying out on a yard, each man perched precariously on foot ropes and hanging on with one hand, the job of handing a sail for furling can become cruel punishment when seas run high and the cold gale bites through heavy jackets. The stout canvas, stiffened by rain and spray, flapping violently as the wind takes charge, burning and blistering hands and tearing out fingernails by the roots, can break the spirit of the hardiest jack-tar.

At the lower mastheads, fifty feet above the deck, are the fighting tops. These are platforms as big as the floor of a fairly large room where, during an action, a midshipman and six sailors use four-pounder howitzers, blunderbusses, and hand grenades to rain down a deadly fire on the enemy's decks.

When the ship is sailing herself in fine weather, the men on deck sit about in little groups, swapping yarns, or pursue the endless job of repairing and overhauling the lines and ropes that is necessary to keep the sails where the Captain wants them. In the *Constellation,* seamen are dressed in duck trousers and striped and checked shirts; although shoes are provided, most of them go barefooted in the tropics. For colder climes, they have blue trousers, round jackets, and woolen caps.[6]

The marines are drilled as soldiers and do none of the ship's work except heaving at the capstan, when all hands are needed to hoist an anchor or set up the stays and braces. They are aboard to do sentry duty, to provide a landing party, and to cover the sailors in a boarding party. Below the tropic, the marines wear white linen overalls. In northern latitudes, they wear blue overalls with red piping; and for dress occasions, short blue coats and blue pantaloons, both garments edged in red, red belts, red vests, and black leather stocks and clasps—from which comes the term "leathernecks." [7]

The Navy lieutenants stand out sharply in their long blue coats with buff half lapels and standing collars, buff vests and buff breeches. Their uniforms are slightly less elegant than, though similar to, the Captain's. They wear a single gold epaulet on the right shoulder, while the Captain wears one on each shoulder.[8]

Before leaving the main deck, one must remark the crew's house of comfort. It is a compartment divided into two by the bowsprit and located at the very bows, or head, of the ship.

Going below to the gun deck, first beneath the main, or spar, deck, one finds the heavy twenty-four pounders ranged in two rows, fourteen on a side, each with its muzzle ready to be run out through a gun port when the port covers are swung outward in preparing for action. At the after end of the gun deck, occupying all the space abaft the mizzenmast and walled off by removable bulkheads, is the Captain's great cabin. He shares his quarters with four cannon, which greatly cramp his dining room. Nevertheless, there is room for a mahogany dining table, a dozen Windsor chairs, a mahogany secretary, and a copper coal-burning stove. Opening off the dining room is his stateroom, and off the stateroom, in one of the quarter galleries, his private water closet. Incongruous are the delicate lines of the Windsor chairs and the fine mahogany pieces that sit among heavy gun carriages; most unwarlike is the finishing touch in the great cabin—curtains at the windows! [9]

In the dining room, each day at a quarter past two, the Captain dines with two of his officers and one midshipman. He has told his first lieutenant that he expects "all that reserve when on duty Set aside" during this daily occasion.[10] But it is unlikely that any liberties are ever taken with the Captain as he presides at his table. The midshipmen do well to utter a syllable, so completely discomfited are they by their commander's presence.

Forward on the gun deck, before the mainmast, is the "Complete Camboose," where the crew's daily allowance of a pound of pickled meat per man is soaked overnight in steep tubs to remove some of the salt, and where, in the cook stove, it is rendered vaguely palatable. In addition to the meat, each man is allowed a pound of ship's bread a day (baked in Norfolk before this voyage, or perhaps even the previous one), a quarter-pound of cheese on Mondays, Wednesdays, and Saturdays, two ounces of butter on Fridays, and a quantity of dried peas, beans, rice, or turnips on specified days of the week.

Below the gun deck, the crew is lodged. The lieutenants, surgeon, purser, gunner, carpenter, boatswain, and captain's clerk: each has a tiny cubicle dignified by the name of "State room." Seamen, marines, petty officers, and midshipmen swing their hammocks from the overhead each night. During daytime, the hammocks are carried topside and stowed in the boarding nettings just above the bulwarks surrounding the main deck. This serves to clear the between-decks space and also to provide the crew on deck with additional protection from enemy gun shot and musket balls. When hammocks are swung below, their occupants can stare up at the foot-and-a-half-deep oak beams that support the gun deck. Captain Truxtun has pointed out that "The space of sixteen inches, between each hammock is allow'd, which is two Inches more, than in any other service in the world." [11]

There is yet another deck—the orlop—below this one. It is allotted entirely to storage spaces and ammunition handling rooms, except for one compartment abaft the cable tiers and between the two bread rooms, which is designated as the cock-pit. It is here that the surgeon and his mate labor over the shattered bodies that inevitably result from engagement with an enemy of sufficient force.

In the very bottom of the ship is the magazine, in which a hundred and fifty barrels of gunpowder are stored; the shot locker, containing nearly a hundred rounds of assorted plain, double headed, bar, chain, grape, and canister shot for each of the guns; a spirit room; and finally a coal hole with its cargo of thirty tons of sea coals.[12]

This, then, is the huge machine that constitutes the "petty kingdom." Self-sufficient for perhaps three months without replenishment, this community of better than three hundred men is confined between wooden walls but a few fathoms apart. The men work, eat, sleep, and work again according to the absolute law of the "solitary being" who, in a coffee house or on a city street, appears to be merely another man with the requisite number of eyes, ears, fingers, legs, and feet. Appearances are deceptive, however. As in every vocation, there are superb and good and ordinary and indifferent captains of men-of-war; and the difference between the first and the last consists of the indefinable force of character that inspires or disgusts, leads or coerces, commands or bullies.

In the best military sense of the word, Captain Truxtun commands.

Guadeloupe was still in sight when Captain Truxtun discovered a fleet standing to northwestward. He hove his ship about and ran down before the wind to investigate. After throwing out the private signal for the day, he soon learned that the fleet consisted of some two dozen sail of homeward bound American merchantmen under convoy of two Navy vessels, the ship *Montezuma*, 20, and the brig *Norfolk*, 18. The *United States*, 44, Captain Barry, which had accompanied the convoy on the first leg of its long journey home, was hull down on the horizon, returning to her port of rendezvous at the island of Dominica, next south of Guadeloupe.

Captain Alexander Murray, of the *Montezuma*, came on board the *Constellation* from his own ship and diplomatically requested that Captain Truxtun take charge of the fleet, which the latter was happy to do. Captain Truxtun decided to anchor the convoy in Basseterre Roads, St. Kitts, and to send the *Norfolk* eastward to

*Captain Truxtun. Miniature painting on ivory,
c. 1800. Artist unknown, but perhaps Archibald
Robertson, of New York*

Antigua in order to give homeward bounders there an opportunity to join the fleet before proceeding northward.[13]

He sent Bartholomew Clinch, his Lieutenant of Marines on this voyage, ashore to inform the commanding officer of the British fort that the *Constellation* would salute with thirteen guns if the fort would answer with a like number. Captain Truxtun brought up the rear of the convoy, and by the time all the vessels were safely at anchor and Lieutenant Clinch had returned to the ship, it was too late in the day to salute the fort. However, next morning promptly at seven o'clock, the first bark of the ship's guns rolled in across the water. Shore guns spat answering fire as the etiquette was nicely observed.[14]

The captain of the *Cyane,* British sloop-of-war lying in the roadstead nearby, promptly made his call aboard this new American frigate, and a number of gentlemen of the town came off in boats to pay their respects to Captain Truxtun.[15] As soon as he could do so, he went ashore to call upon the governor and to return the calls that the others had just made.

The town of Basseterre lay between the roadstead and the remarkable green dome of Monkey Hill, which took its name from the chattering, grimacing little animals that lived upon it. Since there was no pier at the landing place, the Captain's heavy boat plunged in through the surf and set him down most unceremoniously on the open beach.[16] "The town Basseterree," he later entered in his journal, "is a very small disagreable place, though the Country about is very delightful. The beautiful Sugar Cane fields interspersed with hansome risings, renders the prospect delightful." [17] This island, like the others in the Leeward chain, was steeply reared in great backbone ridges that often pierced the clouds.

The governor, Robert Thomson, was a gracious host. He offered the Americans every service within his power and invited Captain Truxtun to visit and dine with him whenever he had an opportunity.[18] The governor also brought him up to date on the French situation in the Islands. The notoriously cruel governor of Guadeloupe, Victor Hugues, had been deposed and sent back to France in one of the frigates that brought out his successor, General Desforneaux. It was supposed that *L'Insurgente,* which until recently had been commanded by the disgruntled American, Joshua Barney —who quit the United States Navy rather than be junior to Captain Talbot—had sailed for France, and that only the frigate *La Volontaire* remained in the West Indies. The British had unquestioned control of the sea lanes, but there were still many French privateers operating out of Guadeloupe and skulking among the other islands in search of unescorted merchantmen. One American man-of-war, the schooner *Retaliation,* 14, which had been a French privateer until she was captured by Captain Decatur off the Jersey coast, had been retaken recently by the frigates *L'Insurgente* and *La Volontaire* and sent in to Guadeloupe; her crew was now languishing in a dungeon.[19]

While he may have wished for more excitement than the French forces would be likely to afford, Captain Truxtun could see nevertheless that the mere protection of commerce in these islands, spread out as they were, would keep all available American ships of war quite busy for some time to come.

He thought that his orders, which permitted him to engage only armed French vessels, and which specifically forebade his interfering with ships of any other nation, were not consistent with the honor of a great nation.[20] One must agree that they were poorly conceived and badly stated. He was not even permitted to recapture an American vessel should he find her in the hands of anyone but the French, nor to interfere if anyone but a Frenchman detained or captured a merchantman while under his convoy. While he disagreed violently with the spirit of his orders, he was bound to conform to their letter. As to the requirement that he molest only armed French vessels, he was sure he could abide by this order. He could find at least a case knife aboard any vessel; for him that would be arms enough.[21]

When next he addressed a letter to the Secretary of the Navy, he noted the friendly reception he had been accorded by the British naval and civil authorities. "I am satisfied," he wrote, "we shall find the Station a very pleasant One."

"The Crew of the *Constellation* is in good Health, and fine Spirits," he continued, "all meritoriously wishing to meet the Enemy on equal Ground." He invoked the "kind Indulgence of Heaven to our united Prayers" that the wish might come true. Although he may have been over-optimistic in concluding that his crew felt as he did, it was clear that the Captain of the *Constellation,* at least, was spoiling for a fight.[22]

CHAPTER 33

## *L'INSURGENTE*

   *❧*  . .  *❧*  . .  *❧*  . .  *❧*  . .

WITHIN a short time after his arrival at Basseterre, Captain Truxtun had established the routine he and his squadron would follow. He informed Captain Barry, two hundred miles to windward, that he would arrange for convoys of homeward bound merchantmen to leave St. Kitts periodically; he suggested that Barry escort vessels from the windward station as far as St. Kitts, whence they could be added to the regular northbound convoys. When his men-of-war were not occupied with convoys, he ordered them to cruise throughout the area in search of privateers.[1]

In the *Constellation,* he cruised for several days to northward among the islands of St. Eustatius, St. Bartholomew, and St. Martin. This was his assigned cruising ground; but since his orders gave him considerable leeway and because he had found nothing of much promise, he stretched to the south of St. Kitts and Nevis, past Montserrat, and on toward the French stronghold at Guadeloupe.[2]

One day he spied a frigate lying at anchor in a Guadeloupe roadstead, under the guns of a French fort. Tauntingly he hoisted his colors and stood in as close as he dared, but the enemy ignored his invitation to come out and fight. Two days later, at the other end of the island, he drew the well-directed fire of another fort. Keeping count of the number of rounds fired at him, he stood off just out of range of the fort's guns and returned the "Insult" with double the number of guns. Next day, he returned to the same spot and again kept just out of range, puckishly inviting the enemy to throw away more powder and shot. He circled the island and hovered off its steep-to shores for nearly a week. He chased every sail he saw, but none turned out to be a French vessel.[3]

Within three weeks after his arrival in the West Indies, he had sent three convoys northward and already had another one arranged for; his little squadron had cruised almost continuously throughout the northern half of the Leeward Islands; and now, on the fifth of February, 1799, having satisfied himself that his orders were being carried out by the other vessels under his command, he was off again on another patrol.[4]

On the ninth, a Saturday, the *Constellation* was a few leagues to the east of Nevis, the island next south of St. Kitts. The officer of the watch had just reported to Captain Truxtun, bringing twelve o'clock. As was his custom, the Captain wrote out, on a slip of paper, the remarks to be copied into the ship's journal for the twenty-four hours just ended. "At Noon," he wrote, "saw a Sail standing to the Westward, gave Chase. I take her for a Ship of War." [5]

The strange sail was perhaps fifteen miles to leeward, south and west of the *Constellation*. Running down before the wind, Captain Truxtun meant to speak her. By one o'clock, when he could see her more clearly, he threw out the private signal of the day for a British man-of-war, a blue signal flag at the fore topmast head and a blue, white, and red flag at the main topmast head.[6] The stranger replied by hoisting an American ensign. Since that was not the answer he expected, he tried next the private signal for an American warship. To this the ship made no reply. Concluding that she must be a French frigate, he ordered the drummer to beat all hands to quarters.[7]

At the urgent rattle of the drum, a chill of excitement swept through the *Constellation* as the crew took up battle stations. Men boiled up from the lower decks, running to their posts. The topmen swarmed aloft on shrouds and ratlines. The arms chests were opened and the marines, being mustered on the quarter-deck, helped themselves to muskets and blunderbusses. On the gun deck, the ports were swung outward, the tompions were removed from the muzzles, and the carriages were bowsed out—hauled outboard by heavy rope tackles—so the guns projected beyond the wooden walls of the ship. The bulkheads of the great cabin came down and the furniture was stowed out of harm's way. Slow matches were lighted and passed up and down the line; the handling rooms were manned, scuttles opened to the magazine and shot locker, and the human train that kept the guns supplied with powder and shot was formed. In the cock-pit, the surgeon, surgeon's mate, purser, captain's clerk, and loblolly boy laid out their amputation tools and instruments for the gruesome work they hoped would not be required. The carpenter and his mates, stationed at the pumps, surveyed their stock of wooden plugs and oakum in anticipation of the moment when they might be needed to stop up shot holes below the water line.

On the weather deck, three groups of men, each led by a midshipman, stood by the pin rails at fore, main, and mizzenmasts, ready to trim sails at the Captain's order, and to act as musketeers when the opportunity offered. Two quartermasters were stationed at the wheel; the sailing master and two midshipmen messengers stood near the Captain on the quarter-deck, attending his every word and action.[8]

By this time, the stranger had hauled her wind and was standing northwestward. She replaced the American ensign by the tricolor of France and fired a shot to windward, which was the universal signal to confirm the fact that she was now under her true colors. The *Constellation,* running under the toe of Nevis, bore up slightly to head her off.

At two o'clock an angry squall raced across the sea; the wind, already brisk, suddenly rose to gale force as the squall struck both ships. With a cracking and snapping of sails and rigging as sheets and braces were let go on the run, the *Constellation* weathered the shock, losing only a single studdingsail boom; but the other ship, responding an instant too late, shuddered as her main topmast gave way and crashed downward. While the French frigate's wreckage was being cleared away, her antagonist was coming up fast. Bearing up a point or two closer to the wind, the French captain decided to try to run for shelter in the neutral roadstead of St. Eustatius, thirty miles distant.[9]

By three o'clock, the *Constellation* had nearly ended the chase. Almost due west of Nevis, the two frigates were sailing north-north-westward in sight of Basseterre Roads, St. Kitts.[10] Because his ship was heeled over by the press of sail she carried, Captain Truxtun had his larboard guns housed while those on the weather side were run out, ready to fire.[11]

At a quarter past three, the *Constellation* ranged up on the lee quarter of the French frigate, whose captain began to hail. Captain Truxtun heard the hail but made no move to answer. Only the creaking of timbers, the moaning of the wind in the rigging, and the insistent surging of seas under her bluff bows disturbed the pregnant silence that pervaded his ship. He stood fast on the quarter-deck, narrowly—almost calmly—watching the enemy, trying to anticipate her actions.

On the gun deck, the division commanders already had their orders. Through the gun ports they looked across the rapidly closing stretch of water at their French counterparts, who looked nervously back at them. Lieutenant Rodgers, commanding the first five great guns; Lieutenant Cowper, the next five; and Lieutenant Sterett, the remaining four; all waited until their ship was almost abreast of the enemy at point blank range, scarcely more than a hundred yards distant. Only then was the French captain's hail answered. The three lieutenants gave the signal to fire as their guns were brought to bear; matches were put to the touchholes, and a broadside of twenty-four-pound balls crashed into the enemy's hull. Belching fire and acrid smoke, the *Constellation*'s cannon leapt back from the ports. Each gun and its carriage—three tons of iron and oak suddenly come alive—were checked by a heavy breeching rope. When the brutish contraption came to rest, its gun crew sprang into action to reload. The bore was sponged out, the flannel powder cartridge was rammed home and wadded, two balls were loaded, and the whole charge was secured by another wad. The cartridge was pricked through the touchhole and the train was poured from a powder horn. After each gun was served, its carriage was bowsed out to firing position again; in a few short moments the battery was again ready to fire.

The first broadside was almost instantly returned by the enemy. Thus began a close action that lasted for an hour and a quarter. The French frigate wore as though to come alongside for boarding, but the *Constellation* raced ahead and crossed her bow, making the most of an opportunity to rake her, each gun of the battery firing in its turn. Ranging now ahead and now astern, the *Constellation* raked her several times during the battle, the heavy balls inflicting terrible losses as they crashed down the length of her deck.

The howitzers in the *Constellation*'s tops and the twelve-pounders on her quarter-deck took their toll of the enemy's top hamper. The French frigate's running rigging was badly cut up, her foretopsail was riddled, her mizzen topmast was shot away, and her spanker was cut to ribbons. Her situation soon became critical. Repeated hails from the deck got no answer from the tops; no quartermasters attended the wheel; men by the dozens lay about the decks, dying and dead.

Her guns were aimed high; the sails and rigging of the *Constellation* were cut up, but few if any shot landed in her hull between wind and water. At half past four, the *Constellation,* still under control, stood up athwart her antagonist's stern, ready once more to rake. The French captain was discussing his next move with his officers. He wanted to surrender, but he also wanted to share the responsibility for his decision. His first lieutenant said, "Do as you please." The others offered no objection.[12] Thereupon he hauled down his flag and gave to the Americans a valuable prize.

Lieutenant Rodgers was sent to take possession of the ship. He described the scene in a letter home a few days later, after the casualties had been counted. "I must confess," he wrote, "the most gratifying sight my eyes ever beheld was seventy French pirates (you know I have just cause to call them such) wallowing in their gore, twenty-nine of whom were killed and forty one wounded." [13]

On board the *Constellation* there was no such carnage. In spite of the close and general action, the men in the tops were the only ones hurt by the enemy. Midshipman David Porter, commanding in the foretop, reported the injuries of three of his men: "John Andrews, shot through both of his legs—George Walters, back broke by the wind of a cannon ball—Samuel Wilson, in the side." In the maintop, Midshipman James Macdonough [14] lost a foot; and in the mizzentop Thomas Wilson, a seaman, had a leg shot off and died next day.[15]

The only American killed during the action was on the gun deck. Neal Harvey, a seaman in one of Lieutenant Sterett's gun crews, was terrified by the action and ran from his station. Andrew Sterett, a young man just twenty-one, apparently hypnotized by the tumult of battle, ran him through with a sword. "And so," he said, "put an end to a *coward.*" Writing to his brother, he continued, "You must not think this strange, for we would put a man to death for even looking pale on board *this* ship."[16] Captain Truxtun's reaction to Sterett's deed is unknown. Apparently he wrote it off to the impulsiveness of youth. Perhaps he reprimanded him privately, but he praised him publicly for his zeal. In the ship's roll, opposite Neal Harvey's name, he entered simply "Killed in Action." [17]

When the vanquished captain was brought across to the *Constella-*

*tion,* he came on board sputtering with indignation. "Why have you fired upon the national flag?" he demanded of his captor; "Our two nations are not at war."[18]

Captain Truxtun made no reply because he was busy with the several tasks of transferring prisoners from the other ship, arranging for repairs sufficient to make her weatherly, and supervising the repairs in his own ship. Taking time only to learn that he had captured the forty-gun frigate *L'Insurgente,* Captain Citizen Barreaut, he relieved the captain of his sword and sent him below.

*L'Insurgente!* This fast-sailing frigate, reputed to be the fastest in the French Navy, able to outrun all the British ships that had chased her, was the one that Joshua Barney only recently commanded. She had not, after all, gone home to France. Remarking on the coincidence, Captain Truxtun said, *"It is singular she should be the first taken."* [19] It would have been even more singular had he taken the French frigate while the American, Joshua Barney, still commanded her.

Next morning, he talked with his chief prisoner. Barreaut, claiming that he had orders not to fire on the American flag, was still highly incensed by the unfair advantage that had, in his view, been taken of him. If he had known that he might be attacked, he said, he could have used his eighteen-pounders on the quarter-deck as stern chasers, and the *Constellation* might not have been able to come up with him at all. He was surprised, he continued, to see the Americans declare war, because he thought their differences were being settled peaceably.

Captain Truxtun told him the United States had not yet declared war on France. "Pardon me," said Barreaut, "your taking me . . . is a Declaration of War."

If that is so, Captain Truxtun replied, what about your capture of the *Retaliation,* an American man-of-war?

Here the conversation ended, with this one further observation by Captain Truxtun, "that be it War, or be it Peace," he should certainly attempt to take every French frigate he met.

In his report to the Secretary of the Navy, he wrote, "The french Captain tells me, I have caused a War with France, if so I am glad of it, for I detest Things being done by Halves." [20]

Whether the battle might have turned out otherwise had Barreaut been instructed differently, or whether, as he claimed later, the loss of his main topmast was the "source of all our misfortune," is a subject for idle speculation. Because his report of the action [21] is full of inconsistencies, one is inclined to agree with Captain Truxtun's verdict that the Frenchman was "as fully prepared for meeting an Enemy, as she could have been, if an Express had been sent to the Commander, that I should make an Attack on him, whenever we met." [22]

By the time *L'Insurgente* was ready to spread sail, the two ships had drifted far to leeward. In their present crippled state, it was doubtful whether they could beat up to St. Kitts at all. However, Captain Truxtun decided to try. On Monday morning, the ships were sailing in company, now on the starboard and now on the larboard tack, clawing up into a contrary wind, when a sail appeared in the offing. The *Richmond,* one of the ships of his squadron, was on her way north with a convoy when she sighted the two crippled ships and ran down to investigate. Captain Truxtun had his dispatches ready to send to Secretary Stoddert, but he was afraid that if he hove to in order to send them across to the *Richmond* it would take him "half a Day's hard Beating" to regain the ground he would lose. Therefore, the first word of the action to reach the United States was compounded of what Captain Barron could understand of the account Captain Truxtun shouted through his speaking trumpet and of the outward appearance of the two frigates.[23]

Nearly three days after the battle, the *Constellation* and *L'Insurgente* made Basseterre roadstead, coming to anchor under the guns of the fort on Bluff Point, just north of town. When he reported his arrival to Secretary Stoddert, Captain Truxtun wrote, "It is impossible for me to state to you the Joy demonstrated by the Inhabitants on this Occasion." [24]

British gentlemen of the first rank came on board his ship to congratulate the intrepid commander. Governor Thomson sent him a congratulatory letter in which he repeated his offer to help the Americans in any way he could. A member of the King's Council asked the Captain to fire a salute in order that the fort might return it. A British frigate and a sloop-of-war, standing near his ship, manned their yards and gave him three hearty cheers.[25]

Captain Truxtun basked in the warmth of applause that greeted him at every turn. He sent off word of his exploit to Captain Barry, asking him incidentally to send down several score men from his squadron to help man his prize ship. He hired a schooner to take his dispatches to America, but not until after he had ordered a search of the roadstead to find an eligible captain, the first one approached "being too extravagant in his Terms." He asked Secretary Stoddert to write a line to Mary at Perth Amboy telling her he was well, because, he said, "I have not Time." He distributed the enemy lieutenants' swords to his own lieutenants, and he sent a beautiful plume, part of Captain Barreaut's battle array, to his "God Son, John Williams Truxtun," in St. Kitts. However, consumed though he was by his increasing fame, he did not neglect his principal task as commodore of the American squadron in the northern Leeward Islands.

He sent the wounded from both ships to a hospital ashore, and he disposed of his prisoners by sending the French officers—fifty-two in all—in a cartel to Guadeloupe after exacting from them a promise that they would not take up arms against the United States, by putting a hundred men in the Basseterre jail, and by sending the rest —180 men—to a British prison hulk lying in the roadstead.[26]

Captain Barreaut, on taking his leave, was moved to write to his captor, "You have united the two Qualities, which characterize a Man of Honor: Courage and Humanity. Receive from me the most sincere Thanks, and be assured, I shall make it a Duty, to publish to all my fellow Citizens, the generous Conduct, which you have observed towards us." [27]

Captain Truxtun sent word with the cartel to Desforneaux, Governor of Guadeloupe, that he might have the rest of the prisoners if he would send down all of the Americans he was holding there.

Instead of returning the Americans, General Desforneaux, who was still inclined to maintain the fiction of peace between France and America, sent an envoy to demand the instant return of L'Insurgente. "If you do not act according to this Demand," he threatened, "I will confiscate all American Property, which is in this Colony, and consider the Americans, as Prisoners." [28]

Captain Truxtun of course had no distant idea of returning the ship; however, because the French prisoners were expensive to maintain and because Governor Thomson was stretching his authority by permitting prisoners taken by another nation to be held in St. Kitts, the envoy was able to return to Desforneaux not entirely empty-handed. Except for a dozen men who had already entered the United

States Navy, all the prisoners were released and sent back to Guadeloupe with the understanding that Americans being held there would be set free. As for peace and amity between the two countries, Captain Truxtun told the French general, "I, like my Government, and Countrymen in general, wish Peace with France, and all the World on fair, and honorable Terms, but on any Other we disdain it, Yes Sir, we spurn at the Idea." [29]

Lieutenant John Rodgers was put in command of *L'Insurgente;* he made every effort to repair and refit her for immediate service in the United States Navy. Captain Truxtun enjoined him to "be as frugal as possible in the Outfit" and reminded him that "Character is always concerned in the Expenditure of public Money." But that was not the only reason for frugality. The Captain warned him that "when the United States value the Ship, we shall have to pay perhaps our Proportion of her Outfit." [30] This was a reminder of the fact that the Captain and crew had a pecuniary interest in the prize ship, although she would have to be regularly condemned by an American Court of Admiralty before the prize money was paid.

One day, shortly after the two ships had anchored in Basseterre Roads, Lieutenant of Marines Bartholomew Clinch dined in the great cabin with the Captain. After dinner was cleared away and wine was served tête à tête, the conversation turned to the action and the dispatches concerning it that had been sent home. While they were speculating on how soon the news would reach America and how it would be received, Captain Truxtun called to Edward, his servant, to open the secretary and hand him his letter book, in which he kept copies of all his letters and dispatches. Taking the book, he opened it to February 14th and began reading the report he had written upon his arrival at St. Kitts.

The Lieutenant listened while the Captain named off the first three lieutenants, Rodgers, Cowper, and Sterett. "The Zeal of these 3 Officers in performing their Duty, and complying strictly with my Orders," he continued, "cannot be surpassed, but I must not in Praise of them be silent as to the good Conduct of Mr. Shirley, the Master, and Mr. Archer, the 4th Lieut. . . . I must declare that it is impossible for Officers and Men in any Service to have behaved better, than my People generally did on this Occasion, it must therefore not be understood because I have mentioned the Names of a few of the principal Gentlemen, that those of an inferior Grade in their Stations are less deserving. On the Contrary, to the latter I always feel myself most indebted for their Exertions in the Hour of Battle, as they have generally much less at Stake, than those in higher Stations [for example, a smaller share of prize money], and consequently less Inducement to display their Valor."

He closed by professing his own zeal for "the Good of the Service, and I hope and trust for its Honor too." [31]

Lieutenant Clinch wondered out loud why all the commissioned officers in the ship except him had been specifically named, and why his own name was missing.

In reporting the incident to the Commandant of the Marine Corps (recently formed by an Act of Congress), Clinch said in defense of his own honor and fame: "The question seemed to embarrass him for untill that moment I am well convinced the omission never occured to him. He desired however that I would not feel uneasy . . . his Conduct towards me on every other occasion has been of such a nature as to make me regard esteem & respect him during Life." Moreover, he was convinced that the sword Captain Truxtun had given him as a trophy was "the second best" of the six he had to distribute. [32]

When, after nearly a month of hard work, *L'Insurgente* was materially ready for sea, she still had a crew of only one hundred and twenty-four men. This did not even remotely approach her complement of four hundred, but in order to man her at all, Captain Truxtun had taken out more men than he could conveniently spare from the *Constellation* and other ships of his squadron.

While he wrestled with this latest of his many problems ("He creates his own difficulties by his own zeal," was Secretary Stoddert's opinion), the news of his victory had at last arrived in the United States. [33]

## CHAPTER 34

## TRUXTUN'S VICTORY

℘ . . ℘ . . ℘ . . ℘ . .

THE news of "Truxtun's Victory" trickled slowly into America.[1] By the first of March, 1799, three weeks after the battle, the Secretary of State had "undoubted intelligence" of its occurrence.[2] It was reported in Norfolk about the same time. Captain Truxtun's first account appeared in a Baltimore newspaper on the ninth; it was not until four days later that Secretary Stoddert received the official dispatches.[3] By the middle of March the news was beginning to spread all up and down the eastern seaboard.

President Adams was about to send another trio of peace envoys to France when the news arrived. On the strength of assurances by Talleyrand, French Minister of Foreign Affairs, he was hopeful that the humiliating "XYZ" treatment would not be repeated. The occurrence of this clear-cut naval victory would go a long way toward convincing the French government that the Americans meant business when their diplomats stated that they would meekly submit to no more indignities or depredations. At the same time there were those who, like the Secretary of State, questioned the wisdom of another attempt at diplomacy. "The only negociation compatible with our honor or safety," he said, "is that begun by Truxtun in the capture of L'Insurgente." [4]

Toward the end of April, when the one-year enlistments in the *Constellation* were beginning to run out, Captain Truxtun was forced to return from the West Indies in order to keep faith with his men. Leaving orders for the vessels under his command—by this time four in number—to continue cruising for another month or six weeks, he took his prize ship *L'Insurgente* with him on a last look about the Islands, and the two ships, still keeping company, sailed leisurely northward toward home. On the twentieth of May, they stood triumphantly into Hampton Roads, the prize ship wearing the tricolor of France beneath her American ensign.[5]

Captain Truxtun was welcomed ashore, presented with a handsome address by the "Mayor, Recorder, and Alderman of the Borough of Norfolk," and deluged with invitations to dine at the homes of his many friends and acquaintances.[6] As soon as it could be arranged, a lavish public celebration was held in his honor. The festivities were opened by a parade of volunteer companies of the Fifty-fourth Regiment of militia. A rifle salute of sixteen rounds was fired, after which the citizens gathered in Lindsay's Gardens, adjoining the Hotel, for an elegant dinner. Presumably entertained by a "Concert of Instrumental Music" while they dined and perhaps later on by a "country dance band," the afternoon and evening were spent in an atmosphere of the "utmost harmony and conviviality."[7]

Throughout the country the name and exploits of the gallant Captain became the subject of dinners, toasts, and songs. In Baltimore, a public dinner was given at the Fountain Inn; the Sons of St. George, at another dinner, toasted "Captain Truxtun, and success to the *Constellation*, the *Vanguard* of Columbia's naval glory," and followed the toast with nine cheers. Mr. Fox, at the theatre, sang a song cranked out for the occasion, "Huzza for the *Constellation*."[8] In Philadelphia, the New-Theatre presented "a dramatic sketch interspersed with song and spectacle, called the '*Constellation*, or a Wreath for American Tars.'"[9] In Boston, a day of celebration was declared. The populace was urged to assemble in State Street at one o'clock where, after salutes had been fired from batteries on Copps Hill and Fort Hill and from a ship in the harbor, they could unite in giving three resounding cheers for "Capt. Truxtun, the officers and crew of the *Constellation*, and success to the Wooden Walls of America." The holiday came off as planned, and an additional crowd filled Liberty Square and Washington Street. In Merchant's Row, one could buy "brave Truxtun cock'd & round hats, in the Military and Naval stile"; and in the Federal Street Theatre, the singing of "a new patriotic song written by Mrs. Rowson," called "Truxtun's Victory," was followed by the display of a view of the frigates as they lay in Basseterre Roads after the action.[10]

Fourth of July celebrations, far and wide, sang the praises of brave Truxtun and the United States Navy. In one New Hampshire town, the thirteenth toast was drunk to "Captain Truxtun: our popular Envoy to the French, who was accredited at the first interview"; and in upstate New York, three cheers followed the toast to "Our rising

Navy: may its canvass soon cloud the face of the deep, scourge pirates from our coast, and may its Commanders inherit the firmness and valor of Truxtun." [11]

His fame spread even across the ocean. It was reported that the Merchants and Underwriters at Lloyd's, in the London Exchange, had subscribed five hundred guineas to buy him a handsome sword as a token of their gratitude for ridding the seas of an enemy frigate, thus making safer their West Indian commerce. [12] The trophy from Lloyd's finally arrived nearly two years later; it was not a sword but an extravagantly handsome silver urn encased in a brass bound mahogany box. [13] As soon as he received it, Captain Truxtun sent off his thanks to the gentlemen at Lloyd's, "many of whom," he wrote, "are my old friends and acquaintances."

"This mark of your attention," he continued, "will leave an impression of respect and esteem on my mind, that will only cease with my existence, and will be remembered after by my offspring." [14]

More details of the action were broadcast when the letters of Lieutenant Rodgers and Midshipman Porter were printed in the newspapers; and alas, there was the one by Lieutenant Sterett. Rodgers had only praise for "Our brave commander, who well deserves the appelation"; [15] Porter did not mention Captain Truxtun in this letter, but he remembered him, years later, as a "proud and tyrannical, though gallant naval commander." [16] Sterett unfortunately invited a storm of abuse when he boasted that he had killed Neal Harvey for cowardice, and that "we would put a man to death for even looking pale on board *this* ship."

The Antifederalist press, hostile to the Navy and opposed to war with France in any form, capitalized on Sterett's indiscreet remark. The Philadelphia *Aurora* turned pale immediately. Here, said its editor, was a perfect illustration of the arrogance that always accompanies military command. In the same paper was printed a spurious letter from "Ruby Nose," who requested that "you will have the charity to publish immediately a list of all the shops in the United States, where the best *rouge* is sold, in order that every *pale-faced* subject may purchase a quantity to give their cheeks a courageous appearance." The Federalist newspapers, on the other hand, saw nothing wrong with Sterett's deed. Discipline, they said, must be maintained. [17]

Captain Truxtun failed to notice publicly his subordinate's contumely, which amounted to his condonation of an inexcusable performance.

Nevertheless, Captain Truxtun deserved the praise he enjoyed. While he was remote from the seat of government, he had acted with decision in many matters affecting foreign relations of the United States. He had maintained, and even strengthened, the cordial relations with the British that he had established upon his arrival in St. Kitts. He had kept his little squadron busy with the work he had been sent out to do. He had carried on negotiations with Desforneaux, often resorting to his French-English dictionary in order to answer his notes. These exchanges were accomplished "as you would suppose, with good sense and dignity," according to Timothy Pickering, Secretary of State.[18]

Often he had felt the need of more specific, less ambiguous instructions. Although he wondered at times whether his moves would be approved by his government, he was never inactive; he always did what he considered best for the "Good of the Service" and for the national honor. "I hope," he told Secretary of the Navy Ben Stoddert, "my Zeal in the Cause will entitle me to expect, if not altogether the Approbation, the Protection of the President of the United States."[19]

He received the protection in full measure, and much approbation, too. President Adams, writing to Stoddert, wished that "all the other officers had as much zeal as Truxtun. What has become of them? We hear nothing of any but Decatur, Truxtun, and Murray."[20]

The President thought that Captain Truxtun's admission to Desforneaux, that his orders forbade him to molest unarmed French vessels, was a case of giving away information that "might as well have been concealed." Apparently he did not recognize that Captain Truxtun expected this admission to influence Desforneaux's future policy with regard to American merchantmen. However, the President instructed Secretary Stoddert to use the utmost tact in dealing with matters affecting his zeal. "If you correct Truxtun's ardor a little, as you ought to do," he wrote, "I pray you to do it very gently and with great delicacy. I would not have it damped for the world."[21]

Stoddert, past master of the useful art of flattery, wrote Captain Truxtun a congratulatory letter as soon as he heard of his taking *L'Insurgente*. He assured him of the President's "high approbation of the whole of your able and judicious conduct in the West Indies," and then added, "I must however add, that he observes . . . indeed all others I have heard speak on the subject, join in the observation, that this is nothing but what we expected from Truxtun." [22]

When first he learned that Captain Truxtun had returned to America, the President had told Secretary Stoddert, "Capt. Truxtun has deserved well of his country and will as he ought, have their thanks, as well as yours and mine. But I should have been much easier on account of the safety of our commerce, if he had remained longer in the West Indies." But if he had stayed longer, he would have broken faith with his men, who had enlisted only for one year. Furthermore, American seamen were the most precious commodity in the West Indies. He had been unable completely to man *L'Insurgente,* and his squadron was never large enough to effect a rotation of crews in homeward bound vessels. Nevertheless, both Adams and Stoddert had hoped that he would find a way to resolve all difficulties.[23] While serving a government that wished to carry on a war without declaring war and while attending to instructions that were equivocal and in constant need of clarification, Captain Truxtun made many difficult decisions. It is small wonder that he was unable always to divine what the President and the Secretary of the Navy would have him do every time a choice had to be made.

The *Constellation*'s crew was discharged shortly after her arrival in American waters. To men who would enlist for another year, Captain Truxtun gave—according to one of those who did—a beaver hat, a black silk handkerchief, two months' pay in advance, and two weeks liberty on shore.[24] To every man he gave a prize ticket, which entitled him to his share of prize money when—and only when—the prize had been legally condemned and the money had been delivered to the prize agent, who would redeem the tickets.

It was an intricate business, this settlement for a prize taken by a ship of war. Officers and crew received one-half the value of a prize if it was inferior to its captors; if the prize was adjudged superior, then it became the sole property of those who took it. And there were exceptions to this rule. If other naval vessels were in sight when a capture was made, all crews shared the prize money, dividing it according to the number of guns and men on board each vessel. If a prize was taken by a vessel operating in a squadron, the commodore of the squadron was entitled to a share, and the captain who took the prize had his share reduced accordingly. This last regulation made some junior captains reluctant to fall in with a commodore, and it was the source of much litigation. In order to recover his (commodore's) share of one prize, Captain Truxtun finally had to sue a subordinate captain who claimed he had not yet joined his squadron when the prize was taken; the legal contest dragged on for years.[25]

Soon after he took *L'Insurgente,* Captain Truxtun appointed as prize agent Henry Benbridge, who had married his eldest daughter. Benbridge, son of a Philadelphia portrait painter, was, in Charles Biddle's estimation, "a very good young man, . . . sober and industrious," but "not prudent." His father-in-law had set him up in the grocery business with a capital of some ten thousand dollars. Without Captain Truxtun's knowledge, the young man's capital had shrunk most alarmingly in the space of less than three years. When Benbridge received the bills of exchange for prize cargoes that had been sold in the West Indies, he foolishly used them to bolster his tottering credit.[26]

When he finally realized that he was facing serious trouble, he called on Charles Biddle for advice. Biddle immediately saw that the prize agency would become hopelessly, entangled in Benbridge's other affairs if his business failed, and that the prize money might never be paid to those who had earned it. Always solicitous for his friend Truxtun's welfare, he wrote him a letter which the Captain received in Norfolk.

"I am the most unfortunate man alive," was the Captain's immediate reaction; "every attempt even, to serve a child, turns out to my disadvantage." He was aware of the consternation that would arise if the prize tickets were not paid off, and he implored Biddle to take over the agency. "I pray you," he wrote, "not to suffer him to ruin me . . . and oblige me to resign my station besides. . . . That will be a pretty business." [27] Biddle, a little reluctantly, accepted the job.

*L'Insurgente* was regularly condemned by a Court of Admiralty sitting in Norfolk. When it came to the decision as to whether she was superior or inferior to the *Constellation,* Lieutenant Rodgers, who commanded the prize ship, was called to testify. He knew well the details of both ships. The *Constellation,* mounting twenty-eight 24-pounders and ten 12-pounders, was sailed by 316 men. *L'Insurgente* had twenty-four 12-pounders in the main battery, and four

36-pounders, two 24-pounders, two long eighteens, and eight 6-pounders on quarter-deck and forecastle, for a total of forty guns; she had a crew of 409 men.[28] The American's battery could hurl a broadside of nearly four hundred pounds, while that of her antagonist was somewhat less than three hundred pounds. There was really little question about which ship had the material advantage; the *Constellation* was physically the larger ship, and her main battery of 24-pounders was unquestionably superior to the French battery of 12-pounders. Before he had talked himself into his now firm conviction that he had vanquished a superior foe, Captain Truxtun had tacitly admitted that the French frigate was nominally inferior to his ship.[29] However, Lieutenant Rodgers in court stated the bare facts, and because he was not pressed to do so, he did not elaborate. Forty guns to thirty-eight, he said; 409 men to 316.[30] Thereupon the Court decreed that *L'Insurgente* was the stronger ship.

"I cannot but think," Secretary Ben Stoddert told Captain Truxtun when he heard the Court's decree, "on a full consideration of all circumstances, the opinion of the Court erroneous." [31] Moreover, he thought that the estimate of the prize's value—$120,000—that had been made by a board of six men convened by William Pennock, the Norfolk Navy Agent, was entirely too high.[32] Therefore he called on Joshua Humphreys, who, without ever leaving Philadelphia, produced an estimate of $84,500, which was much more to the Secretary's liking.[33] Declaring his confidence that a higher court would reverse the decree, and at the same time proclaiming his aversion to starting a legal contest between the United States and the crew of a United States ship, he tactfully but very firmly offered Captain Truxtun and his crew $84,500, practically on a take-it-or-leave-it basis.[34]

After sailing the *Constellation* round to New York at the end of June, 1799, to complete her refitting, recruiting, and provisioning, and after visiting his family for the first time in over a year and a half, Captain Truxtun hurried down to Philadelphia.[35] Finding the Secretary adamant in his decision and realizing that his reasoning was probably correct even though it was unnecessarily arbitrary, he accepted the $84,500 on behalf of his crew.

The Captain's share of the prize was three-twentieths, over $12,000; the four sea lieutenants and the sailing master each received about $1,600; the other officers received lesser shares; lowest on the scale, seamen and marines were entitled to $106.80 each.[36] Every share was reduced below its nominal value because Biddle, as prize agent, received five per cent of the whole. However, his acquisitive friend Truxtun claimed half of this commission for the trouble he was put to in settling the accounts of the business.[37] This was after Captain Truxtun had told William Pennock, who had assembled the board to value his prize: "Not one Dollar of Commission will you or any one else receive on that Prize. . . . You are capital Fellows for Commissions at Norfolk; let me ask you, if you dont dream of Commissions every Night. . . . no Commission, No, No, on *L'Insurgente*." [38]

Most of the officers drew their shares with no difficulty, but relatively few of the seamen and marines received what they were entitled to. According to Biddle, nineteen out of every twenty sold their shares to speculators or friends for a mere trifle, some for not more than ten dollars. Some lost their tickets, and others never made the journey to Philadelphia to collect their money.

With his ship anchored in New York harbor, Captain Truxtun supervised the complete replacement of her armament with guns that he had decided would be more suitable. He had been forced, when approaching *L'Insurgente,* to run under the enemy's lee in order to keep his gun deck dry, so far did the stiff breeze heel his ship over. The main battery 24-pounders, being too heavy and thus making the ship tender, were supplanted by eighteens; on the quarter-deck, he replaced the long twelves with 32-pounder carronades mounted on sliding carriages.[39] Effectively he lowered the center of gravity of the ship without materially changing the weight of her broadside.

Many of the details of provisioning he left to his Purser with the admonishment to carry out his general orders without delay. "I say without Delay," he said, "for naval Agents often love to take their time, and you have no Aversion to your Bed of a Morning." [40]

While the work went forward in his ship, he lived in New York, taking up lodgings at Mrs. Gallop's boarding-house in Cortlandt Street, across town from the Tontine Coffee House.[41] He frequented the Tontine, a commodious brick building in Wall Street; he was often seen in the public room where the shipping books were kept, and which served gentlemen and merchants as a stock exchange.[42] On Thursday, the twenty-fifth of July, he attended a dinner given in his honor by the Washington Troop and Rifle Company.[43] He greatly admired the painting—on silk—of his renowned action, which was displayed at the head of the table, and also "two other figuers suitable on such a complimentary occasion" at the other end of the table.[44]

On the following Tuesday, the Chamber of Commerce and two insurance companies gave him another sumptuous dinner at the Tontine. In spite of the hot weather, the Mayor and a large company of gentlemen attended. The cosmopolitan diplomat, Gouverneur Morris, and Alexander Hamilton were there; the dinner was presided over by the President of the Chamber of Commerce, John Murray, a wealthy and venerable Quaker merchant; indeed, according to the guest of honor, "every man of distinction, in the City" was present.[45]

These were pleasant days for Captain Truxtun. However, his ship was almost ready for sea, and he was eager to be out once more. Planning to visit his family again for a day or two, he told his friend Biddle that he would have "one frolic more in Jersey before I embark, and then Sir for another *Insurgente* if they please to come in the way of the *Constellation*." [46]

Already riding the crest of a wave of fame that had greatly increased the popularity of the Navy at home and established it abroad as a power to be reckoned with, he was about to go out in search of new laurels when suddenly—precipitously—he made a decision that threatened to end his whole naval career.

On the first day of August, 1799, he resigned his commission as a captain in the United States Navy.

CHAPTER 35

TALBOT, DALE, AND TRUXTUN

&⁀ﾠ . . &⁀ﾠ . . &⁀ﾠ . . &⁀ﾠ . .

IT HAD been nearly a year since Secretary Ben Stoddert had told President Adams that a decision on the ranking of Talbot, Dale, and

Truxtun would shortly be needed. Finally the President had determined the ranking in that order—Talbot, Dale, and Truxtun—and exactly as Stoddert had predicted, Truxtun had instantly resigned. Stoddert, in conveying the President's decision to Captain Truxtun, told him to "Take at least one day to consider before you answer this Letter." [1]

Captain Truxtun took no day to consider. In an unused room of his mind, a letter of resignation, fully composed, had been gathering dust for a year or more. It took only a glance at Stoddert's letter to bring all the full round phrases expressing pain and indignation together; in an instant they were crowding to get out, to be put down on paper, to be scrawled out in immoderate haste in order to be finished in time for return of the post.

President John Adams, who was accused by responsible Federalists of "shifting conduct . . . indiscretion, vanity, and jealousy," [2] and of governing "by fits and starts—without the advice of friends around him . . . in order to be characterised as an independent man," [3] had certainly lived up to his critics' estimates in handling this affair of Talbot, Dale, and Truxtun.

In 1794, when the first captains were appointed, Silas Talbot had ranked ahead of Richard Dale, and Dale ahead of Truxtun. Captain Truxtun was without any doubt or question junior to Captain Talbot then  But the building of three of the frigates was halted, and Captains Dale and Talbot were returned to private life. Later, when the first commissions were signed by President Washington, Captain Truxtun's bore the notation "No. 3." He was the third ranking captain of those still active, junior only to Barry and Nicholson.

When, in 1798, Adams asked Talbot and Dale to return to the Navy, he sent their appointments to the Senate for approval.[4] This was as though they had never served at all.

Ben Stoddert, looking at the affair from this angle, had decided that Captain Truxtun's claim to rank ahead of Talbot and Dale was justified, and his opinion was seconded by those of the Secretaries of State, War, and Treasury.[5] President Adams' cabinet, then, had agreed on an answer to the question. But Adams chose to be "an independent man."

Stoddert had already informed Captain Truxtun of his own opinion. "My register stands," he wrote, "Barry—Truxtun—Talbot &c. Nicholson is well content to remain on shore [as superintendent of

Boston Navy Yard] where I think he will certainly remain, as long as I remain in Office." [6] For two years now, ever since he had received his commission, Captain Truxtun had believed that he was indeed "No. 3." Now he had learned otherwise. Therefore, he could see no other course to follow, compatible with his honor, except the one he had immediately chosen.

John Adams was summering, as he always did, in Braintree, ten miles from Boston, when Captain Talbot was ordered to relieve Captain Nicholson as commander of the *Constitution*. Stoddert sent to Adams, in Braintree, a commission for Captain Talbot, since none had been issued to him previously, and the President forwarded it to him with "as handsome a letter from myself as I could pen." [7]

Captain Talbot had the President just where he wanted him. He was close at hand, and the President was anxious to get the *Constitution* to sea again. Talbot, deciding to force the issue, returned his commission to Adams because he had not been restored to his original rank.

Soon he received another letter from the President, asking him to come down to Braintree. Adams started out with the admission that "I know not the facts at present, with precision enough to decide between your pretensions and those of Captain Truxtun." From that statement he went on to a promise. "If you would accept the commission," he wrote, "altered so as to leave the question of rank undecided, to be determined hereafter by a council of officers, this shall be done." And finally came the invitation: "It will be impossible for me to arrange any thing without a personal conference with you." [8]

Coming down in his boat, Captain Talbot bearded the "independent man" at his home. He refused to accept the commission, altered as Adams suggested. He said he would gladly resign if the President "from political or any other motives whatever" wanted Truxtun to remain in service. He freely granted that Captain Truxtun had much merit, but then perhaps he—Talbot—had "some small share also." Admittedly, Truxtun had captured a frigate "of nearly his own force," for which he had received great praise. "I have done some things," he continued, "that were, perhaps, thought at the time equally clever, and if the rules of delicacy would allow a detail of them, they might easily be brought to view, and I should glory in the comparison." [9]

At some time during the interview his sense of delicacy must have failed him, because from none other could Adams have heard so complete a recital of his prowess on land and sea.

Now, apparently, the President had the facts with precision enough. "My resolution is irrevocable," he soon wrote to Secretary Stoddert, "that Talbot shall go in the *Constitution*. All things are settled." He continued, "In point of merit & services there is not an officer in our Navy, who can bear any comparison with Talbot, as I will ere long convince you." [10]

Three days later he sent off a very long letter designed to convince Stoddert that his decision to give Talbot rank over Truxtun was a just one, the "result of mature deliberation" and an "impartial consideration of the whole subject." Dale was never once mentioned, no doubt because he was not importuning the President at the moment. He was off on another private China voyage.

Adams based his argument, as he should, on the fact that Talbot had at one time ranked above Truxtun, observing that "the suspension of his pay and subsistence was no deprivation of his office, any more than shaking off the apples is cutting down the tree." But he was not content to leave it at that, with the apples shaken off. He composed a laudatory essay on Talbot's services during the Revolution, when he was successively a captain, major, and lieutenant-colonel in the Continental Army, commanded a sloop fitted out by General Gates, and finally received as reward a captain's commission in the Continental Navy, although no Navy vessel was ever provided for him to command. "His services, last war," Adams wrote, "far outweigh all the services which were ever performed by Truxtun, to the United States, during his whole life. . . . Truxtun is a new man in the service of the United States. Talbot has served them very long."

Still, he hoped Captain Truxtun would not resign. "I respect, I esteem, and, especially since his late glorious action, I love the man," he wrote. [11]

This contention over rank was the result of a series of errors, starting with that of President Washington's making no provision for the displaced captains when he issued the commissions in 1797, and ending with President Adams' unpardonable indiscretion of settling the issue with the advice and counsel of only one of the interested parties, after ignoring the question until the necessity for getting a ship to sea had forced him to settle it under pressure. The question might have been settled, as both Adams and Secretary Stoddert suggested, by a board of officers, and neither man would have had room for complaint. No matter. The debate was ended; the President had spoken.

On board the *Constellation*, the officers prepared a glowing tribute to their departing Captain. It began with "a degree of regret scarcely to be conveyed in words," continued with "grateful thanks for the kind & Paternal Care you have uniformly exercised towards us," and concluded with "fervent & Cordial Wishes for Your Prosperity here & hereafter." [12]

Next day, Captain Truxtun replied in a similar vein. He was sure that no greater harmony could have prevailed in any ship than that which he had enjoyed in his. Long might this "band of brothers," cultivating good order and a patriotic spirit, continue to do its duty, "as I have seen you like brave Americans do it before."

"Farewell." [13]

Talk of Truxtun's resignation soon replaced that of Truxtun's victory. In Hampton Roads, Captain Barry was entertaining some gentlemen from Norfolk at dinner on board the *United States* when word of the resignation was brought by a pilot boat that had just arrived from Philadelphia; it also brought orders for Captain Samuel Barron to repair immediately to New York, in order to take command of the *Constellation*. "Our pleasure," said one of the guests, "was in a great measure destroy'd." Another said, "Not a countenance was seen, in which sorrow & dejection were not strongly depicted." Several days later, one of Captain Truxtun's friends in Norfolk told him, "I have not recovered my Spirits yet." [14]

On the other hand, a Lieutenant of Marines who was stationed in Norfolk, wrote to his Commandant, "I am sorry to hear of the resagnation of Capt. Truxtun but see in todays paper he will act as his own Trumpeter." [15]

Thomas Truxtun, who at forty-four was a private citizen once more, was not satisfied with being merely a trumpeter. He might more aptly have been likened to a full brass band.

He had retired to "Pleasant View," his home in Perth Amboy, opposite the onetime Royal Governor's mansion. His big house was approached through a long avenue of Lombardy poplars; it was surrounded by a generous ten acres of ground, which sloped toward the east, down to the water's edge.[16] From his front porch he could look beyond the lower tip of Staten Island out across Raritan Bay; on a clear day he could see the lighthouse fifteen miles distant on Sandy Hook, and an occasional sail coming into New York's lower bay. Perth Amboy, only a few hours' ride from New York, was a quiet town where, according to Captain Truxtun, "Sickness is scarcely known," where "a Physician cannot get Bread by the Calls of Patients." Less than half a mile from the Court House was a mineral spring that had proved efficacious for some complaints. Added to his pleasure at being with Mary and his "little Brats" were the diversions of an "admirable Society" of "worthy Gentlemen, . . . charming Girls, and elegant Ladies." To one thirsting less after glory and fame, this would have been a fine place to put aside the cares and responsibilities of a command at sea, to sip the finest old Madeira in company with John Angus, retired merchant shipmaster, and to pass the time of day with the Mayor and other worthy gentlemen.[17] However, he found little time for anything besides assuaging his wounded feelings by publishing "to the World" his side of the story of his resignation.

"I have received a volume of letters," he told a friend in New York, "making inquiry as to the cause" of the resignation. Rather than answer each letter individually, he sent out copies of a letter he had written to William Pennock in Norfolk. Inevitably, the letter soon appeared in the public prints. Here was the whole affair laid out in tedious detail. Parading "honor" and "candor" and "injustice," even quoting Ben Stoddert's words "My register stands, Barry—Truxtun—Talbot," he told his side of the story.[18] Pennock and his other friends in Norfolk were sorry to see the letter in print, because they had hoped there might be some way left to reconcile differences and to get him back into the Navy. A captious letter like this, they felt, could do no good.

Ben Stoddert, taking no official notice of the trumpeting, still tried to get him to change his mind. He tried to lure him out to sea by telling him about a French frigate someone had sighted that was probably steering for the American coast. Captain Truxtun struck at this bait and agreed to go out if Captain Barron did not immediately come to relieve him; but Barron arrived promptly, and matters remained as they were.[19]

Charles Biddle, in Philadelphia, had a dozen carpenters hard at work on his house in Islington Lane, well out of reach of the dreaded fever that had again attacked the city. He and his family were living there, even though they had but three habitable rooms. No outside doors were yet hung, and the wind whistled through the corridors.

One day, around the first of September, 1799, rain was pouring down in steady streams. Biddle heard a familiar voice at his gate, demanding to know his whereabouts. There, drawn up in a carriage, was Captain Truxtun. He had disembarked from the stage at Frankford and in a hackney had come to call on his good friend. He was, he explained, on his way to Mount Vernon. The General, he continued, had asked him to come down.

Torn up as his home was, still Biddle invited him to wait out the storm under his roof. He made up a bed for him in the parlor, and there the Captain slept for three or four nights. At length, when the weather improved, Biddle hitched up his carriage and took his friend as far as Naaman's Creek, almost half a day's ride, where he embarked again in the stage for Mount Vernon.[20]

General Washington had returned to Mount Vernon two years before, after his second term as President. He was at last retired, as much as a great public figure could ever retire. He no longer had to spend all of his time on the national business but he was, as he described it, continually importuned by a procession of "Applicants, recommenders of applicants, seekers of information with their servants and horses . . . to aid in the consumption of my forage, and what to me is more valuable, my time." [21] Situated as he was, nine miles from the nearest inn, he felt obliged to house and feed his callers for a night or for a few days, perhaps for a week. In spite of all this, he had taken the trouble to invite Captain Truxtun to visit him. The General was always a good friend of the Navy. He understood the important part it could play in increasing the stature of the United States among the nations of the world. In order to act its role effectively, it needed men of spirit, men with zeal, audacious men, brave men, men who could not rest as long as the ocean held out a promise of honor and glory—men like Captain Truxtun.

On Thursday, the twelfth of September, 1799, Captain Truxtun dined at Mount Vernon.[22] He ate and drank with the great General and looked with him down the long reaches of the Potomac River. For a few hours at least, he was under the spell of an incomparable presence. Although no record survives to witness the meeting, it is possible that this was another important turning point in his life.

After he returned to Perth Amboy it was not long until the weeks of inactivity began to pall. "I must confess," he soon told Charles Biddle, "that it mortify's me to be Idle, in a moment like the present, when every mind and every hand should be employed, to save our country." [23] Perhaps the seed of that idea was sown by the master of Mount Vernon, who may have made the observation that even though he himself was an old man, "far advanced into the vale of life," he stood ready to serve his Country whenever and wherever his help might be needed.[24]

"I want," continued Captain Truxtun, "I want to have another touch at these Frenchmen." [25]

From Trenton, again the temporary seat of government, came at last a straw for his grasping. Secretary Ben Stoddert told him his resignation had never been formally accepted. Would he care to reconsider? This was an embarrassing question. Of course he would like to reconsider his decision, but could he do so without some loss of face, some degradation of his personal honor? That was the problem. He had already taken his stand, and it ill became a gentleman to shift his ground when he fancied that his elaborately conceived honor was threatened. Gentlemen fought duels rather than admit to the error of an impulsive action or a thoughtless word.

Very circumspectly, he sounded the Secretary to learn how he might escape from the corner into which his overweening pride had forced him. He asked his friend Biddle to "take a ride to Trenton" —a day's journey from Philadelphia—to see Stoddert and to find out what compromise might be reached. If both commissions—his and Talbot's—were "of same date, and neither to be superior, and never to act together, but in some case of evident necessity," then perhaps he could be persuaded to serve again.[26]

Charles Biddle, happy to oblige him because he thought "it would be a loss to the Navy for Truxtun to leave it," rode off to Trenton in company with his friend General James Wilkinson, who was also a friend of Captain Truxtun. Together they called on Stoddert. Wilkinson was a fluent talker; Biddle was forever the politician. "Mr. Stoddert made some difficulty," Biddle later recalled, "on account of the other captains, who he thought would resign." Perhaps they would, was the retort, but Biddle did not think it likely. "Although most of them were very brave men," he said, "as a naval officer none of them were equal to Truxtun."[27]

And so, when the nights were beginning to hint of frost and splashes of brilliant color appeared on New Jersey hillsides, General Wilkinson rode eastward from Trenton across Middlesex County toward "Pleasant View." The handsome general, who had learned his soldiering—and more besides—from Benedict Arnold, and who at the moment was looking for a suitable conveyance to take him to New Orleans, carried Captain Truxtun's commission and another letter from Stoddert.

The advice of his friends at last had its effect on the headstrong Captain. He accepted the commission this time with only a single proviso. "Talbot's ever having a controul over me," he said, "is out of the question. It must be clearly understood, that he is never to attempt it—and then I accept."[28]

Secretary Stoddert assured him that his wishes would be respected as far as possible. Captain Talbot would have the Santo Domingo station, and since Captain Barry was expected to take the new peace envoys to France, Captain Truxtun would have the whole of the Windward Islands—after General Wilkinson had been delivered to New Orleans. There he would be the commodore of a sizable squadron; there he could improve on Barry's indifferent performance of the winter before.[29]

To still the clamor that immediately arose among the captains who were junior to Truxtun before he resigned and who thought that he should now, having once resigned, take his place at the very end of the list, Stoddert explained that his resignation had never been accepted by the President and that his commission had lain in the Navy Office waiting merely for the opportunitiy to return it to him. The reaction of one junior captain, Stephen Decatur the elder, who had been a privateer captain during the Revolution, was relayed to Captain Truxtun by his friend Biddle as an idle bit of gossip, or perhaps—there was a waggish streak in the Captain's friend—as a juicy morsel of bait.

"You write me that Decature is reconciled to my return to service," was the instant reply; "Why Dam his impudence, for dareing to make an observation—this is all that is necessary for me to say on that subject."[30]

To get to sea once more in the *Constellation* was now Captain Truxtun's obsession. He inquired for a vessel about to sail for Norfolk, where his ship lay. Finding none, he decided to go overland, and then at the last moment a likely sloop sailed by, and in that he took passage.[31] Meanwhile, General Wilkinson found another conveyance to New Orleans.

When he climbed aboard his own ship in Hampton Roads, Captain Truxtun's face still had a slight greenish cast as a result of a late November storm off the Atlantic coast, but he soon shook that off and was back in the routine that had long since become an integral part of his existence.[32]

While he prepared his ship for departure, he may well have repeated the address he had made to his crew when last he was in these roads. "On the ocean is our field to reap fresh laurels," he had said; "let the capstan, then, be well manned, trip cheerfully our anchor, spread the sails, give three cheers, and away to hunt up our enemies, as we have done before, until we find them." [33]

After a maddening wait for a favorable wind, the *Constellation*, on the day before Christmas, 1799, sailed once more out through the door to the ocean. On Christmas day, the crew was busy shaking down the ship for the passage to St. Kitts; the anchor cables were unbent and the anchors were stowed for sea; the boatswain, carpenter, and sailmaker were all busily employed at their trades; and the Captain was rejoicing over smooth waters and pleasant weather, "delightfull for the Season." [34]

CHAPTER 36

## LA VENGEANCE

℘ . . ℘ . . ℘ . . ℘ . .

IN THE roadstead of Basseterre, St. Kitts, Captain Truxtun found five American men-of-war lying peacefully at anchor. Three frigates and two brigs, these were five of the eight vessels that had been ordered to put themselves under his command.

It was a respectable force, but of little use as long as it remained at anchor. This was what had irked Secretary Ben Stoddert so very much. The orders he wrote for his squadron commanders repeatedly stressed his injunction to keep all vessels "constantly cruising." In no other way could the enemy be met and taken. Not that he wanted the vessels to go out as a squadron: the French privateers nearly always cruised alone, so the protection afforded by cruising together was unnecessary. Besides, six or eight vessels cruising alone could cover six or eight times as much territory as a squadron sailing snugly together. "Nothing fills the President with more disgust," Stoddert had written, than "Three or four vessels sailing in company when there is no prospect of meeting an Enemy equal to the smallest of them." [1]

The *Constellation* anchored in the roadstead as the sun was going down. Early the next morning, Captain Truxtun dispatched the first of his vessels. Within a week, he had sent all of his squadron off on independent cruises. And while he prodded the other vessels out of the roadstead, he hurried to get his own ship again ready for sea. He had heard that there was another French frigate and a corvette at Guadeloupe.[2] Unloading some lumber from the orlop deck, down in the bowels of the ship, one of the seamen heard Captain Truxtun tell the carpenter to have the space cleared out completely and not to leave behind so much as a single rope yarn, because, within a week from that day, he was determined to have five hundred prisoners aboard.[3]

Captain Truxtun was down in the West Indies for "another touch at these Frenchmen," and he was impatient to be out. His ship was remarkably healthy; there were only ten men on the surgeon's list, and six of those were "under Venereal complaints, of long standing." [4] He felt sure that his crew was ready to do battle with any French vessel he might find. After scarcely more than a week in port, he laid down his course toward the latest reported position of the largest enemy ship in the Islands.

Early Saturday morning, February 1, 1800, the *Constellation* was beating up under Guadeloupe, keeping her tacks on board as she worked her way against the unceasing breeze that swept up from the southeast. While she was yet a few leagues from the island, a sail was sighted far to the south, standing westward.[5] As she bore away to take a closer look at the stranger—a large ship, probably a British frigate from Martinique—Captain Truxtun ordered up English colors to entice the ship to come halfway to speak him. For him to run down in pursuit of the stranger was to abandon, for the time being, his chosen cruising grounds, where he supposed that the French were lurking. To regain the lost ground would take many more hours of laborious beating. But the stranger did not come halfway. She made no sign of recognition, threw out no signals. Instead, she blossomed forth with studdingsails and every rag of canvas that could be set. It was plain that she did not wish to speak anyone.

After examining the stranger more carefully through his long glass, Captain Truxtun decided finally that she was a heavy French frigate, mounting perhaps fifty guns or more. The pursuit began at once. Although he gained rapidly throughout the morning, his advantage was threatened when the wind fell light and the chase held way with him. For a brief moment, the question of whether he could overhaul the enemy before nightfall must have entered his head. He was running his own ship to leeward at a great rate. If he could not come up with the other ship at all, he would have lost a couple of days' hunting under Guadeloupe. Only for an instant was the question entertained, however, for here was a ship even larger than *L'Insurgente,* which he had captured a year before. A ship in sight was worth a whole harborful of ships lying secure under the guns of a French fort.

The drum had long since beat to quarters; his ship was cleared for action almost as soon as the chase began. The yards were slung with chains, replacing ropes that might be carried away by a lucky shot; and the running rigging was reinforced with stopper ropes as a further precaution. The *Constellation,* pressed on at last by a freshening wind, began to gain way once more.

Captain Truxtun had his every sail set, but he prudently kept bag reefs in his topsails in order to give him better control of his ship should the chase, which was now running dead away, suddenly haul up on the wind and prepare to give battle. "But this," he observed, "did not prove to be her commanders intention." [6]

Through the long afternoon, the pursuit continued, and on into the evening hours. For twelve hours the crew stood at quarters. "Oh! sir," wrote an observer aboard the *Constellation,* "it is not for my feeble pen to describe the ardor of Columbia's sons of the waves on this great and solemn occasion, seated among the engines of death, some at their gambols, others combing out their hair like Spartan sons of old." [7]

As daylight dwindled, the distance between the ships grew shorter. About eight o'clock, Captain Truxtun ordered the American colors hoisted, the candles in the battle lanterns lighted, and the great speaking trumpet rigged at the lee gangway. Standing at the trumpet, the gallant Captain prepared to demand the surrender of the French frigate. At that moment, a puff of smoke from the enemy's deck, followed by the concussive report of an eighteen pounder, signaled the beginning of the action. The enemy, upon finding that the American ship was gaining rapidly, had hauled two great guns aft to fire through stern ports. With these stern chasers, the French captain hoped to discourage his adversary before her battery could be brought to bear.

The division commanders on the gun deck, Andrew Sterett, Ambrose Shirley, and Samuel Brooks, first, second, and third lieutenants respectively, all of them veterans of the battle with *L'Insurgente,* already had their orders; but Captain Truxtun sent one of his midshipmen messengers to repeat his instructions to the lieutenants. Henry Vandyke, unquestionably impressed by his Captain's unhurried demeanor, carried the word forward to Lieutenant Sterett's division and then brought it back through the length of the ship. The orders were "not to throw away a single charge of powder and shot, but to take good aim, and fire directly into the Hull of the enemy, and load principally with two round shot, and now & then with a Round Shot and Stand of Grape . . . to Encourage the Men, at their Quarters, to cause or suffer no noise or confusion whatever; but to load and fire as fast as possible, when it could be done with certain effect." [8]

With the new and lighter guns on her gun deck, the *Constellation* was much stiffer than she had been the year before. There was no need now to run under the enemy's lee, in order to keep her gun ports dry. Therefore, she gained and held the weather gauge as she drew up swiftly on the weather quarter of her harried opponent.

Captain Truxtun, cool as ever a man could be, waited now for the battle to unfold. He and his little retinue—sailing master, marine lieutenant, and midshipmen messengers—were planted on the quarter-deck. Quietly, with full confidence in his ship and men, he took into battle as smart a ship as ever spread a sail.

When the space between ships had been closed to less than half-range of the great guns, perhaps three hundred yards, Lieutenant Sterett's larboard bow gun was brought to bear, and the Frenchman's defiance, offered by his stern chasers, was returned in kind. As the *Constellation* still gained, other guns of the larboard battery were soon brought to bear, and acrid smoke belched forth from their muzzles all down the line. Cannon balls crashed into the enemy between wind and water, some of them going clear through the hull and out the other side.[9]

The enemy kept up a furious fire for half an hour. Firing at the rigging and firing without aiming, the French battery made a wonderful great noise. The French captain, impressed by the clamor in his own ship, thought that the *Constellation*'s fire was but badly sustained. Captain Truxtun's order "not to throw away a single charge of powder and shot" was completely foreign to his understanding.

Enemy shot carried away the *Constellation*'s head sails early in the action. Falling away for a few moments to repair the damage, Captain Truxtun could see—now by moonlight—his adversary crowding on all sail again, even rigging out studdingsails, trying again to escape. He drew up again and resumed the fight. For another three hours or more, the action was general, with the two ships running almost board and board. The *Constellation* kept up a continuous fire from her main battery; the carronades on the quarter-deck were well served; the howitzers in the tops added to the din; and the marines sent along a well-directed rain of musket balls. Twice, at least, Captain Truxtun attempted to maneuver his ship into a raking position, once ahead and once astern of the enemy, but each time the French captain anticipated his move and was able to avoid being raked. When he saw the American's flying jib-boom run afoul of his mizzen shrouds, the Frenchman thought he was about to be boarded. He shouted a command to repel boarders, and his crew swarmed up onto the quarter-deck. It was at this juncture that the Americans, taking advantage of the opportunity, let fly a shower of grape shot.[10] Through it all, as the tense minutes lengthened into hours, Captain Truxtun fought his ship with the audacity of one who knows not the meaning of personal fear. Here, indeed, was a tradition-maker at work. No extravagant poses (although he never for a moment forgot his role as "petty tyrant"), no histrionics, no ringing phrases of derring-do: his was tradition of a different sort. He pressed home the attack with coolness and deliberation born of complete control of and confidence in his ship and his crew.

Aboard the French frigate, the carnage was great. Three gun ports were blasted into one. A cannon ball knocked the captain's speaking trumpet out of his hand and took off the arm of a lieutenant nearby.[11] Men by the score were writhing on decks slippery with blood or lying deathly still in their last contorted postures.

Nor were the decks of the *Constellation* free of pools of blood turned black by the moon's pale light. Surgeon Isaac Henry, at his station far below in the cock-pit, was hard at the gruesome work of patching shattered bodies and of trying to relieve the last agonies of those already beyond help. A seaman standing near the pumps amidships lost his right arm and had his entrails laid bare by a cannon ball. John Baptist, a boy, had his leg shot off. Arms and legs were broken; musket balls pierced hands and necks and thighs and buttocks. In all, the surgeon amputated six limbs and dressed a number of very severe flesh wounds.[12]

As the moon dipped low on the western sea rim, after nearly five hours of fierce and almost constant action, the enemy's fire was completely silenced. Twice, perhaps three times, her captain had struck her flag and cried for quarter. But the action had been too intense. His cries had gone unheard and the battle had continued.[13] When at last she sheered off to gain respite from the unflagging American fire, it was within a few minutes of one o'clock.

The *Constellation* was still close under the enemy's weather quarter, less than a half pistol-shot away. Fifth Lieutenant Robinson, commanding a division on the quarter-deck, reported to Captain Truxtun, who stood nearby. "I cannot, sir," he said, "bring the carronades to bear."

"Never mind, Robinson," the Captain replied, "she is all our own, we have nothing to do but get alongside of her." [14]

But the *Constellation* never quite got alongside her antagonist.

While he was trying to trim his shattered sails, news of the most alarming sort reached the Captain. The mainmast was in danger of going over the side at any moment. The towering pole, a hundred and fifty feet high and nearly three feet in diameter at the deck, was normally supported by shrouds, backstays, and forestays. Now it was steadied by nothing at all above the main deck; every stay and shroud had been shot away. Captain Truxtun acted instantly. He tried first to rig stoppers, rejoining the separated rope ends; but there were almost no rope ends long enough to be joined. He then ordered the men up from the gun deck, planning to use all hands in getting up temporary stays.

Within a few minutes, his exertions proved to be in vain. The great stick was wracked by the rolling of the ship; with a final shattering report, it broke off just above the deck, taking full charge for a few terrifying seconds until it was thrown clear of the ship into the water alongside.

Overboard with the mast went the topmen. Midshipman James Jarvis, commanding in the maintop, had been warned by one of his men that the mast would soon give way. Captain Truxtun journalized the incident. "He had already so much of the principle of an officer engrafted on his mind," he wrote, "not to leave his Quarters on any account, that he told the men if the mast went, they must go with it, which was the case, and only one of them were saved." [15]

It was two o'clock before the wreckage was all cleared away, and by that time the moon was down. Limping badly, the *Constellation* was again ready to meet the enemy, but the enemy was nowhere in sight. The Frenchman's pumps had been going when last seen; it was evident, even in the gloom, that the hull had been badly hurt; and masts and spars were so badly shattered that only a single sail —the mizzen topsail—could be spread.[16] It was only reasonable to assume that the enemy had been sunk.

Except for keeping a sharp lookout, there was little that Captain Truxtun could do about the vanquished but missing ship. The safety of his own ship had become his main concern. Although his hull was not badly damaged, his rigging was almost completely wrecked, with scarcely anything standing. Faced with the task of getting his unweatherly ship into port, he gave up any idea of beating back up to St. Kitts, which by now was a hundred and fifty miles to windward. Instead, he bore away for Jamaica, over seven hundred miles to leeward.

Next morning, while all hands toiled to square the ship away for the long run down to Jamaica, Captain Truxtun published and proclaimed his "thanks to the officers of every description, seamen, marines, and others, for the gallantry they displayed on this occasion, which under a beneficent Providence, has enabled me to add another laurel to the American character, on the records of the Navy." [17] By the nature of command at sea, the Captain was not merely asserting his ego when he used the personal pronoun in a sense that must include the men and ship under his control. Dead, wounded, and live heroes he carried in his ship, but it was Captain Truxtun's incomparable skill in the art of command at sea that had won the day for the *Constellation*. The men in his crew possessed more brawn, more brains, more proficiency in many branches of practical gunnery and seamanship than he could ever hope to have. But it was he, after all, who possessed the rare and peculiar ability to make his ship and crew a wieldy weapon. It was he who fought his ship as a single instrument; it was he who hammered to the point of submission a ship of greater force than his own.

The Secretary of the Navy, commenting later on the "Heroic Action," pointed out that while every officer and man on board must have "nobly performed" his duty, it should be remembered that "The praise of having pursued for many hours a Ship of force so greatly superior to his own, to bring her to action, and of conducting that action with so much skill as to compensate for his great inferiority of force, belongs exclusively to the gallant Commander." [18]

Men on both sides in this duel of the frigates acknowledged Captain Truxtun's bravery and skill. His officers, replying on behalf of the ship's company to his proclamation of thanks, said, "They [officers and men] with one Voice proclaim, That under such a Commander whose Example would have made even Cowardice Brave, they must have been less than Men, not to have Acted" as they did. More often than not, when the Captain was mentioned in a personal letter by a member of his crew, he was "brave Truxtun," or "the brave Commodore." [19]

On Monday, February 3, two days after the action, her jury-rig was carrying the *Constellation* toward Jamaica, when an American man-of-war hove in sight. The schooner *Enterprize,* Captain John Shaw, was immediately designated to carry the news of the battle back to the continent. Because Thomas Truxtun, junior, was a midshipman in the *Enterprize,* Shaw was ordered to take his vessel to Perth Amboy, where he could anchor almost in the Truxtun front yard, and carry the dispatches overland to the Navy Office in Philadelphia.[20]

Next day, when the United States frigate *Insurgente* happened by, Captain Truxtun ordered her to accompany him down to a safe harbor.[21] After the late action, it was appropriate that he should be convoyed by this former French frigate, which his zeal and audacity and skill had just a year before brought under the American flag.

Finally, on Saturday, a week after the engagement, the *Constellation* came to anchor in the harbor of Port Royal at the island of Jamaica. Captain Truxtun sent an officer to the British admiral's flagship, proposing that a salute be exchanged between the British and American ships; but the admiral took the same stand as had Admiral Vandeput in Norfolk. He said he would be glad to return a salute, but because of his superior rank he would return two guns less than he received. As before, no salute was fired by American guns.[22]

Surgeon Isaac Henry sent nine badly wounded survivors of the action ashore to the hospital at Port Royal. Henry, who was greatly fatigued in body and in mind after attending night and day to the wounded aboard ship, noted dejectedly that "some of them have died since we got in with Lock Jaw." [23]

Three weeks after the action, when American casualties stood at eighteen dead and twenty-one wounded, nothing at all had been heard of the French frigate.[24] "It is hard to conjecture," Captain Truxtun wrote to Secretary Ben Stoddert, "whether she sunk, or whether she got into St. Thomas's or Curracoa. If she is still above water, she must be irreparable in the West-Indies. Her loss of men must have been prodigious in an action of five hours, with 600 men on board: My fire was directed principally at her hull."

"Several of my officers have told me," he continued, "that they thought they saw her go down—certain it is, that the ship and her lights disappeared of a sudden, and we ought to have seen her at day light. But I was so employed myself, in preserving our fore-mast and mizen-mast, after the main-mast went over the side, that I attended to nothing else." [25]

His skill as a mariner was put to the test again while the *Constellation* lay in Port Royal. In order to replace his mainmast alone, even disregarding all the yards and other missing spars, he needed three pieces of timber. The lower mast was a stick a hundred feet long and nearly three feet in diameter; above the lower mast was the topmast, sixty feet long; and above that was the topgallant mast, nearly fifty feet long. Given the timbers, the hoisting and shipping of the masts would still be a formidable task. But in Jamaica he found that no masts of the kind he wanted could be bought at any price, so he decided to take his ship under a jury-rig back to an American port, where such timbers were available. It was only the indefatigable zeal and ingenuity of the Captain that enabled the ship to sail forth from Port Royal on the first day of March, 1800. Exactly what sort of rig she wore is unknown, but she took fourteen sail of merchantmen under convoy, and her journal of the homeward bound passage gave no hint that she was disabled. She could beat to windward and she weathered some violent squalls.[26] After arriving in Hampton Roads, Captain Truxtun sent up to Norfolk for more than a score of masts and yards to replace his jury-rig, in order to make permanent repairs to his ship. The smallest of the spars he ordered, a mizzen royal yard, was twenty-two feet long.[27]

It was only after he had anchored in home waters, nearly two months after the action, that he heard for the first time the name and fate of his antagonist. She was *La Vengeance*, Captain Citizen Pitot; she had not been sunk as he supposed, but survived the battle and made her way to the Dutch island of Curaçao.

*La Vengeance*, a large frigate mounting fifty-four guns, had just departed from Guadeloupe for France when she was sighted by the Americans. She had on board a crew of 320 men and carried, in addition, 80 military passengers, many of them artillery officers. Also on board were thirty-six American seamen, prisoners of war, who were being transported to France. The French passengers had gone to quarters and fought alongside the seamen throughout the battle; but the Americans, who refused to fight against their flag, had been sent below and had no part in the action. However, she might never have reached port again if the American prisoners had not been on board.

When the French ship bore away after the long conflict, her upper works were in ruins, and she had nearly two hundred shot holes in her hull. There was already more than five feet of water in her hold, and the water was gaining fast. As soon as the firing ceased, the American prisoners sprang willingly to her pumps, while the French passengers manned buckets and even wooden bowls; before daybreak they had gotten the better of the inundation that threatened to swamp the ship. During the next five days, while she limped southward toward Curaçao, the prisoners did duty as seamen alongside the surviving Frenchmen. They won the gratitude of Captain Citizen Pitot for their exertions in helping to bring his ship into port "in a most distress'd situation without a Mast standing except the lower Fore and Mizen Masts, and not an original rope to be seen except the fore and bobstay that was not knotted or spliced."[28]

While the number of casualties in *La Vengeance* cannot accurately be determined, it is certain that her crew fared much worse than that of the *Constellation*. Contrasted with the final count of eighteen Americans killed and twenty-one wounded was the French captain's report which minimized his losses but admitted to twenty-eight killed and forty wounded. Other reports claimed as many as 160 French casualties. The truth lay somewhere between these extremes; probably *La Vengeance* lost about a hundred killed and wounded.[29]

Captain Citizen Pitot, in his anxiety to justify his defense of his ship, paid Captain Truxtun a few unwitting compliments in his official reports. "The ship which we fought," he wrote on the day after the action, "is a ship of the line, quite long and very high in the stern. . . . She had a very numerous crew and a well-served musketry." Even after he had learned the name of his adversary, he told his seniors that she carried "60 guns and a complement of 500 men." In actual fact, the *Constellation* carried 38 guns and 320 men.[30]

While the French captain was forced to exaggerate the strength of his assailant in order to give his story credibility, Captain Truxtun had no such need. From the American viewpoint, it was a glorious action; it should have insured the undying fame of the gallant Captain. But about this time he began to indulge an unfortunate tendency to magnify his own accomplishments, to embroider his statements, and in time to become convinced that his extravagances were bona fide facts. Instead of 400 men in *La Vengeance* he chose a figure that varied between 560 and 600. In comparing the weight of metal in a broadside that each ship could hurl at the other, he was not content to list a total of fifty-four twelve- and eighteen-pounders and thirty-six-pounder carronades, all of which gave the French frigate an advantage of 516 pounds to 372; he felt compelled to claim, without a sound reason, that a French eighteen-pound ball weighed twenty pounds and that a thirty-six-pound ball weighed forty-two.[31] Eventually, his eagerness to display his prowess in the best possible light was to become wearisome. It annoyed and repelled those who might have been warm in his praise. If his positive accomplishments had been less durable, he would have within a few years dulled the luster of his fame beyond repair.

But only two months had passed since the action; most of his troubles still lay in the future. Judging by the acclamation that followed him wherever he went, his future was never brighter than it was at this moment.

## CHAPTER 37

## SENIOR OFFICER PRESENT

   *ও*  .  .  *ও*  .  .  *ও*  .  .  *ও*  .  .

THE news of this latest sea fight, which resulted in an apparent victory for the gallant Captain, brought him a new round of applause, dampened only a little by political undertones.

In Norfolk, the public acclaim of the year before was repeated. At the Exchange Coffee House an elegant dinner, prepared by Mr. Rourke, was served at three o'clock to a numerous and distinguished company. The usual toasts, "interspersed with songs," were proposed and drunk. After he had listened to all the toasts save one, the guest of honor, full of wine and proper modesty, retired from the room in order that a resounding toast might be proposed to "Commodore Truxtun."

"The day was spent in harmony and cheerful mirth," ran the account in the newspaper, "inspired with the pleasure which every one felt in paying a tribute of respect to the gallant Commodore and his brave Officers and Crew." [1]

When Charles Biddle, in Philadelphia, heard the outcome of the battle, he hurried down the street to see Congressman Josiah Parker, chairman of the House Committee on Naval Affairs. Since brave Truxtun would collect no prize money for this encounter, Biddle thought it would be fitting for Congress publicly to recognize his great achievement.

Shortly afterwards, Parker proposed a resolution calling for a golden medal to be presented to him. He pointed out at the same time that "in other countries monuments have been erected to commemorate such splendid victories."

A congressman from Maryland objected to the resolution. All he knew about the action was what he had read in the papers; he didn't like the idea of going around giving away golden medals just on the strength of newspaper stories. He would like to see the official reports. Besides, he thought the young officer who had chosen to lose his life rather than shrink from his duty deserved some honor, too. Congressman Parker admitted that he had gotten his information from the newspapers, but he saw no reason why there should be any doubt about it; and as for the dead midshipman hero, he was just about to propose that his bust be placed in a niche in the new Capitol building, after the government moved to the new city of Washington by the Potomac.

Another member of the House, representing Virginia, said that he just could not bring himself to vote for a medal for Captain Truxtun. He didn't think the Captain's conduct was particularly gallant; it seemed merely rash to him. The comment by the gentleman from Vermont was yet more caustic. He had voted at some time in the past for the employment of three frigates, he said, under the impression that they were to be used for the protection of commerce. And now he was called upon to vote a medal to a captain who was off his station, chasing a ship of superior force, and reducing his own as well as his enemy's ship almost to wreckage.

These gentlemen, members of the opposition in a predominantly Federalist Congress, expressed their views, but the golden medal was approved. The resolution of Congress commended Captain Truxtun for an engagement "honourable to the American name, and instructive to its rising navy."

The proposal for a bust of Midshipman Jarvis was dropped after another resolution was passed. This one is unique in the history of Congress: "*Resolved,* That the conduct of James Jarvis, a Midshipman in said frigate, who gloriously preferred certain death to an abandonment of his post, is deserving of the highest praise, and that the loss of so promising an officer is a subject of national regret." [2]

Secretary of State Timothy Pickering read the eulogy on Jarvis and immediately sat down to write a letter to his son, who was a midshipman in another American frigate. "Face every danger which duty presents;" he wrote, "but I shall derive no consolation from vulgar applause, nor even for an act of Congress, because you remained on the tottering mast, and perished, rather than quit your post, when no possible good could be derived from your keeping it." [3]

The discordant notes in the song of praise were not all within the Government. The Antifederalist press was quick to deplore the battle and the adulation that followed it. This "hideous transaction," said the Philadelphia daily *Aurora,* was in direct opposition to the will of the people. Were we not even now treating for peace with the great Republic? The fact that the hand of a diplomat is strengthened by such evidence of naval vigor apparently never occurred to the editor.

"Of the bravery of Captain Truxtun and his crew there can be no doubt," the attack continued; "his prudence however is very questionable." The editor thought it was considerate of the French frigate not to come back and renew the fight and to let the *Constellation* escape into a friendly port. [4]

Pierre S. du Pont de Nemours, who had narrowly escaped the guillotine during the most violent period of the French Revolution, asked in a letter to Thomas Jefferson, then Vice President, "Whence comes this madness for killing foreigners and for getting one's fellow countrymen killed, when it is evident that both nations are reconciled or arbitrating?" [5]

But the cries of doubters were effectively stilled by the acclamation, public and private, for the doer of mighty deeds by the sword. Most of the faultfinding was of the carping sort. It quite ignored the clear facts of the situation. Here was a squadron commander who carried explicit orders to capture or destroy enemy vessels in the Caribbean Sea. To him, there could be no alternative: the French were either friends or they were enemies. His instructions told him that they were enemies. Captain Truxtun, who was more concerned about the honor and dignity of the national flag than he was, even, about his own fame and glory, could recognize only one possible interpretation of his orders. When he saw a vessel, he demanded to know if it was French; if it was French, he used every means at his disposal to capture or destroy it.

The criticizers ignored the facts, but they probed a sore that had festered for two years, unchecked by the Government. This war with France was still undeclared. The national policy was no clearer than it had been when hostilities began.

The medal voted
by Congress in
1800 to honor
Truxtun (engrav-
ing c. 1807)

Secretary Ben Stoddert, starting two years before with only three frigates and a single armed merchant ship, had laced the national backbone with oak and iron. His fleet of more than thirty men-of-war, carrying in all nearly one thousand guns to punish and annoy the enemy, was more a tribute to his energy and tenacity than the result of any clear-cut national policy.[6]

Within a few months after his appointment to the Navy post, Stoddert had begun advocating a greatly expanded naval program. He wanted to build seventy-fours, heavy-gunned ships of the line, and he wanted admirals for command of his battle fleets. Although the political tide was running strong against the Federalist Administration in which he served, he was still hopeful that at least some of his numerous plans might be carried out.[7]

He was lavish in his praise of Captain Truxtun after his engagement with *La Vengeance*. He hoped that Congress would soon pass a law permitting naval officers of flag rank: two admirals, two vice-admirals, and two rear admirals. Had this act been passed while Stoddert was still in office, there is no question as to who would have been the first American admiral.[8] But while he could not yet offer Captain Truxtun anything more than the broad pennant of a squadron commander, which carried with it by tradition and courtesy the title of commodore, he could and did offer him a new and larger ship to succeed the *Constellation*.

His new ship was the *President*, one of the original forty-fours that had been temporarily laid aside four years before. She had just been launched; and as soon as he could get away from Norfolk, he was scheduled to take command of her in New York. In her, he might speedily return to the West Indies, where, Stoddert told him, "I hope your future glory will equal, & your future success exceed the past." [9]

All praise and smooth sailing, with no violent squalls of adversity, proved too much for the gallant Commodore. Tasting too often the heady wine of public acclaim, he was beginning to exceed his capacity and to reel from its effects.

When he sent up to Josiah Fox, in Norfolk, the list of masts and spars that he needed for the *Constellation,* he expected him to put a gang of men to work on them immediately; but Fox, the naval constructor, already was working at capacity. For more than a year he had been building and fitting out the new frigate *Chesapeake,* and for more than a month he had been worrying with the *Congress,* the New England-built thirty-six that had been totally dismasted in a strong gale off the coast.[10] The *Constellation* was but another frigate, standing on Fox's calendar at the bottom of the list. But when Captain Truxtun spoke, Fox's calendar instantly became the most unimportant document in Norfolk.

"You come to me and make a complaint," wrote Captain Truxtun, "that Captain Sever wished your men all employed on the *Congress*'s spars &c—and a few minutes after—produce me a letter from the Secretary of the Navy—desiring that no Object should interfere with the dispatch of that ship—I am not pleased with this sort of proceeding."[11]

The brave Commodore, expecting ashore the same instant obedience to his will that he enjoyed afloat, impatiently brushed aside Fox's objections to setting the *Constellation* before everything else on the eastern seaboard.

"You will," he told Fox imperiously, "for the good of the Service—the honor of this Yard, and your own honor, Compleat the main mast procurred for the *Congress*—for the *Constellation* . . . and every other article ordered for the latter ship, without loss of time."[12]

"There is one thing Certain," observed one of the Commodore's friends, "that his Word is a Law here."

"Which may not be his fault," he added, "as Mankind will be sometimes Blinded in the radiance of Glory."[13]

Captain Truxtun, fuming at the delays that kept him from his new ship in New York, had more than repairs to the *Constellation* to keep him occupied. Because he was senior officer in Chesapeake Bay, the captains of other naval vessels came to him for help when their own problems confounded them.

James Sever, the unpopular captain of the dismasted frigate *Congress,* wanted to have a court-martial convened to try several men in his crew for mutinous conduct. When Secretary Ben Stoddert was consulted, he wrote to Captain Truxtun, "As Commander of the Squadron, you might have ordered a Court Martial at once, without appealing, to me, & I am sorry you did not do it." The Secretary was mildly annoyed. "I do not like," he continued, "this method of appealing to the head of the Department, by officers, who are themselves competent to the object of appeal."[14]

Next day, Secretary Stoddert wrote again. "You must," he charged the Commodore, "assume all the authority belonging to your rank, at Norfolk, which is as much as if you were already an Admiral, as I hope you will quickly be—or as if you had Command of the whole Navy." [15] The Secretary's quill had slipped. For months afterwards he must have wished that he had never written that sentence.

Given the choice, Commodore Truxtun chose command of the whole Navy. When, a few weeks later, he reviewed the sentence of the court-martial he had convened, he signed himself "Thomas Truxtun, Vested with the powers of Commander in Chief of the Navy of U.S." To his credit, however, he mitigated a death sentence to one hundred lashes and dishonorable discharge from the service, realizing no doubt that an American seaman hanging from a yard-arm of the *Congress* would have an unhappy effect upon the public's opinion of the Navy.[16]

Meanwhile, also to his credit, he had presided over the Court of Inquiry that cleared Captain Sever of blame for the dismasting of his ship. The proceedings of the Court were submitted to President Adams, who observed that the whole affair had been conducted "in a manner to do yourself as much honor as you had so well merited by your gallantry and skill on the ocean." [17]

Aside from his ostentatious display of the ill-advised phrase in Secretary Stoddert's letter to him, there were two occasions upon which his overweening sense of personal importance got the better of him.

When he made plans for his new ship's organization, he decided, since he had been satisfied with all the officers in the *Constellation,* that he would take them all with him to the *President* in New York.

"You must not think of it," came back Secretary Stoddert's reply to this proposal; "if you have made these, you can make others—the men will be enough dissatisfied to change their Commander—an entire Sett of new Officers would produce a mutiny."

"Such things," he concluded, "are unprecedented in any Service." [18]

Secretary Stoddert indulged the whims and vanity of his officers with more patience than a lesser man could have found; he realized that the loyalty of his captains was more important than strict adherence to rules and form; but he always retained full control of his Department's business—except for one situation that arose in Norfolk.

Captain Alexander Murray took over command of the *Constellation* from Captain Truxtun, and before the middle of May the frigate was completely repaired and in all respects ready for sea. Impatient to see his former ship again employed against the French, Captain Truxtun suddenly assumed more authority than Secretary Stoddert ever meant to bestow—more, indeed, than he could have dreamed a man would take. Before sailing orders could reach Captain Murray, Captain Truxtun ordered him to sail for the West Indies. Incidentally, he also ordered Murray to take young Tom Truxtun on board the *Constellation* should he fall in with the *Enterprize,* in which he was serving as a midshipman.

Captain Murray was happy to comply with orders given him by his friend Captain Truxtun. He wrote to Secretary Stoddert, telling him that his early departure from Norfolk was "much to the credit and Zeal of our Worthy Commodore who has been indefatigable & had an immensity of trouble and vexation among the Workmen on Shore." The trouble was that the *Constellation* was bound for St. Kitts, while Secretary Stoddert wanted her on the Santo Domingo station, five hundred miles from St. Kitts. When word of Captain Murray's departure reached the Navy Office, the air was suddenly filled with agonized expletives.

"I am extreamly mortified," the Secretary wrote to the Commodore, "at the unwarrantable step which your too great Zeal has prompted you to take. . . . It was in every way improper . . . and God knows what inconveniences may result from it. You must avoid such interference in future."

Three times within the week, he chastised his errant officer. Captain Truxtun learned that he had assumed one of the prerogatives of the President of the United States, because orders coming from the Secretary of the Navy were, in name at least, the orders of the President. He learned by stinging repetition in Secretary Stoddert's letters that he had let his suddenly distended sense of personal importance impair his judgment.[19]

It was on this note that Captain Truxtun wound up ten arduous weeks in Norfolk and turned his attention to his new ship in New York.

The latest letter he had received from Secretary Stoddert informed him of the Navy Department's move to the new federal city on the Potomac, where the Government expected to establish permanent headquarters. Because he wanted to see Secretary Stoddert, but perhaps more particularly because he wanted to see for himself what manner of place this federal city might be, he set out on his northern journey along the road to Washington.

## CHAPTER 38

## PRESIDENT

 ℰ  .  .  ℰ  .  .  ℰ  .  .  ℰ  .  .

TO THOSE who were accustomed to Philadelphia's conveniences, its cobblestoned streets, its brick sidewalks, and the luxury of its inns and boarding-houses, the new capital city in 1800 was indeed a desolate place. Work was going ahead on one wing of the Capitol and on the President's house, but almost nothing was yet complete. Those two white sandstone buildings stood out in bold contrast to the largely undisturbed woods and fields round about. Pennsylvania Avenue, running from Capitol to President's house, was a quaggy morass, dense with elder bushes.

A congressman, viewing the city for the first time, reported that "the roads in every direction were muddy and unimproved. A sidewalk was attempted, in one instance, by a covering of chips hewed from the Capitol. It extended but a little way and was of little value; for in dry weather the sharp fragments cut our shoes, and in wet weather covered them with white mortar." [1] The accommodations for congressmen were so bad that "they were within an ace of adjourning" to another city, where there was an established society and where the boarding-houses were better and the mud not quite so deep. [2]

Captain Thomas Tingey, who had been at the capital laboring to establish a Navy Yard while winter snows were still deep, was already one of the veteran inhabitants of the place. It was in Captain Tingey's carriage that Captain Truxtun appeared, riding about the city, during the oppressively hot June weather that greeted him. [3]

Although Secretary Stoddert had already arrived when Captain Truxtun reached Washington, his office was still on the way, the papers and records rumbling overland in a wagon, and the furniture and fittings rolling round by water.[4] No papers were needed, however, to satisfy Captain Truxtun that the most important job in the world was that of fitting out and manning the frigate *President:* the Secretary's expertness in handling his people apparently saw to that. Almost as soon as the interview ended, Captain Truxtun set out for New York. He was gone even before he could be invited to the dinner party that Mrs. Thornton was giving for the Secretaries of Navy, War, and State.[5] His friends in Baltimore urged him to stay over with them for a day or two, but he refused their hospitality. He sent word ahead to Charles Biddle, in Philadelphia, asking him to bring some money and papers out to Frankford, on the stage line, in order to avoid the loss of a moment on his journey to New York. He wanted to go over some personal accounts with his friend, but the only solution he could see was for Biddle to follow him to New York, or at least to his home in Perth Amboy.[6]

At once, he was deep in the manifold problems, details, vexations, and delays that always attended the fitting out, manning, and provisioning of a ship of war. The *President,* a 44-gun frigate, built by the same drafts and molds as the *Constitution* and the *United States,* had been in the water for scarcely more than two months.[7] She was one of the original 1794 frigates—Captain Talbot's ship until she was discontinued in 1796. The superintendence of her building and launch had finally fallen to Lieutenant Isaac Chauncey, who, Secretary Stoddert supposed, would be her first lieutenant. But he had not reckoned with Captain Truxtun's imperiousness. The Captain had brought with him his first lieutenant, Andrew Sterett; therefore, Chauncey had to be content with the post of second lieutenant. Surgeon Balfour, who had been with Captain Truxtun when he took *L'Insurgente,* was ordered to the *President;* and four midshipmen, all of whom were made lieutenants, and James Morgan, faithful gunner, were transferred with their captain to the new ship.[8]

Twenty new midshipmen were entered in the *President,* as compared to the dozen or fourteen carried in each of the other forty-fours. Here indeed was a school of the sea, providing for young gentlemen who aspired to the command of a ship the best that the Navy could offer in the way of precept and example. In order to supplement the practical work of the day at sea, Robert Thomson, chaplain and schoolmaster, was assigned to the ship to help teach the theory and practice of navigation.[9]

Captain Truxtun wanted Lieutenant Clinch to follow him to his new ship in order to continue as lieutenant of marines, but Lieutenant Colonel William Burrows, Commandant of the Marine Corps, had other ideas. He had already had his fill of naval captains' interference with his marine officers. He contended that if he were not to make the assignments of men of his corps, then there would be no use for him nor for his staff. With this opinion, Captain Truxtun was in complete agreement. He said that he was "sensible of the unimportance of the Marine corps." [10] Whatever he thought of the Marine Corps at the moment was bound to grow worse as time revealed to him the shortcomings of the two lieutenants who had been assigned to him in lieu of Lieutenant Clinch.

Near the end of June, 1800, Charles Biddle brought two of his sons —James, seventeen years old, and Edward, a little younger—to New York to see them safe aboard the *President* as midshipmen under his good friend's especial care. Before and during the Revolution, Charles Biddle had spent twenty years at sea in the merchant service, and it was only natural that his sons should want to taste sea life; but all during this journey, he later related, he secretly wished that something might happen that would prevent their going. If only the ship would burn or sink, then they might return home and forget the sea. He understood, as well as did Captain Truxtun, the many and various vicissitudes that faced the boys as they looked forward with keen anticipation to their life afloat. When he left his boys in Captain Truxtun's ship, he enjoined him to take good care of them and then added, "and you, I suppose, will make them good officers. They know the advantage of being with you, and are informed that nothing will gratify me so much as meeting your approbation, nothing give me more pain than their not doing it." [11]

James and Edward were immediately favored by their captain. In August, 1800, when the *President* was nearly ready to sail, he took them down to his home in Perth Amboy while their father and mother paid them another farewell visit. The final parting scene was in the best melodramatic tradition. Mrs. Biddle, greatly distressed by the whole affair, was finally reconciled to her sons' going when old faithful black Tom, a slave who had been born and brought up in the Biddle household, agreed to go with them in the frigate in order to look after them during the cruise.[12]

Throughout the whole summer Captain Truxtun took little time off from his ship, but there was one celebration that he willingly attended. He was invited to the annual Fourth of July dinner of the Society of the Cincinnati, an organization of officers of the Revolutionary Army; and although he was not eligible for full membership, he had been elected an honorary member and was admitted to the brotherhood on that day.[13]

Except when something special lured him away, he appeared regularly on board his ship each day. As each article was received from the naval agents in New York, he personally checked it off in his record book.[14] At the same time, he kept close tally on recruiting, being carried on in Philadelphia as well as New York. By the middle of August, his crew was complete except for a few petty officers.[15] Scarcely two months after he took command of the *President,* Captain Truxtun had his ship completely equipped, manned, and ready for sea.

On a clear and windy evening early in September, 1800, he sailed out to sea past Sandy Hook lighthouse, from which he took his departure.[16] He laid down his course once more for Basseterre Roads at the island of St. Kitts.

"I see in the papers," du Pont de Nemours wrote to Vice-President Jefferson, "that Truxtun is leaving and will do the impossible in order to have a second fight with the *Vengeance. . . .* And it is said that he hastened for fear of getting official news of an armistice. What vain and unreasonable creatures most men are!"[17]

The naval war with France was fast running out. In spite of Secretary Stoddert's urgent pleas that he get to his station as soon as possible, because of the sudden increase of French raids on American vessels, Commodore Truxtun found no French cruisers on his station, nor did he hear of any that he might hunt down nearby. *La Vengeance,* he was told, had been forced by a change of political weather in Curaçao to leave that island while she was still in a poor state of repair and badly undermanned, and that she had been taken shortly afterwards by a British forty-four gun frigate, following a sharp and severe action.[18]

Commodore Truxtun kept his squadron cruising constantly, and his own ship was seldom at anchor; but in spite of all the cruising there were only a half-dozen captures made by his squadron during the four months he commanded it. French vessels of all kinds were becoming *"scarce,"* he said, "so much so, that what I formerly found (chasing) an amusement, and pastime, is now insiped, Urksome & tiresome, and the life I lead may be truly called sedentary." [19]

When the latest newspapers from London, which he received in November, 1800, reported that a French-American treaty had been signed in Paris, he was ready to go home. He was tired of the duty, and he was tormented by "an obstinate complaint of my bowels, that has debilitated me so much that the pure Northern air of America, can only restore the usual, and natural action, to my languid and emaciated frame; for such I assure you it has become, by being constantly under the muzzle of the sun for such a length of time." Contrary to his surgeon's advice, he dosed himself with calomel. When Doctor Balfour had him read a chapter in one of his weighty medical tomes in order to carry his point, Commodore Truxtun told him that since his indisposition was caused "intirely by wind or bile, or perhaps both," he was sure that it was the disease and not the remedy that made him suffer.[20]

Along with his lingering ailments and the complex business of keeping a squadron constantly employed, he was bedeviled by problems of discipline on board his own ship. A seaman threw a marlinespike at Lieutenant Sterett, was promptly clapped in irons, and finally sent ashore to prison. Sailing Master John King, who on the quarter-deck menaced Lieutenant Chauncey with a bayonet, threatening to drive a thunderbolt through his soul, was placed under arrest in his cabin to await court-martial. Chaplain Thomson, continually at odds with the lieutenants in the gun room ("a sycophant and a tatler," said one), was permitted to return home before the cruise was six weeks old. Captain Truxtun had no fault to find with his chaplain, but he could see no other way to restore some semblance of harmony among his officers. Some of his midshipmen, as usual, tried his patience. Archibald Kearney was punished for an "impropriety" by being sent to another ship in the squadron, but when the *President* was ready to go home he was brought back on board.

Many an insufferable young gentleman was sent to a midshipman's berth by influential parents who had despaired of his rearing, but still hoped that the Navy could do something with him. Such a one was John Harris, son of one of Captain Truxtun's friends. Almost admitting his failure in "reclaiming, and yet making you a man," the long-suffering Captain decided, more than once, to give him one more chance.[21]

Of all those who ran afoul of Captain Truxtun's will, none was as bitter as Marine Lieutenant John Lewis. A misunderstanding in New York, before the ship sailed, had caused him to read all sorts of sinister motives into every order the Captain issued. Because he, as an officer in the Marine Corps, reported to the Commandant of the Corps, he felt that he should somehow be excused from being ordered around by a naval officer. He took Captain Truxtun's insistence upon discipline among marines, as well as seamen, as a mark of personal animosity. "Capt. T," he wrote midway in the cruise, "has been accustom'd to receive homage, he now demands it without bounds. His officers, and they are those who have sail'd with him in the *Constellation,* with one voice lift up their hands and are astonished at his insolence and tyranny."

"I hold him now in the most contemptible light," he continued, "and with such an oppinion it is possible to be happy." [22]

His nagging sickness undoubtedly made the Captain sharp and irritable. It irked him, too, to have to spend his time on petty details of shipboard administration when he was responsible for the performance of a squadron of men-of-war. He may have recognized that he played an important role in his country's foreign affairs; or perhaps his hat was fitting him badly, pinching at the temples.

Any unusual charges of contumely must be viewed in the light of a personal tragedy that had occurred while he was down under Guadeloupe searching for the enemy. Midshipman Edward Biddle, ailing for a few days with a fever that Captain Truxtun supposed was "generated on board during the calms and intense warm weather, we have experienced during the Hurricane season," suddenly became worse. Chaplain Thomson, who visited the sick youth, found faithful black Tom huddled under his cot, sobbing as though his heart would break. Tom told the chaplain that his master was very, very sick; but Edward told him, a bit impatiently, that he was feeling better. Half an hour later, he was dead.[23]

Deeply hurt by the loss of his particular friend's son and acutely aware of his helplessness in the face of death, he could not bring himself to write directly to Charles Biddle; but he said requiem over the boy in other letters that he wrote. "He was," he wrote to Captain Tingey, in Washington, "without a vice of any kind, or ever a foible that I ever heard of, his disposition was of the most friendly, & benevolent kind, his education, Mental qualifications, studious habits, becoming Pride, discernment and good sense, bid fair to make him a Naval Ornament, . . ." And so on, and on, trying as men will to fill the terrible vacuum with words.[24]

When, in the middle of January, 1801, Commodore Barry arrived in the frigate *United States* to relieve Commodore Truxtun, there still was no news of the impending peace that could implicitly be relied upon. The French governor at Guadeloupe had sent down a flag of truce, bearing a proclamation of peace, a few days before; while Commodore Truxtun replied graciously enough that he was happy to hear the good news, he added that he could not recognize the existence of peace until he received instructions from his own government. Thereupon he had sailed off on another cruise in search of Frenchmen, during which he was fired upon by a French fort on Guadeloupe.[25]

He was pleased to see Commodore Barry for two reasons. First, he could now return to the "pure Northern air of America"; and second, since the peace settlement seemed imminent, he was no longer interested in remaining on a station that offered only the routine task of showing the flag among the islands of the Caribbean.

He showed Commodore Barry the courtesy due his rank by hauling down the broad pennant he had been wearing in the *President*, but in view of a letter from the Secretary of the Navy that told him that "His [Barry's] Seniority entitles him to this command, & it could not be denied to him," and the "roving Commission" that Truxtun was given rather than being placed under Barry's direction, it is no wonder that he addressed him as a friend and not as a senior officer. Giving freely of his friendly advice, Commodore Truxtun within a fortnight weighed anchor, took with him the thirty-six gun frigate *Chesapeake,* and after a final look about the islands laid down his course for the mainland.[26]

## CHAPTER 39

# RANK RANKLES

ᢞ  .  .  ᢞ  .  .  ᢞ  .  .  ᢞ  .  .

ON MARCH 4, 1801, the death knell of the Federalist party might well have been sounded. At noon, in the crowded Senate chamber of the new Capitol building, Thomas Jefferson became President of the United States.[1] The Federalist party, representing men of property and high social status, had been in the majority throughout the eight years of George Washington's administration; its banners had been spattered and torn during John Adams' four years in office; and now it was well on its way toward oblivion. The new President, leader of the opposition, was committed to an immediate reduction of government expenditures, and that boded ill for the future of the Navy.

Two days after the inauguration ceremonies, Captain Truxtun, attended by his servant, arrived in Washington.[2] When he called at the President's house to pay his respects, he was cordially received. His interview with the new Chief Executive was quite pleasant.[3] Perhaps this man, symbol of the Antifederalists, was not as bad as he had been painted.

His talk with Ben Stoddert, who was staying on as Secretary of the Navy until a successor could be found, was not quite so encouraging. Secretary Stoddert knew that the old Congress, working desperately to jam through the last of the Federalist bills before the new President took office, had passed an act having to do with the Navy, but as yet it was too early to learn exactly what the act contained, since copies of it had not arrived from the printer. He was afraid that his recommendations had been disregarded and that the Navy might be hopelessly disrupted by a hastily drawn and poorly considered law.[4]

Leaving the Navy's future in a gloom of uncertainty, Captain Truxtun pushed on to Perth Amboy, there to undertake the repair of his health.

Captain Truxtun, forever the Federalist, might well have tendered his resignation at this time and with honor it might have been accepted. The war with France—Truxtun's War—was over. There was no question of his pre-eminence on the ocean. Of the ninety-odd French vessels of all sizes captured or engaged by the United States Navy, *L'Insurgente* and *La Vengeance* were by far the largest.

The future political atmosphere should not have been too hard to estimate. There was little likelihood now of admirals and ships of the line; it appeared inevitable that the Navy would have to fight for its very existence. The Antifederalists for years had tried to scuttle every measure that favored the Navy.

Captain Truxtun was rounding out his seventh year as a naval officer; for five years he had given all of his time and all of his energy to the rising Navy. He had divorced himself from trade. Had it not been for the windfall of prize money from *L'Insurgente,* he would have been poorer by some twelve thousand dollars, which he had spent above his pay and rations since entering the Navy.[5] At that rate, he could never grow rich as a naval captain. However, during his half a lifetime in merchant vessels, he had built up an estate that would keep him and his family in comfortable circumstances, and he had so arranged his affairs that he might give to the service the rest of his life's effort. He was not ready to resign—not just yet.

If he had been more objective in appraising his situation, he might have gone on to greater glories, most probably writing his name in the annals of the sea so boldly that posterity could not for an instant ignore, and certainly never forget, his part in establishing a naval tradition of bravery, audacity, and fierce devotion to the good of the service. Had he been less blind in his convictions and less vain in his estimate of his own reputation, he might again have carried his broad pennant in the van of many a proud frigate squadron. Always, he could be depended upon to be cool and resourceful when physical danger threatened, but, unfortunately for his future, when he imagined that his reputation was under attack he was neither cool nor resourceful. He never learned that detractors are silenced most quickly by silence.

As soon as the new Administration was fairly in possession of Washington, Captain Truxtun renewed his claim to rank third among the naval captains, or in any case to rank above Captain Talbot.

Before the Vice-President, Aaron Burr, had been in office a week, he was informed by Captain Truxtun of this pretension.[6] General Sam Smith, acting as Secretary of the Navy after the search for a successor finally exceeded the limit of Ben Stoddert's patience, evaded the issue because he expected to be in the Navy Office for a few weeks only.[7]

President Jefferson, when the question was put to him, promptly and firmly put it down. Captain Truxtun, who admitted that he should lay his claim before the Secretary of the Navy rather than the President, nevertheless asked his indulgence "for the liberty I have taken in writing to you this letter as *Mr. Jefferson* and not as President Jefferson."

To this the President replied: "Altho' this communication was expressly made to me in my private character . . . it is only as a public officer that my opinion can be of any consequence." He freely granted that Captain Truxtun's arguments were "undoubtedly weighty," but then, so were Captain Talbot's. He would not say with certainty that he would have arrived at the same decision as President Adams, but since the question had once been settled by "an authority equally competent with myself," he had no intention of unsettling it.[8]

The Federalists, anticipating Jefferson's fervent cry, "peace is our passion," were convinced that the new Administration would be hostile to the Navy and at the first opportunity would try to get rid of it entirely. Better, then, it seemed to them, to get something on the statute books than to leave all of the initiative to the Antifederalists. Accordingly, on the third of March, 1801, in a frantic rush to get under the legislative wire, the dying Congress had passed the Peace Establishment Act and President Adams had signed it.[9]

Based entirely upon the recommendations of the outgoing Secretary of the Navy, Ben Stoddert, the Act provided that only a part of the existing Navy be maintained. Of thirty-odd vessels in service during the war with France, all but thirteen—the largest and best— were to be sold; and of the thirteen, seven were to be laid up in port. The officer corps was to be reduced from twenty-eight captains to nine, with lieutenants and midshipmen in proportion.

Although the Act appeared to have decimated the Navy that it was designed to protect, the statesmanship of Ben Stoddert was evident in the stipulation that a squadron of six vessels "be kept in constant service in time of peace." This was the important provision of the Act. Here was the opportunity for continuous drill and training of officers and crews, a veritable school of the sea. Aside from insuring a seasoned foundation upon which a larger force could be built quickly when it was needed, the principle of "constant service" would enable the Navy to show the flag in the Mediterranean, and perhaps to maintain peace with the Barbary rulers, who understood only the language of force.[10]

On April 2, 1801, Captain Truxtun was ordered to the command of a squadron preparing to cruise in the Mediterranean. He returned to his ship in Hampton Roads after having spent less than a month at home, but ostensibly because "peace can afford no field for me on the ocean," he informed Acting Secretary Sam Smith that he would much prefer to see the command given to another officer. Through a friend in Washington, he let Smith know that he would not be interested in taking out the squadron "unless It should be intended to act decisively" against the states of Barbary. To another friend he wrote, "If I get foul of those Barbary pirates, or any other pirates enemies to our country, if I have anything like equal force I will bang them into submission." The Bashaw of Tripoli was currently demanding increased tribute from the United States as the price for continued peace, but the Navy was to take no punitive measures unless he first declared war. Acting Secretary Smith, informing Captain Truxtun that the purposes of the cruise were to show the flag and to acquaint naval officers with the coasts and waters of the Mediterranean, was considerate enough to transfer the squadron command to Captain Dale, at the same time assuring Captain Truxtun that he would be retained in service and receive half pay until his services were again required. Had the Administration been disposed to be arbitrary at this time, the Captain could easily have been forced either to take the squadron or to give up his commission. As it was, he went ahead with preparation of ships, men, and provisions while waiting to be relieved by Captain Dale.[11]

While he was yet in Norfolk, Captain Truxtun persuaded some of his friends to buy Washington city lots from Ben Stoddert, whose three years in office had so deranged his business and drained his resources, that he left the Navy Office a poor man except for the land that he owned in the capital city. In a short time, Captain Truxtun raised twenty-five thousand dollars, subscribing one-tenth of it himself. Exhorting his friend Charles Biddle, in Philadelphia, to raise a similar fund there, he observed, "We are poor creatures & require much the aid of each other in our passage through this life." [12]

It was also in Norfolk that he again crossed swords with the Marine Corps. Writing to Commandant Burrows, he complained of the constant bickering between marine and naval officers that he had observed in his squadron, and even within his own ship. If harmony between the two sets of officers was not soon established, he thought it would be best to remove all marines from Navy ships. In their place, an equal number of ordinary seamen, drilled by a good master-at-arms, could in a short time be trained to do marine duty. In addition, they would still be useful as seamen, which the marines were not. [13] Complaining at the same time to the Navy Office, he insisted that if "something is not done to effect a due observance of propriety in the marine officers, I shall address another copy of this letter with some remarks directly to the President, and this I do not wish to do as I am sensible of the unimportance of the Marine corps, especially in time of peace, and of the injury it might be of to the Colonel of Marines [Burrows]." [14]

Marine Lieutenant Keene, lately assigned by Burrows to the *President,* was aware of Captain Truxtun's differences with the Corps. "I can never," he told his Commandant, "think of Sailing with a man who Views the Corps to which I belong in the Most contemptuous light."

"In Justice to Capt. Truxtun," he wrote, however, "I must say he treated me with the utmost Politeness." [15]

On May 22, 1801, on board the *President,* moored in Hampton Roads, Captain Truxtun gave up the command of his squadron to Captain Dale. He wished his successor well, and assured him that his flagship was "the finest frigate that ever floated on the waters of this Globe." [16]

There was more to Captain Truxtun's declining to take the squadron out to the Mediterranean than his desire to follow a decided course of action when he arrived there. This cruise was, after all, for the purpose of instructing younger naval officers, and there were few objects that he thought more important. He quit his command because of the sore subject of rank.

As far as his rank was concerned, he thought all along that he had been treated shamefully by the government; now President Jefferson had refused to reopen the question. When he left Norfolk after turning over his command to Captain Dale, he had fully resolved to resign his commission as soon as he reached Perth Amboy; but his friends from north and south had anticipated his intention, and when he arrived home, he found a tall stack of letters awaiting him, all of them admonishing him to postpone his resignation until he was very sure that he could never again serve the Navy under terms that would satisfy his wounded feelings.[17]

He yielded to the importunate counsel of his friends and decided to sit awhile at home, nursing his ills and his ravaged sense of self-esteem. While he drew half pay, he resumed his role as a gentleman of Amboy, master of the large and prosperous household at "Pleasant View." Whether or not he ever returned to the Navy, he had already made up his mind that he would never go back to the merchant service. When reports that he was going out as captain of a merchantman reached him, he was quick to deny the rumor. "In a squadron," he said, "I may sail by & by but in pursuit of Commerce Never no more from this land." [18]

While he was sitting home at "Pleasant View," Captain Truxtun noted in passing that the large frigates, conceived in the minds of Federalists and built to last for half a century or more, were already beginning to show signs of decay. The *United States* was rotten above the water line; his own *Constellation* had proved not much better.[19] Even a piece of live oak in the *Chesapeake* had decayed.[20] Joshua Humphreys, after inspecting the rotting ships, declared that the trouble was caused "by the foul air in the hold." He thought it might be prevented by the application of salt and by adequate ventilation.[21] Captain Truxtun was nearer to the truth when he blamed the decay on insufficient seasoning of the timber.

When the list of captains to be retained under the Peace Establishment Act was published, Captain Truxtun still ranked fifth, after Barry, Nicholson, Talbot, and Dale, exactly as he had when the Navy was first organized seven years before. He had now come the full circle, and it appeared that he had gotten nowhere. Still, he did not resign. For the moment he turned his attention to domestic problems.

Mary, who had been ailing for some time, was growing more and more dissatisfied with Perth Amboy. Particularly during the dreary winter months, she longed for the greater convenience and more numerous society of a large city. When her husband was gone, Mary's situation became quite intolerable. Neither did Captain Truxtun look forward to the isolation of winter at "Pleasant View." Therefore, he was thinking about moving his family to one of the cities, but he could not immediately decide which one. He enjoyed New York, and he had a host of friends there and in Norfolk; but the houses he owned were in Philadelphia, and he had just bought some ground in the new city of Washington.[22] Facing so many alternatives, the Captain reached no decision for several years.

Desolate though the town might be, "Pleasant View" never wanted for activity. Of the eight Truxtun children, six were at home. Sarah, the eldest, wife of Henry Benbridge, was living in Norfolk. Eighteen-year-old Thomas was away at sea, making a voyage to the Mediterranean in a merchant schooner, after having resigned his warrant as midshipman in the Navy. Elizabeth, his twin sister, was back home after an unsuccessful marriage with Sam Cox. That "scoundrel," that "infamous villain," that "Sad fellow Cox," apparently ran away from his business obligations and from his wife. William, eleven years old, was being schooled by the Reverend Mr. Elias Riggs, master of the Academy on the Market square in Perth Amboy. All the others were at home, down to the baby of the family, just three years old. Toward the end of 1801, another baby was on the way to add to the general confusion.[23]

Up the street lived one of the younger naval captains, William Bainbridge—not to be confused with the Benbridges. Captain Bainbridge, who was hounded by misfortune, had just returned home from the command of the first American warship to call in a Barbary port. His ship, the *George Washington,* had been dispatched in August, 1800, to carry the annual tribute of the United States to the Dey of Algiers. In September, while he was at anchor in the harbor of Algiers, under the guns of the fort, Captain Bainbridge was directed by the Dey to prepare his ship for a voyage to Constantinople. He wanted passage for his ambassador and a numerous retinue to the Court of the Ottoman Empire.

Captain Bainbridge, guided by the American consul in Algiers, who in turn was influenced by the policy of appeasement that had characterized American relations with the Barbary states, meekly agreed to the Dey's demand rather than risk war with Algiers. The crowning indignity, which marked the absolute nadir in the history of the United States Navy, was the Dey's order that the Algerian flag must fly above American colors while the ambassador was on board.[24] How many epithets the proud master of "Pleasant View" flung in the direction of the Bainbridge home no one can know, but he could scarcely have held his tongue in view of the shameful conduct of Captain Bainbridge's ship.

However, there was one brilliant exploit, occurring shortly after Captain Dale's squadron reached the Mediterranean, in the summer of 1801, that tended to allay the humiliation that followed in the wake of the *George Washington*'s cruise.

Lieutenant Andrew Sterett, commanding the twelve-gun schooner *Enterprize*—which command he had been given by Captain Truxtun in the West Indies during the previous winter—and seconded by Lieutenant David Porter, had captured a Tripolitan man-of-war after a battle that raged for nearly three hours. The corsair, which mounted fourteen guns, lost thirty men killed and thirty wounded. Aboard the *Enterprize* none was killed; moreover, not a man was even hurt. The American officers had learned their lessons well when they were in Captain Truxtun's ships.[25]

This news came shortly after it was learned in America that the Bashaw of Tripoli had in the traditional manner—by chopping down the flag staff in front of the American consul's office—declared war on the United States.[26]

Except for Lieutenant Sterett's victory, the year had gone badly for the Navy. Even the thought of the cruise of the *George Washington* was enough to make any naval officer cringe. In Washington, the business of the Navy had been carried on by General Sam Smith for nearly four months before a permanent Secretary of the Navy could be found. It was only after the President had suffered five refusals that he finally found a man who would sit in the chair. Samuel Smith's younger brother, Robert, a Baltimore gentleman of quite inconsiderable talents, took office near the end of July, 1801.[27]

Midway through January, 1802, in the dead of winter at Perth

Amboy, the call came to Captain Truxtun to take out a second squadron to the Mediterranean to relieve Captain Dale.[28]

While the preparations for his departure were going forward at "Pleasant View," a caller took the trouble to set down his impressions of the Truxtun household after partaking of its hospitality.

"We have visited the Commodore and Lady," wrote the guest, "and seen all their Eastern magnificence. Mrs. Truxtun is quite agreeable, and the Commo. extremely genteel, and their children beautiful. Their tea was excellent, their china handsome, and the silver Urn the most dazzling utensil I ever saw on a tea table. . . . Commo. T. is preparing to join the squadron in the Med., heartily tired of Amboy where he has been confined with gout, . . . Hercules at his distaff, and Achilles in female attire were not stranger figures than the brave Commo., sitting at his desk, penning his instructions for the American Navy, arrayed in his uniform coat, cocked hat and cockade, a flannel petticoat in place of breeches, and his feet rolled up in pieces of the same texture. But he is now to leave us, perhaps forever, and as he rises in his wrath, let the Dey of Algiers and all perfidious pirates tremble at his approach." [29]

CHAPTER 40

## TO QUIT THE SERVICE

ℰ  ·  ·  ℰ  ·  ·  ℰ  ·  ·  ℰ  ·  ·

ON MONDAY, the first day of February, 1802, Captain Truxtun was in the Navy Office in Washington.[1] Sniffling with a cold he had caught on the stage journey down, he had come to learn from the Secretary of the Navy more about his assignment.

Secretary Robert Smith—this was the same Robert Smith who had been spurned and ignored by Captain Truxtun while he was in Baltimore building the *Constellation*—was most agreeable. He complied immediately with the Captain's request that an additional captain, to be responsible for management of the flagship, be assigned to his squadron. After all, Commodore Dale had a junior captain in his flagship in order to relieve him of the petty details of daily routine, leaving him free to spend his time on his principal duties as commodore; and when captains to be retained under the Peace Establishment Act were selected, an extra one was held over in order to act as captain of the ship in which a commodore carried his flag.[2] Secretary Smith turned to his chief clerk and asked him to write out a list of the officers who would be under Captain Truxtun's command. Heading the list as flag captain was Hugh Campbell, who had commanded the brig *Eagle* in his squadron in the West Indies.

Captain Truxtun observed to Secretary Smith that the flagship, *Chesapeake,* was a very small frigate in which to carry his flag, but he made no issue of it because he intended to shift to the *Constitution* when she reached Gibraltar, after undergoing necessary repairs in Boston. Neither of the other large frigates was immediately available. The *United States* was laid up, out of commission, and the *President* was already in the Mediterranean.[3]

After they had settled the details of his command, Secretary Smith took Captain Truxtun to call on the President. Mr. Jefferson was quite distant—coldly polite and nothing more—during the short interview. Therefore, the Captain was quite surprised a few hours later to receive a card from the President, inviting him to dinner on Wednesday afternoon.

The dinner party on Wednesday was a strange affair. Still plagued by his cold, Captain Truxtun thought he would have been better off in bed, but he attended in order to "prevent anything like an appearance of disrespect to the Chief Magistrate."[4] A dozen gentlemen, at least, were present. The President, plainly dressed, acted the host. Soft-spoken, mild in manner, a rambling but often brilliant conversationalist: this was the man who presided at the table that was the social focus of the unfinished and desolate city of Washington.[5]

Compounding the discomfort of his cold was Captain Truxtun's icy reception in the President's house. Throughout the whole afternoon, the subject of the squadron that he was on his way to command was never broached, nor were the deteriorating relations with the Barbary powers. In fact, during the course of the conversation, President Jefferson astonished him by asking him whether he was traveling northward or southward.

Certainly, as Captain Truxtun pointed out, the dispatch of a squadron to the Mediterranean station was not a matter too trifling for the President's attention. Probably, as he also observed, his appointment to the command of the squadron "was by No Means Congenial to the President's feelings." Nevertheless, he gulped a bit, got his pride down out of his craw, and pressed on to Norfolk.[6]

His flagship, the *Chesapeake,* tied up at a wharf in the Norfolk Navy Yard, was a disheartening sight. She had lain there, unattended and almost forgotten, for nearly a year. There was but a single officer on board, and he had been unable to make much progress with necessary repairs.

With characteristic vigor, Captain Truxtun fell to this latest task. Within three weeks, he had completed the repairs and had on board provisions enough for a cruise; still, he lacked officers and men to take his ship to sea.[7]

By the third of March, 1802, he had only two lieutenants out of four promised him, and a letter from Secretary Smith led him to believe that he would receive no more, because Smith suggested that he promote a deserving midshipman to the post of third lieutenant. The letter also informed him that Captain Campbell, his flag-captain-to-be, would not be able to join him because of a recent injury.[8] No mention was made of a possible replacement.

Two lieutenants, both of them young and inexperienced, and no flag captain: that was more than he could endure. He could see ahead the bitter prospect of having to train, from the very beginning, the crew of the *Chesapeake* as he had trained the *Constellation's* crew four years before; and while this was going on, he would also have the duties of commodore to perform. Under the circumstances, he thought that the two jobs—captain and commodore—were too complex to be handled by a single officer. "Not only too hard," he told his friend Charles Biddle, "but highly improper, and should neither be attempted by an individual or permitted by the Government." All in all, the situation was highly unpromising. He was tempted again to give up his command to anybody who would take it.[9]

Having worked himself into a high state of agitation, he decided to bring the matter to a head. He sat down and wrote a letter to Secretary Smith, asking once more for a flag captain.

"Having a reputation to lose, which I am very tenacious of," he wrote, "I should consider myself wanting in that duty which I owe to myself and to my family if I was to proceed without being placed in a situation similar to the Commander of the Squadron now in the Mediterranean and if this cannot be done I must beg leave to quit the service." [10]

If Secretary Smith had been half the judge of men his predecessor Ben Stoddert was, this would have been but another incident in the story of a Mediterranean cruise. He would have recognized that Captain Truxtun had been battling successively the gout, a cold, and the frustrations that fairly surrounded him in Norfolk while he labored with his undermanned ship. He would have answered the Captain's letter by offering him a few words of helpful encouragement. His first move would have been propitiatory, because he would have realized that the Navy could not afford to lose a Truxtun. But judgment and tact were not among the Secretary's few positive attributes. Most of his letters were unnecessarily blunt; many of them bore the stamp of insolent authority. The one he wrote to Captain Truxtun was of the same variety. He left no loophole in case the Captain should change his mind. Regarding his wish to "quit the service," he told him flatly, "I cannot but consider your notification as absolute." He then sent off for Captain Richard Morris, in Boston, to hurry to Norfolk to assume the vacant command.[11]

As soon as Ben Stoddert caught wind of the affair, he went to call on Secretary Smith. The Secretary showed him the correspondence and declared that there was nothing that could be done about sending a flag captain to serve under Captain Truxtun. Stoddert, after visiting the Secretary, wrote to his friend in Norfolk: "You will not, I presume be considered out of the Navy, indeed Smith said you would not, unless you resign."

"I think you had better not resign." [12]

Ben Stoddert's letter reached Captain Truxtun too late. Already he was telling the world—individual by individual inhabitant thus far—that he had resigned and why he had done it. He wrote a long letter to his alter ego, Charles Biddle, detailing for his judgment the reasons and motives for "having quit the Navy." [13] He told Vice-President Aaron Burr, who was always pleased to hear evil of the President, that the master of the "palace . . . never intended that I should proceed on the command in question, if it could be decently avoided."

"It was," he wrote, "with pain & reluctance I quit the Navy but it was unavoidable, as you will see. . . ." [14]

These were but the first of hundreds of letters that came from under his hurrying quill. As time went by, the writer became more incensed, the script grew larger, the strokes bolder, the commas and dashes more splattered as he stabbed indignantly at the white pages. Eventually, he came to rue his decision and to wish that he might return to the Navy. But it was too late. Do what he might, he could never unwrite that letter of the third of March, 1802, in which he had said "I must beg leave to quit the service."

# PART FIVE

# Commodore Ashore

## CHAPTER 41

## IN OR OUT?

ಲ   •   •   ಲ   •   •   ಲ   •   •   ಲ   •   •

THE man who arrived home in Perth Amboy, late in April, 1802, had suddenly grown old. Feeling "extremely Ill indeed," he climbed into bed at once; he roused himself only enough to explain in a letter to his friend Captain Dale, that "My indisposition has been brought on from various causes, too perplexing to await the human mind at any one time." [1] He was not full of years; he was only forty-seven; but he was out of the service that he had thought he would follow for the rest of his life. Already, he had done important work, but now it appeared that he had forever closed the door on the opportunity to do more.

He found little to do at Amboy besides write letters. "I want to employ Money," he told Captain Dale, "but am either afraid or have forgot how." [2] The management of his financial affairs he left in

Charles Biddle's capable hands. Finding himself with more time than he could make use of, he brooded. As he brooded, his thoughts went round and round in an ever tightening circle. Always at the center of the circle was the Navy Department, and always at the center of the Navy Department was the man whose policy was constant as a weather vane, Secretary Robert Smith. As he turned his troubles over and over in his mind, he became more firmly convinced that he was, in one way or another, the object of a calculated course of persecution being followed by the new Administration. As long as Secretary Smith interspersed his yesses and noes with maybes, Commodore Truxtun was never quite sure whether the Secretary was the author of all the cruelty, or whether it stemmed from his elder brother General Sam, or perhaps even from President Jefferson himself. He made much of the warning he had received "from high authority"—a Federalist Congressman [3]—that he would be cunningly removed from his post. "They will not dismiss you," he had been told, "because you are too popular, but they will work you out of the Navy, by contrivance." [4]

Cunningly? By contrivance? What signifies a word—had he not resigned? Here the Commodore shifted his ground. The more he thought about it, the more positive he became that he had merely begged leave to quit the Mediterranean service, and that it was a deliberate misconstruction of his letter that enabled his tormenters to work him out of the Navy.

He believed that time would do him justice and "convince the world," as he was convinced, that "it was a national misfortune" that he did not go to the Mediterranean.[5] Judging by the news that came back from the Barbary coast, there was more than a little truth in his bombastic assertion. With the exception of Lieutenant Sterett's exploit, all the news was bad. Commodore Dale's squadron had accomplished little. Commodore Richard Morris, whose squadron relieved Dale's after Commodore Truxtun quit, found the job too much for his abilities. Upon his return home, his conduct was censured by a Court of Inquiry; and Secretary Smith, with the President's permission, revoked his commission.[6] Captain Murray, who was left in charge in the interim between Dale's departure and Morris's arrival, was not active enough to suit the soldier-adventurer William Eaton, American consul in Tunis. "Government may as well send out *quaker meeting-houses* to float about this sea," he informed the Secretary of State, "as frigates with Murrays in command."

"Have we but one Truxtun," he asked, "and one Sterett in the United States?" [7]

The master of "Pleasant View," following the progress of the Navy off the Barbary coast, observed that "We have lost many opportunities of establishing a National Character on the ocean." It appeared to him that the operations thus far had done naught but give the officers an airing.[8]

It may indeed have been a national misfortune that he did not take the squadron out to the Mediterranean. Certainly, he would have pursued an active and decided course of action in dealing with the pirate kings. He expected to concentrate his force in an attack on the city of Tripoli, whose Bashaw had declared war on the United States. If he could pound the city to submission, or at least alarm the Bashaw, then he might expect to make an honorable peace with that country. A peace won by force alone, without tribute and without expensive presents to please the arrogant ruler and his court, would make it easier to deal with the other despots of Barbary.

The Secretary of the Navy managed to avoid showing any great concern over the "national misfortune" he was responsible for. He sent ships and men, singly and in squadrons, across the Atlantic and beyond Gibraltar, and he never once considered Commodore Truxtun in any of his plans. His acts, if not his words, left no doubt as to the Commodore's status as far as the Administration was concerned. He was out of the Navy, as completely removed as though he had been stripped of his uniform and commission.

Nevertheless, after he had been home for a year, and when yet another squadron was being talked about, he swallowed his pride for a moment. He had no need for the money he might earn, but he was tired of idleness. Bracing himself, he wrote to Secretary Smith and again offered his services. The Secretary need only command, and he would be ready on a moment's notice to sail in pursuit of all perfidious pirates.

The Secretary did not deign to answer his letter.

Swallowing a little harder, he tried diplomatically to enlist the aid of Secretary Smith's brother, General Sam, in securing his reinstatement in the Navy. "I never had a desire," he told the General, "to shelter myself behind an Embrasure in time of such danger—or when the public weal required real exertions—nor do I now feel a disposition to be an Idle spectator of scenes to be performed."

"I offered my services to Mr. Secy. Smith last summer," he concluded wistfully, "but I suppose they were not considered necessary." [9]

As the memory of the third of March, 1802, grew to spectral proportions in the mind of the distraught Commodore, the details became blurred. As he dwelt upon his mind's picture of the day when his quill raced over the paper, scrawling out the fateful phrase, "I must beg leave to quit the service," even the colors of the picture began to change. He had ended that letter with a characteristic "I am very busy this morning and write you in great haste." [10] At length, so distorted had the image become, he came to believe that the letter had been written when he was not in full possession of his faculties. Finally, he told all who would listen that the letter was "written in extreme illness, on a day I was twice bled, and when confined in my bed, as is well known in Norfolk." [11]

To anyone who would commiserate with him, he related his version of the whole affair in full and ofttimes wearisome detail. His correspondents included Federalists of the first rank. Former President Adams, former Chief Justice John Jay, and unreconstructed Senators Timothy Pickering and Gouverneur Morris were among the dozens of Jefferson-hating gentlemen who agreed with him that he had been badly used by the new Administration. His correspondence with Senator Pickering was born of their common distrust of anything that President Jefferson's myrmidons might do. "The tyranny exhibited to the friends of former administrations" was for them the rallying call.[12] Both of them were archenemies to those who did not espouse true Federalist principles. And what were true Federalist principles? Let Ben Stoddert, another of Commodore Truxtun's friends and communicants, give the definition. "To be a good Federalist," he said, "a man must be fond of power, only that he may use it, for the benefit of deserving men. The greatest objection I have to the present administration arises from their inability to distinguish who deserves, & who does not, those little offices the Public have to give." [13] The Commodore became quite intimate with the suave and always sympathetic Aaron Burr, Vice-President of the United States; and to Charles Biddle he confided his deepest hurts and bitterest disappointments.

Dogmatic as his correspondents were, it is little wonder that the Commodore became less and less balanced in his treatment of the all-consuming sore that festered in his mind. The wonder is that his mind did not become quite unhinged.

Even the President was not spared from the flood of complaining words that issued from the big house at Perth Amboy. After explaining and re-explaining his position to others for nearly two years, the Commodore had all the details in a fixed order when finally he sat down in 1804 to write directly to Mr. Jefferson. He first enumerated all of the wrongs and slights he had suffered since the beginning of the new Administration. Then he went on to say that if justice were not soon done to him, he would be forced to advertise his case to the public. To give substance to his threat, he enclosed a few copies of a printed letter addressed to his "Fellow Citizens of the United States." Would Mr. President like to reconsider his case before he started to distribute these printed letters? [14]

Apparently not. The President merely filed the Commodore's letter away. He made no reply because he knew that any letter he wrote might very shortly appear in the public prints; and even if it did not, he realized that he could not expect to assuage the Commodore's bitterness. To acknowledge this letter would be to invite more. He had no desire to fan the fires of resentment that burned on the shores of Raritan Bay; therefore he made no reply.

At about this same time, Commodore Truxtun was reminding the Vice-President of the pitiful showing the Navy had made in the Mediterranean. "Since the present administration," he wrote, as though Burr were not a part of it, "every thing they have done in Marine affairs seems to have been studied for the worst—and we have been the laughing stock of foreigners."

"I again repeat," he repeated, *"the Navy is all aback."* [15]

Throughout the years of controversy, he was sustained by the letters that his friends wrote to him and by a firm conviction of his rectitude. Viewed from a distance, the conviction looks a bit ridiculous, but he was not viewing it from afar.

He confided it to his friend Richard Dale. For past services, he wrote, "I have the Nations approbation, which will remain on record when Jefferson and his sect are sunk into obscurity—yes my friend when they are no More, and Not a bone or vestige of them is to be found under the surface of the earth." [16]

Old John Adams sent him a warm letter on another occasion that harked back to more glorious days. The golden medal, voted to Captain Truxtun shortly after his action with *La Vengeance,* had been delivered to him just before he left the service in 1802, more than two years after the event. He had an additional hundred copies of the medal struck at the Mint; Adams was one of those to whom he sent a copy. This was the occasion for the former President's letter.

"I accept [the medal] with great pleasure," Adams wrote, "not only from a personal regard to the giver, but I esteem every laurel conferred upon you for the glorious action of the first of February, 1800, as an honour done to our beloved country. . . ."

"I regret that the artist had not completed the Medal in season, that I might have had the satisfaction of presenting it [the presentation was made by President Jefferson on the day of the fateful dinner party in February, 1802] to an officer who had so greatly deserved it; and I lament still more that I had not the power of promoting merit to its just rank in the navy, that of an admiral. . . ."

"All reasonable encouragement," he concluded in perfect tune with his reader, "should be given to a navy. The trident of Neptune is the sceptre of the world." [17]

Although his thoughts were seldom on domestic matters, life went on all around the ailing master of "Pleasant View."

Another baby girl had arrived in the spring of 1802. Only a few weeks later, the melancholy news of the loss at sea of young Tom, nineteen years old, while he was yet returning from his first voyage to the Mediterranean, was a blow that had greatly disturbed the equanimity of the household. In the spring of 1804, Mary was again pregnant. For the eleventh time, she awaited the arrival of another addition to her family.

"The promise of name," Commodore Truxtun wrote to Charles Biddle, "is not forgot should a boy arrive." [18] But the baby was not named Charles. This latest—and last—arrival was another girl. In all, Mary Truxtun bore twelve children. Thomas and Elizabeth had arrived as twins. Two girls had died, one in infancy and one at the age of twelve; the sea had claimed Tom. Still, there were eight girls, ranging all the way from Sarah, now married for eight years, to

Gertrude, the new baby; and there was one boy left—William, going on fourteen.

William, like his elder brother, was born to the sea. When he was fourteen, his father arranged a berth for him in a China trader under the command of Captain William Jones, who had been one of Captain Truxtun's officers in the *St. James,* more than twenty years before.[19]

"He is a healthy, active & I think every way smart boy," he told Charles Biddle. "I would sooner he would go with Jones," he continued, "than any other person—as good manners and a dignified deportment are essential in forming the Young Mind and such are not as frequent as I could wish on ship board generally." [20]

Daughter Elizabeth, whose first husband had run away, was married for the second time; and as though the fates had all contrived to remind her father of his woes at every turn, her second husband was Theodore Talbot, son of none other than Captain Silas Talbot, onetime senior officer of the triumvirate Talbot, Dale, and Truxtun.[21]

Even the inexorable march of years did little to mend the wounded feelings of Commodore Truxtun. Throughout all of his days, he had a skin that was excessively tender. He found insult and injury in the slightest indiscreet utterance of enemy or friend. Too often he thought, when two men talked together or when a coffee house crowd conversed, that he was the subject of conversation. He never quite understood the ephemeral quality of public acclaim. He never realized that the public memory was so very slight.

He had already been grievously hurt by the events that followed his impetuous withdrawal from the Navy. He had yet in store an almost unendurable measure of insult, injury, and humiliation. He would bear the scars of it to his lonely grave.

## CHAPTER 42

## BURR-HAMILTON INTERLUDE

&ℴ  .  .  &ℴ  .  .  &ℴ  .  .  &ℴ  .  .

ON THE Fourth of July, 1804, Commodore Truxtun was in New York, having traveled the twenty-five miles from Perth Amboy in order to celebrate the day with his "brothers in arms," members of the Society of the Cincinnati. At Ross's Hotel, a dinner and "suitable entertainment" were given, the usual toasts were drunk, and the hall resounded with the noise of convivial fellowship.[1] General Alexander Hamilton presided at the dinner; seated next to him was Vice-President Aaron Burr, one of the guests of honor. The two men did not speak. Burr was glum and morose during most of the celebration; but when the General, in good voice, favored the company with a song, the Vice-President seemed to rouse himself from his thoughts. He raised his head and watched intently as the General performed.[2]

Commodore Truxtun knew that Hamilton and Burr were violently opposed to each other in politics. The Vice-President's political ambitions had been thwarted by Hamilton many times during the past dozen years or more. It was the General, for example, who tipped the scales in Jefferson's favor when the House of Representatives, as the result of a tie in the electoral college vote, had to decide between Jefferson and Burr for President; and it was he who most lately had caused the defeat of Burr for governorship of New York. But when the Commodore saw them side by side at dinner, he had no remote idea that they were already committed to a meeting on the field of honor.[3] An indiscreet publication by Hamilton had come to Burr's attention, and Burr had issued the challenge.

Just a week later, Wednesday the eleventh of July, Alexander Hamilton lay dying on the dueling ground at Weehawken on the Jersey shore, while Aaron Burr, the man who killed him, was being rowed back across the river to New York.[4]

Commodore Truxtun, who was in New York not long after the duel was fought, caught the spirit of the situation in the opening line of his next letter to Charles Biddle. "There is the devil to pay in this city," he wrote, "about the late duel."

"I am abused," he added, "as being a friend of Col. Burr." [5]

Indeed, any friend of Colonel Burr was thoroughly castigated in the newspapers. The press of New York, which the day before had damned or praised General Hamilton and his Federalist principles according to the principles or pleasure of the various editors, sprang as a body to attack the man whom all of them hated. In the newspapers, Colonel Burr was charged, indicted, and convicted of murder, all without even so much as a sidelong glance at the truth.

Pistol duels between gentlemen were commonplace in a society that maintained a meticulous and elaborate code of honor. Both of the principals in this contest had been on the field before, and the son of the loser had been killed in a duel. "There is no doubt," Commodore Truxtun said, "but the duel was a fair one according to the laws in such cases."

"Why," he demanded, "this abomoniable persecution? I detest and dispise it." [6]

A New York Coroner's jury, disregarding the fact that the duel did not take place in New York, was called when public clamor had reached alarming proportions. It sat day after day, trying to arrive at the verdict that had patently been reached in advance. The Coroner's jury had not been called until after the dead man was shut up in his coffin, when even the corpse could no longer be positively identified. Commodore Truxtun recounted that not one of the jurors recognized the corpse when it was examined, "owing to its having been painted with Lamp black & tar as also the winding sheet, to insure its keeping without being offensive, untill the desired arrangements for the procession were made."

"I found a great disposition," he told Charles Biddle, "to have me up and examined before the inquisition." All the while he was in New York, he kept receiving calls from men who thought he might have heard Colonel Burr say something that could be used to insure an indictment. But he gave no comfort to those who cried murder. [7]

"I lament the Death of Hamilton," he wrote, "as much as I could the death of a brother of equal talents and worth to human society, but I must at the same time justify Burr, and will everywhere justify him. . . ."

"If the laws of honor in any case between man and man will justify the practice of duelling," he continued, "(and there are some cases in which I think a devout Bishop would almost countenance it) surely [this] must be admitted as one of those cases, and if men and soldiers once go to the field there ought to be no trifling."[8]

On Saturday, July 14, the funeral procession moved slowly up Broadway to Trinity Church; on Sunday the Anglican churches of New York were hung in black, and funeral orations were said for the late departed.[9] Some read a portent in the thunderbolts that were released by an angry heaven just as churches were beginning the evening service.[10]

By the following Sunday, July 22, 1804, cities all up and down the coast were half-masting flags, tolling muffled bells, and listening to the melancholy rite of minute guns.[11] Here was a national misfortune that the people could participate in and enjoy. The public orgy of grief was to be sustained for as long as possible. Finally, the cry for vengeance that had accompanied the lugubrious wailing of the public prints had had its effect. Colonel Burr was afraid to remain any longer in New York.

Shortly after breakfast on this Sunday morning, Commodore Truxtun busied himself in his study at "Pleasant View."[12] A servant interrupted to tell him that a gentleman outside would like to see him. Thinking that it was a neighbor making a call, the Commodore sent the servant back to show the visitor into the drawing room and to tell him that he would be down in a few minutes. Before he had reached a stopping place, his wife halted his train of thought abruptly by telling him that the Vice-President of the United States was waiting to see him.

Downstairs he found only a negro boy, who told him that his master was waiting outside and would he please come outside to see him. Hurrying down the lawn toward his landing place, the master of "Pleasant View" at last caught sight of his caller. In a boat, lying off a short distance from shore, was the fugitive Aaron Burr. The watermen rested on their oars, prepared to pull away at once if the reception of their passenger was hostile. Here was the Vice-President, second officer in the government of the United States. He had spent most of the night on the water; he had abandoned his house in New York; and even now, at the home of an avowed friend, he was acting with extreme caution.[13] He had already learned that his wide circle of acquaintances, attracted to him by his worldwise charm, had shrunk alarmingly when he found himself in trouble.

Commodore Truxtun was still friendly, however. Within a few minutes, the Vice-President was warming himself with a hot dish of coffee. He informed his host that he was fleeing southward, that he had been assured a haven in Philadelphia by Charles Biddle, and that he might go on from there to South Carolina, where his daughter Theodosia—wife of one of the prominent Alstons—lived.[14] He did not wish to intrude himself upon his host's hospitality, he said, and if the Commodore would just hire him horses and a carriage, then he would be gone at once. But it was Sunday and no conveyance was to be had, so Colonel Burr spent the rest of the day and the night at "Pleasant View."

In their conversation that day, the duel was avoided for a while, but Commodore Truxtun could not keep away from the painful yet attractive subject. He told his distressed visitor that he "had esteemed as an invaluable friend, statesman, and soldier" the dead man, adding as an afterthought that he "always had an unfeigned and sincere regard" for Colonel Burr. While he extended to the Colonel a "hearty welcome," he told him that had the fates been reversed he would as readily have welcomed General Hamilton. The day must have been something less than restful for Colonel Burr.[15]

On Monday morning, Commodore Truxtun ordered up his own carriage. Together the two men rode out of Perth Amboy, bound for Cranbury, a village located not far from Trenton. In Cranbury, the Vice-President hired a light wagon to take him on the next stage of his journey. Perhaps before nightfall he could be safe across the Delaware River, in Pennsylvania, out of the state where the duel was fought, and far from New York, where the shrill public outcry had changed his status from that of a gentleman who had satisfactorily settled a point of honor to that of a common murderer who had taken the life of one of his country's first citizens.

This was by no means the last to be heard of him, nor was this the last journey that Commodore Truxtun would undertake because of his association with the brilliant but troublesome Colonel Burr.

Although the Commodore and his lady had wanted for years to move away from "Pleasant View," it was not until the next spring —1805—that he was able to rent the place and to move his family to one of his houses in Philadelphia. He had wanted to go to Washington or Norfolk, to New York or Baltimore—anywhere but Philadelphia. There was something about that city that made him vaguely uneasy. It was as though by public agreement he was being ignored, ostracized. "Never," he told Charles Biddle, "was I in a town City or place in any part of the world where I felt my self so uncomfortable and so humble as in Philadelphia." But he owned property in Philadelphia, he had been unable to sell it, and he had no ready cash to buy a house in another city. "In this world," he wrote dejectedly, "we can have Nothing exactly as it is most desirable." [16]

As his fretful retirement dragged on into its fourth year, his correspondence with friends—among them Colonel Burr—sustained him and at the same time kept all of his doubts and resentments alive. In the fall of 1805, when the Colonel was making an extended tour through the western country, he commented upon seeing the Commodore's name in Nashville.

"Who would have thought," he wrote, "that Naval Talents were in such estimation at 600 miles from salt water?" He had just heard of the racehorse named "Truxtun," which had been recently acquired by Andrew Jackson. "General Jackson, who is the owner of this celebrated quadruped," he continued, "is one of the most distinguished men in that State. He says that as the Commodore stands unrivalled at sea, so is the horse Truxtun on land, and that if he should ever be beaten, he will change his name." [17]

Unrivaled at sea. This letter was idle chatter, of course, but that phrase was a reminder to Commodore Truxtun. The Navy was still fighting the Barbary Wars. Perhaps he still could bring that seemingly endless affair to an expeditious end—if only he could get back into uniform.

Strangely enough, there were signs that the Administration had changed its mind and that it was preparing to make amends for the anguish it had caused him. It appeared to him that he might soon be on his way to the Mediterranean to take command of all American forces there. [18]

## CHAPTER 43

## OUT FOR SURE

ৈ   •   •   ৈ   •   •   ৈ   •   •   ৈ   •   •

THE beginning of the second term of the Jefferson Administration, in 1805, was the occasion for only one change in the President's cabinet, and that change was of no concern to Commodore Truxtun. Robert Smith, "that Dark designing Gentleman," was still Secretary of the Navy.[1]

Through Alexander James Dallas, presently a United States District Attorney, Charles Biddle was able to reopen the question of the 1802 resignation, and at the same time to raise the hopes of the displaced Commodore that he might soon be back in an important command. Biddle had known Dallas since the French craze of 1793, when both of them were active in the Democratic Society; Dallas was intimate with Robert Smith. Biddle wrote to Dallas, saying that he was "very certain the Commodore had no intention whatever of resigning his commission when he resigned the command of the Mediterranean squadron, and that I understood the Secretary, after the appointment of Morris, said he hoped Commodore Truxtun would not resign." Dallas sent this letter on to Secretary Smith.[2]

Within the last year or so Ben Stoddert, the former Secretary, had passed along an encouraging bit of news. Secretary Smith had made the declaration that, with the exception of old Sam Nicholson, Commodore Truxtun was at the head of the Navy.[3] Commodore Barry was dead. Silas Talbot had resigned, as had Richard Dale. Captain Sam, "glittering with his broad golden brassards," [4] had been merely serving his time ashore, ever since Ben Stoddert took him out of the *Constitution* back in 1799, and there was no likelihood that he would ever be sent to sea again. Nevertheless, Secretary Smith made no move at that time to call Commodore Truxtun back to active duty.

It was after Charles Biddle's circumspect prodding that the Secretary opened a private correspondence with the Commodore. In the summer of 1805, they exchanged several letters, and as Secretary Smith turned each reassuring phrase, he led Commodore Truxtun further down the path toward shattered illusions. Aaron Burr warned his friend, when he heard of the letter writing, that no good could come of it; nevertheless, by the end of summer, the Commodore was expecting that he would be called to service any day. Secretary Smith told him as much, promising action "as soon as I shall have the opportunity of speaking with the President in person, and of knowing his sentiments." [5]

What the President had to say to his Secretary of the Navy is unknown; but the President was not the only one whose sentiments the Secretary sounded. In a round of letters that kept the mails from Maine to Virginia busy for several weeks, Mr. Secretary Smith held a consultation-by-post. Writing to four senior naval captains who were in America, he asked for their interpretation of Commodore Truxtun's letter of the third of March, 1802, heretofore construed as his letter of resignation, and of Smith's reply of the thirteenth of March, in which he considered the notification as absolute. When these two letters were written, were their authors talking about a resignation from the Navy, or weren't they? He then instructed the four captains to exchange their sentiments with the others before sending their replies to him. Of all the letters thus written in round robin fashion, a fair sample found its way back to the Navy Office.[6]

Captain Edward Preble, writing from Portland, Maine, extolled the virtues of the gallant Commodore. His "professional talents," he said, have "ever commanded my highest consideration, and his retiring from service has been a subject of regret with me, as our Navy cannot well afford to lose so valuable an officer." [7] Captain Preble had long ago expressed his willingness to serve under Commodore Truxtun in the Mediterranean at any time; [8] but the question now was whether the letter of March third said what the Secretary wanted it to say. Captain Preble could not deny that the Commodore had begged "leave to quit the service" and that the Secretary had agreed that he should do so. He was forced to conclude, he said, that the two men, when they wrote the letters, considered "leave to quit the service" as another name for absolute resignation.

Captain William Bainbridge, in Perth Amboy, had no room in his letter to praise the officer in question, but he readily agreed with Captain Preble that Commodore Truxtun was indeed out of the service.

Captain Samuel Barron, ill at his home in Hampton, Virginia, and barely able to see the paper on which he wrote, answered "aye" to Secretary Smith's request for an answer of "aye." His brother, Captain James Barron, made the opinion unanimous.[9]

After the replies from the four captains were received, Captain Alexander Murray was asked by Secretary Smith to give his opinion of the much-discussed letters. This was the man who commanded the *Constellation* in 1800, when Commodore Truxtun had sent her off to the West Indies without reference to the Navy Office. Captain Murray was shown copies of some of the letters the Secretary had already received, and he was then instructed, as the others had been, to consult with his brother officers before returning his opinion. Captain Murray thought it over for only a few minutes; his reply was almost immediately on its way to the Navy Office. He told the Secretary that he could see no reason to correspond or even to confer with anyone else in "an affair so clear" to his mind. He felt sure that the letter written by Commodore Truxtun was not a resignation, and he hoped it would not be considered as such.[10] Captain Murray's loyalty to his former commander, rather than honest conviction, probably could be thanked for this lone dissenting opinion.

When Secretary Smith wrote again to Commodore Truxtun, on February 10, 1806, it was for the last time. "According to the opinion, nearly unanimous," he wrote, "of professional men consulted thereon, . . . you cannot now be reinstated consistently with the Privileges of the Captains and other Officers of the Navy of the United States." You are, his letter said in a word, out.[11]

After a performance like this, a performance calculated to keep alive old resentments and animosities and to stir up new ones, a performance in which Mr. Secretary Smith demonstrated the extreme paucity of his administrative talents, it was with ample reason that the gallant old Commodore exclaimed,

*"O, Heavens what a man."* [12]

The Secretary's letter, written almost four years after the question first arose, finally laid to rest any ideas Commodore Truxtun had that he could ever return to the Navy. This was the definitive answer that he had sought, whether he realized it or not, during all that time.

This "consultation business," he said, "clears up the whole affair and puts the saddle on the right horse." No longer did he blame the machinations of a vague "Administration" for all of his various troubles. "Robert Smith, (the apology for a Secretary of the Navy)" was the author of all the wicked designs, of all the persecution that had so plagued and harassed him.

He wished that Smith would come out and fight like a man. If only Commodore Truxtun could seize upon a word or a phrase that would give him an excuse for a challenge, then on the field of honor he might teach the little man a thing or two. But no, "he shelters himself," the Commodore said, "behind the embrasures of his office where he will lie skulking until [Smith was being talked of as a possible Supreme Court justice] he is pop'd into another skulking place still more secure." [13]

The embrasures of his office were not the only battlements he sought. The Washington *National Intelligencer,* Administration newspaper, printed column after column in defense of the Navy Department's stand in order "to correct the errors and misrepresentations of certain *printed* sheets, that have been *privately* circulated by Commodore Truxtun." Letters from the Navy Office files were quoted at length, and the whole production bore the heavy-handed imprint of Secretary Smith's strange anxiety to appear as merely a victim of circumstances entirely beyond his control.[14]

Dragging the delicious controversy out beyond all conscionable limits, Commodore Truxtun took up his quill and answered the *Intelligencer*'s arguments one by one. The resulting explanation and vindication of his position was published "to the World" in another pamphlet that added little except bulk to the tedious literature of the subject.[15]

As the months wore on, his correspondence continued apace, growing so monotonous and repetitious that he was at length forced to move back a step or two to survey the cluttered field.

"I am tired of the subject," he said. "An octavo volume would not record the whole history of this business, and all I have heard and know of it." His letters, already written, would fill many octavo volumes; but, fortunately for the reputation he still had left, he did not carry through his earlier plan to publish a book exposing to public view the infamous behavior of Secretary Smith and his "mismanagement" of the Navy Department.[16]

"Had I died the death of Nelson in my last battle," he mused as the news of Admiral Lord Nelson's great victory off Cape Trafalgar reached Philadelphia, "I should Now have been out of the way and it would have been for the better, . . ."

"But that did not please god," he continued, "and I must Spin out the remainder of life as well as I can." [17]

## CHAPTER 44

BURR'S "TREASON"

୧ଡ଼  .   .   ୧ଡ଼   .   .   ୧ଡ଼   .   .   ୧ଡ଼   .   .

THROUGHOUT the years, ever since he had quit the service, and while he was becoming increasingly embittered by his treatment at the hands of the Jefferson Administration, Commodore Truxtun had been encouraged by the smooth and charming Colonel Burr to maintain the self-righteous position he took. If the Commodore should occasionally temper his hatred of the Administration with a suggestion of reasonableness, the Colonel was quick to revive his suspicions and resentments in order to re-establish the status quo. For all of Colonel Burr's overtures there was, of course, a reason. Filled as his busy mind was with schemes, plots, and intrigue, there was always the possibility that an able naval commander, unalterably hostile to the men in Washington, might at some time or in some place be useful to him.

He had often mentioned, in the course of conversations with Commodore Truxtun, his schemes for settlement of the far southwest, embracing at times the southern part of the new Louisiana Territory, at times Texas, and at other times all of Mexico; but the Commodore had listened with only half an ear because he thought Colonel Burr was merely talking. The only thing he regarded seriously was the possibility of speculation in western lands if they could be bought cheaply enough.

One day in the summer of 1806, after the Colonel had asked for his opinion as to the best method for reducing and capturing several widely separated Spanish ports in the Caribbean Sea, Commodore Truxtun began to wonder whether he was witnessing the formulation of some grandiose plan of conquest like that of Miranda, the adventurer who dreamed of ruling all the vast domain of Spanish America. Perhaps also, as the newspapers were beginning to intimate, the Burr plan involved the separation of a slice of western United States territory and its eventual annexation to whatever kingdom the Colonel might cut out for himself. Not that there was anything particularly wrong, at the time, about the whole affair. Commodore Truxtun's good friend Senator Pickering and a band of New England Federalists were campaigning earnestly for the secession of New England from the rest of the states.[1] The concept of an inviolable Union was something that came later, long after the men who fought in the Revolution were in their dotage.

The answer to the question of Colonel Burr's objectives was not long in coming. He sent a message to the Commodore that he would come and take a glass of wine with him one afternoon, provided no other gentlemen were present at his table.

Commodore Truxtun dined with his family, but after the meal was cleared away he sat alone with Colonel Burr. When the wine was poured and cigars were lighted, the Colonel brought forth his plans.[2] He had expected for some time to head an expedition into the western territory, west and north of New Orleans. In case of war with Spain—and such a war seemed probable if not quite inevitable—he intended to invade Mexico with his personal army and to drive the Spaniards out of that part of the world. He would set up a new government over all the conquered territory, and if his plans worked out as he hoped they would, his new kingdom would include a big chunk of the lately acquired Louisiana Territory.[3]

"He said," Commodore Truxtun later recalled, "he wanted to see me perfectly unwedded from this Navy and to determine not to think more of those men at Washington." [4]

His plan to "liberate" Mexico required the assistance of a naval force under able leadership. The Colonel himself could lead troops on land, with General Wilkinson, United States Army, as his second. If the Commodore would take command of the naval end of the expedition, Burr was sure that it could not possibly fail. When the objective—the conquest of Mexico—was achieved, then Commodore Truxtun could at last become an admiral. Under Emperor Burr's new government, he would be given chief command of "a formidable Navy."

The Commodore asked the Colonel whether the President of the United States knew about this scheme.

No! Decidedly not!

In that case, said Commodore Truxtun, he could not think of playing any part in such an expedition. Sanctimonious as his declarations sounded, they were nevertheless sincere and true. His honor as an officer and his unwavering devotion to his country, no matter how the present Administration might treat him, forbade any further discussion of the matter. He could not fathom how General Wilkinson, or anyone holding a commission in the service of the United States, could ever dream of becoming involved in such a plan. "I consider with pain," he told a friend, "the sacred honor of a soldier . . . prosterated for Villainous purposes." [5]

As the months slipped by, reports from the western country gave substance to Colonel Burr's words, and Commodore Truxtun watched "the speck that appeared in the summer to the westward, growing into a heavy and threatening cloud, which darkened the whole horizon in that quarter." [6] The public prints kept conjecture and suspicion on tip-toe, and the Commodore was ever sensitive to the mood and meaning of their often capricious columns.

Meeting his good friend Charles Biddle one morning, he complained that he had not closed his eyes all night.

"What ailed you?" Biddle asked.

"Did you not see in the *Aurora* of yesterday," Truxtun replied, "the mention that 'a distinguished American commander was concerned with Burr'?"

"Yes," Biddle said, "I saw that in the *Aurora,* but why should that give any uneasiness?"

"Why," Truxtun said, "because the person alluded to must be me."

"And are you concerned with Colonel Burr?"

"You know I am not."

"Then why uneasy," Biddle said, "at anything said in the papers about this 'distinguished commander'?"

"Let me ask you, my friend," Truxtun said, "if you would not be hurt at such a publication?"

"Not in the least," Biddle replied. "I should not have the vanity to suppose it was intended for me."

Charles Biddle ended his recollection of this conversation with the waggish reflection that "He was highly offended at some part of what was said, and for a month did not speak to me." [7]

But Commodore Truxtun was unable to let the piece in the *Aurora* pass. He called on the printer Duane and demanded of him an explanation.[8] William Duane, who maintained a line direct to the President's ear in Washington, assured the Commodore that he was not the "distinguished commander" alluded to. Before his caller departed, Duane had gotten from him a complete and detailed recital of all he knew and surmised about the Burr-Wilkinson cabal; and President Jefferson soon had a full report of the interview from Duane.[9]

Commodore Truxtun had said nothing that he wanted to keep from the President's notice. Quite the contrary. When the stories that came back from the western country began to hint at conspiracy and proceedings that threatened the safety of government there, the Commodore carefully recollected all that had passed between him and Colonel Burr, and he sent off direct to the President a full statement of his knowledge of the affair. Moreover, he worked out a plan to employ a small naval force at the mouth of the Mississippi in order to frustrate Colonel Burr's plan to use New Orleans as his base of operations. This naval expedition, he pointed out to President Jefferson, would have control over any commerce carried on with New Orleans and would prevent the arrival of foreign aid; in short, it would be much more effective than an army.[10]

Then came the famous cipher letter.

Colonel Burr's grand schemes went completely awry when his fellow conspirator, General Wilkinson, saw in the situation a chance for personal glory to be gained at the Colonel's expense. Burr's fond hopes of conquest and empire evaporated when General Wilkinson, who far outshone him as a master of intrigue and double-dealing, publicly accused him of treason and published a letter he had received from Burr concerning the expedition to Mexico.

The letter, originally in cipher—they had been using code for their personal correspondence for several years—stated flatly, according to Wilkinson's version of it, "Naval protection of England is secured. Truxtun is going to Jamaica to arrange with the admiral on that station. It will meet us at the Mississippi." [11]

Colonel Burr resolutely denied that he had made any such statement in the cipher letter; and of course Commodore Truxtun had no remote idea of going to Jamaica.

Whether Colonel Burr made the assertion or whether the words were written in General Wilkinson's fine hand can never definitely be known. Nor does it really matter. According to this letter, Commodore Truxtun was clearly implicated in the conspiracy.

Commodore Truxtun met Colonel Burr and General Wilkinson in the spring of 1807, but not "at the Mississippi," nor indeed anywhere in the western country. He met his former friends in Richmond, where Colonel Burr was on trial before a United States Court. The charge was treason.

He made the long journey down to Richmond in order to clear his name of the slightest suggestion of his being involved in the Burr-Wilkinson intrigues. Against his enemies, whoever they might be, he had long since hoisted "the flag of defiance at the main," but he was, as usual, dreadfully afraid that his friends and the public at large might misunderstand, might be gulled by some statement made during the trial, if he were not present immediately to set the record straight.[12]

The imagined urgency of his mission added zest to his overland passage, and certain it is that no other traveler on the road considered his own journey quite as vital as did Commodore Truxtun. He stopped over in Washington only long enough to pay a gentlemanly call on the President and to pick up his old friend Ben Stoddert, who also was bound for the promised excitement in Richmond.[13]

These friends, who rode down from Washington together, were but two members of a vast and brilliant assemblage that converged on Richmond for the celebrated trial. John Marshall, Chief Justice of the Supreme Court, was sitting as trial judge. The Randolphs were there, Edmund acting as chief counsel for the defense, John of Roanoke as foreman of the grand jury. General Andrew Jackson came to Richmond for much the same reason as Commodore Truxtun. He would defend at all costs his fair name and reputation. Colonel Burr's charming daughter Theodosia and her husband had come up from South Carolina, in order to be with the defendant. Printer Duane, of the Philadelphia *Aurora,* and the young author, Washington Irving, were on hand to report and interpret the proceedings to those unable to attend.[14]

While he was yet nearly fifty miles from his destination, Commodore Truxtun found awaiting him a warm invitation from Major James Gibbon to spend his stay in Richmond under his roof. Major Gibbon, a gallant old soldier of the Revolution, would not hear of his friend's going to a common tavern or lodging-house.[15] In a letter to Charles Biddle a few days later, the Commodore remarked on the hospitality of his host and "charming family."

"Richmond I am delighted with," he wrote, "and from the Governour down, throughout the Society of '*Worthies,*' of all politicks, I have been at home and had welcome shown me in every house, *Most Conspicuously*—I Dine every day at ½ past 4, rise at 8 from dinner and be at an evening party at ½ past 8, and in bed at 12—up at 6—go to Court at 10, adjourn at 3."[16] It was almost enough to make him forget why he had come. But not quite.

One morning, he sent to the grand jury an unsolicited note in which he disclaimed any knowledge of the Jamaica expedition to which his name had been tied. Before the day was over, he was summoned before that body "in the most polite and respectful manner" and assured by the foreman that not a single member of the jury ever believed a word of the tale. On that score the Commodore could rest easy.[17]

Before the trial was fairly under way, it became clear that the evidence against Colonel Burr was exceedingly flimsy. He consistently denied ever having had any thought of treason; uniformly he stated that he had never mentioned Commodore Truxtun's name in connection with his schemes. General Wilkinson's obvious lies and distortions made the careful observer wonder how he avoided indictment for crimes and misdemeanors far more serious than Colonel Burr's.

But the public already had condemned Burr. President Jefferson had publicly declared his guilt, and General Wilkinson was the State's star witness.[18] The Administration was leaving no stone unturned in its anxiety to win a conviction. It would be difficult for one to avoid lamenting the sad plight of the persecuted Colonel Burr. Commodore Truxtun saw the defendant in court, and because he "felt compassion for his degraded Situation and recollecting his former standing in Society," he called on him at his lodgings.[19]

He saw General Wilkinson, too. In the midst of a "large & respectable party of Gentlemen," the fat, importantly strutting General recognized him and advanced with outstretched arms of friendship. From the Commodore he got no sign of recognition, no word of greeting. He was snubbed into a completely disordered retreat.[20]

Meanwhile, Charles Biddle was receiving letters from all three—Burr, Truxtun, and Wilkinson—while they were in Richmond.

"Truxtun abused Wilkinson as having acted the part of a base hypocrite," he said later; "and Wilkinson wrote of him in such a manner that they would have fought had they seen each other's letters." [21]

Perhaps they would have, but the Code concerned itself only with the conduct of gentlemen in affairs of honor; and if even half the adjectives Commodore Truxtun used to describe General Wilkinson were accurate—actually, nearly all of them were—then the General was so far beneath the rank of gentleman that no self-respecting follower of the Code would accept his challenge. He could be considered only fit for the "cow skin," a whip wielded by the strong hand of a "Negro hired for the purpose." [22]

Commodore Truxtun testified at the trial as a State's witness, but he gave no comfort to the Administration. His testimony was calm and deliberate. He told the whole truth as he saw it. He made it clear that he had suspected Colonel Burr's designs from the beginning, but he could not by any stretch of language consider anything that Burr had told him as treasonable. His demeanor could not help but impress the jury; for a fleeting moment, just before he stepped down from the stand, the court heard an echo of the zeal that had helped to make him a great ship commander. Colonel Burr, conducting his own cross-examination, ended his questions with, "Would you not have joined in the expedition if sanctioned by the government?"

"I would," he answered, "most readily get out of my bed at twelve o'clock at night, to go in defence of my country, at her call, against England, France, Spain, or any other country." [23]

Eventually, Colonel Burr was acquitted. General Wilkinson, who should have been on trial in the first place, found himself caught up in his own tangle of lies and accusations, and he emerged from Richmond with a badly tarnished reputation. For Commodore Truxtun, although he did not recognize it as such, the trial had provided occupation for a harassed mind and an excuse for a most enjoyable outing.

The trial held the center of the national stage for many months, and it would have provided grist enough to keep the Commodore's mills turning for years; but the *Chesapeake* and *Leopard* affair, coming as it did in the middle of the trial, put a new face on the whole proceedings. Here was Mr. Jefferson's government bending all its efforts toward punishing a citizen who was a political enemy, while off the nearby Virginia capes the national honor was being compromised as a result of the deplorable state of the Navy. Commodore Truxtun knew by heart the whole catalog of events, deeds, and misdeeds that had brought the Navy to its present state. That it was yet to suffer further loss of stature was already manifest, and in this he was destined to play—for the last time—a characteristically vigorous role.

CHAPTER 45

## JEFFERSON'S EMBARGO

℘ . . ℘ . . ℘ . . ℘ . .

THE *Leopard* was a British frigate that had recently lain in Hampton Roads. Several members of her crew had deserted and, according to her captain, had enlisted in the United States frigate *Chesapeake,* which was preparing to sail for the Mediterranean. Fitted out as a flagship, the *Chesapeake* was commanded by Master Commandant Charles Gordon and carried Captain James Barron as commodore of the Mediterranean squadron. The British captain, after vainly demanding the return of the deserters, watched the American vessel narrowly as she lay moored nearby. When at length the *Chesapeake* weighed for sea, the *Leopard* followed close astern. When the frigates were a few miles at sea, the British captain again demanded the deserters. He was met again by a refusal to deliver up the men, so he resorted to his guns to enforce his demands. The *Leopard* attacked the *Chesapeake.* The American ship was hopelessly unready for battle. Some of her guns were not securely mounted in their carriages; matches were not lighted, and only a few powder horns were filled; her marines had no musket cartridges that would fit their pieces. Moreover, the ship had not been cleared for action, and even when the attack was imminent, her men were not called to quarters. Before she was able to fire a single shot, her colors were struck and she was surrendered to her attacker. The captain of the *Leopard* took out of her the men he had been demanding, and contemptuously he returned her to her captain.[1]

If this was not an act of war—and Commodore Truxtun could see it as nothing else, while the Administration was anxious to say as little about it as possible—then this humiliating transaction was at least a warning that ought not to be ignored.[2] The treatment of the incident was consistent with the rest of naval policy, policy that more than once had sacrificed national honor on the altar of expediency, and which now seemed calculated to remove the United States from the place it had once earned as a naval power.

Commodore Truxtun, who had set an example of enterprise and audacity for the young Navy, saw better than most Americans that Mr. Jefferson's compromising policy was likely to lead to complete impotence on the ocean. He understood the fallacy in the argument that America could get along perfectly well without a Navy. Many of his naval lessons he had learned at sea; in addition, he had for more than a decade studied every work on naval and military strategy and tactics and military philosophy that he could contrive to add to his library. For Thomas Dobson, printer of the *Encyclopedia,* he had edited for publication some extracts from "the best authors" on naval tactics, and added a commentary on the genius of Admiral Lord Nelson's brilliant but unorthodox tactical concepts as demonstrated at Trafalgar. He examined the battle from every angle in order to encourage young American naval officers to become more proficient in the naval art.[3] "We have many good Seamen but very few tactitians among them," he wrote, "and this will be the case until a National marine academy is established. . . . But such an Institution is not likely to be created in our day, as we have no Naval Pride."[4]

Indeed, naval pride reached a dangerously low ebb during Mr. Jefferson's administration. The President finally arrived at the delusion that the way to keep out of trouble with foreign powers was to keep American vessels off the ocean. That idea, so popular with Antifederalists during the early years of the Navy, was revived during the public outcry that followed the *Leopard*'s attack on the *Chesapeake*. Jefferson proposed the building of a gunboat Navy, composed of fleets of small vessels for the defense of coastal cities, bays, and rivers, but he did nothing to bolster the sagging strength and morale of the sea-going Navy.

Commodore Truxtun agreed with his policy of building gunboats for harbor defense, but at the same time he did not want the Navy to consist of gunboats alone. He realized that the nation's maritime trade could not survive unless it had the protection of a fleet capable of sailing anywhere and of fighting at sea. The gunboats could only be effective in smooth waters, and without an ocean fleet it was vain to believe that commerce could venture into the open sea. As far as the deep sea Navy's relation to national honor was concerned, there was never any question in his mind. One could not survive without the other. As Mr. Jefferson pursued his unhappy course to its ultimate end, the Commodore could only conclude that both the Navy and national honor were irrevocably doomed.

In December, 1807, the end was reached. The Embargo Act was passed and—according to law—American foreign trade ceased. As might have been expected, the embargo was not complete. A few unscrupulous men always find a way to circumvent the law when the law threatens to diminish their influence or their income. Heavily freighted coasting vessels, carefully observing all of the prescribed forms for registry and clearance, could easily contrive to be blown off the coast during foul weather and, after seeking refuge in the West Indies, could as easily manage to dispose of their cargo at a handsome profit. By law, however, America was, by its own choice, isolated from the rest of the world.

Strange as it seems at first glance, Commodore Truxtun was not opposed to the Embargo Act—only to the emasculation of the Navy that accompanied it. In his opinion, the embargo could not last for long, and while it lasted it would hurt nobody but the French in the West Indies. The British, supreme upon the seas, would not be affected seriously by the removal of American bottoms from the carrying trade; but the French, already sorely distressed by the military extravagance of their emperor Napoleon, would be hard put to find a substitute for the supplies and vessels that Americans had furnished them with. Forever, in Commodore Truxtun's mind—in spite of the *Leopard* incident—France was the enemy across the sea.

He thought he saw everywhere the signs of an approaching day when his beloved country would have acceded to every demand of the arrogant Napoleon and when the United States would be merely another of the growing company of satellites in the French Empire.[5]

During the first year of the embargo, his interest in national affairs was dulled by his disgust with the way they were being conducted. As relief, perhaps, he turned to the soil. The spring of that year, 1808, found him hard at work in the role of gentleman farmer. In exchange for one of his houses in Philadelphia, he acquired more land near Cranbury, New Jersey. His farm, which he called "Cranberry Place," grew, through small purchases from neighbors, to well over two hundred acres.[6] It was situated on the Brunswick Road beyond Trenton, a long day's drive from Philadelphia. "Cranberry Place" had extensive buildings, a large timber lot, an orchard of some five hundred apple trees, a fine flock of English sheep, quantities of poultry and other animals, and fields set out in Indian corn, oats, wheat, rye, flax, and vegetables.[7]

At times, he seemed almost happy again as he planned the spring planting, concerned himself with the breeding of his sheep, or totted up the loads of compost manure manufactured from "lime and rich earth from a swamp I have." [8]

After the embargo had been in effect for a year, and the Enforcing Act, which gave local customs officers dictatorial powers in refusing clearance to vessels and in confiscating cargoes, had been added to the original law, the results of this unhappy legislation were increasingly evident. Forests of empty spars, rising from fleets of rotting hulks, stood stark against the sky in every harbor town. Export goods were valueless. Foreign wares that found their way to American shores were daily becoming scarcer, and speculators were making exorbitant profits. Prices had gone up to a price-and-a-half within a season; within another few months it seemed certain that they would go to twice or thrice normal unless the embargo was lifted at once.[9]

The Enforcing Act, according to merchants and traders, was "a direct invasion of the established principles of civil liberty." To continue the embargo any longer, they added, was "unjust, oppressive, and impolitick." [10]

Commodore Truxtun agreed with them. In January, 1809, he found himself again embroiled in a public controversy.

On a clear, crisp Tuesday morning, the last day of January, a deputation of merchants and traders ("Friends of the Constitution, Union and Commerce," they called themselves), swelled to mob proportions by Federalists, by sympathizers with their cause, by unemployed seamen, and by the merely curious, appeared in Chestnut Street before the State House—the building in which both the Declaration and the Constitution were born.[11] Nearly two thousand strong, they surged up the steps, through the hallway, and out the other side into the State House yard. Following them was a crowd from the opposite political camp.

A stage had recently been erected in the yard by the Antifederalists—now called Democrats. They had used it the week before for a meeting during which they gave voice to their approval of the Enforcing Act.[12] The crowd that was now filling the yard had provided no other rostrum for the leaders of its meeting. It was well known, having been advertised in the press for several days, that the Democrats were determined to prevent the opposition from using their property.[13]

No Democrat had yet made a move to seize the stage when the merchants and traders began to shout for their leader to take the chair. Two unemployed seamen mounted the platform and planted an American flag at each end of it. A group of prominent men, members of the committee that had organized the affair, followed. Then the chairman, none other than "the gallant TRUXTUN," ascended and took his seat.

The portly, graying Commodore—he was nearly fifty-four years old this day—was in distinguished company. His friends Commodore Dale and Joshua Humphreys were alongside him. George Clymer, nearing seventy, a signer of the Declaration of Independence, was the secretary; and several old soldiers of the Revolution were there.

"Eleven o'Clock was the hour of meeting," the chairman recounted a day or two later; "it was now ¾ after ten—the people called aloud to proceed to business—the Democrats said they had erected the stage and demanded it—we had possession and was determined to maintain it. And I told the seamen along side of me to support the Colours at all events—that the flag of the U S had never been disgraced under my auspices. They swore support. . . ."[14]

Just as the meeting was being called to order, the Democrats, several hundred strong, accompanied by numerous well-served drums, pressed forward to make good their threats. "They came up furiously at first," he continued, "to dispossess us of the stage—but having the fort, we maintained it, and they were drove back by the citizens of our party and the hardy tars." Foiled in their attempt to halt the proceedings, they dropped back a little and continued to beat their drums and to shout and hiss all the while the meeting lasted.

The resolutions to be approved by the assembly were read. The first—there was no hint of hypocrisy in it—was "That the committee will support the government, right or wrong." The others, urging repeal of the Embargo Act and the Enforcing Act, included the "earnest advice to our fellow citizens everywhere to avoid and discourage violation" of the acts until regularly repealed. In all, a moderate and honorable production.

The chairman put the question: "Do you agree to these Resolutions?"

As he recounted it, "A unanimous cry of Aye resounded through the air."

The resolutions having been approved, the meeting adjourned. The "hardy tars" assisted Commodore Truxtun off the platform; they handed down his chair; and without further ado they demolished the stage. Leaving the splinters for the Democrats to fret over, the crowd made its way back through the State House into Chestnut Street once more.

The Commodore was at the center of a throng in high good spirits. Again and again, the name of Truxtun echoed up from the narrow street. The sailors brought the chair they had taken from the stage; they crowded around "their adored Truxtun" and in a moment seated him in the chair. Amidst the repeated shouts of "huzza!" he was carried above their heads in a triumphant procession toward the Coffee House.

Lurching along in his seat of honor, he looked down upon a sea of a thousand heads of sailor men. He had commanded men like these —men who had toiled at a rope-end, who had swarmed up icy shrouds and lain out on plunging yards to fist and hand brutally thrashing sails whipped about by biting winds, men who knew the feel of heaving decks and lonely nights a thousand leagues from home. These were fearless men, men who knew no master ashore, men who paid homage only to those who had earned their respect.

Commodore Truxtun still stirred the popular imagination as a leader of men. Once again—for the last time during his lifetime—he was being publicly acclaimed as the gallant Commodore, the brave warrior, the famous son of Neptune. It was an unforgettable tribute.

At the Coffee House, he was carried into the gallery. "I then addressed the Multitude," he said, "in an appropriate manner." The multitude applauded. The air was filled for a time with sailors' cheers; and then the crowd dispersed "in good order and in high spirits." [15]

The old guard of Federalism, revived by this demonstration of strength, was active for a few days after the meeting. Commodore Truxtun was caught up in an exhausting round of committee meetings, attending as many as four in a single day.

On the tenth of February, 1809, this spurt of activity reached its second climax—some would say anticlimax. On that day, in the Mansion House Hotel, a lavish dinner was given in honor of the Commodore's friend, Senator Pickering, and the other "Federal members" of the Senate and House of Representatives. Over two hundred and fifty Federalists, filling three dining rooms, sat down to the meal. Commodore Truxtun, a member of the committee on arrangements, presided in one of the rooms.[16]

The whole catalog of Federalist toasts was proposed and drunk. One, anticipating President Jefferson's return to private life—his term was to end less than a month later—was to "A Philosopher in Dignified Retirement: may he find full employment in forcing exotics, coercing bullfrogs, and pinning beetles by the side of butterflies." [17]

As a memento of the occasion, Commodore Truxtun presented to Senator Pickering a song "Composed particularly in honor of your Zeal and meritorious exertions in the Senate, to preserve the Independence and promote the real and true Interest of this Country, as a well proven patriot of old." [18] The song may have been composed by the Commodore. One wonders whether he sang it for the entertainment and instruction of the assembled company.

## CHAPTER 46

# THE LAST CHAPTER

    ❧  .  .  ❧  .  .  ❧  .  .  ❧  .  .

WHILE the echoes of this applause still reverberated in the streets and alleys of Philadelphia, while the ink that recorded this last taste of public acclaim was still fresh in the newspapers, this book might appropriately be brought to a close. Commodore Truxtun still had thirteen tedious years of existence left to him; but already he was seven years away from the sea, seven years removed from the work at which he excelled, from the life he loved. If the years of his retirement thus far had been occasionally interesting and amusing, the bleak years that lay ahead could excite in the bystander only pity— sometimes pity for the Commodore, perhaps nearly as often pity for those around him.

The endless months at home, engaged in no useful or important pursuit, plagued the aging Commodore and taxed his good wife, Mary. Accustomed as they were, throughout their first twenty-five years of married life, to the long months apart and the few intense weeks together between voyages, they were finding that for them too much time together was indeed worse than too little. Mary had for years managed a large household without the advice or interference of her husband; his years of command had taught him to expect instant obedience from everyone about him; and now both of them found that the necessary adjustments could not be conveniently made in middle age.

In the Trenton *Federalist*, a public notice appeared during the spring of 1811. Commodore Truxtun used this means to warn all readers that he would be responsible for no debts incurred by anyone "other than by myself *in person*. . . . Circumstances extremely unpleasant," he informed the public, "have obliged me to have recourse to giving this notice generally."[1] It seems that Mary had bought a pair of shoes and had charged them to her husband's account.

In a pathetic letter to Charles Biddle, Mary told her side of the quarrel that led to the public notice. For the past eight years, she wrote, life for her had been nearly unbearable. Her husband was forever complaining about her spending money on one or another of their married daughters' families. Often he raved and ranted, swore at her, and even ordered her out of the house. The immediate reason for the public notice was that she had bought a pair of shoes at a store in Cranbury without consulting him. What, she asked, could she possibly do to keep her household intact, for the protection at least of the youngest children? [2]

Indeed, it was a disagreeable situation. Thomas Truxtun was a commander of ships and of men, not a fit subject for retirement in any form. In long—almost interminable—indignant letters to the same confidant, Charles Biddle, he poured out his troubles and grievances.[3] So many beloved daughters there were; and so many unworthy suitors and worthless sons-in-law.

The ungrateful Benbridge, Sarah's spouse: what a profligate, what a scoundrel! Many a dollar of the Commodore's hard earned fortune had been spent by Mrs. Truxtun to help support that family. Then there was the scrape that daughter Anna Maria, already married to another man, had had with Paul Hamilton, son of the new Secretary of the Navy. More unpleasant incidents and execrable people to trouble the master of "Cranberry Place." More indignant letters to Charles Biddle. And there was daughter Mary's husband John Swift, whom he had never liked. Even their wedding seemed to be planned to humiliate him. The wedding date was set for a Friday. Commodore Truxtun arrived in town the Tuesday before in order to attend the wedding, but behold! they already had been married on Monday. Even William, his only surviving son, at the age of twenty-one was "So Extreemly bad" that his father would have nothing more to do with him.[4]

Mrs. Truxton finally refused to stay any longer at "Cranberry Place," so their next move was to another farm much closer to Philadelphia. In exchange for "Cranberry Place" they acquired a property near Moorestown, New Jersey, twelve miles beyond Cooper's ferry across the Delaware, and in addition "631½ acres of *choise* lands in Otsego County State of New York." Their new home, a two-story brick house, complete with a "piazza" facing south, they named "Woodlawn."[5]

From piazza and parlor of "Woodlawn" Commodore Truxton

restlessly surveyed the passing parade. Incredulously, he watched the War of 1812 develop. Until nearly the day of war's declaration, the enemy had not been settled upon. He could see no enemy in Europe but Napoleon; and yet war was declared against Great Britain. He was convinced that this war was but an electioneering scheme to insure the re-election of President Madison. Whatever the cause or justification of the war, he could not expect to be asked to help fight it. It was during this war that the Navy came into its own, but only vicariously could he hear the noise and smell the acrid smoke of sea battles that once again brought honor to his beloved flag.

Although his list of correspondents grew shorter as the years passed, he was never entirely forgotten by the men with whom he served. He kept in touch with Captain Tingey; he heard occasionally from his sometime surgeon Balfour; [6] and Robert Harrison, once a lieutenant in the *Constellation* and later a consul in the West Indies, sent him a butt of old rum, and again a quarter cask of well-aged Madeira and a large sea-turtle as marks of "profound admiration and esteem for your character."

Consul Harrison wrote, "Since I left the *Constellation* I have been in every part of the world, . . . and amidst courtiers and princes, I have never forgot the Father of our Glorious little navy, whose consummate skill and perseverance gave the first impulse of Naval enterprize and enthusiasm to a band of young officers, whose deeds [in the War of 1812] have astonished all Europe." [7]

Once during the idle years, Commodore Truxtun let Charles Biddle enter his name on the Federalist ticket for Congress as a Representative from Philadelphia County. Even though he did no campaigning and stayed on his farm until after the election, he lost out by only a score of votes.[8]

In the fall of 1816, Charles Biddle thought he might do his old friend a service by putting him forward as a candidate for High Sheriff of Philadelphia County. There was some difficulty about his living in New Jersey, but he was placed on the ticket and won the office by a comfortable margin. After the election, there was still some question as to whether he could be seated; that being so, his friend and counselor, Charles Biddle, hustled him into a carriage, and the two of them set off for the state Capitol in Harrisburg, where his commission as sheriff would be issued. They left Philadelphia one morning in a downpour, and they stayed on the muddy road all day and all night, in order to secure the commission before the opposition could organize any attempt to prevent its issuance.[9] The two friends were old men to undertake such a harrowing journey. Commodore Truxtun was nearly sixty-two; Charles Biddle was past seventy.

For three years he served the public as High Sheriff. When his term was over in 1819, he was at last content to sit by his fireside, which by this time he had established in Philadelphia, at 328 Arch Street, out beyond Eleventh.[10] With advancing age had come lingering illnesses that grew worse with each new season. The gout was now constantly with him, and it was becoming more and more painful to hold a quill.[11]

He revised his will for the last time "after due consideration and long and cool deliberation." He provided for his wife an income for the rest of her life, "or until she should marry again." She survived him for only about a year.[12] Disowned were his son and two of his daughters. His valuable library was to be divided among his other daughters. The "elegant rich silver urn" was to go to Cornelia and the golden medal to Gertrude. His gold watch and badge of the Cincinnati were to be given to his grandson Truxtun Swift; his "excellent Brass sextant . . . and telescope" were intended for his grandson Truxtun Henderson; and his other instruments and clothes were to go to a third grandson, Truxtun Beale.[13]

There were twenty-four states in the healthy, growing nation in the early spring of 1822. There had been but fifteen when Commodore Truxtun first nurtured the infant Navy.

America was now a respected power upon the seas. No longer were corsairs suffered to plunder vessels that sailed under her flag. No longer did her colors endure humiliation at the hands of arrogant kings and admirals. Her Navy now had ships of the line—seventy-fours—in service, and first-raters that would mount more than a hundred guns were being planned.[14] No longer was the Navy in danger of annihilation in the halls of Congress. Commodore John Rodgers, who had entered the service as first lieutenant of the *Constellation,* was senior officer of the Navy.[15] David Porter and Isaac Chauncey, both of whom had started their naval careers under Commodore Truxtun's command, were high ranking commodores. Both Rodgers and Porter were members of the influential three-man board of Navy Commissioners, which aided and advised the Secretary of the Navy on policy matters.

Throughout the naval service, although his name might be forgotten by younger officers, was the indelible stamp of Commodore Truxtun. He had established a system where no system existed. By precept and example, he had founded a tradition of command. His attributes of personal bravery, audacity, and tenacity were being encouraged within the service. His tradition was being carried on and preserved for generations of naval officers yet unborn.

An aging Quaker widow, Deborah Logan, entered a few lines in her diary on the eighth of May, 1822, the day after the body of Commodore Truxtun was carried down Arch Street to his grave in the Christ Church burying ground—where he yet lies in the company of his friends Benjamin Franklin, Charles Biddle, Richard Dale, and many others.

"I should have mentioned in my acct. of yesterday," the widow Logan wrote in her fine hand, "that Commodore Truxtun was buried. I have always respected him as a worthy Citizen, and a very brave officer, indeed the Father of our American Navy. He has been hardly dealt with by the Government, and others permitted to reap the Harvest that he had sowed, as in the affair of Tripoly. I have not seen him for several years." [16]

Two years later, Commodore Rodgers, upon his resignation from the board of Navy Commissioners in order to assume a command at sea, was honored by a public dinner in Washington. Present were the Secretaries of State, War, and Navy and a distinguished group of Army and Navy officers. As the wine was poured and the toasts were drunk, Commodore Chauncey proposed a toast to "The memory of Commodore Truxtun, the officer under whose auspices our gallant guest first distinguished himself as a naval officer." [17] This was nearly a quarter of a century after either Rodgers or Chauncey had served under the brave Commodore.

The tradition of Thomas Truxtun still lives. His concept of command at sea has stood the test of a century and a half of time. As long as the United States Navy ranges the waters of the globe, his spirit will ride the bridge of every ship in every ocean, strutting his few fathoms of scoured plank, ordering his helmsman to steer wherever "the good of the service" dictates, keeping always uppermost in his thoughts the honor and glory of his country's flag.

# REFERENCE NOTES

*ℰ⁹* . . *ℰ⁹* . . *ℰ⁹* . . *ℰ⁹* . .

ABBREVIATIONS

(a) Abbreviated Titles of Works Frequently Cited.

> *Barbary Wars*. U.S. Naval Records and Library Office, *Naval Documents Related to the United States Wars with the Barbary Powers, 1785–1807*. 7 vols. Washington, D.C., 1939–44.
>
> *Navy 1790–98 LB*. Navy Department Records in the National Archives, *Correspondence on Naval Affairs when Navy was under War Department 1790–1798*. A Ms. Letter Book.
>
> *Quasi-War*. U.S. Naval Records and Library Office, *Naval Documents Related to the Quasi-War Between the United States and France, 1797–1801*. 7 vols. Washington, D.C., 1935–38.

(b) Depositories of Manuscript Collections. For more complete description, see Bibliography: Manuscripts.

> APS. American Philosophical Society, Philadelphia.
>
> HSPa. Historical Society of Pennsylvania, Philadelphia.
>
> LC. Library of Congress, Washington, D.C.
>
> MassHS. Massachusetts Historical Society, Boston.
>
> NDA. Navy Department Records in the National Archives.
>
> NYHS. New York Historical Society, New York.
>
> NYPL. New York Public Library, New York.
>
> PMS. Peabody Museum, Salem, Mass.
>
> PhilaLC. Library Company of Philadelphia.

A NOTE ON QUOTATIONS

I have tried, throughout this book, to make entirely honest use of quotations. However, because of my frequent use of short—sometimes fragmentary—passages, I have made a few departures from the strictly literal method of quoting.

My subject's name was often misspelled "Truxton" in his day, as it is today. I have used "Truxtun" throughout, in order to avoid repeated insertions of the disturbing *sic*. For clarity and consistency, I have shown names of vessels in italics, whether or not the writer underlined the names. I have omitted marks of elision at the end of phrases when their omission has not distorted the sense of the quotation. In a very few cases, spelling, capitalization, or punctuation have been altered; I have resorted to this only when the modern reader would find the original unintelligible. Finally, I have occasionally omitted italics that appeared in the original, particularly when whole sentences were underlined and I used only a sentence or so from a letter. Once or twice, I have ignored italics when the author obviously used them capriciously and indiscriminately.

CHAPTER 1 (pp. 1–6)

1. The first biographical notice of Commodore Truxtun appeared in *Port Folio*, Philadelphia, 2nd ser., 1 (1809), 30–36. It is quite accurate despite its elegance. For life on Hempstead plain, see Benj. D. Hicks, ed., *Records of the Towns of North & South Hempstead* (Jamaica, 1900), IV, 215, 376, 424–25; V, 97.
2. *New York Mercury*, October 13, 1760.
3. E. B. O'Callaghan, ed., *Documents Relative to the Colonial History of the State of New York* (Albany, 1853–61), VI, 133, 392, 550; VIII, 450, 457.
4. *History of Queens County, N.Y., with Illustrations, Portraits, and Sketches of Prominent Families and Individuals* (New York, 1882), p. 58.
5. Island Record Office, Spanish Town, Jamaica, B.W.I.: *Wills*, liber 30, fol. 94. This is the will of estranged wife Mary Truxtun (1702–1755). She was his second or perhaps third wife. See also J. H. Lawrence-Archer, *Monumental Inscriptions of the British West Indies from the Earliest Date* (London, 1875), p. 142.
6. New York Historical Society, *Genealogical and Biographical Record*, XII, 145.
7. Esther Singleton, *Social New York under the Georges, 1714–1776* (New York, 1902), Part 4.
8. *Ibid.*, Part 5.
9. *History of Queens County*, p. 176.
10. Clifford K. Shipton, *Biographical Sketches of Those Who Attended Harvard College in the Classes 1722–1725* (Boston, 1945), pp. 432–40.
11. Henry Onderdonk, Jr., *Annals of Hempstead, 1643–1832* (Hempstead, 1878), p. 76.
12. Quotation from account book of Rev. Mr. Samuel Seabury, entry of August 29, 1761. In collection of the Honorable Samuel Seabury (1947). For remarriage of the elder Truxtun, see his will, note 14 below.

13. Shipton, *op. cit.*, pp. 432–40; *New York Mercury*, March 27, 1762; Henry Onderdonk, Jr., *Antiquities of the Parish Church, Hempstead* (Hempstead, 1880), pp. 22–23.
14. Thomas Truxtun, Sr., *Will*, New York, State and County, Surrogate's Court, *Liber 25 of Wills* (November 18, 1761), p. 172; E. B. O'Callaghan, *N.Y. Colony—Names of Persons for Whom Marriage Licenses Were Issued by the Secretary of the Province prior to 1784* (Albany, 1860), p. 399.
15. E. B. O'Callaghan, *Calendar of Historical Manuscripts in the Office of the Secretary* (Albany, 1865–66), II, 675; *New York Mercury*, July 11, 1757.
16. *Port Folio*, Philadelphia, 2nd ser., I (1809), 31.

## CHAPTER 2 (pp. 6–10)

1. No description of the *Pitt* survives. This description is based on fairly intimate knowledge of sailing vessels of this period. For some general statistical evidence, laboriously assembled, see Murray G. Lawson, "The Boston Merchant Fleet of 1753," *American Neptune*, IX (July, 1949), 207–15.
2. Robert G. Albion, *Square Riggers on Schedule* (Princeton, 1938), pp. 15–16.
3. I have found no satisfactory single account of sea life in eighteenth-century merchant vessels. This account is compounded of many clues derived from a wide variety of source material. A few references are listed in the bibliography. Under Biography, see Andrews, Bullen, Dana, and Roberts; under Naval and Maritime History, see Lever.
4. E. B. O'Callaghan, ed., *Documents Relative to the Colonial History of the State of New York* (Albany, 1853–61), VIII, 451; HSPa: Ratzer Map of 1767, "Plan of the City of New York."
5. *Port Folio*, Philadelphia, 2nd ser., I (1809), 31.

## CHAPTER 3 (pp. 10–13)

1. Isaac Schomberg, *Naval Chronology* (London, 1802), I, 406.
2. *Ibid.*, I, 394.
3. *Ibid.*, I, 406.
4. Truxtun Hare Collection: Truxtun to Secretary of State, December 1, 1796.
5. *New York Gazette, and the Weekly Mercury*, April 15, 1771.
6. Truxtun Hare Collection: Truxtun to Secy. of State, December 1, 1796.
7. *Port Folio*, Philadelphia, 2nd ser., I (1809), 31.
8. *New York Gazette, and the Weekly Mercury*, June 10, 1771.
9. *Port Folio*, Philadelphia, 2nd ser., I (1809), 31.

CHAPTER 4 (pp. 13–16)

1. Peter Force, ed., *American Archives* (Washington, D.C., 1837–53), 4th ser., I, 248–51; II, 134; E. B. O'Callaghan, ed., *Documents Relative to the Colonial History of the State of New York* (Albany, 1853–61), VIII, 431; Alexander C. Flick, ed., *History of the State of New York* (New York, 1933), III, 220–25; Herbert M. Morris, "Sons of Liberty in New York," Richard B. Morris, ed., *Era of the American Revolution* (New York, 1939), pp. 269–89.


CHAPTER 5 (pp. 17–19)

1. Truxtun Family Bible, in private collection of Truxtun Brodhead, Esq.
2. *New York Gazette, and the Weekly Mercury*, April 10, 1775; *Rivington's New York Gazeteer*, April 13, 1775.
3. *New York Gazette, and the Weekly Mercury*, November 13, 1775.
4. *Port Folio*, Philadelphia, 2nd ser., I (1809), 31.
5. Lowell J. Ragatz, *The Fall of the Planter Class in the British Caribbean, 1763–1833* (New York, 1928), pp. 88–89.
6. E. B. O'Callaghan, ed., *Documents Relative to the Colonial History of the State of New York* (Albany, 1853–61), VIII, 446–49.
7. Peter Force, ed., *American Archives* (Washington, D.C., 1837–53), 4th ser., IV, 458.
8. *Ibid.*, 4th ser., III, 1036.
9. *New York Gazette, and the Weekly Mercury*, July 31, September 25, November 13, 1775.


CHAPTER 6 (pp. 20–23)

1. *Pennsylvania Gazette*, Philadelphia, February 21, 1776; *Pennsylvania Evening Post*, Philadelphia, April 23, 1776.
2. *Port Folio*, Philadelphia, 2nd ser., I (1809), 31.
3. J. Thomas Scharf and Thompson Westcott, *History of Philadelphia* (Philadelphia, 1884), I, 309–10.
4. Edmund Cody Burnett, ed., *Letters of Members of the Continental Congress* (Washington, D.C., 1921–38), I, 399, 400; E. C. Burnett, *The Continental Congress* (New York, 1941), p. 138.
5. Burnett, *Continental Congress*, p. 139.
6. U.S. Library of Congress, *Naval Records of the American Revolution 1775–1788* (Washington, D.C., 1906), pp. 249, 258.
7. W. C. Ford, *et al.*, eds., *Journals of the Continental Congress, 1774–1789* (Washington, D.C., 1904–37), IV, 250.

8. [*Colonial Records of Pennsylvania, 1683–1790*] (Philadelphia, 1852–53), x, 542.
9. *Ibid.*, x, 536; Ford, *op. cit.*, IV, 250.
10. Robert W. Neeser, ed., *Despatches of Molyneux Shuldham* (New York, 1913), p. 128.
11. [*Colonial Records*], x, 542.
12. *Ibid.*


CHAPTER 7 (pp. 23–27)

1. Lowell J. Ragatz, *The Fall of the Planter Class in the British Caribbean, 1763–1833* (New York, 1928), pp. 89–90; John Almon, ed., *Remembrancer, or Impartial Repository of Public Events* (London, 1775–82), III, 238.
2. HSPa: Court of Admiralty Docket, June 24, July 1, 1776.
3. *New England Chronicle*, Boston, June 8, July 4, 18, August 2, 1776.
4. Almon, *op. cit.*, III, 174, 238.
5. *New York Gazette, and the Weekly Mercury*, June 10, 1776.
6. Almon, *op. cit.*, III, 174.
7. *Daily Advertiser*, London, August 5, 1776.
8. *Pennsylvania Gazette*, Philadelphia, June 19, 1776; *New England Chronicle*, Boston, August 15, 1776; *Pennsylvania Evening Post*, Philadelphia, June 13, 1776.
9. *Pennsylvania Gazette*, Philadelphia, June 19, 1776.
10. Peter Force, ed., *American Archives* (Washington, D.C., 1837–53), 4th ser., VI, 1026–27.
11. *New England Chronicle*, Boston, August 15, 1776.


CHAPTER 8 (pp. 27–33)

1. B. J. Lossing, *Pictorial Field Book of the Revolution* (New York, 1860), II, 594.
2. E. C. Burnett, ed., *Letters of Members of the Continental Congress* (Washington, D.C., 1921–38), II, 7.
3. Lossing, *op. cit.*, II, 79.
4. Peter Force, ed., *American Archives* (Washington, D.C., 1837–53), 5th ser., I, 374.
5. *Port Folio*, Philadelphia, 2nd ser., I (1809), 32.
6. Thomas Truxtun, *Instructions, Signals, and Explanations Offered for the U.S. Fleet* (Baltimore, 1797), p. 35.
7. *Public Advertiser*, London, October 2, 1776; *Newport Mercury*, September 30, 1776.
8. *Whitehall Evening Post*, London, November 5, 1776.

9. *Independent Chronicle*, Boston, October 24, 1776; *Newport Mercury*, September 30, 1776.

10. Force, *op. cit.*, 5th ser., III, 1498.

11. *Ibid.*, 5th ser., III, 872.

12. *Ibid.*, 5th ser., III, 1072, 1513.

13. *Ibid.*, 5th ser., III, 1223.

14. G. W. Allen, *A Naval History of the American Revolution* (Boston, 1913), p. 50.

15. *Independent Chronicle*, Boston, October 31, November 21, 1776.

16. Secretary of the Commonwealth of Massachusetts, Archives Division: Petition of Isaac Sears for letter of marque for *Mars*, May 24, 1777.

17. Samuel Hazard, *et al.*, eds., *Pennsylvania Archives* (Harrisburg, 1852–1949), 5th ser., I, Letters of Marque, October 25, 1781, *St. James*.

18. *Public Advertiser*, London, August 23, September 8, 1777; *Independent Chronicle*, Boston, July 10, October 30, November 13, December 4, 1777; February 26, 1778.

19. Allen, *op. cit.*, p. 258 and chap. 8.

20. New York Hist. Soc., *Collections* (New York, 1887), Deane Papers, II, 143.

21. *Independent Chronicle*, Boston, November 13, 1777.

22. Of the twenty-one ships owned by Sears & Co. from 1776 through 1782, none was larger than *Mars*. For list of vessels, see U.S. Library of Congress, *Naval Records of the American Revolution 1775–1788* (Washington, D.C., 1906), *passim;* and G. W. Allen, "Massachusetts Privateers of the Revolution," Massachusetts Hist. Soc., *Collections,* LXXVII (1927).

23. Truxtun Family Bible, in private collection of Truxtun Brodhead, Esq.

CHAPTER 9 (pp. 33–38)

1. U.S. Library of Congress, *Naval Records of the American Revolution 1775–1788* (Washington, D.C., 1906), p. 226; Samuel Hazard, *et al.*, eds., *Pennsylvania Archives* (Harrisburg, 1852–1949), 2nd ser., I, 1779—Pennsylvania Navy commissions.

2. Truxtun Hare Collection: Truxtun to William Constable, September 23, 1779.

3. Evangeline W. Andrews, ed., *Journal of a Lady of Quality* (New Haven, 1934), pp. 135–36.

4. *Ibid.*, pp. 136–37.

5. The name *Lydia* appears only in HSPa: Etting Papers, Navy, p. 82, August 26, 1779, a bill of lading.

6. *Ibid.;* Truxtun Hare Collection: Truxtun to William Constable, September 23, 1779.

7. Truxtun Hare Collection: Truxtun to William Constable, September 23, 1779; Truxtun to A. & J. Caldwell, April 21, 1780.

8. Truxtun to A. & J. Caldwell, September 25, October 2, 1779; April 21, 1780.

9. *Ibid.*, February 11, 1780; *Hazard's Register of Pennsylvania* (Philadelphia, 1828–35), VIII, 384.
10. Truxtun Hare Collection: Truxtun to A. & J. Caldwell, February 11, 1780.
11. *Ibid.*, April 21, May 3, 1780.
12. *Pennsylvania Packet*, Philadelphia, June 22, 1780.
13. HSPa: Misc. Ship Papers [Am 677], Thomas Truxtun, *re* brig *Phoenix* and prize brig *Clyde,* June 16, 1780.
14. HSPa: Admiralty Court Papers, June 7, 1780; R. V. Harlow, "Aspects of Revolutionary Finance," *American Historical Review,* XXXV (1930), 49–51.
15. John C. Miller, *Triumph of Freedom* (Boston, 1948), pp. 440–45. Chapter 22, "Inflation and its Consequences," is outstanding on this subject.
16. Josiah Quincy, ed., *Journals of Major Samuel Shaw* (Boston, 1847), p. 58. The actual statement, altered for the sake of uniformity, was "30 for 1."

CHAPTER 10 (pp. 39–42)

1. Truxtun Hare Collection: Truxtun to A. & J. Caldwell, July 27, 1780.
2. Anne Bezanson, *Prices and Inflation during the American Revolution* (Philadelphia, 1951), pp. 135–37; Quotation is from John C. Miller, *Triumph of Freedom* (Boston, 1948), p. 481.
3. Miss Betham-Edwards, ed., *Arthur Young's Travels in France, 1787–1789* (London, 1900), p. 129.
4. LC: John Paul Jones Papers, Jones to Truxtun, October 24, 1780.
5. John S. Barnes, ed., *Fanning's Narrative* (New York, 1912), p. 86.
6. *Ibid.*, p. 78n.
7. U.S. Library of Congress, *A Calendar of John Paul Jones Manuscripts in the Library of Congress* (Washington, D.C., 1903), p. 170, October 13, 1780. In Truxtun Hare Collection: Truxtun to A. & J. Caldwell, L'Orient, September 28, 1780, Tom mentioned the expected departure of the French fleet that made the Yorktown victory possible. The fleet, eventually commanded by de Grasse, was scheduled to sail from Brest (70 miles from L'Orient) on October 8, 1780. Actually, it got under way in January, 1781. Tom listed by name eight ships of the line, as well as the number of transports and troops. This points up the ease with which intelligence might be obtained by the enemy.
8. Barnes, *op. cit.*, pp. 87–89.
9. *Ibid.*, p. 124.
10. LC: John Paul Jones Papers, Jones to Truxtun, October 24, 1780.
11. LC: Continental Congress Papers, vol. 193, fol. 311.
12. *Ibid.*
13. HSPa: Etting Collection, John Paul Jones to Robert Morris, October 26, November 8, 1780.
14. LC: John Paul Jones Papers, Jones to Truxtun, October 24, 1780. For example, see *Quasi-War,* III, 74—Truxtun to Secretary of the Navy, Bas-

seterre, St. Kitts, April 20, 1799. After discussing proper use of command pennants in naval ships, he concluded, "Some Instructions should also be given respecting Merchantmen, hoisting Pendants, and fancy Colours, instead of the regular Ensign of the United States."

15. Truxtun Family Bible.
16. Truxtun Hare Collection: Truxtun to A. & J. Caldwell, December 29, 1780.

## CHAPTER 11 (pp. 42–47)

1. MassHS: Pickering Papers, Truxtun to Pickering, December 8, 1807.
2. Franklin Institute, Philadelphia: Lenthal Collection, Mast yard papers of Turner & Thompson, "Dementions of [masts and spars of] the Ship Sainte James Capt. Truxon."
3. Truxtun Hare Collection: Truxtun to A. & J. Caldwell, November 17, 1781; *Pennsylvania Packet,* Philadelphia, October 23, 1781.
4. Charles W. Goldsborough, *United States' Naval Chronicle* (Washington, D.C., 1824), I, 28n.
5. HSPa: Jones & Clarke Papers, William Jones to Truxtun, January 18, 1809.
6. *Diary of Frederick Mackenzie* [1775–81] (Cambridge, Mass., 1930) II, 660–61.
7. Truxtun Hare Collection: Truxtun to A. & J. Caldwell, November 17, 1781; *Pennsylvania Mag. of Hist. and Biog.,* Philadelphia, XIX (1895), 399.
8. APS: Franklin Papers, vol. 23, fol. 45, Thomas Barclay to Franklin, November 15, 1781.
9. Frederick B. Laidlaw, "History of the Prevention of Fouling," U.S. Naval Inst. *Proceedings,* LXXVIII (July, 1952), 772.
10. Truxtun Hare Collection: Truxtun to A. & J. Caldwell, November 17, 1781.
11. Thomas Truxtun, *Reply of Commodore Truxtun to an Attack Made on Him in the National Intelligencer, in June 1806* (Philadelphia, 1806), pp. 23ff.
12. *Pennsylvania Packet,* Philadelphia, January 6, 1781.
13. *Ibid.,* March 19, 21, 1782.
14. For example, LC: Continental Congress Papers, vol. 193, fol. 311, John Paul Jones to Board of Admiralty, October 26, 1780.

## CHAPTER 12 (pp. 47–52)

1. U.S. Library of Congress, *Naval Records of the American Revolution 1775–1788* (Washington, D.C., 1906), p. 327; Truxtun Hare Collection: Truxtun to A. & J. Caldwell, April 21, 1780.
2. *Naval Records,* p. 327. For other business of Randall and Truxtun, see LC: Robert Morris Diary in Office of Finance, II, 190, 193, 220–21, 227–28.

3. *Pennsylvania Packet,* Philadelphia, September 24, 1782.
4. *Ibid.,* December 12, 1782; *Independent Gazeteer,* Philadelphia, December 14, 1782.
5. *Pennsylvania Packet,* Philadelphia, January 7, 1783.
6. Truxtun Family Bible.
7. Samuel Hazard, *et al.,* eds., *Pennsylvania Archives* (Harrisburg, 1852–1949), 3rd ser., xv, xvi—Effective Supply Tax for 1780 and 1782.
8. HSPa: Society Collections, Truxtun to Hannah, September 22, 1793.
9. HSPa: Assessment Books of Philadelphia, vol. 617 (entries regarding Truxtun in 1781–83). See also *ibid.,* vol. 96 (1783 Tax on Carriages).
10. *Autobiography of Charles Biddle . . . 1745–1821* (Philadelphia, 1883), p. 189.
11. *Ibid.*
12. *Pennsylvania Gazette,* Philadelphia, October 1, 1783.
13. *Ibid.; Pennsylvania Packet,* Philadelphia, June 3, 1783; *Connecticut Courant,* Hartford, October 14, 1783.
14. HSPa and Philadelphia Bourse: Customs House, Outward entries, April 21, 1784, Inward entries, March 22, September 14, 1784; *Pennsylvania Packet,* Philadelphia, June 3, 1783; *Independent Gazetteer,* Philadelphia, September 27, 1783; *Pennsylvania Gazette,* Philadelphia, October 1, 1783; HSPa: Joshua Humphreys Account Books (1784–1813), v, January 21, April 26, 1785.
15. *Pennsylvania Packet,* Philadelphia, January 11, 1785.
16. *Ibid.,* June 24, 1783.
17. *Autobiography of Charles Biddle,* p. 189.
18. *Ibid.*
19. Truxtun Family Bible.
20. HSPa: Joshua Humphreys Account Books (1784–1813), v, March 23, 1785.
21. *Pennsylvania Packet,* Philadelphia, February 18, 1785.

CHAPTER 13 (pp. 52–59)

1. Benjamin Franklin, *Writings,* A. H. Smyth, ed. (New York, 1905–1907), ix, 364.
2. *Ibid.,* ix, 181.
3. *Ibid.,* ix, 327.
4. I. Minis Hays, *Calendar of the Papers of Benjamin Franklin in the Library of the American Philosophical Society* (Philadelphia, 1908), iii, 260–61, 266; iv, 142.
5. Franklin, *op. cit.,* ix, 360.
6. *Ibid.,* ix, 371.
7. Charles F. Jenkins, "Franklin Returns from France—1785," Amer. Philosophical Soc., *Proceedings,* xcii (1948), 417–32, p. 420 cited.
8. *Pennsylvania Packet,* Philadelphia, September 16, 1785.
9. Jenkins, *op. cit.,* p. 427.

10. *Ibid.*, p. 430.
11. APS: Franklin-Bache Papers, Diary of Benjamin Franklin Bache, July 27, 1785, referred to hereinafter as Bache Diary.
12. Jenkins, *op. cit.*, p. 423.
13. Franklin, *op. cit.*, x, 458–59.
14. Carl Van Doren, *Benjamin Franklin* (New York, 1938), pp. 723–24; Franklin, *op. cit.*, x, 459; Jenkins, *op. cit.*, p. 423.
15. Franklin, *op. cit.*, ix, 346.
16. Jenkins, *op. cit.*, p. 431.
17. Franklin, *op. cit.*, ix, 370.
18. Bache Diary, July 24, 1785.
19. Franklin, *op. cit.*, ix, 369.
20. APS: Franklin Papers, vol. 38, fol. 162.
21. *Ibid.*, vol. 38, fol. 163.
22. Bache Diary, July 27, 28, 1785.
23. Franklin, *op. cit.*, x, 461.
24. *Ibid.*, ix, 410–13. Distance covered during 24 hours ranged all the way from 4 to 190 miles, averaging 93.
25. APS: Franklin Papers, Journal of William Temple Franklin.
26. Franklin, *op. cit.*, ix, 371.
27. *Ibid.*, ix, 372–406.
28. MassHS: Pickering Papers, Truxtun to Pickering, March 17, 1806.
29. HSPa: Joshua Humphreys Account Books (1784–1813), v, November 24, 1785.
30. Franklin, *op. cit.*, ix, 400–401.
31. Jenkins, *op. cit.*, p. 430.
32. Franklin, *op. cit.*, ix, 402.
33. *Ibid.*, ix, 413 ff.
34. Bache Diary, August 23, 24, 1785.
35. Franklin, *op. cit.*, x, 471. For evidence of moonlight, see HSPa: Christopher Marshall's Diary (1783–91), September 13, 1785.
36. *Connecticut Courant,* Hartford, September 26, 1785.
37. Jenkins, *op. cit.*, p. 430.
38. Franklin, *op. cit.*, x, 471.


CHAPTER 14 (pp. 60–67)

1. *Pennsylvania Packet,* Philadelphia, September 16, 1785.
2. HSPa: Philadelphia Customs House Record Books, Inward entries, March 22, 1784; Outward entries, March 22, 1784.
3. *Pennsylvania Packet,* Philadelphia, March 2, 1784.
4. Hosea Ballou Morse, *Chronicles of the East India Company Trading to China* (Oxford, 1926–29), ii, 95; HSPa: Misc. Coll., Samuel Shaw to Winthrop Sargent, November 10, 1785.

5. Samuel W. Woodhouse, "Log and Journal of the Ship *United States,*" *Pennsylvania Mag. of Hist. and Biog.,* LV (1931), 225–58; William Bell Clark, "Postscripts to the Voyage of the Merchant Ship *United States,*" *ibid.,* LXXVI (July, 1952), 294–310; *Pennsylvania Packet,* Philadelphia, September 16, October 7, 1785.

6. HSPa: Benjamin Fuller Letter Books, III, December 31, 1785.

7. HSPa: Joshua Humphreys Account Books (1784–1813), V, October 19, 1785.

8. That the *London Packet* became *Canton* was a conclusion I reached after a thorough study of Customs House Record Books at HSPa, and Captains' Reports, April 20, 1785–June 8, 1786, and Tonnage Book of Entries, 1785–1786, at the Navigation Commission Office, Philadelphia Bourse Bldg. Nowhere does *Canton* appear inward nor *London Packet* outward.

9. Ray W. Irwin, *Diplomatic Relations of the United States with the Barbary Powers 1776–1816* (Chapel Hill, 1931), p. 37.

10. *Pennsylvania Packet,* Philadelphia, November 22, 1785.

11. HSPa: Gratz Collection, Box 2, Petition of Donnaldson & Coxe and others, n.d.; LC: Continental Congress Papers, Memorial of Coxe & Frazier, Donnaldson & Coxe, and others, December 22, 1785.

12. *Pennsylvania Packet,* Philadelphia, January 17, 1786.

13. C. P. Fitzgerald, *China, A Short Cultural History* (New York, 1938), pp. 551–52.

14. *Pharmaceutical Journal,* London, 2nd ser., III, 197, 333; IX, 77; 3rd ser., I, 665; "Ginseng," *Encyclopedia Britannica,* 11th ed.; NYPL: Constable-Pierrepont Collection, William Constable Shipping Papers, Box 2—two notes on ginseng, n.d. [c. 1787].

15. HSPa: Philadelphia Customs House Record Books, Outward entries, December 30, 1785.

16. HSPa: Benjamin Fuller Letter Books, III, December 31, 1785.

17. HSPa: Society Collections, *Delaware* ship Papers (1793–97), Ship's account book.

18. R. L. Brunhouse, "Lascars in Pennsylvania, a Sidelight on the China Trade," *Pennsylvania History,* VII (January, 1940), 20 ff.; Samuel Hazard, *et al.,* eds., *Pennsylvania Archives* (Harrisburg, 1852–1949), 4th ser., IV, 7–8; Pennsylvania State Library, Harrisburg: Post-Revolutionary Papers, XXII, no. 25; XXIV, no. 8. It was Capt. John O'Donnell who built a house called "Canton" in Baltimore; for description of house, see Thomas Twining, *Travels in America One Hundred Years Ago* (New York, 1894).

19. PhilaLC: Truxtun-Biddle Letters, Truxtun to Biddle, December 16, 1789.

CHAPTER 15 (pp. 67–71)

1. Thomas Truxtun, *Remarks, Instructions, and Examples, Relating to the Latitude and Longitude* (Philadelphia, 1794), pp. 72 ff.

2. *Ibid.*
3. George Dixon, *A Voyage Round the World* (London, 1789), p. 30; Josiah Quincy, ed., *Journals of Major Samuel Shaw* (Boston, 1847), Journal of first voyage.
4. *Pennsylvania Journal*, Philadelphia, August 2, 1786.
5. Compare the passage of *London Packet* from Europe to America, 93 miles per day (note 24, Chap. 13, above), with the first passage of *Empress* to Canton, 134 miles per day (Quincy, *op. cit.*, p. 211).
6. Samuel Dunn, *A New Directory for the East-Indies* (5th ed., London, 1780), pp. 348–49; *Pennsylvania Journal*, Philadelphia, August 2, 1786.
7. NYPL: Constable-Pierrepont Collection, William Constable Shipping Papers, Box 2, Truxtun to Isaac Hazelhurst, March 30, 1790.
8. Hepburn Collection Transcripts: Barry Papers, Patrick Hayes' Journal of the China Voyage.
9. *Ibid.*
10. Dunn, *op. cit.*, p. 348.
11. *Ibid.*, p. 347.
12. By plotting fixes given in Truxtun, *op. cit., passim,* the separate tracks for Truxtun's four Eastern voyages can be clearly established.
13. Truxtun, *op. cit.*, "Lunar Observations," p. 3; Quincy, *op. cit.*, p. 154.

## CHAPTER 16 (pp. 71–77)

1. C. N. Parkinson, *Trade in the Eastern Seas 1793–1813* (Cambridge, England, 1937), p. 57.
2. Hepburn Collection Transcripts: Barry Papers, Memorandum relating to the trade at Canton [1789], referred to hereinafter as Barry's memorandum; George Dixon, *A Voyage Round the World* (London, 1789), pp. 288–90.
3. Dixon, pp. 305–306.
4. *Ibid.*, pp. 291, 305–306; Barry's memorandum.
5. Dixon, *op. cit.*, pp. 305–14; Foster Rhea Dulles, *The Old China Trade* (Boston, 1930), pp. 15–16.
6. Hosea Ballou Morse, *Chronicles of the East India Company Trading to China* (Oxford, 1926–29), II, 119.
7. NYHS: Sloop *Experiment* Papers—*Experiment* arrived about June 15, 1786; Josiah Quincy, ed., *Journals of Major Samuel Shaw* (Boston, 1847), p. 113—*Hope* arrived August 15, 1786; *Empress of China* probably arrived early August, 1786. She was spoken by Truxtun on April 5 in lat. 31° 30′ S, long. 18° W (*Pennsylvania Journal*, Philadelphia, August 2, 1786), and she did not call at Cape Town. Truxtun in *Canton* departed from Cape Town early in May, 1786. *Grand Turk* did not leave Isle de France until July 1, 1786.
8. Robert E. Peabody, *Log of the Grand Turk* (Boston, 1926), p. 233. *Grand Turk* arrived Canton in September, 1786.

9. B. J. Lossing, *Pictorial Field Book of the Revolution* (New York, 1860), II, 591; Quincy, *op. cit.*, p. 227.
10. Barry's memorandum; Dixon, *op. cit.*, p. 292.
11. Barry's memorandum; Quincy, *op. cit.*, p. 176.
12. Dixon, *op. cit.*, p. 309.
13. *Ibid.*, p. 308.
14. Peabody, *op. cit.*, p. 80; Barry's memorandum.
15. Quincy, *op. cit.*, p. 174.
16. Barry's memorandum.
17. C. P. Fitzgerald, *China, A Short Cultural History* (New York, 1938).
18. Peabody, *op. cit.*, pp. 82–84.
19. Dixon, *op. cit.*, pp. 296, 313.
20. *Ibid.*, p. 296; Barry's memorandum.
21. Barry's memorandum; Peabody, *op. cit.*, p. 85.
22. Barry's memorandum.
23. Dixon, *op. cit.*, p. 296.
24. *Ibid.*, pp. 296–97; Barry's memorandum.
25. Quincy, *op. cit.*, p. 175.
26. NYHS: Sloop *Experiment* Papers (1785–87).
27. Peabody, *op. cit.*, pp. 94–96.


CHAPTER 17 (pp. 77–81)

1. *Pennsylvania Packet,* Philadelphia, May 23, 1787.
2. John F. Watson, *Annals of Philadelphia* (Philadelphia, 1927), I, 583.
3. HSPa: Misc. Coll., Samuel Shaw to Winthrop Sargent, January 12, 1787.
4. J. Thomas Scharf and Thompson Westcott, *History of Philadelphia* (Philadelphia, 1884), I, 425; MassHS: Eleazar Oswald to Gen. Henry Knox, June 23, 1787.
5. HSPa: Misc. Coll., Samuel Shaw to Winthrop Sargent, January 12, 1787.
6. HSPa: Philadelphia Customs House Record Books, Outward entries, December 6, 1787.
7. Josiah Quincy, ed., *Journals of Major Samuel Shaw* (Boston, 1847), p. 303.
8. William Bell Clark, *Gallant John Barry* (New York, 1938), pp. 329–30.
9. NDA: *Alliance,* Indiaman, Log Book of Richard Dale (1787–88).
10. Carl Van Doren, *The Great Rehearsal* (New York, 1948), p. 10.
11. *Ibid.*, pp. 180–82.
12. Scharf and Westcott, *op. cit.*, III, 2167.
13. HSPa: Benjamin Fuller Letter Books, IV, December 8, 1787.
14. *Ibid.*, IV, p. 55.
15. PhilaLC: Truxtun-Biddle Letters, Truxtun to Biddle, December 1, 1787.
16. HSPa: Philadelphia Customs House Record Books, Outward entries, December 8, 1787; NYPL: Constable-Pierrepont Collection, William Constable Shipping Papers, Box 1, *Canton* and *New York* folder; HSPa: Benjamin Fuller Letter Books, April 18, 1788.

## CHAPTER 18 (pp. 81-86)

1. Josiah Quincy, ed., *Journals of Major Samuel Shaw* (Boston, 1847), p. 319. The geography of the strait was changed and the town of Anjer was wiped out when Krakatau erupted in 1883. With the possible exception of the Siberian meteor of 1908, this still remains the greatest explosion known to modern man.
2. Hepburn Collection Transcripts: Barry Papers, Patrick Hayes' Journal of the China Voyage; HSPa: Benjamin Fuller Letter Books, April 18, 1788; William Bell Clark, *Gallant John Barry* (New York, 1938), p. 341.
3. LC: Washington Papers, vol. 274, Truxtun to Edmund Randolph, July 27, 1795; Quincy, *op. cit.,* p. 169; NYPL: Constable-Pierrepont Collection, William Constable Letters (1774-91), Truxtun to Isaac Hazelhurst, July 2, 1789.
4. Quincy, *op. cit.,* pp. 221-26; see also "Batavia," *Encyclopedia Britannica,* 11th ed.
5. *Ibid.*
6. *Philadelphia Gazette,* October 5, 1797, Letter of Truxtun to "A Physician" in Philadelphia, October 1, 1797, regarding yellow fever.
7. NDA: *Alliance,* Indiaman, Log of Richard Dale, November 27, 1787, April 4, 1788.
8. HSPa: Benjamin Fuller Letter Books, February 20, 1788.
9. Quincy, *op. cit.,* p. 303; Hepburn Collection Transcripts: Barry Papers, memorandum relating to the trade at Canton [1789]. A photograph of a typical agreement is shown in Robert E. Peabody, *Log of the Grand Turks* (Boston, 1926), facing p. 88; William Bell Clark, *Gallant John Barry* (New York, 1938), p. 346.
10. Quincy, *op. cit.,* pp. 113, 175.
11. Benjamin Franklin, *Writings,* A. H. Smyth, ed. (New York, 1905-1907), IX, 206.
12. *Ibid.,* IX, 207.
13. *Ibid.*
14. John F. Watson, *Annals of Philadelphia* (Philadelphia, 1927), I, 290; Tippecanoe Historical Soc. Museum, Lafayette, Ind.: Truxtun to Sarah Truxtun, January 5, 1789 [transcript].
15. William Bell Clark, *Gallant John Barry* (New York, 1938), pp. 349-50.


## CHAPTER 19 (pp. 86-91)

1. NYPL: Constable-Pierrepont Collection, William Constable Letters, Truxtun to Constable, November 9, 1789.
2. J. Thomas Scharf and Thompson Westcott, *History of Philadelphia* (Philadelphia, 1884), III, 2215.
3. NYPL: Constable-Pierrepont Collection, William Constable Shipping Papers, Box 2, e.g., May 10, 1784.

4. *Ibid.,* William Constable Letters, Truxtun to William Constable, October 18, 1789.
5. *Ibid.*
6. *Ibid.,* Truxtun to [?], October 24, 1789.
7. *Ibid.,* Truxtun to William Constable, November 25, 1789.
8. *Ibid.,* William Constable Shipping Papers, Box 1, *Canton* and *New York* folder, *Canton* cargo, December, 1789.
9. *Ibid.,* Truxtun to William Constable, November 25, 1789; *ibid.,* Orders to Capt. R. Mercer and Mr. John Houston, December 4, 1789.
10. HSPa: Journal of ship *United States,* Capt. Thomas Bell, from Philadelphia bound toward China.
11. Carl Van Doren, *The Great Rehearsal* (New York, 1948), p. 1; PhilaLC: Truxtun-Biddle Letters, Truxtun to Biddle, December 12, 1789.
12. PhilaLC: Truxtun-Biddle Letters, Truxtun to Biddle, December 12, 1789.
13. *Ibid.,* Truxtun to Biddle, December 16, 1789.
14. *Ibid.;* NYPL: U.S. Navy Collection, Truxtun to John Barry, September 7, 1788.
15. NYPL: Constable-Pierrepont Collection, William Constable Letters (1774–91), Truxtun to Isaac Hazelhurst, March 17, 1790.
16. Josiah Quincy, ed., *Journals of Major Samuel Shaw* (Boston, 1847), p. 269.
17. LC: Washington Papers, vol. 274, Truxtun to Edmund Randolph, July 27, 1795.
18. NYPL: Constable-Pierrepont Collection, William Constable Letters (1774–91), Truxtun to Isaac Hazelhurst, March 17, 1790.
19. *Ibid.,* William Constable Shipping Papers, Box 1, *Canton* and *New York* folder, account of disbursements for *Canton,* March 31, 1791.
20. George Dixon, *A Voyage Round the World* (London, 1789), pp. 22, 23, 28, 31, 38, 49, 231, 336.
21. HSPa: Benjamin Fuller Letter Books, April 27, 1791.

CHAPTER 20 (pp. 91–99)

1. Charles R. King, ed., *Life and Correspondence of Rufus King* (New York, 1894–1900), I, 222.
2. John F. Watson, *Annals of Philadelphia* (Philadelphia, 1927), I, 581–82.
3. Thomas M. Griffiths, *Maine Sources in the House of the Seven Gables* (Waterville, 1945), pp. 33, 34, 36.
4. *The Journal of William Maclay, 1789–91* (New York, 1927), p. 371.
5. Navy 1790–98 LB, October 30, 1790; Harold and Margaret Sprout, *Rise of American Naval Power, 1776–1918* (Princeton, 1946), pp. 26–28.
6. Carl C. Cutler, *Greyhounds of the Sea* (New York, 1930), p. 393.
7. *American Daily Advertiser,* Philadelphia, November 19, 1791; HSPa: Dreer Collection, Joshua Humphreys shipyard notebook, pp. 224–30.
8. NYPL: Constable-Pierrepont Collection, William Constable Shipping Papers, Box 1, *Delaware* folder, bill of lading, Madras, September 20, 1792.

9. *Ibid., St. Jean de Lone* folder, Truxtun to George Lawson, October 4, 1792; *ibid.,* William Constable Letters, Truxtun to Constable, March 12, 1793.

10. *Ibid.,* William Constable Letter Book, August 23, 1793.

11. Watson, *op. cit.,* I, 179–80; J. T. Scharf and Thompson Westcott, *History of Philadelphia* (Philadelphia, 1884), I, 473–74; *Autobiography of Charles Biddle* (Philadelphia, 1883), pp. 252–53.

12. Scharf and Westcott, *op. cit.,* I, 474.

13. NYPL: Constable-Pierrepont Collection, William Constable Letter Book, July 14, 1793. Refers to advice sent on May 29, 1793.

14. Alexander Graydon, *Memoirs of a Life* (Edinburgh, 1822), p. 383.

15. *Ibid.; Philadelphia Gazette,* October 5, 1797.

16. J. H. Powell, *Bring Out Your Dead* (Philadelphia, 1949), pp. 22–24, 65, 99, 106, 114; Mufford Stough, "The Yellow Fever in Philadelphia, 1793," *Pennsylvania History,* VI (January, 1939), 6.

17. *Autobiography of Charles Biddle,* p. 259.

18. *Philadelphia Gazette,* October 5, 1797.

19. Kenneth and Anna M. Roberts, ed. and trans., *Moreau de St. Méry's American Journey, 1793–1798* (New York, 1947), p. 325.

20. *Autobiography of Charles Biddle,* p. 256.

21. *Ibid.,* p. 257.

22. *Philadelphia Gazette,* October 5, 1797.

23. PhilaLC: Truxtun-Biddle Letters, Truxtun to Biddle, October 2, 1793.

24. NYPL: Constable-Pierrepont Collection, William Constable Letter Book, William Constable to H. F. Constable, June 17, 1793.

25. *Ibid.,* William Constable Shipping Papers, Box 1, *St. Jean de Lone* folder.

26. *Ibid.,* William Constable Letter Book, Constable to Truxtun, September 27, 1794.

27. *Ibid.,* (1793–94), p. 167, Constable to S. Ward, October 10, 1793.

28. *Ibid.,* p. 198, Constable to Truxtun, November 20, 1793; HSPa: *Delaware* ship Papers, deposition by William Constable *re* ownership of vessel.

29. PhilaLC: Truxtun-Biddle Letters, Truxtun to Biddle, June 29, 1799.

30. *Ibid.,* December 16, 1789; MassHS: Pickering Papers, Truxtun to Pickering, February 1, 1806.

31. George Washington, *Writings,* J. C. Fitzpatrick, ed. (Washington, D.C., 1931–44), XXXII, 29; XXXIII, 109–10, 294; XXXIV, 34, 47.

32. *Ibid.,* XXX, 475; XXXII, 40.

33. HSPa: *Delaware* ship Papers.

34. NYPL: Constable-Pierrepont Collection, William Constable Letter Book (1793–94), p. 198, November 20, 1793.

35. Truxtun Hare Collection: Truxtun to Timothy Pickering, Secretary of State, December 1, 1796.

36. *American Daily Advertiser,* Philadelphia, April 21, 1794.

37. For arrival in Philadelphia, see *ibid.*

38. HSPa: *Delaware* ship Papers, agreement with Thomas Mills, December 24, 1793.

CHAPTER 21 (pp. 100–103)

1. Ray W. Irwin, *Diplomatic Relations of the United States with the Barbary Powers 1776–1816* (Chapel Hill, 1931), pp. 60–61; Charles W. Goldsborough, *United States' Naval Chronicle* (Washington, D.C., 1824), I, 53; *Barbary Wars*, I, 25.
2. Goldsborough, *op. cit.*, p. 50.
3. *Barbary Wars*, I, 10.
4. [Annals of Congress.] *Debates and Proceedings in the Congress of the United States, 1789–1824* (Washington, D.C., 1834–56), 3 Congr., 485–98; quotation from p. 494.
5. Harold and Margaret Sprout, *The Rise of American Naval Power, 1776–1918* (Princeton, 1946), pp. 28–32; *Barbary Wars*, I, 70.
6. G. W. Allen, *A Naval History of the American Revolution* (Boston, 1913), p. 704.
7. William Bell Clark, *Gallant John Barry* (New York, 1938), pp. 366–67.
8. George Washington, *Writings*, J. C. Fitzpatrick, ed. (Washington, D.C., 1931–44), XXXIII, 294.
9. Clark, *op. cit.*, p. 367.
10. HSPa: *Delaware* ship Papers, Truxtun's orders to William Hawks, May 26, 1794.
11. *Barbary Wars*, I, 75.
12. Lincoln Lorenz, *John Paul Jones* (Annapolis, 1943), pp. 88, 152.
13. Navy 1790–98 LB, June 24, 1794.
14. NYPL: U.S. Navy Collection, Truxtun to Richard Dale, August 3, 1805.


CHAPTER 22 (pp. 103–108)

1. Thomas Truxtun, *Remarks, Instructions, and Examples, Relating to the Latitude and Longitude* (Philadelphia, 1794).
2. *Ibid.*, pp. * 5– * 7.
3. APS: Franklin-Bache Papers, Diary of Benjamin Franklin Bache; Benjamin Franklin, *Writings*, A. H. Smyth, ed. (New York, 1905–1907), IX, 412.
4. Josiah Quincy, *Journals of Major Samuel Shaw* (Boston, 1847), p. 210.
5. Truxtun, *op. cit.*, "Lunar Observations," p. 3.
6. According to A. Wolf, *A History of Science, Technology, and Philosophy in the Eighteenth Century* (2nd ed., London, 1952), p. 159, Royal Navy vessels were furnished with chronometers from about 1825. On the initial success of Harrison's chronometer, see D. C. Holly, "All for the Purpose of Marking Time," U.S. Naval Inst. *Proc.*, LXXIX (March, 1953), 303–309.
7. Truxtun, *op. cit.*, "Lunar Observations," pp. 3–6; "Navigation," *Encyclopedia Britannica*, 11th ed.
8. Truxtun, *op. cit.*, p. * 5.
9. Samuel Eliot Morison, *Maritime History of Massachusetts, 1783–1860* (Boston, 1921), pp. 114–16.

10. *Autobiography of Commodore Charles Morris, USN* (Annapolis, 1880), p. 12.

11. The similarity between this chart of the world and the one in William Guthrie, *Maps Belonging to Guthrie's System of Geography* (London, 1786), must be remarked. The engraver apparently copied Guthrie's chart.

12. Nathaniel Bowditch, *The New American Practical Navigator* (First ed., Newburyport, 1802), p. 235.

13. LC: Washington Papers, vol. 274, Truxtun to Edmund Randolph, July 27, 1795.

14. Navy 1790–98 LB, p. 103.


CHAPTER 23 (pp. 108–111)

1. Navy 1790–98 LB, April 1, May 12, 1794.
2. *Commerce, London Packet, Delaware.*
3. HSPa: Joshua Humphreys Letter Books, iii, October 7, 1801.
4. *Ibid.*, i, Humphreys to Robert Morris, January 6, 1793. The basis for this statement is *Shipbuilder's Repository, or a Treatise on Marine Architecture* (London, 1789), p. 41. See also statement by Josiah Fox to this effect in PMS: Fox Papers, Fox to Secretary of the Navy, November 27, 1826.
5. HSPa: Joshua Humphreys Letter Books, i, 203; *American State Papers: Documents, Legislative and Executive* (Washington, D.C., 1832–61), Naval Affairs, i, 6–8.
6. HSPa: Joshua Humphreys Letter Books, i, 165, June 5, 1795; Navy 1790–98 LB, May 12, 1794.
7. *Ibid.*, June 26, July 17, 1794.
8. Thomas Truxtun, *Remarks, Instructions, and Examples, Relating to the Latitude and Longitude* (Philadelphia, 1794), Part ii, i, ii, iv, viii.
9. HSPa: Joshua Humphreys Letter Books, i, 31.
10. *Barbary Wars*, i, 120.
11. Truxtun, *op. cit.*, Part ii, viii; *Quasi-War*, i, 564.
12. *Barbary Wars*, i, 128.
13. PMS: Fox Papers, Truxtun to Fox, November 21, 1794.
14. Navy 1790–98 LB, December 18, 1794.


CHAPTER 24 (pp. 111–114)

1. George Washington, *Writings*, J. C. Fitzpatrick, ed. (Washington, D.C., 1931–44), xxxiii, 333; LC: Jefferson Papers, vol. 142, Truxtun to Jefferson, July 10, 1804.
2. Hulbert Footner, *Sailor of Fortune, The Life and Adventures of Commodore Barney, USN* (New York, 1940), pp. 193–203.
3. *Barbary Wars*, i, 76.

4. Navy 1790–98 LB, August 8, 1794.
5. Thomas Twining, *Travels in America One Hundred Years Ago* (New York, 1894).
   Enoch Pratt Free Library, Baltimore: 1792 Folie MS Map of Baltimore; Twining, *op. cit.* Rebuilding of the fort on Whetstone Point (later Fort McHenry), employing sodded dirt and some timber cribbing, was approved by Congress about the same time the new Navy was, in 1794. Its cost was estimated at $4225.44, which included $500 for contingencies. Perhaps $15,000 was spent on it from 1794 through 1797. In 1798, building of the masonry fort was begun, and by the end of 1801 at least $100,000 had been spent upon it. *American State Papers: Documents, Legislative and Executive* (Washington, D.C., 1832–61), Military Affairs, I, 63, 87–89, 111, 116, 153, and *passim.*
7. Maryland Historical Society: Truxtun to James McHenry, May 20, 1798.
8. *American State Papers,* Naval Affairs, I, 6.

## CHAPTER 25 (pp. 114–119)

1. *American State Papers: Documents, Legislative and Executive* (Washington, D.C., 1832–61), Naval Affairs, I, 6; HSPa: Joshua Humphreys Letter Books, I, 113–26.
2. *American State Papers,* Naval Affairs, I, 8.
3. Navy 1790–98 LB, April 21, 1794.
4. *Barbary Wars,* I, 77, 80, 98; HSPa: Joshua Humphreys Letter Books, I, 28–29, 190; *American State Papers,* Naval Affairs, I, 8, 18.
5. American State Papers, Naval Affairs, I, 17.
6. HSPa: Joshua Humphreys Letter Books, I, 28.
7. *American State Papers,* Naval Affairs, I, 9, 10.
8. HSPa: Joshua Humphreys Letter Books, I, 28–29, Morgan to Humphreys, October 21, 1794.
9. *American State Papers,* Naval Affairs, I, 8.
10. *Barbary Wars,* I, 103.
11. HSPa: Joshua Humphreys Letter Books, I, 190; *American State Papers,* Naval Affairs, I, 18.
12. Navy 1790–98 LB, December 31, 1795.
13. HSPa: Joshua Humphreys Letter Books, I, 182.
14. HSPa: Joshua Humphreys Correspondence, (1775–1831), I, 28, Truxtun to Humphreys, June 26, 1795.
15. Truxtun Hare Collection: Truxtun to Joshua Humphreys, October 8, 1795; HSPa: Joshua Humphreys Correspondence (1775–1831), I, 132.
16. *Quasi-War,* I, 337; Navy 1790–98 LB, p. 85; HSPa: Joshua Humphreys Letter Books, I, 14, Humphreys to Tench Coxe, September 29, 1794.
17. Navy 1790–98 LB, November 2, December 5, 1796.
18. HSPa: Joshua Humphreys Letter Books, I, 14, Humphreys to Tench Coxe, September 29, 1794.

19. PMS: Fox Papers, Fox to Truxtun, April 2, 1795.
20. LC: Jefferson Papers, vol. 142, Truxtun to Jefferson, July 10, 1804.
21. HSPa: Joshua Humphreys Correspondence (1775-1831), Truxtun to Humphreys, April 19, 1795.
22. Maryland Historical Society: David Stodder to Secretary of War, April 20, 1797.
23. Navy 1790-98 LB, April 7, 1795.
24. Maryland Historical Society: Truxtun to Secretary of War, May 20, 1798.
25. HSPa: Joshua Humphreys Letter Books, I, April 27, 1795.
26. *Barbary Wars,* I, 122-25.
27. *Ibid.,* I, 121-22.

CHAPTER 26 (pp. 119-122)

1. Truxtun Hare Collection: Truxtun to Phyn, Ellice and Ingalls, September 13, 1795.
2. *Ibid.,* Truxtun to Thomas Mills, March 27, 1795.
3. PhilaLC: Truxtun-Biddle Letters, Truxtun to Biddle, October 2, 1793.
4. *Ibid.,* Truxtun to Biddle, August 3, 1799, August 14, 1800; HSPa: Gratz Collection, Truxtun to Willing and Francis, February 14, 1796; Truxtun Hare Collection: Truxtun to John Blackburn, January 3, 1797; *Federal Gazette & Baltimore Daily Advertiser,* March 16, 1796.
5. Truxtun Hare Collection: Truxtun to Fauchet, August 7, 1794; Truxtun to Secretary of State, April 7, 1795.
6. NYPL: Constable-Pierrepont Collection, William Constable Letter Books, December 10, 1795; PhilaLC: Truxtun-Biddle Letters, Truxtun to Biddle, August 3, 1799; HSPa: Thomas Truxtun Letter Book, 1798-99, p. 52.
7. LC: Washington Papers, vol. 274, Truxtun to Edmund Randolph, July 27, 1795.
8. Middlesex County Deeds (Court House, New Brunswick, N.J.), II, 58-59; V, 881, 884-85, 889-90, 892; Truxtun Hare Collection: Truxtun to Fauchet, August 7, 1794.
9. HSPa: *Delaware* ship Papers, Truxtun's personal account in London, 1793; PhilaLC: Truxtun-Biddle Letters, Truxtun to Biddle, December 19, 1799.
10. HSPa: Truxtun to Hannah, his slave, September 22, 1793; HSPa: Dreer Collection, Book of Rush Letters, Benjamin Rush to Truxtun, March 5, 1813.
11. MassHS: Pickering Papers, Truxtun to Pickering, November 27, December 8, 1807.
12. *Barbary Wars,* I, 70; PMS: Fox Papers, Truxtun to Fox, January 4, 1796.

1. *Barbary Wars,* I, I, 119, 143.
2. Ray W. Irwin, *Diplomatic Relations of the United States with the Barbary Powers 1776–1816* (Chapel Hill, 1931), pp. 80–81; G. W. Allen, *Our Navy and the Barbary Corsairs* (Boston, 1905), p. 56.
3. *Barbary Wars,* I, 83.
4. *Ibid.,* I, 141.
5. *Ibid.,* I, 139.
6. [Annals of Congress.] *Debates and Proceedings in the Congress of the United States* (Washington, D.C., 1834–56), 4 Congr., 870, 872–73, 879, 882, 893.
7. PMS: Fox Papers, Truxtun to Fox, January 4, 1796.
8. HSPa: Wayne Papers, vol. 43, p. 104, Truxtun to Wayne, January 23, 1796.
9. LC: Washington Papers, vol. 277, Truxtun to Washington, February 4, 1796.
10. *Barbary Wars,* I, 150–51.
11. NDA: War Department Letter Book, Arming and Equipping Frigates, 1795–98, p. 2; NYHS: Barry Papers, John Barry to Truxtun, May 22, 1796.
12. NYHS: Barry Papers, John Barry to Truxtun, May 22, 1796; *Barbary Wars,* I, 172–74; Navy 1790–98 LB, May 20, 1796.
13. George Washington, *Writings,* J. C. Fitzpatrick, ed. (Washington, D.C., 1931–44), XXXIV, front., March 14, 1795; HSPa: Joshua Humphreys Letter Books, I, 36, 81, 87. *Chesapeake* was named later—*Quasi-War,* III, 63.
14. *Pennsylvania Packet,* Philadelphia, September 2, 1777.
15. HSPa: Joshua Humphreys Correspondence, William Rush to Humphreys, April 30, 1795. Printed in *Pennsylvania Mag. of Hist. and Biog.,* XXXI (1907), 239–40; see also *American Neptune,* VII (1947), 256.
16. For evidence of this and other "raisings," see *Philadelphia Gazette,* February 9, 1796; HSPa: Joshua Humphreys Letter Books I, 187 (President Washington attended raising of stern in Philadelphia); *ibid.,* I, 200 (six weeks later several frames had been raised).
17. *American Daily Advertiser,* Philadelphia, February 10, 1796, copied from *Maryland Journal,* Baltimore, February 5, 1796.
18. PMS: Fox Papers, Truxtun to Fox, February 7, 1796.
19. HSPa: Joshua Humphreys Letter Books, I, February 22, 1796.
20. Kenneth and Anna Roberts, ed. and trans., *Moreau de St. Méry's American Journey, 1793–1798* (New York, 1947), pp. 76–81.
21. PhilaLC: Truxtun-Biddle Letters, Truxtun to Biddle, August 3, 1799; MassHS: Pickering Papers, Truxtun to Pickering, December 15, 1803, March 23, 1806, March 5, 1810.
22. Great Britain, Admiralty, *Regulations and Instructions Relative to His Majesty's Service at Sea* (13th ed., London, 1790).
23. Truxtun Hare Collection: *Signal Book for the Ships of War,* n.d. [watermark: GR].
24. MassHS: Pickering Papers, Truxtun to Pickering [1806], fol. 308.

25. Thomas Truxtun, *Instructions, Signals, and Explanations Offered for the U.S. Fleet* (Baltimore, 1797).
26. Navy 1790–98 LB, June 16, 1797.
27. This copy is in Navy Department, Office of Naval Records and Library.
28. *Documents Accompanying a Message from the President of the United States, with Sundry Statements of Expenditures of Public Monies, by Naval Agents, from the 1st of January, 1797 to the 31st of December, 1801* (Washington, D.C. 1803), part III. Approximately 27 tons of copper in sheets, bolts, nails, etc., were purchased from Alexander Bisland & Co., London.
29. *Barbary Wars,* I, 188.
30. HSPa: Joshua Humphreys Letter Books, II (1797–1800), 26–27.
31. Navy 1790–98 LB, July 25, 1797; *Quasi-War,* I, 9.
32. HSPa: Joshua Humphreys Letter Books, II, 36.
33. *Telegraphe and Daily Advertiser,* Baltimore, August 29, 1797.


CHAPTER 28 (pp. 130–135)

1. Dimensions of the ship are given by Truxtun in HSPa: U.S. Frigate *Constellation* Orders, Muster Rolls, Stores, etc.
2. *American State Papers: Documents, Legislative and Executive* (Washington, D.C. 1832–61), Naval Affairs, I, 50.
3. *Barbary Wars,* I, 188.
4. Navy 1790–98 LB, July 24, 1797.
5. *Barbary Wars,* I, 188.
6. Navy 1790–98 LB, August·8, 1797; *Federal Gazette,* Baltimore, August 9, 1797.
7. *Federal Gazette,* Baltimore, August 9, 1797.
8. *Maryland Historical Magazine,* XXVIII (1933), 197 ff, October 29, 1796.
9. Navy 1790–98 LB, July 24, 1797.
10. *Federal Gazette,* Baltimore, September 6, 1797; see also Eugene S. Ferguson, "Figure-head of the United States Frigate *Constellation*," *American Neptune,* VII (October, 1947), 255–60.
11. *Quasi-War,* I, 9; HSPa: *Constellation* Orders.
12. *Documents Accompanying a Message . . .* (Chap. 27, note 28 above).
13. *American Daily Advertiser,* Philadelphia, September 11, 1797; *Telegraphe and Daily Advertiser,* Baltimore, September 8, 1797.
14. *Quasi-War,* I, 10–11; New Jersey Hist. Soc., *Proceedings,* 4th ser., III, 15.
15. *American Daily Advertiser,* Philadelphia, September 11, 1797; *Telegraphe and Daily Advertiser,* Baltimore, September 8, 1797.
16. *Federal Gazette,* Baltimore, September 19, 1797.
17. *Ibid.*

CHAPTER 29 (pp. 135-138)

1. *Maryland Historical Magazine,* xxviii (1933), 197 ff, September 10, 1797.
2. *Philadelphia Gazette,* October 5, 1797.
3. *American State Papers: Documents, Legislative and Executive* (Washington, D.C., 1832-61), Naval Affairs, i, 37-39.
4. *Columbian Centinel,* Boston, September 20, 1797.
5. *American State Papers,* Naval Affairs, i, 56; *Columbian Centinel,* Boston, October 25, 1797.
6. HSPa: U.S. Frigate *Constellation* Orders, Muster Rolls, Stores, etc.
7. NDA: War Dept. Letter Book, Arming and Equipping Frigates, 1795-98, November 15, 1797.
8. *American State Papers,* Foreign Relations, i, 748-59.
9. HSPa: Governors of Pennsylvania Collection, Charles Biddle to Truxtun, March 15, 1797.
10. [Annals of Congress.] *Debates and Proceedings in the Congress of the United States, 1789-1824* (Washington, D.C., 1834-56), 4 Congr., 879, 2050, 2140.
11. *Barbary Wars,* i, 202-203, 224, 232.
12. James Brown Scott, ed., *Controversy over Neutral Rights between U.S. and France, 1797-1800* (New York, 1917), p. 17.
13. Thomas Twining, *Travels in America One Hundred Years Ago* (New York, 1894); John B. McMaster, *A History of the People of the United States* (New York, 1888-1913), ii, 374
14. *Quasi-War,* i, 42.

CHAPTER 30 (pp. 138-144)

1. *Federal Gazette,* Baltimore, April 11, 1798; *Telegraphe and Daily Advertiser,* Baltimore, April 13, 1798.
2. *Quasi-War,* i, 7, 49.
3. Simon Gross, a lieutenant in the Continental Navy, was appointed first lieutenant before August 17, 1797 and served for a few weeks at least. However, no mention of him appears after September 18, 1797. *American Daily Advertiser,* Philadelphia, August 17, 1797; *Quasi-War,* i, 12-16, 28; C. O. Paullin, *Commodore John Rodgers* (Cleveland, 1910) pp. 22-29.
4. *Quasi-War,* iv, 159.
5. Paullin, *op. cit.,* front. and pp. 27, 172; *Quasi-War,* v, 435.
6. *Quasi-War,* i, 49-50, 304-12.
7. *An Impartial Examination of the Case of Captain Isaac Phillips* (Baltimore, 1825), p. 47; *Quasi-War,* i, 304-12; vi, 34, 188.
8. *Quasi-War,* i, 77-78, 114.
9. *Ibid.,* i, 41, 304-12.

10. HSPa: U.S. Frigate *Constellation* Orders, Muster Rolls, Stores, etc.

11. *Quasi-War*, I, 82, 298–99, 362.

12. *Ibid.*, I, 12–15.

13. *Ibid.*, I, 61, 70–71, 98–99, 103, 144.

14. *Ibid.*, I, 13, 99, 144.

15. HSPa: *Constellation* Orders; *Quasi-War*, I, 105, 125, 132.

16. *Quasi-War*, I, 102.

17. *Ibid.*, I, 104, 134; Secretary of the Commonwealth of Massachusetts, Archives Division: Petition of Isaac Sears for letter of marque for *Mars*, May 24, 1777.

18. *Quasi-War*, I, 118, 135.

19. *Ibid.*, I, 133–35, 139, 143.

20. *American State Papers: Documents, Legislative and Executive* (Washington, D.C., 1832–61), Foreign Relations, I, 152.

21. George Washington, *Writings*, J. C. Fitzpatrick, ed. (Washington, D.C., 1931–44), XXXVI, 394.

22. Bernard C. Steiner, *Life and Correspondence of James McHenry* (Cleveland, 1907), p. 379; Nathan Schachner, *Alexander Hamilton* (New York, 1946), pp. 374–75, 379.

23. Steiner, *op. cit.*, p. 479; *Quasi-War*, I, 410.

24. [Annals of Congress.] *Debates and Proceedings in the Congress of the United States, 1789–1824* (Washington, D.C., 1834–56), 5 Congr., 534–35, 539–41, 1522, 1545–47, 1553–54.

25. *Quasi-War*, I, 101, 236; William Bell Clark, *Gallant John Barry* (New York, 1938), p. 414.

26. *Quasi-War*, I, 118–19, 132–33.

27. *Ibid.*, III, 30.

28. *Ibid.*, II, 331.

29. Kenneth and Anna M. Roberts, ed. and trans., *Moreau de St. Méry's American Journey, 1793–1798* (New York, 1947), p. 28; *Quasi-War*, I, 143.

30. *Quasi-War*, I, 141, 148.

CHAPTER 31 (pp. 144–151)

1. *Quasi-War*, I, 152–53, 291.

2. *Ibid.*, I, 156–58.

3. *Ibid.*, I, 160.

4. *Ibid.*, I, 233, 291.

5. *Ibid.*, I, 158–59.

6. Irving Anthony, *Revolt at Sea* (New York, 1937), pp. 68–95.

7. *Dictionary of National Biography* (London, 1885–1901), XLV, 281–82.

8. *Quasi-War*, I, 312, 365; cf. *Aurora*, Philadelphia, October 7, 1816; MassHS: Pickering Papers, Truxtun to Pickering, October 26, November 22, 1807.

9. *Quasi-War*, I, 370; II, 11, 296, 298.

10. *Ibid.*, VII, 223. One-half pint of rum was mixed with 1½ pints of water to make 2 pints of grog (*ibid.*, I, 152).

11. *Ibid.*, I, 254, 290–91, 298–99; HSPa: Thomas Truxtun Letter Book, 1798–99, p. 26.

12. [David Porter], *Constantinople and Its Environs* (New York, 1835), II, 10. I have rejected the statement and quotation made by David D. Porter in his *Memoir of Commodore David Porter* (Albany, 1875), p. 24, that Captain Truxtun, "the honest hearted old seaman," took Midshipman Porter "by the hand and said, 'My boy, you shall never leave the navy if I can help it; why you young dog, every time I swear at you, you go up a round in the ladder of promotion; and when Mr. Rodgers blows you up it is because he loves you and don't want you to become too conceited.' " This does not ring true, and Admiral Porter was not discriminating in his use of sources. For example, he swallowed the Goldsborough version of the sequel to the *Constellation-Insurgente* action. See my comment in note 24, chapter 33, below.

13. *Quasi-War,* IV, 159.

14. *Life in Letters: American Autograph Journal,* Merion Station, Pa., June, 1941, Truxtun to Charles Biddle, October 16, 1805.

15. *Quasi-War,* I, 288.

16. *Ibid.,* I, 319, 467.

17. HSPa: Thomas Truxtun Letter Book, 1798–99, p. 44, October 8, 1798.

18. *Quasi-War,* I, 460–61.

19. *Ibid.,* I, 146, 278, 330, 339, and *passim.* See index: Navy, Secretary of; Charles W. Goldsborough, *United States' Naval Chronicle* (Washington, D.C., 1824), I, 94.

20. *Quasi-War,* I, 430; III, 25, 66.

21. *Ibid.,* I, 106, 555–56; II, 519; G. W. Allen, *Our Naval War with France* (Boston, 1909), p. 71.

22. *Quasi-War,* I, 542–43.

23. HSPa: Thomas Truxtun Letter Book, 1798–99, Truxtun to William Pennock, October 30, 1798.

24. *Quasi-War,* II, 5, 15; III, 455.

25. *Ibid.,* II, 55–56, 522; Leland P. Lovette, *Naval Customs, Traditions, and Usage* (Annapolis, 1939), p. 61. "Rules for Regulation of the Navy of the United Colonies" were compiled in 1775 by John Adams [G. W. Allen, *Naval History of the American Revolution* (Boston, 1913), p. 24; the rules are quoted in *ibid.,* pp. 686–95; also in Peter Force, ed., *American Archives* (Washington, D.C., 1837–53), 4th ser., III, 1929–32]. More than half of these rules were lifted, nearly intact, from Great Britain, Admiralty, *Regulations and Instructions Relating to His Majesty's Service at Sea* (11th ed., London, 1772). Over half of the 1799 regulations, in turn, were lifted from the 1775 rules. Several articles were added to prescribe the conduct of courts-martial and the distribution of prize money. See references above and *Statutes at Large of the United States of America, 1789–1873* (Boston, 1850–73), I, 709–17—Navy regulations adopted March 2, 1799.

26. *Quasi-War*, II, 35, 110.
27. *Dictionary of National Biography* (London, 1885-1901), LVIII, 99-100; *Quasi-War*, II, 127-28.
28. *Quasi-War*, II, 28, 144, 439. Martinique was in British hands, having been taken in 1794.

CHAPTER 32 (pp. 152-159)

1. *Quasi-War*, II, 144, 234, 258.
2. *Ibid.*, II, 238.
3. HSPa: *Constellation* Journal, January 15, 1799.
4. *Quasi-War*, I, 301.
5. *Barbary Wars*, VII, 70.
6. Details of clothing are from HSPa: U.S. Frigate *Constellation* Orders, Muster Rolls, Stores, etc.
7. *Quasi-War*, I, 12, 404.
8. *Ibid.*, I, 10-11.
9. Details of compartments and furnishings are from HSPa: *Constellation* Orders.
10. *Quasi-War*, I, 14, 155.
11. HSPa: *Constellation* Orders.
12. *Ibid.*
13. *Quasi-War*, II, 246-47.
14. *Ibid.*, II, 247, 253.
15. *Ibid.*, II, 253, 272.
16. Evangeline W. Andrews, ed., *Journal of a Lady of Quality* (New Haven, 1934), p. 121.
17. *Quasi-War*, VI, 412.
18. *Ibid.*, II, 257.
19. *Ibid.*, I, 175; II, 122; VII, 370.
20. *Ibid.*, II, 73-74, 135, 241.
21. *Ibid.*, II, 332.
22. *Ibid.*, II, 259-60.

CHAPTER 33 (pp. 160-169)

1. *Quasi-War*, II, 269, 304. By contemporary custom and usage, Truxtun's title was "Commodore" whenever he commanded a squadron. However, it was a title of courtesy only. He never held a rank higher than captain for the reason that no higher rank existed in the United States Navy until some sixty years later. In order to avoid needless confusion of titles, he will continue to be referred to as "Captain" for the present.
2. *Ibid.*, II, 73-74, 272, 275, 280-83, 287-88.

3. *Ibid.*, II, 292, 296–97, 300, 302, 305.

4. *Ibid.*, II, 307–309.

5. *Ibid.*, II, 328; HSPa: *Constellation* Journal. One of the slips was found in the Journal. The Journal itself was not written in Truxtun's hand.

6. *Quasi-War*, II, 328; IV, illus. facing 426.

7. Most of the information for this encounter is in *Quasi-War*, II, 326 ff. A few other sources are listed below.

8. Quarter Bill is in HSPa: U.S. Frigate *Constellation* Orders, Muster Rolls, Stores, etc.

9. John Hoxse, *The Yankee Tar* (Northampton, 1840); Edgar S. Maclay, *History of the Navy* (New York, 1895), I, 183.

10. *Federal Gazette*, Baltimore, March 12, 1799; *American Daily Advertiser*, Philadelphia, March 12, 1799.

11. Hoxse, *op. cit.*

12. Maclay, *op. cit.*, I, 185.

13. *Quasi-War*, II, 337; Rodgers' ship *Hope* had been taken by a French privateer (*ibid.*, I, 26, 28).

14. Captain Thomas Macdonough, famed for his exploits on Lake Champlain during the War of 1812, and whose name is enshrined along with Thomas Truxtun's in the Arlington amphitheatre, was a younger brother of James.

15. *Federal Gazette*, Baltimore, March 12, 1799, letter from David Porter to his father; *Quasi-War*, I, 306.

16. *Quasi-War*, II, 335.

17. *Ibid.*, I, 306.

18. Maclay, *op. cit.*, I, 185.

19. *Quasi-War*, II, 357, 427.

20. *Ibid.*, II, 327, 357–58.

21. Maclay, *op. cit.*, I, 183–86, translated from the French.

22. *Quasi-War*, II, 470.

23. *Ibid.*, II, 329.

24. *Ibid.*, II, 329, 346; Evangeline W. Andrews, ed., *Journal of a Lady of Quality* (New Haven, 1934), map facing p. 120. There is no basis in fact for the exciting story that probably appeared first in Goldsborough's *Naval Chronicle* in 1824 (pp. 132–33). It has been copied numberless times, sometimes with variations. Goldsborough related how John Rodgers and David Porter boarded *L'Insurgente* after the action. He wrote, "night set in, and it came on to blow so hard as to separate the ships, leaving one hundred and seventy-three prisoners on board the *Insurgente*, to be guarded by lieutenant Rodgers, and his small party." Two officers and eleven men then kept the prisoners below for three nights and two days while they brought the ship to St. Kitts.

Actually, *Constellation's* Journal indicates that the ships were constantly in company while they beat their way up to St. Kitts (*Quasi-War*, II, 328–29, 343, 346). John Hoxse in his *Yankee Tar* wrote that they "bore away for St. Kitts, where we arrived two days afterwards, with our prize, all safe."

25. Hoxse, *op. cit.; American Daily Advertiser,* Philadelphia, March 29, 1799; *Quasi-War,* II, 329.
26. *Quasi-War,* II, 327, 331-32, 351, 353-56, 379.
27. *Ibid.,* II, 354.
28. *Ibid.,* II, 378.
29. *Ibid.,* II, 332, 378, 392, 409.
30. *Ibid.,* II, 358-59.
31. *Ibid.,* II, 329-31, 481.
32. *Ibid.,* III, 318.
33. *Ibid.,* III, 40.


CHAPTER 34 (pp. 170-178)

1. "Truxtun's Victory" was one of many songs written to celebrate the victory. A copy of the broadside "Truxtun's Victory together with the Beggar Girl and Two Strings to My Bow" is in Boston Public Library.
2. MassHS: Pickering Papers, Pickering to William Smith [March 1, 1799], fol. 443.
3. *Quasi-War,* II, 333, 421, 450.
4. MassHS: Pickering Papers, Pickering to Rufus King, March 6, 1799.
5. *Quasi-War,* III, 122, 210-13, 217.
6. NYHS: Address to Truxtun by Citizens of Norfolk, n.d. [1799].
7. Truxtun Hare Collection: Officials and Citizens of Norfolk to Truxtun, May 22, 1799; *Norfolk Herald,* May 25, 30, June 6, 1799.
8. *American Daily Advertiser,* Philadelphia, March 19, 1799; *Telegraphe and Daily Advertiser,* Baltimore, March 12, 13, 1799; *Federal Gazette,* Baltimore, April 24, 1799. Maryland Historical Society has framed a leaf of the song.
9. *American Daily Advertiser,* Philadelphia, March 20, 1799.
10. *Columbian Centinel,* Boston, March 23, 27, 1799; *Independent Chronicle,* Boston, March 14, 1799.
11. *Spectator,* New York, July 11, 27, 1799.
12. *Ibid.,* June 1, 1799.
13. NYHS: Truxtun to Rufus King, April 15, 1801; Maria Scott Beale Chance, *A Chronicle of the Family of Edward F. Beale* (Haverford, 1943), p. 216.
14. NYHS: Truxtun to Merchants and Underwriters at Lloyd's Coffee House, April 15, 1801.
15. *Quasi-War,* II, 336.
16. [David Porter], *Constantinople and Its Environs* (New York, 1835), II, 10; *Federal Gazette,* Baltimore, March 12, 1799.
17. John B. McMaster, *A History of the People of the United States* (New York, 1888-1913), II, 433; *Aurora,* Philadelphia, March 16, 1799.
18. *Quasi-War,* III, 60; MassHS: Pickering Papers, Pickering to William Smith, [March 15, 1799] fol. 532.
19. *Quasi-War,* II, 458.

20. *Ibid.*, III, 84.
21. John Adams, *Works*, C. F. Adams, ed. (Boston, 1850–56), VIII, 630; *Quasi-War*, III, 84.
22. *Quasi-War*, II, 450.
23. *Ibid.*, III, 50, 273, 312.
24. John Hoxse, *The Yankee Tar* (Northampton, 1840).
25. PhilaLC: Truxtun-Biddle Letters, Truxtun to Biddle, March 6, 1802, and throughout this collection.
26. *Quasi-War*, III, 143, 358; *Art in America*, VI (February and June, 1918); *Autobiography of Charles Biddle* (Philadelphia, 1883), pp. 278–79.
27. PhilaLC: Truxtun-Biddle Letters, Truxtun to Biddle, June 29, 1799.
28. *Quasi-War*, II, 329–33.
29. *Ibid.*, II, 359.
30. *Ibid.*, III, 552.
31. *Ibid.*, III, 480.
32. PMS: Fox Papers, Letter Book II, certificate of *Constellation's* value dated May 27, 1799.
33. *Quasi-War*, III, 450; HSPa: Joshua Humphreys Letter Books, II (1797–1800), p. 224.
34. *Quasi-War*, III, 480.
35. *Ibid.*, III, 455.
36. *Statutes at Large of the United States of America, 1789–1873* (Boston 1850–73), I, 709–17—Navy regulations, adopted March 2, 1799; *Autobiography of Charles Biddle*, p. 279.
37. PhilaLC: Truxtun-Biddle Letters, Truxtun to Biddle, July 13, 26, 1799.
38. *Quasi-War*, III, 386.
39. *Ibid.*, III, 394; PhilaLC: Truxtun-Biddle Letters, Truxtun to Biddle, July 31, 1799.
40. *Quasi-War*, III, 456.
41. *Spectator*, New York, July 18, 1799.
42. W. Harrison Bayles, *Old Taverns of New York* (New York, 1915), pp. 356, 360.
43. NYPL: Elizabeth de Hart Bleeker MS Diary, 1799–1806, July 25, 1799.
44. PhilaLC: Truxtun-Biddle Letters, Truxtun to Biddle, July 31, 1799.
45. *Ibid.*
46. *Ibid.*


CHAPTER 35 (pp. 178–187)

1. *Quasi-War*, III, 568. See also *supra*, Chapter 31.
2. Bernard C. Steiner, *Life and Correspondence of James McHenry* (Cleveland, 1907), p. 473. Charles Carroll of Carrollton is quoted.
3. Charles R. King, ed., *Life and Correspondence of Rufus King* (New York, 1894–1900), III, 33, Robert Troup to Rufus King, June 5, 1799.
4. *Quasi-War*, III, 491.

5. *Ibid.*, III, 463.
6. *Ibid.*, III, 340.
7. *Ibid.*, III, 400, 466.
8. *Ibid.*, III, 474–75.
9. *Ibid.*, III, 312, 479.
10. *Ibid.*, III, 519.
11. *Ibid.*, III, 528–32
12. *Ibid.*, IV, 48.
13. *Ibid.*, IV, 51.
14. *Ibid.*, IV, 22, 61; NYHS: William Pennock to Truxtun, August 14, 1799; Moses Myres to Truxtun, August 15, 1799.
15. *Quasi-War*, IV, 122.
16. HSPa: MS Map of Perth Amboy, 1831; Middlesex County Deeds (Court House, New Brunswick, N.J.), V, 881, 884–85, 889–90.
17. Truxtun Hare Collection: Truxtun to Secretary of War, February 17, 1798; *Quasi-War*, II, 356.
18. *Quasi-War*, IV, 97–99.
19. *Ibid.*, IV, 69; *Norfolk Herald*, August 22, 1799.
20. *Autobiography of Charles Biddle* (Philadelphia, 1883), p. 281.
21. George Washington, *Writings*, J. C. Fitzpatrick, ed. (Washington, D.C., 1931–44), XXXVII, 360.
22. George Washington, *Diaries*, J. C. Fitzpatrick, ed. (Boston, 1925), September 12, 1799.
23. PhilaLC: Truxtun-Biddle Letters, Truxtun to Biddle, October 21, 1799.
24. Washington, *Writings*, XXXVII, 349.
25. PhilaLC: Truxtun-Biddle Letters, Truxtun to Biddle, October 17, 1799.
26. *Ibid.*
27. *Autobiography of Charles Biddle*, p. 282.
28. PhilaLC: Truxtun-Biddle Letters, Truxtun to Biddle, October 26, 1799.
29. *Quasi-War*, IV, 311–12.
30. PhilaLC: Truxtun-Biddle Letters, Truxtun to Biddle, December 3, 1799.
31. *Quasi-War*, IV, 375; PhilaLC: Truxtun-Biddle Letters, Truxtun to Biddle, November 12, 1799.
32. PhilaLC: Truxtun-Biddle Letters, Truxtun to Biddle, November 28, 1799.
33. John Hoxse, *The Yankee Tar* (Northampton, 1840).
34. *Quasi-War*, IV, 561, 566.


CHAPTER 36 (pp. 187–198)

1. *Quasi-War*, IV, 170, 377–79; V, 112.
2. *Ibid.*, V, 112, 115, 159.
3. John Hoxse, *The Yankee Tar* (Northampton, 1840)
4. *Quasi-War*, V, 44. The surgeon was entitled to $5 for curing a seaman and $10 for curing an officer of a "Venereal complaint." See *ibid.*, VII, 127–28.
5. *Ibid.*, V, 160, 162.

6. *Ibid.*, v, 160.
7. *Ibid.*, v, 165.
8. *Ibid.*, v, 160–61.
9. *Ibid.*, v, 170.
10. *Ibid.*, v, 167–68, 198.
11. *Ibid.*, v, 165, 170.
12. *Ibid.*, v, 163, 208. See also John Hoxse, *op. cit.* "Soho Hurst" in *Quasi-War*, v, 163, is undoubtedly John Hoxse.
13. *Quasi-War*, v, 171.
14. *Ibid.*, iv, 48. Robinson is indicated as 6th Lieut.; however, Lt. Archer was not on the Quarter Bill (HSPa: U.S. Frigate *Constellation* Orders, Muster Rolls, Stores, etc.) and apparently Robinson had advanced to 5th Lieut.; *Quasi-War*, v, 172.
15. *Quasi-War*, v, 161.
16. *Ibid.*, v, 167–68.
17. *Ibid.*, v, 172–73.
18. *Ibid.*, v, 333.
19. *Ibid.*, v, 165–66, 173, 392.
20. *Ibid.*, v, 183, 193, 538; vii, 354.
21. *Ibid.*, v, 193.
22. *American Neptune*, v (April, 1945), 156.
23. *Quasi-War*, v, 208, 211.
24. *Ibid.*, v, 162–63, 211. Probably there were more dead. See *ibid.*, v, 208.
25. *Ibid.*, v, 210.
26. *Ibid.*, v, 259–348 *passim;* e.g., 294.
27. PMS: Fox Papers, Truxtun to Josiah Fox, April 1, 1800, List of spars wanting. Size of spars in *Barbary Wars*, vii, 70.
28. *Quasi-War*, v, 166, 168–70, 197–98.
29. *Ibid.*, v, 168, 198, 333, 473.
30. *Ibid.*, v, 164, 168; vii, 461.
31. *Ibid.*, iv, 52–53; v, 163–64, 210.

CHAPTER 37 (pp. 198–206)

1. *Norfolk Herald*, April 5, 1800.
2. [Annals of Congress.] *Debates and Proceedings in the Congress of the United States, 1789–1824* (Washington, D.C., 1834–56), 6 Congr., 629–32, 640–42.
3. Octavius Pickering, *Life of Timothy Pickering* (Boston, 1867), iii, 329.
4. *Aurora*, Philadelphia, February 25, 26, 1800.
5. Dumas Malone, ed., *Correspondence between Thomas Jefferson and Pierre S. du Pont de Nemours, 1798–1817* (Boston, 1930), p. 22.
6. *Quasi-War*, vii, 364–71.
7. *Ibid.*, v, 296.
8. *Ibid.*, v, 421.

9. *Ibid.*, v, 295; 405–406.
10. *Ibid.*, III, 63; v, 62–66.
11. *Ibid.*, v, 373.
12. *Ibid.*, v, 430.
13. *Ibid.*, III, 552.
14. *Ibid.*, v, 419.
15. *Ibid.*, v, 421.
16. *Ibid.*, v, 520–21.
17. *Ibid.*, v, 492.
18. *Ibid.*, v, 415–16.
19. *Ibid.*, v, 538, 545, 555, 573; VI, 72.


CHAPTER 38 (pp. 206–212)

1. H. P. Caemmerer, *A Manual of the Origin and Development of Washington* (Washington, D.C., 1939), pp. 39–40.
2. Charles R. King, ed., *Life and Correspondence of Rufus King* (New York, 1894–1900), III, 461.
3. *Quasi-War*, v, 113, 201; "Diary of Mrs. William Thornton," Columbia Hist. Soc. *Records*, x (1907), 154, Thursday, June 12, 1800.
4. *Quasi-War*, v, 577; VI, 26, 59, 111; NYHS: Truxtun to Charles Biddle, June 19, 1800, in Cooper's Extra-Illustrated *History of the Navy*.
5. "Diary of Mrs. William Thornton," *loc. cit.*, p. 157.
6. NYHS: Truxtun to Charles Biddle, June 19, 1800, in Cooper's Extra-Illustrated *History of the Navy*.
7. *Quasi-War*, v, 405.
8. *Ibid.*, III, 329; VI, 122, 566.
9. *Ibid.*, VI, 521, 531.
10. *Ibid.*, VI, 175, 547; VII, 195.
11. *Autobiography of Charles Biddle* (Philadelphia, 1883), pp. 6, 188, 286–87, 370.
12. *Ibid.*, p. 288.
13. John Schuyler, *Institution of the Society of the Cincinnati* (New York, 1886), pp. 85, 97.
14. *Quasi-War*, VI, 240; HSPa: Thomas Truxtun Letter Book, 1800–1801 [Am 681], August 2, 1800.
15. HSPa: Thomas Truxtun Letter Book, August 13, 1800.
16. *Quasi-War*, VI, 321.
17. Dumas Malone, ed., *Correspondence between Thomas Jefferson and Pierre S. du Pont de Nemours, 1798–1817* (Boston, 1930), p. 22.
18. *Quasi-War*, VI, 198–200, 267–70, 419; VII, 86–90, especially 88.
19. *Ibid.*, VII, 1, 86–89, 373.
20. *Ibid.*, VI, 547; VII, 1. Doctor Balfour had Bell's *System of Surgery*, 4 vols. See Naval Academy Museum: Truxtun to Dr. George Balfour, December 25, 1800.

21. *Quasi-War,* VI, 241, 359, 496, 516, 530–31; VII, 106, 123; HSPa: Thomas Truxtun Letter Book, 1800–1801, pp. 21, 81–82; Truxtun to Gentlemen of the Gun Room Mess, November 12, 1800.

22. *Quasi-War,* VI, 240–41.

23. *Ibid.,* VII, 1; *Autobiography of Charles Biddle,* p. 292.

24. *Quasi-War,* VII, 1.

25. *Ibid.,* VII, 74–75, 77–78, 85.

26. *Ibid.,* VII, 20, 90–91, 106–107, 109, 111.


CHAPTER 39 (pp. 213–221)

1. Margaret Bayard Smith, *First Forty Years of Washington Society,* Gaillard Hunt, ed. (New York, 1906), pp. 25–27.

2. NDA: E. Truxtun Beale Photostats, Almanac and notebook, Antigua, 1801, with notations by Truxtun.

3. Thomas Truxtun, *Reply of Commodore Truxtun to an Attack Made on Him in the National Intelligencer, in June 1806* (Philadelphia, 1806).

4. *Quasi-War,* VII, 140.

5. *Ibid.,* VII, 214.

6. LC: Jefferson Papers, vol. 110, Truxtun to Vice-President of U.S., March 10, 1801.

7. *Barbary Wars,* I, 439.

8. LC: Jefferson Papers, vol. 112, Truxtun to Jefferson, May 10, 1801; Jefferson to Truxtun, May 28, 1801.

9. *Quasi-War,* VII, 134–35.

10. *Ibid.,* VII, 134–35; cf. *American State Papers,* Naval Affairs, I, 74–78, Stoddert's report and recommendations to H.R. of January 15, 1801. Stoddert's important role in this Act is ably set out in Robert G. Albion, "Distant Stations," U.S. Naval Inst. *Proc.,* LXXX (March, 1954), 265–73, p. 266 cited.

11. *Barbary Wars,* I, 426, 428, 432; PhilaLC: Truxtun-Biddle Letters, Truxtun to Biddle, October 24, 1801; Charles W. Goldsborough, *United States' Naval Chronicle* (Washington, D.C., 1824), I, 188–92.

12. *Quasi-War,* VII, 230; PhilaLC: Truxtun-Biddle Letters, Truxtun to Biddle, July 28, 1802.

13. *Quasi-War,* VII, 187–89.

14. *Ibid.,* VII, 195.

15. *Ibid.,* VII, 197–98.

16. *Barbary Wars,* I, 474.

17. Truxtun Hare Collection: Truxtun to James Watson, October 8, 1801.

18. PhilaLC: Truxtun-Biddle Letters, Truxtun to Biddle, July 14, 1801.

19. *Quasi-War,* VI, 198; HSPa: Joshua Humphreys Letter Books, III, October 28, 1800.

20. PMS: Fox Papers, Josiah Fox to William Pennock, May 13, 1801.

21. HSPa: Joshua Humphreys Letter Books, III, September 5, 1812.

22. Truxtun Hare Collection: Charles Biddle to Truxtun, June 16, 1801;

Truxtun to James Watson, October 8, 15, 1801; PhilaLC: Truxtun-Biddle Letters, Truxtun to Biddle, June 19, 1801.

23. PhilaLC: Truxtun-Biddle Letters, fols. 39, 40, 43, 44, 48, 58; Truxtun Hare Collection: Thomas Truxtun, Jr., to Truxtun, October 23, 1801; *Quasi-War*, VII, 354; *United States' Gazette*, Philadelphia, March 16, 1802.

24. G. W. Allen, *Our Navy and the Barbary Corsairs* (Boston, 1905), chapter VI; *Barbary Wars*, I, 365–67, 433.

25. *Barbary Wars*, I, 536–37.

26. *Ibid.*, I, 459.

27. *Ibid.*, I, 425; C. O. Paullin, "Naval Administration under Secretaries of the Navy Smith, Hamilton, and Jones, 1801–14," U.S. Naval Inst. *Proc.*, XXXII (1906), 1289 ff.

28. *Barbary Wars*, II, 19.

29. Katharine M. Beekman, "A Colonial Capital," N.J. Hist. Soc. *Proc.*, 4th ser., III, 15.

## CHAPTER 40 (pp. 221–225)

1. PhilaLC: Truxtun-Biddle Letters, Truxtun to Biddle, March 31, 1802, gives date erroneously as c. February 25, 1802; NYHS: Truxtun to Biddle, February 4, 1802, tells of receiving medal from President the day before.

2. *Barbary Wars*, I, 460, 488, 498.

3. Thomas Truxtun, *Reply of Commodore Thomas Truxtun to an Attack Made on Him in the National Intelligencer, in June 1806* (Philadelphia, 1806); *Quasi-War*, VII, 265; *Barbary Wars*, II, *passim* (see index: *Constitution*); PhilaLC: Truxtun-Biddle Letters, Truxtun to Biddle, March 6, 1802.

4. PhilaLC: Truxtun-Biddle Letters, Truxtun to Biddle, March 31, 1802.

5. Henry Adams, *The Formative Years*, Herbert Agar, ed. (Boston, 1947), pp. 101–102; Margaret Bayard Smith, *First Forty Years of Washington Society*, Gaillard Hunt, ed. (New York, 1906), p. 6.

6. PhilaLC: Truxtun-Biddle Letters, Truxtun to Biddle, March 31, 1802.

7. NYPL: U.S. Navy Collection, Truxtun to Richard Dale, June 8, 1802.

8. *Barbary Wars*, II, 26; *National Intelligencer*, Washington, D.C., June 16, 1806.

9. PhilaLC: Truxtun-Biddle Letters, Truxtun to Biddle, March 6, 31, 1802.

10. *Barbary Wars*, II, 76.

11. *Ibid.*, II, 82–83.

12. Truxtun Hare Collection: Benjamin Stoddert to Truxtun, March 29, 1802.

13. PhilaLC: Truxtun-Biddle Letters, Truxtun to Biddle, March 31, 1802.

14. *Barbary Wars*, II, 94.

CHAPTER 41 (pp. 226–232)

1. HSPa: Dreer Collection, Truxtun to Richard Dale, May 2, 1802.
2. *Ibid.*
3. Congressman Josiah Parker, sometime Chairman, Committee on Naval Affairs. See Truxtun Hare Collection: Truxtun to Aaron Burr, June 27, 1803.
4. PhilaLC: Truxtun-Biddle Letters, Truxtun to Biddle, May 31, 1814.
5. MassHS: Pickering Papers, Truxtun to Pickering [April, 1806], fol. 308.
6. G. W. Allen, *Our Navy and the Barbary Corsairs* (Boston, 1905), pp. 134–37.
7. *Barbary Wars,* II, 229.
8. Truxtun Hare Collection: Truxtun to Aaron Burr, June 27, 1803.
9. MassHS: Truxtun to Samuel Smith, March 31, 1804.
10. *Barbary Wars,* II, 76.
11. MassHS: Pickering Papers, Truxtun to Pickering, May 13, 1806.
12. *Ibid.,* December 15, 1803.
13. *The Collector* (Mary A. Benjamin), LXI, no. 1, p. 16, Stoddert to Gideon Granger, April 8, 1806.
14. LC: Jefferson Papers, vol. 142, Truxtun to Jefferson, August 20, 1804.
15. NYHS: Truxtun to Aaron Burr, March 19, 1804.
16. NYPL: U.S. Navy Collection, Truxtun to Richard Dale, June 8, 1802.
17. *Quasi-War,* V, 174–75; VI, 503, 513.
18. PhilaLC: Truxtun-Biddle Letters, Truxtun to Biddle, March 18, 1804.
19. Charles W. Goldsborough, *United States' Naval Chronicle* (Washington, D.C., 1824), I, 28.
20. PhilaLC: Truxtun-Biddle Letters, Truxtun to Biddle, November 27, 1804.
21. Truxtun Hare Collection: Truxtun to Aaron Burr, June 27, 1803; MassHS: Pickering Papers, Truxtun to Pickering, February 1, 1806.


CHAPTER 42 (pp. 233–237)

1. John Schuyler, *Institution of the Society of the Cincinnati* (New York, 1886), p. 100.
2. *Guardian, or New Brunswick Advertiser,* August 16, 1804; S. H. Wandell and Meade Minnigerode, *Aaron Burr* (New York, 1927), I, 285.
3. *Autobiography of Charles Biddle* (Philadelphia, 1883), p. 303.
4. Wandell and Minnigerode, *op. cit.,* I, 288–89.
5. PhilaLC: Truxtun-Biddle Letters, Truxtun to Biddle, July 26, 1804.
6. *Ibid.*
7. *Ibid.,* July 30, 1804.
8. *Autobiography of Charles Biddle,* p. 406.
9. Wandell and Minnigerode, *op. cit.,* I, 298.
10. NYPL: Elizabeth de Hart Bleeker MS Diary, 1799–1806, July 15, 1804.
11. *American Daily Advertiser,* Philadelphia, July 21, 24, August 2, 1804.

12. *Philadelphia Gazette,* August 10, 1804.

13. *Ibid.*

14. *Autobiography of Charles Biddle,* pp. 406–407; Wandell and Minnigerode, *op. cit.,* I, 222–23.

15. *American Daily Advertiser,* Philadelphia, August 1, 1804; *Philadelphia Gazette,* August 10, 1804.

16. *Barbary Wars,* v, 544; PhilaLC: Truxtun-Biddle Letters, Truxtun to Biddle, December 5, 1804, December 24, 1805 "(highly confidential)."

17. *Autobiography of Charles Biddle,* p. 408; Marquis James, *Life of Andrew Jackson* (New York, 1938), pp. 105–106.

18. *Autobiography of Charles Biddle,* p. 311.


CHAPTER 43 (pp. 238–242)

1. Huntington Library, San Marino: HM 25447, Truxtun to Benjamin Stoddert, April 14, 1806.

2. *Autobiography of Charles Biddle* (Philadelphia, 1883), p. 311.

3. NYHS: Truxtun to Aaron Burr, March 19, 1804.

4. MassHS: Pickering Papers, Pickering to Truxtun, November 25, 1803.

5. Thomas Truxtun, *Reply of Commodore Thomas Truxtun to an Attack Made on Him in the National Intelligencer, in June 1806* (Philadelphia, 1806), pp. 23 ff.; Huntington Library: HM 25447, Truxtun to Stoddert, April 14, 1806.

6. NDA: Captains Letters (1805), III. Between November 1 and December 7, 1805 there were at least eight letters on the subject.

7. *Ibid.,* Preble to Secretary of the Navy Smith, November 3, 1805.

8. LC: Jefferson Papers, vol. 143, enclosure (n.d.) following Truxtun to Jefferson, September 25, 1804.

9. NDA: Captains Letters (1805); see note 6 above.

10. Huntington Library: HM 25447, Truxtun to Stoddert, April 14, 1806.

11. NDA: Letters to Officers of Ships of War, VII, 83, Secretary of the Navy to Truxtun, February 10, 1806.

12. Huntington Library: HM 25447, Truxtun to Stoddert, April 14, 1806.

13. *Ibid.; Autobiography of Charles Biddle,* p. 406.

14. *National Intelligencer,* Washington, D.C., June 16, 18, 20, and 23, 1806.

15. Truxtun, *Reply,* cited note 5, above.

16. MassHS: Pickering Papers, [copy] Truxtun to Robert Smith, May 1, 1806; Massachusetts Hist. Soc. *Proc.,* 2nd ser., xx (May, 1906), 292.

17. PhilaLC: Truxtun-Biddle Letters, Truxtun to Biddle, December 24, 1805.

CHAPTER 44 (pp. 242–249)

1. Henry Adams, *The Formative Years,* Herbert Agar, ed. (Boston, 1947), pp. 203–15.
2. MassHS: Pickering Papers, Truxtun to Pickering, January 13, 1807; Huntington Library: Deposition by Thomas Truxtun, March 27, 1807.
3. S. H. Wandell and Meade Minnigerode, *Aaron Burr* (New York, 1927), II, 37–40.
4. MassHS: Pickering Papers, Truxtun to Pickering, January 13, 1807.
5. *Ibid.,* February 12, 1807.
6. Huntington Library: HM 25449, Truxtun to Caesar Rodney, April 30, 1807.
7. *Autobiography of Charles Biddle* (Philadelphia, 1883), p. 317.
8. MassHS: Pickering Papers, Truxtun to Pickering, January 13, 1807.
9. Massachusetts Hist. Soc. *Proc.,* 2nd ser., xx (May, 1906), 292, Duane to Jefferson, December 8, 1806.
10. LC: Jefferson Papers, vol. 160, August 10, 1806, copy of Truxtun's "Minutes"; vol. 164, Truxtun to Jefferson, January 23, 1807.
11. Wandell and Minnigerode, *op. cit.,* II, 79.
12. *Autobiography of Charles Biddle,* p. 413.
13. LC: Jefferson Papers, vol. 169, Truxtun to Jefferson, July 23, 1807.
14. Walter F. McCaleb, *Aaron Burr Conspiracy* (New York, 1936), pp. 265–68.
15. Eulogies in *Richmond Courier,* July 2, 1835, and *Richmond Enquirer,* July 3, 1835.
16. PhilaLC: Truxtun-Biddle Letters, Truxtun to Biddle, May 30, 1807.
17. LC: Jefferson Papers, vol. 168, Truxtun to John Randolph, Foreman, and Grand Jury, June 23, 1807; MassHS: Pickering Papers, P.S. to Pickering on MS copy of above letter.
18. McCaleb, *op. cit.,* p. 269.
19. PhilaLC: Truxtun-Biddle Letters, Truxtun to Biddle, July 11, 1807.
20. *Ibid.;* LC: Jefferson Papers, vol. 169, Truxtun to Jefferson, July 23, 1807.
21. *Autobiography of Charles Biddle,* p. 316.
22. Truxtun mentioned the cow-skin in connection with another former gentleman who had fallen from grace—PhilaLC: Truxtun-Biddle Letters, Truxtun to Biddle, May 26, 1809.
23. Albert J. Beveridge, *Life of John Marshall* (Boston, 1916–19), III, 451; David Robertson, *Reports of the Trials of Aaron Burr* (Philadelphia, 1808), I, 485–91.


CHAPTER 45 (pp. 249–255)

1. *Barbary Wars,* VI, 535–41, 561–70.
2. MassHS: Pickering Papers, Truxtun to Pickering, October 26, 1807.
3. Thomas Truxtun, *A Few Extracts from the Best Authors on Naval Tactics* (Philadelphia, 1806).

4. MassHS: Pickering Papers, Truxtun to Pickering, February 1, 1806.
5. PhilaLC: Truxtun-Biddle Letters, *passim;* MassHS: Pickering Papers, Truxtun to Pickering, February 2, 1809 and *passim.*
6. PhilaLC: Truxtun-Biddle Letters, Truxtun to Biddle, May 16, 1801; NYPL: U.S. Navy Collection, Truxtun to Isaac Snowden, August 11, 1808; Middlesex County Deeds (Court House, New Brunswick, N.J.), VII, 515; VIII, 23, 29, 50, 244; IX, 441.
7. PhilaLC: Truxtun to Thomas Biddle, June 7, 1809.
8. MassHS: Pickering Papers, Truxtun to Pickering, January 1, 1810.
9. *Ibid.,* December 1, 1808.
10. *United States Gazette,* Philadelphia, January 31, 1809.
11. HSPa: William Page MS Diary, January 31, 1809.
12. J. T. Scharf and Thompson Westcott, *History of Philadelphia* (Philadelphia, 1884), I, 538.
13. *United States Gazette,* Philadelphia, January 26–30, 1809.
14. MassHS: Pickering Papers, Truxtun to Pickering, February 2, 1809.
15. *Ibid.; United States Gazette,* Philadelphia, January 31, 1809.
16. Scharf and Westcott, *op. cit.,* I, 539; MassHS: Pickering Papers, Invitation to dinner, n.d. [February 10, 1809].
17. Scharf and Westcott, *op. cit.,* I, 539.
18. MassHS: Pickering Papers, Truxtun to Pickering, March 9, 1809.


CHAPTER 46 (pp. 256–260)

1. *Trenton Federalist,* May 13, 1811.
2. PhilaLC: Truxtun-Biddle Letters, Mary Truxtun to Biddle, May 9, 26, 1811.
3. *Ibid.,* fols. 83–109, *passim.*
4. *Ibid.*
5. *Ibid.,* Truxtun to Biddle, January 30, 1812.
6. NDA: Truxtun to Dr. George Balfour, November 15, 1817.
7. Truxtun Hare Collection: Robert Harrison to Truxtun, December 4, 1816, June 14, 1817.
8. PhilaLC: Truxtun-Biddle Letters, Truxtun to Biddle, September 17, 24, October 3, 1810; *Aurora,* Philadelphia, October 12, 15, 1810.
9. *American Daily Advertiser,* Philadelphia, October 10, 1816; *Autobiography of Charles Biddle* (Philadelphia, 1883), pp. 354–55.
10. Truxtun Hare Collection: William Truxtun to Mrs. Truxtun, February 15, [1820?].
11. LC: Thomas Truxtun Papers (1795–1820), Truxtun to William S. Biddle, December 3, 17, 1819; June 7, 1820; NYHS: Truxtun to David Lewis, December 29, 1818.
12. *Long Island Star,* Brooklyn, September 18, 1823.
13. Maria Scott Beale Chance, *A Chronicle of the Family of Edward F. Beale* (Haverford, 1943). Truxtun's will is printed in full.

14. Howard I. Chapelle, *History of the American Sailing Navy* (New York, 1949), p. 338.
15. C. O. Paullin, *Commodore John Rodgers* (Cleveland, 1910), p. 324.
16. NDA: [ZB] Invitation to attend Truxtun's funeral, May 6, 1822; HSPa: Deborah Norris Logan MS Diary, v (1821–22), May 8, 1822.
17. C. O. Paullin, *op. cit.*, pp. 330–31.

# BIBLIOGRAPHY

❧ . . ❧ . . ❧ . . ❧ . .

## MANUSCRIPTS

American Philosophical Society, Philadelphia
Franklin Papers; Franklin-Bache Papers.
Franklin Institute, Philadelphia
Lenthal Collection, Mast Yard Papers of Turner & Thompson.
Hare, T. Truxtun, Esq. *See* Truxtun Hare Collection.
Hepburn Collection Transcripts, Courtesy of William Bell Clark, Esq., Brevard, N.C.
John Barry Papers.
Historical Society of Pennsylvania, Philadelphia
Admiralty Court Papers; *Constellation* Journal; *Constellation* Orders, Muster Rolls, Stores, etc.; *Delaware* ship Papers (1793–97); Dreer Collection; Etting Collection; Benjamin Fuller Letter Books; Gratz Collection; Joshua Humphreys Letter Books, Account Books, and Correspondence (1774–1831); Jones & Clarke Papers; Deborah Norris Logan Diary (1815–39); Christopher Marshall Diary (1783–91); Misc. Collection; Misc. Ship Papers; William Page Diary (1808–12); Philadelphia Assessment Books; Philadelphia Customs House Record Books; Society Collections; Thomas Truxtun Letter Books (1798–99 and 1800–1801); Journal of ship *United States,* Capt. Thomas Bell, from Philadelphia bound toward China; Wayne Papers; Wharton & Humphreys Shipyard Accounts (1774–95).
Henry E. Huntington Library, San Marino, Calif.
Truxtun Letters (1795–1815).
Library Company of Philadelphia (Free Library of Philadelphia, Librarian)
Truxtun-Biddle Letters. For description and index see Eugene S. Ferguson, *Commodore Thomas Truxtun 1755–1822, A description of the Truxtun-Biddle Letters* . . . Research Bull., Free Library of Philadelphia, Philadelphia, 1947, 31 pp.
Library of Congress, Washington, D.C.
Continental Congress Papers; Jefferson Papers; John Paul Jones Papers; Thomas Truxtun Papers (1795–1820); Washington Papers.
Middlesex County, Deeds, Office of Recorder, Court House, New Brunswick, N.J.
Massachusetts Historical Society, Boston
Pickering Papers.

Navy Department Records, National Archives, Washington, D.C.

  *Alliance,* Indiaman, Log of Richard Dale (1787–88); T. Truxtun Beale Photostats; Captain's Letters (1805); Correspondence on Naval Affairs when Navy was under War Dept. 1790–98, 1 vol. [Navy 1790–98 LB]; Letters to Officers of Ships of War; War Dept. Letter Book, Arming and Equipping Frigates, 1795–98.

New York Historical Society, New York

  Barnes Collection; John Barry Papers; Sloop *Experiment* Papers (1785–87).

New York Public Library

  Elizabeth de Hart Bleeker Diary (1799–1806); Constable-Pierrepont Collection; U.S. Navy Collection. The Constable-Pierrepont Collection provided solid information on the China voyages that I should not have found elsewhere.

Peabody Museum, Salem, Mass.

  Josiah Fox Papers.

Pennsylvania State Library, Harrisburg

  Post-Revolutionary Papers.

Truxtun Family Bible, in private collection of Truxtun Brodhead, Esq. This is the source for dates of birth, marriage, and death of Truxtun, his wife, and children.

Truxtun Hare Collection

  Private manuscript collection of the late T. Truxtun Hare, Esq. My account of Captain Truxtun's Revolutionary service would have been sketchy indeed had it not been for this collection; and for many other circumstances of his career, these letters have provided essential color and background.


## PUBLIC DOCUMENTS

*American State Papers: Documents, Legislative and Executive.* 38 vols. Washington, D.C., 1832–61.

[Annals of Congress.] *Debates and Proceedings in the Congress of United States, 1789–1824.* 42 vols. Washington, D.C., 1834–56.

Force, Peter, ed., *American Archives.* 9 vols. Washington, D.C., 1837–53.

Ford, W. C., *et al.,* eds., *Journals of the Continental Congress, 1774–1789.* 34 vols. Washington, D.C., 1904–37.

Great Britain, Admiralty, *Regulations and Instructions Relative to His Majesty's Service at Sea.* 9th ed., London, 1757; 13th ed., London, 1790.

U.S. Library of Congress, *A Calendar of John Paul Jones Manuscripts in the Library of Congress.* Washington, D.C., 1903.

———, *Naval Records of the American Revolution 1775–1788.* Washington, D.C., 1906. A calendar of Mss. and letters of marque.

U.S. Naval Records and Library Office, *Naval Documents Related to the Quasi-War Between the United States and France, 1797–1801.* 7 vols. Washington, D.C., 1935–38.

———, *Naval Documents Related to the United States Wars with the Barbary*

*Powers, 1785–1807.* 7 vols. Washington, D.C., 1939–45. [Vol. 7 is *Register of Officer Personnel . . . and Ships' Data, 1801–1807.*]

The last two titles, abbreviated in reference notes as *Quasi-War* and *Barbary Wars,* respectively, are indispensable to a work of this kind. Well planned and executed, they have brought to my desk a great deal of source material that otherwise would have been difficult and expensive to collect. Their value to me has been inestimably great.

## HISTORY JOURNALS AND SOCIETY PUBLICATIONS
Volumes given are those actually cited in reference notes, above.

*American Historical Review.* New York. xxxv (1930).
*American Neptune.* Salem, Mass. v, vii, ix (1945, 1947, 1949).
American Philosophical Soc., *Proceedings.* Philadelphia. xcii (1948).
Columbia Hist. Soc., *Records.* Washington, D.C. x (1907).
*Maryland Historical Magazine.* Baltimore. xxviii (1933).
Massachusetts Hist. Soc., *Collections.* Boston. lxxvii (1927).
——, *Proceedings.* Boston. 2nd ser., xx (1906).
New Jersey Hist. Soc., *Proceedings.* Newark. 4th ser., iii.
New York Hist. Soc., *Collections.* New York. xx (1887).
*Pennsylvania History.* Philadelphia. vi–vii (1939–40).
*Pennsylvania Mag. of Hist. and Biog.* Philadelphia. xix (1895), xxxi (1907), lv (1931), lxxvi (1952).
*Port Folio.* Philadelphia. 2nd ser., i (1809).
U.S. Naval Inst., *Proceedings.* Annapolis. xxxii (1906), lxxviii (1952), lxxx (1954).

## NEWSPAPERS
Years given are those actually cited in reference notes, above.

Baltimore: *Federal Gazette & Baltimore Daily Advertiser* (1796–99); *Maryland Journal* (1796); *Telegraphe and Daily Advertiser* (1797–99).
Boston: *Columbian Centinel* (1797, 1799); *Independent Chronicle* (1776–78, 1799); *New England Chronicle* (1776).
Hartford, Conn.: *Connecticut Courant* (1783, 1785).
London, England: *Daily Advertiser* (1776); *Public Advertiser* (1776–77); *Whitehall Evening Post* (1776).
New Brunswick, N.J.: *Guardian; or, New-Brunswick Advertiser* (1804).
New York: *New York Gazette, and the Weekly Mercury* (1771, 1775–76); *New York Mercury* (1757, 1760, 1762); *Rivington's New York Gazetteer* (1775); *Spectator* (1799).
Newport, R.I.: *Newport Mercury* (1776).

Norfolk, Va.: *Norfolk Herald* (1799–1800).
Philadelphia: *American Daily Advertiser* (1794, 1796–97, 1799, 1804, 1816);
*Aurora* (1799–1800, 1810); *Independent Gazetteer* (1782–83); *Pennsylvania Evening Post* (1776); *Pennsylvania Gazette* (1776, 1783); *Pennsylvania Journal* (1786); *Pennsylvania Packet* (1777, 1780–83, 1785–87); *Philadelphia Gazette* (1796–97, 1804); *United States Gazette* (1802, 1809).
Trenton, N.J.: *Trenton Federalist* (1811).
Washington: *National Intelligencer* (1806).

## BIOGRAPHY, WRITINGS, DIARIES, JOURNALS

Adams, John, *Works*. Chas. F. Adams, ed. 10 vols. Boston, 1850–56.
Andrews, Evangeline W., ed., *Journal of a Lady of Quality*. New Haven, 1934.
Barnes, John S., ed., *Fanning's Narrative, being the Memoirs of Nathaniel Fanning, an Officer of the Revolutionary Navy*. New York, 1912.
Beveridge, Albert J., *Life of John Marshall*. 4 vols. Boston, 1916–19.
Biddle, Charles, *Autobiography . . . 1745–1821*. Philadelphia, 1883.
Bullen, Frank T., *The Log of a Sea-Waif, being Recollections of the First Four Years of My Sea Life*. New York, 1899.
Burnett, Edmund Cody, ed., *Letters of Members of the Continental Congress*. 8 vols. Washington, D.C., 1921–38.
Chance, Maria Scott Beale, *A Chronicle of the Family of Edward F. Beale*. Haverford, 1943.
Clark, William Bell, *Gallant John Barry*. New York, 1938.
Cook, Lewis D., "Commodore Thomas Truxtun . . . and his Descendants . . . ," *Pennsylvania Genealogical Magazine*, xvii (June, 1949), 3–32. A carefully compiled genealogy of a large family.
Dana, Richard Henry, *Two Years Before the Mast*. New York: Modern Library, 1936.
*Dictionary of American Biography*. 22 vols. New York, 1928–44.
*Dictionary of National Biography*. 63 vols. London, 1885–1901.
Dixon, George, *A Voyage Round the World*. London, 1789.
Footner, Hulbert, *Sailor of Fortune, Life and Adventures of Commodore Barney, USN*. New York, 1940.
Franklin, Benjamin, *Writings*, A. H. Smyth, ed. 10 vols. New York, 1905–1907. [For *Papers*, see Hays, I. Minis; for biography, see Van Doren, Carl.]
Graydon, Alexander, *Memoirs of a Life, Chiefly Passed in Pennsylvania within the Last Sixty Years*. Edinburgh, 1822.
Hays, I. Minis, *Calendar of the Papers of Benjamin Franklin in the Library of the American Philosophical Society*. 5 vols. Philadelphia, 1908.
Hoxse, John, *The Yankee Tar*. Northampton, 1840. [To be used with caution.]
James, Marquis, *Life of Andrew Jackson*. New York, 1938.
King, Charles R., ed., *Life and Correspondence of Rufus King*. 6 vols. New York, 1894–1900.
Lorenz, Lincoln, *John Paul Jones*. Annapolis, 1943.

Maclay, William, *Journal, 1789–1791*. New York, 1927.

MacKenzie, Frederick, *Diary* [1775–81]. 2 vols. Cambridge, Mass., 1930.

Malone, Dumas, ed., *Correspondence between Thomas Jefferson and Pierre S. du Pont de Nemours, 1798–1817*. Boston, 1930.

Morris, Commodore Charles, USN., *Autobiography*. Annapolis, 1880.

Neeser, Robert W., ed., *Despatches of Molyneux Shuldham, 1776*. New York, 1913.

*News from Home* (Home Insurance Co., New York), xv, no. 1, Spring, 1954. Fifteen of 28 pages in this issue were devoted to Captain Truxtun and the *Constellation*. Profusely illustrated.

Paullin, Charles O., *Commodore John Rodgers*. Cleveland, 1910.

Pickering, Octavius, *Life of Timothy Pickering*. Boston, 1867.

[Porter, David,] *Constantinople and Its Environs, in a Series of Letters . . . by an American*. 2 vols. New York, 1835.

Quincy, Josiah, ed., *Journals of Major Samuel Shaw*. Boston, 1847.

Roberts, Kenneth and Anna, ed. and trans., *Moreau de St. Méry's American Journey, 1793–1798*. New York, 1947.

Schachner, Nathan, *Alexander Hamilton*. New York, 1946.

Shipton, Clifford K., *Biographical Sketches of Those Who Attended Harvard College in the Classes 1722–1725*. Boston, 1945.

Smith, Margaret Bayard, *First Forty Years of Washington Society*. Gaillard Hunt, ed. New York, 1906.

Steiner, Bernard C., *Life and Correspondence of James McHenry*. Cleveland, 1907.

Truxtun, Thomas, *Reply of Commodore Truxtun to an Attack Made on Him in the National Intelligencer in June 1806*. Philadelphia, 1806.

Van Doren, Carl, *Benjamin Franklin*. New York, 1938.

Wandell, S. H. and Minnigerode, Meade, *Aaron Burr*. 2 vols. New York, 1927.

Washington, George, *Diaries*. John C. Fitzpatrick, ed. 4 vols. Boston, 1925.

——, *Writings*. John C. Fitzpatrick, ed. 39 vols. Washington, D.C., 1931–44.

NAVAL AND MARITIME HISTORY, NAVIGATION,
SHIPBUILDING, SIGNALS, TACTICS

Albion, Robert G., *Square-Riggers on Schedule, the New York Sailing Packets to England, France, and the Cotton Ports*. Princeton, 1938.

Allen, Gardner W., *A Naval History of the American Revolution*. 2 vols. Boston, 1913.

——, *Our Naval War with France*. Boston, 1909.

——, *Our Navy and the Barbary Corsairs*. Boston, 1905.

Anthony, Irvin, *Revolt at Sea*. New York, 1937.

Bowditch, Nathaniel, *The New American Practical Navigator*. First ed., Newburyport, 1802.

Chapelle, Howard I., *History of the American Sailing Navy*. New York, 1949.

Cutler, Carl C., *Greyhounds of the Sea*. New York, 1930.

Dulles, Foster Rhea, *The Old China Trade*. Boston, 1930.

Dunn, Samuel, *A New Directory for the East-Indies*. 5th ed., London, 1780.

Goldsborough, Charles W., *United States' Naval Chronicle*. Vol. I (no more published), Washington, D.C., 1824.

Lever, Darcy, *The Young Sea Officer's Sheet Anchor*. First Philadelphia from 2nd London ed., Philadelphia, c. 1819.

Lovette, Leland P., *Naval Customs, Traditions, and Usage*. Annapolis, 1939.

Maclay, Edgar S., *History of the Navy*. 2 vols. New York, 1895.

Morison, Samuel Eliot, *Maritime History of Massachusetts, 1783–1860*. Boston, 1921.

Morse, Hosea Ballou, *Chronicles of the East India Company Trading to China*. 5 vols. Oxford, 1926–29.

Parkinson, C. N., *Trade in the Eastern Seas 1793–1813*. Cambridge, England, 1937.

Peabody, Robert E., *Log of the Grand Turks*. Boston, 1926.

Schomberg, Isaac, *Naval Chronology*. 5 vols. London, 1802.

*Shipbuilder's Repository, or a Treatise on Marine Architecture*. London, 1789.

Sprout, Harold and Margaret, *Rise of American Naval Power, 1776–1918*. Princeton, 1946.

Truxtun, Thomas, *A Few Extracts from the Best Authors on Naval Tactics . . . and Some Short Notes Made Merely to Show the Advantages of a Curve Line of Battle*. Philadelphia, 1806. 15 pp.

———, *Instructions, Signals, and Explanations Offered for the U.S. Fleet*. Baltimore, 1797.

———, *Remarks, Instructions, and Examples Relating to the Latitude and Longitude* [Appendix 1: "Masting of Ships of War"; Appendix 2: "General Duties of Officers"]. Philadelphia, 1794.

Wroth, Lawrence, *Some American Contributions to the Art of Navigation, 1519–1802*. Providence, 1947. 41 pp.

OTHER WORKS

Adams, Henry, *The Formative Years*. Herbert Agar, ed. 2 vols. Boston, 1947.

Almon, John, ed., *Remembrancer, or Impartial Repository of Public Events*. 17 vols. London, 1775–84.

Bayles, W. Harrison, *Old Taverns of New York*. New York, 1915.

Betham-Edwards, Miss, ed., *Arthur Young's Travels in France, 1787–1789*. London, 1900.

Bezanson, Anne, *Prices and Inflation during the American Revolution*. Philadelphia, 1951.

Burnett, Edmund Cody, *The Continental Congress*. New York, 1941.

Caemmerer, H. P., *A Manual on the Origin and Development of Washington*. Washington, D.C., 1939.

[*Colonial Records of Pennsylvania, 1683–1790.*] 16 vols. Philadelphia and Harrisburg, 1851–59.

Fitzgerald, C. P., *China, A Short Cultural History.* New York, 1938.

Flick, Alexander C., ed., *History of the State of New York.* 10 vols. New York, 1933.

Griffiths, Thomas M., *Maine Sources in the House of the Seven Gables.* Waterville, 1945.

Hazard, Samuel, *et al.,* eds., *Pennsylvania Archives.* 9 ser., 138 vols. Philadelphia and Harrisburg, 1852–1949. For earlier series, see *Colonial Records,* above.

Hicks, Benjamin D., ed., *Records of the Towns of North and South Hempstead.* 5 vols. Jamaica, 1900.

Irwin, Ray W., *Diplomatic Relations of the United States with the Barbary Powers 1776–1816.* Chapel Hill, 1931.

Lawrence-Archer, J. H., *Monumental Inscriptions of the British West Indies from the Earliest Date.* London, 1875.

Lossing, Benson J., *Pictorial Field Book of the Revolution.* 2 vols. New York, 1860.

McCaleb, Walter F., *Aaron Burr Conspiracy.* New York, 1936.

McMaster, John B., *A History of the People of the United States, from the Revolution to the Civil War.* 8 vols. New York, 1888–1913.

Miller, John C., *Triumph of Freedom.* Boston, 1948.

Morris, Richard B., ed., *Era of the American Revolution.* New York, 1939.

O'Callaghan, E. B., *Calendar of Historical Manuscripts in the Office of the Secretary.* Albany, 1865–66.

——, ed., *Documents Relative to the Colonial History of the State of New York.* 15 vols. (index in Vol. XI). Albany, 1853–61.

——, *New York Colony—Names of Persons for Whom Marriage Licenses Were Issued by the Secretary of the Province prior to 1784.* Albany, 1860.

Onderdonk, Henry, Jr., *Annals of Hempstead, 1643–1832.* Hempstead, 1878.

——, *Antiquities of the Parish Church, Hempstead.* Hempstead, 1880.

Powell, J. H., *Bring Out Your Dead, The Great Plague of Yellow Fever in Philadelphia in 1793.* Philadelphia, 1949.

*Queens County, N.Y., History of, with Illustrations, Portraits, and Sketches of Prominent Families and Individuals.* New York, 1882.

Ragatz, Lowell J., *The Fall of the Planter Class in the British Caribbean, 1763–1833.* New York, 1928.

Robertson, David, *Reports of the Trials of Aaron Burr.* 2 vols. Philadelphia, 1808.

Scharf, J. Thomas and Westcott, Thompson, *History of Philadelphia.* 3 vols. Philadelphia, 1884.

Schuyler, John, *Institution of the Society of the Cincinnati.* New York, 1886.

Scott, James B., ed., *Controversy over Neutral Rights between U.S. and France, 1797–1800.* New York, 1917.

Singleton, Esther, *Social New York under the Georges, 1714–1776.* New York, 1902.

Twining, Thomas, *Travels in America One Hundred Years Ago*. New York, 1894.

Van Doren, Carl, *The Great Rehearsal*. New York, 1948. On the making of the *Constitution*.

Watson, John F., *Annals of Philadelphia, and Pennsylvania, in the Olden Times*. 3 vols. (reprint). Philadelphia, 1927.

# INDEX

Barry, John (*Cont.*)

Navy, 102; building frigates, 110, 112, 115, 124; commission of, 150; revises Articles of War, 150–51; in West Indies, 149, 156, 160, 166–67; in Hampton Roads, 182; takes envoys to France, 186; relieves T, 212; rank under Peace Establishment Act, 218; dies, 238; mentioned, 125, 143, 153, 179, 183

Basseterre, St. Kitts: port of rendezvous, 152, 156; description of, 158; *L'Insurgente* action in sight of, 162; T arrives in, after action, 166; mentioned, 168

Batavia, Java, 66, 82

Beale, Truxtun, grandson of T, 259

Bell, Thomas, 61

Benbridge, Henry, son-in-law of T: prize agent, 175; in Norfolk, 219; T on, 257

Biddle, Charles: declines partnership with T, 50; on T, 51; agent for T, 80–81, 175, 207, 227; and Tench Coxe, 89; and French craze, 94, 137; and yellow fever, 95; takes prize agency, 175; and T's first resignation, 184, 185–86; advocates medal for T, 198; sons in *President*, 208; and T's second resignation, 224, 238; confidant of T and Mary, 229, 256–57; and Burr schemes, 244–45, 248; and political jobs for T, 258–59; mentioned, 88, 120, 143, 177, 178, 211, 217, 223, 231, 232, 234, 236, 247, 260

Biddle, Mrs. Charles, 208

Biddle, Edward: midshipman in *President*, 208; dies, 211; eulogy on, 211–12

Biddle, James, 208

Black Doctor, Lysingsang, 83

Blanchard, François, French aeronaut, 93

Bligh, William, of *Bounty*, 81

Bombay, India, 89

Boston, Massachusetts: tea party, 13; in Revolution, 19, 26, 27; and *Mars* fitting out, 30; in war with France, 111, 222; celebrates T's victory, 171

*Bounty*, H.M. ship, 81

Bowditch, Nathaniel, 104, 106, 107

Bristol, England, 6, 7, 9, 11

British East India Company: goods to America, 7; monopoly of, 61, 90; and

American ginseng, 64; and St. Helena, 69; mentioned, 73, 89

Brooklyn, New York, 2, 6, 9

Brooks, Samuel, 190

Brown, Andrew, schoolmaster, 85, 91

Burr, Aaron: and rank of T, 215, 224, 239; intimate with T, 229, 230; duel with Hamilton, 233–36; and race horse "Truxtun," 237; schemes of, 242–45; trial in Richmond, 246–49

Burr, Theodosia. *See* Alston

Burrows, William, Commandant of Marine Corps, 208, 217

Cabin boy, duties of, 8–9

Caldwell, Andrew and James, 32, 34, 42, 48

Campbell, Hugh, flag captain, 222, 223

Canton, China, 61, 64, 74–75, 83

*Canton*, ship: named, 63, 271n8; first voyage, 64–70 *passim*, 77; second voyage, 79, 83, 86; third voyage, 87, 89–91; scurvy in, 90; T loses confidence in, 91

Canton River, China, 71–73

Cape Town, South Africa: description of, 69–70; T calls in, 69, 81, 86, 89; T omits call in, 90; mentioned, 91

Cape Verde Islands, 67, 81

Capitol building, Washington, D.C., 199, 213

Cargoes: to West Indies, 18, 24; in prize, 29; from West Indies, 34, 36; from Europe, 46, 50–51, 53, 97–98; to Europe, 50; to Far East, 64–65, 82, 87; to Cape Town, 69; from Far East, 61, 77, 93

Carved work in *Constellation*, 125–26, 131–33

Castries, M. de, French minister of marine, 54

Cecil Furnace, Maryland, 124

Chambers, James, master of *London*, 10, 12, 13–16

*Charming Polly*, sloop, 17, 18, 19–21

*Chance*, sloop, 22, 23–27, 29, 49

Chauncey, Isaac: in *President*, 207, 210; Navy Commissioner, 259–60

*Chesapeake*, frigate: building in Norfolk, 202; accompanies T, 212; decay noted, 218; T's flagship, 222, 223; and *Leopard*, 249–50, 251

Dale, Richard (*Cont.*)
   rank, 150, 178–79, 181, 218; commands Mediterranean squadron, 216–17, 220, 221, 227; has flag captain, 221–22; resigns, 238; at Embargo meeting, 253; T complains to, 226–27, 230; mentioned, 218, 226, 232, 260
Dallas, Alexander James, 238
Dawson, Mike, 36
Decatur, Stephen (1752–1808): takes *Retaliation,* 159; on T's reinstatement, 186; mentioned, 150, 173
Declaration of Independence, 27, 53, 150, 253
*Delaware,* ship: built, 93; coppered, 93; India voyage of, 93; sold, 96; 1794 departure from England, 97–99; to France, 102; to Guernsey, 119
Democrats. *See* Antifederalists
Desforneaux, Governor of Guadeloupe, 158, 167, 173, 212
Donnaldson, John, and *London Packet,* 52. *See also* Donnaldson and Coxe
Donnaldson and Coxe, 52, 62
Duane, William, printer, 245, 246
Duel, Burr-Hamilton, 233–36
Dunlap, John, printer, 60
Du Pont de Nemours, Pierre S., 200, 209
Dutch East India Company, 69, 82

*Eagle,* brig, 222
East India Company. *See* British East India, Dutch East India, and French East India Companies
Eaton, William, 227–28
Edward, T's servant, 168, 213
Embargo Act: passed, 251; T approves, 251; effect of Enforcing Act on, 252; public meetings on, 253–55
*Empress of China,* ship: first voyage, 61; second voyage, 62; speaks *Canton,* 68–69; in Whampoa, 73; and navigation errors, 105
England: Thomas Truxtun, jr. educated in, 120; copper from, 129. *See also* England, King of; Great Britain; London, England; Navy, Royal
England, King of, 2, 11, 12, 94
English Channel, 31, 56, 99
*Enterprize,* schooner, 194
Equator, ceremony on crossing, 68

Erwin, Joseph, 45
Ethiopic Sea, 67, 68
Ewing, John, 104
Exchange: New York, 13; Tontine (New York), 177; Royal (London), 80, 97, 172
Exchange Coffee House, Norfolk, 198
*Experiment,* sloop, in Whampoa, 73

Falkland Islands, 10
Faris, William, 132
Farming, T at "Cranberry Place," 252
Father of Navy, 258, 260
Federalists: favor Constitution, 80; decline of, 213; principles of, 229; and Embargo Act, 255; T on ticket for Congress, 258
Fitch, John, 80
Flag captain, 221–22, 223
Flogging. *See* Punishment
Fort McHenry, Whetstone Point, Baltimore: in ruins, 113; named, 142; rebuilt, 279n6; supplies cannon for *Constellation,* 133, 153
Fox, Josiah, naval constructor: draws sail plan for T, 111; and repairs to *Constellation,* 202–203; mentioned, 126
France: French and Indian War, 2; ports used by Americans (1777), 31–32; Yorktown fleet (1781), 267n7; King of, and John Paul Jones, 40; at war with Great Britain, 94, 98–99; razees similar to U.S. frigates, 109; T sends flour to, 120; attacks American vessels, 136; XYZ affair, 137; privateers in Gulf of Florida, 148; T fears, under Napoleon, 251–52. *See also* French East India Company; French Revolution
France, Quasi-War with U.S.: discussed, 142; caused by T, 165; still undeclared, 200; ends, 209, 210, 214
Franklin, Benjamin: Minister to France, 52–53; engages *London Packet,* 53; leaves Paris, 54; arrives Cowes, 55; in *London Packet,* 55–59; arrives home, 58; reported in Algiers, 63; President of Pennsylvania, 66; at Constitutional Convention, 79; on Gulf Stream, 107; on slavery, 121; dies, 92; mentioned, 62, 105, 260

McCall, [?], supercargo in *Canton,* 79

Macdonough, James, injured in *Constellation,* 164

McHenry, James, Secretary of War: on proof of cannon, 124; and launching of *Constellation,* 129, 135; orders T to prepare *Constellation* for sea, 137; incompetence of, 142–43; mentioned, 116

Madison, James, 79, 258

Madras, India, 93

Magee, James, shipmaster, 73

Mansion House Hotel, Philadelphia, 255

Marine academy, T advocates, 128, 250

Marine Corps, U.S.: pay of men, 139; T's opinion of, 208, 217; mentioned, 169

"Maritime Observations" by Franklin, 56

Marque, Letters of. *See* Letters of Marque

*Mars,* ship, 30, 31, 32, 141

Marshall, John, presides at Burr trial, 246

Martha's Vineyard, Massachusetts, 26, 116

Martinique, West Indies, 90, 151, 152, 189

Masting, 110–11

Medal for *La Vengeance* action: authorized by Congress, 199; illustrated, 201; presented by Jefferson, 231

Mediterranean squadron: T to command (1801), 216; relieved by Dale, 217; T ordered for (1802), 221; flag captain for, 221–22, 223; T quits, 223–24, 227; Morris ordered to, 224; T may still command (1804), 237

Mercer, Robert, master of *New York,* 87–88

Mexico, Burr's expedition to, 242–43, 245

Mills, Thomas, 99, 119, 120

Miranda, Francisco, 243

*Montezuma,* ship, 156

Moore, John Hamilton, on navigation, 104, 106

Morgan, James, gunner, 207

Morgan, John, naval constructor, 115–16

Morocco, treaty with U.S., 122

Morris, Gouverneur, 178, 229

Morris, Robert: in China trade, 86–87, 88; mentioned, 92, 96, 102

Morris, Richard V.: to relieve T, 224; commission revoked, 227; mentioned, 238

Morris, Staats, commands Fort McHenry, 133

Mount Vernon, Virginia: Houdon to visit, 54; T visits, 184–85; mentioned, 95

Murray, Alexander: in *Montezuma,* 156; in *Constellation,* 204, 205, 227–28; consulted on T's resignation, 240; mentioned, 173

Murray, John, merchant, 178

Mutiny: threatened in *Constellation,* 145–47; in British fleet, 146; in *Hermione,* 146, 147; threatened in *Congress,* 203–204

*Nancy,* ship, 14, 16

Nantes, France, 31–32

Napoleon, 251–52, 258

*National Intelligencer,* Washington, attacks T, 241

Naval agents. *See* Sterett, Samuel and Joseph; Pennock, William

Naval constructors. *See* Humphreys, Joshua; Stodder, David; Fox, Josiah; Morgan, John; Hackett, John

Navigation: thermometric, 56; errors in British tables, 70; supplies in London, 97; T's book on, 103–108; "Lunars," 106; chronometers in, 106, 277n6

Navy, Continental: sailed from Philadelphia, 22; off Boston, 26; in English Channel, 31; T's opinion of, 40; John Paul Jones in, 40–41; Talbot's commission in, 181

Navy, Pennsylvania, 22

Navy, Royal: T serves in, 10, 12; and Falklands incident, 10, 11; conditions in, 11; takes *Charming Polly,* 19–20; takes *Andrew Caldwell,* 33; detains *John and Joseph,* 120; T adapts customs of, to U.S. Navy, 127; takes *La Vengeance,* 209; to aid Burr, 245. *See also* Mutiny

Navy, Secretary of. *See* Stoddert, Benjamin (1798–March, 1801); Smith, Samuel (April–June, 1801); Smith, Robert (July, 1801–    )

Navy, U.S.: proposed, 92; authorized, 101; pay in, 103, 139; opposition to, 101, 123, 137; to be used only against

FLORIDA
BAHAMA
ISLAN
GULF
OF
FLORIDA
Havana
Matanzas
CUBA
JAMAICA
Port Royal
CARIBBEAN
W
E
S